PAVILION 21 MINI OP ERA SPACE
HOTO FUDO
WADI RUM RESORT
SILVER CLOUD
WELLNESS ORHIDELIA
HOTEL CAL DOR
CO DE UNI QUE
"ROC K IT SUDA"!
CO DE UNI QUE
GEM @ TELFORD
KUGG EN
I WAY
LBBW IMM OBILIEN HEADQU ARTERS
SNOWF LAKE TOWER
PIXEL IN BEIJING MODELROOM
CUBE TUBE IN JINHU A
CORNICHE TOWER
TOWER 123
MIRAMARE TOWER CENTRE
PRISM CONTEMP ORARY ART I PLAST IC SENSATIONS
BIONIC TOWER
VILLAGE CENTER - CENTER PARCS
YELLOW TREEHOUS E REST AURANT
MASD AR PLAZA OASIS OF TH E FUTU RE
MONDE D'EAU RESORT AND TH EMEPARK
LITT LE ONE ROOM HOUS E WITH A CU RVE
HONGODAI CHRIST CHURCH SCHOOL & NURSERY
"JOSEPHINE BAKER" GROUP OF SCHOOLS
CHAPEL OF ST.LAWRENCE
ALMONTE THEATRE IN HUELVA
SOCIAL KINDER GARDENS
TELLUS NURSERY SCHOOL
LU CINAHAVEN - DAY CARE CENTRE TAULOV
OS LO INTERNATIONAL SCHOOL
FLOR DEL CA MPO SCHOOL
NORVEG COAST CU LTURAL CENTER
SVAL BARD SCIENCE CENTRE 78°NORTH
NABITO SENSATIONAL PARK
TRA M STOP

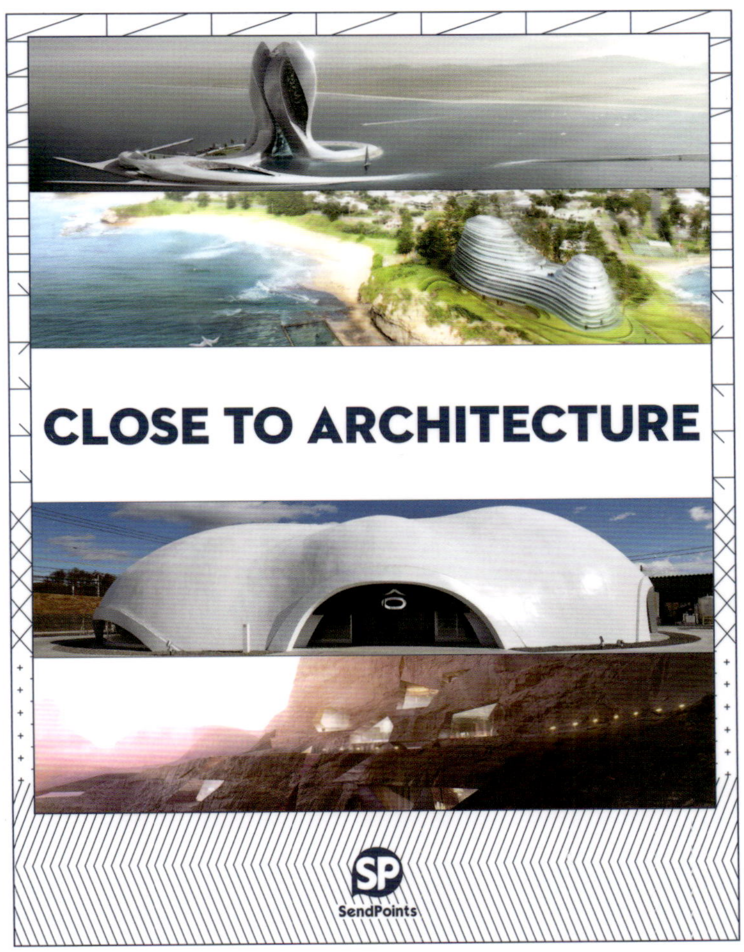

RE-SKIN / MORE WITH LESS
UBUNTU CENTRE
ABUJA NATIONAL COMPLEX
M4 FÓVAM TÉR UNDERGROUND ST ATION
LIGTHS AILS
PERES PEACE HOUSE
SAN PAULO PARISH COMPLEX
KAROO WILDERNESS CENTER
BUENOS AIRES FOOTBALL (BAF)
MEDITATION HOUSE
ANNEX OF THE CHAMBER OF TRADES-VAL DOISE
FAREWELL CHAPEL
TREEHOUSE IN SEATTLE
HOUSE A
FOUR CORNERED VILLA
REFUG E IN LA VALL DE LAGUAR
HOUSE D
INSIDE OUT
VILLA IN DARVISHABAD
HOUSE TRANSFORMATION
DEVO TO HOUSE
THE R HOUSE
HOUSE IN MECO
HOUSE IN PAÇO DE ARCOS
FUGLSANG NAES
HOUSE IN NIKAIA
ORMOND ESPLANADE
REST ORATION OF AN ALPINE BARN
TOWN RESIDENCE
BAMBOO FOREST HOUSE
EDGE HOUSE
FYF RESIDENCE I HOUSE IN ROSARIO
SG LIGHT
HOUSE OF MIST ER R
VILLA G
THE HOUSE ON NIKOLINA GORA
VILLA BH
RESIDENCE IN KURA KUEN
MONTBLANC HOUSE

CLOSE TO ARCHITECTURE

SendPoints

CLOSE TO ARCHITECTURE

SendPoints

Publisher : Lin Gengli
Chief Editor : Lin Shijian
Editorial Director : Jimmy Chai
Executive Editor : Jimmy Chai, Alice
Design Director : Lin Shijian
Designer: Xu Qidong

Address:
RoomC,15/ F Hua Chiao Commercial Centre, 678 Nathan Road, Mongkok, Kl, Hong Kong
Tel: (86)-20-89095121,34108463
Fax: (86)-20-89095206
Email: info@sendpoint.com.cn
Website: www.sendpoint.com.cn

Distributed by
Guangzhou Sendpoints Book Co., Ltd.
Sales Manager: Peng YangHui(China) Limbo(International)

Guangzhou Tel: (86)-02-89095121
Beijing Tel: (86)-10-84139071
Shanghai Tel: (86)-21-63220892
Email: export@sendpoint.com.cn
Website: www.sendpoint.com.cn

ISBN 978-988-18923-5-5
HongKong Davinci Publishing Company Limited

DAVINCI

Printed and bound in China

Acknowledgements
I am very grateful to all of the people and companies who have participated in this book. I would like to thank all of the designers and graphic studios who have collaborated in this project.

COMMERCIAL ARCHITECTURE

PUBLIC CULTURE SPACE

RESIDENCE

INDEX

INTRODUCTION

Everyday we will get in touch with architecture. Architecture is very close to everyone's life and affects our behavior patterns in a profound and subtle way. So when we walk in or go by an architecture, it always arouses our memories, feelings, aspirations and associations.

Architecture is born of the need of human. In the primitive times, two most important things of human life were finding food and inhabiting. At the time of agricultural society which took herding and planting as the most principal thing, human began to put down roots and built beautiful strong houses. At the same time, people built mausoleum to protect the corpse of the dead kings, for example, the pyramids in Egypt reflect Egyptians' belief that people could come alive in later ages. Another important architecture is temple, in order to consecrate gods and collective worship, it needed a space to serve different worship of individual. In the Middle Ages, because of the development of technology and the appear of new ideas, Gothic cathedral turned up, architecture was rooted in this worldly, but seemed could reach to the Kingdom of Heaven, it provided a very important way to connect religious activities and daily life through its multilevel meaning.

The tradition pursues unremitting experiment and scientific truth through out the period of the Renaissance. This new change made people turn the attention from architectural technique to its function and symbolic meaning of the architecture. Marcus Vitruvius Pollio's "De architectura libri decem" regards virtue to be higher than everything, and considers architecture is the tool to preserve and show virtue, so it is necessary for it to be perfect. Architecture could bear the holy relationship of profound ideas between human and society. Most Renaissance architects preferred freestanding, axipetal architecture design. In the middle of sixteenth century, these Renaissance principles were no longer suitable for using, the architects strived to follow the pioneers of classicalism, especially in the aspect of form and detail; on the other hand, people regarded Roman catholic doctrines are important again, as a result, more requests are brought forward to cathedral—a series of Reformation have influenced the design of cathedrals. And the discovery of printing brought Renaissance works to France and England, thus the architecture practice there was deeply affected by foreign concept.

In seventeenth and eighteenth century, the strong ruler in European began the history of establishing absolute state, which was narrated in the architecture at that time. No matter architecture or government, everything was centered on autocracy. At the end of eighteenth century, architects began to observe Gothic, Indian and Chinese architecture, they found that in the irregular scene, nature was overtop of the intelligence and brought the excitement of sense. Their theory brought the trend of scene design which had already existed into intellectual dimension. And scene design started to try to use irregular exotic expressions from the Far East. They began to keep away from academism and classicalism, and even opposed to it. Architects started to use new materials, such as iron and glasses, new technique and social changes brought a breath of fresh air to architecture.

Along with the development of economic, cities in the nineteenth century expanded cosmically, this means the changing of architectural method, economic and social life developed together, brooding a new architectural form, and the great change of society and polity were calling for the request of new institution, street and scene. The concept of city evolved from Renaissance couldn't face this challenge, so architects and town planners put into the method study of new city types. At this time, architects realized that industrial products not only could make forms and structure that never exist before, but also could develop new decorate vocabulary. They wanted to pour spirit or art intension into industrial products which were lifeless or not created personally. This potential opened a door between idea and object.

The First World War provided a starting point for the formation of modern architects. Architect thought that architecture could express individual idea or opinion through traditional and manner technique, hence many architectures of irregular sculpt and dramatic effect appeared. Soviet Union set up after the October Revolution, constructivism boomed and busted, architecture become extremely abstract. In order to reflect the grand figure, they didn't draw on concrete sculpt consciously, suggesting science without decoration and romance could be the spirit connotation of art, thus replaced traditional Russian value system. Western Europe was influenced by cubism at the same time. Modern art and architecture developed new aesthetics.

Architects thought industry could purify material image and made it come to the necessary form, thus the principle rules of architecture design came into being. But functionalism after that thought form could be specially created to adapt the function which it served. Architecture was made for the needs of human, not for the tradition or hierarchy. This turned to be modernism and the most important aspect of its heritage, until now.

In the beginning of twentieth century, the establishment of Bauhaus meant the birth of modern design and it embraced around the globe at that time. Architects began to slip the leash of traditional architecture form, created brand new architecture suitable for the requirement of industrial society with a bold hand. Bauhaus established the leading position of architecture in designing, and raised technology of the same level with visual art, thereby traditional classification was weakened. In the modern industrial design theory, its idea and aesthetic had influenced a whole generation. Although the rise of postmodernism was a crash and advance for the design idea of Bauhaus, some ideas of Bauhaus were still revealing for modern industrial design and technological aesthetics. Its high ideal and goal reflected in the Bauhaus Declaration.

"Close to Architecture" is divided into three parts: commercial architecture, public culture space and residence. We selected the lastest and most special architectures built in recent two years from all over the world. Commercial space is the dynamic and important part in the city. It is the charming part of a city. Today, commercial space is not only a simple shopping environment, but also a spirit space with deep culture intension, influencing the life style and aesthetics. Architecture presents new logical relation and aesthetic value, make people place every visual angle and experience different changes of space and time. While public culture architecture in our book owns strong experimental innovations, blending in more multiculture, region and environment elements, they accommodate people and mould their spirit at the same time. Residences are more humanized and stylized. There are many works which are bionic or using natural materials. The sculpt of these residences is exaggerated, highlighting individualism and advocating character which is out of the ordinary. Every design is a part of the whole culture of the society; it is close related to other parts and influences each other. So our book is tend to show in the first ten years of the new century how architecture continued old ideas and created new theory to affect city and society under the influence of technology and academic thinking at the time.

We believe through this book readers will see the beauty and inconceivability fully and deeply. Here we would like to mention the architects and companies. Thanks for their contribution. We could not finish this book without their help. Thank you.

PUBLIC CULTURE SPACE

RESIDENCE

COMMERCIAL ARCHITECTURE

PAVILION 21 MINI OPERA SPACE

The task which we had to solve with our design was to create a space with 300 seats (or 700 standing spectators) for experimental performances of the Bavarian State Opera. The Pavilion should be dismountable, transportable and re-mountable and make the respective urban space distinctive through its shape. Mass and therefore weight are the decisive criteria for good acoustics. The conception of the Pavilion 21 MINI Opera Space therefore had to overcome a contradiction: to design a lightweight construction which must allow to be disbanded and reassembled quickly, but which at the same time meets the acoustical requirements of a concert hall.

Hence how do we create the conditions for good acoustics despite a reduction of mass? Already the first considerations fixed in drawings show the basic concept of the Pavilion to introduce elements which are on the one hand the spatial transformation of sound sequences, and which on the other hand develop sound reflecting and absorbing properties through their pyramid-like shape: "Soundscaping".

The idea to combine architecture with music is not new. Also the term soundscaping is not new. Similar to landscaping it involves "Gestalt". Soundscaping originates in the 1940's and designates a method of composing. In architecture, Le Corbusier and Iannis Xenakis together engaged in the topic of music and architecture when they thought about three-dimensional implementation of musical compositions (Le Corbusier's Philips Pavilion and the partition of the windows in La Tourette).

Our strategy to achieve soundscaping comprises three steps: firstly, to realize the shielding effect between square and street; secondly, to shape the geometry of the Pavilion in such a way that the surface deflects noise; and thirdly, to design the surface of the Pavilion in such a way that it reflects and absorbs sound.

As a starting point towards the abstraction of music into spatial form, a sequence from the song "Purple Haze" by Jimi Hendrix and a passage from "Don Giovanni" by Mozart were transcribed. Through the analysis of frequency sections from these pieces of music and through the combination with the computer generated 3D model, the sequences are translated into pyramidal "spike constructions" by means of parametric "scripting".

In order to implement the objectives of the interior spatial acoustics, the interior wall and ceiling surfaces were fitted with a combination of perforated absorbing and smooth reflecting sandwich panels. The flooring of the Pavilion is carried out as a reflecting even "stage floor". Sound reflecting, parallel wall and ceiling surfaces are avoided and are therefore tilted or skewed.

The development of the acoustical elements was carried out together with the acoustics department of Arup; the applied construction and materials were worked out with Frener & Reifer.

COMPANY	COOP HIMMELB(L)AU
DESIGN PRINCIPAL	Wolf D. Prix
PHOTOGRAPHER	Markus Pillhofer
CLIENT	The Free State of Bavaria represented by The Bavarian State Opera Munich, Germany
COUNTRY (DISTRICT)	Austria

´SCUSE ME WHILE I KISS THE SKY´
JIMI HENDRIX, PURPLE HAZE

FREQUENZAUSSCHNITT
FREQUENCY SECTION

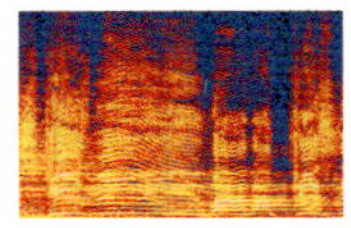

SONAGRAMM
SONAGRAM

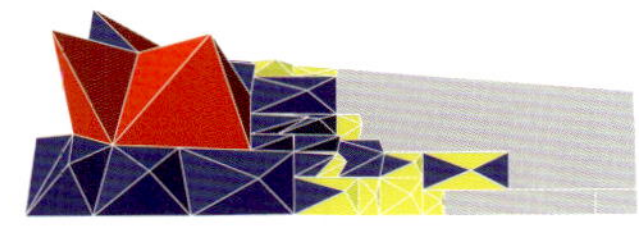

BESTIMMT DIE GRÖSSE DER SPIKES
DETERMINES THE SIZE OF THE SPIKES

NON HO TIMOR: VERRÓ!
WOLFGANG AMADEUS MOZART, DON GIOVANNI, ATTI II, SZENE 15 / SCENE 15

FREQUENZAUSSCHNITT
FREQUENCY SECTION

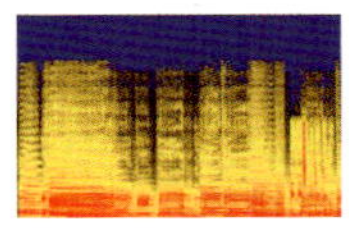

SONAGRAMM
SONAGRAM

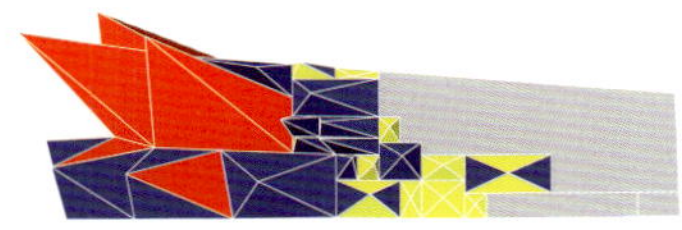

BESTIMMT DIE RICHTUNG DER SPIKES
DETERMINES THE DIRECTION OF THE SPIKES

SCRIPTING-KONZEPT / SCRIPTING CONCEPT

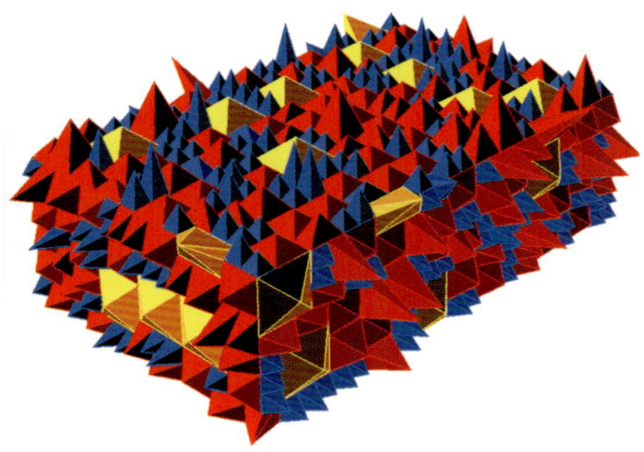

Pavilion 21
SCRIPTING-KONZEPT
SCRIPTING CONCEPT

CONTROL 0

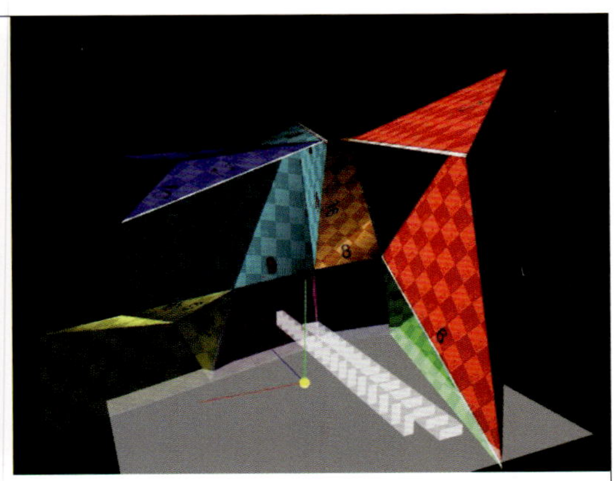

CONTROL 1

PROJECTION 1

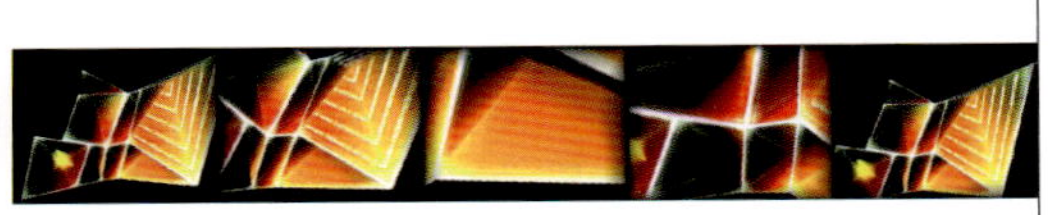

PROJECTION 2

MEDIENTECHNIK BAR- UND LOUNGEBEREICH / CAT-X
MEDIA TECHNOLOGY BAR AND LOUNGE AREA / CAT-X

Pavilion 21
MEDIENTECHNIK
MEDIA TECHNOLOGY

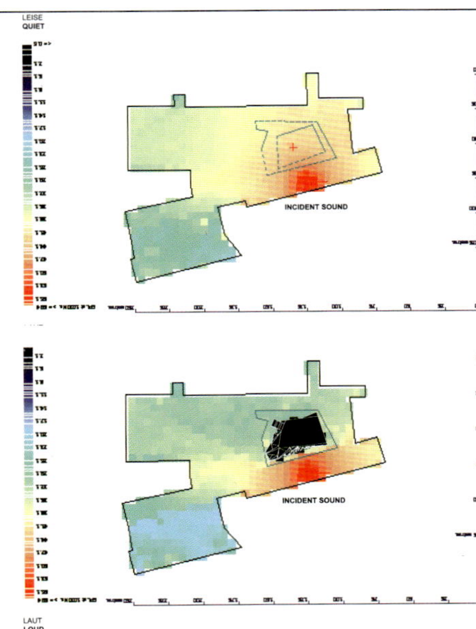

MIT PAVILLON
WITH PAVILION

Pavilion 21
GERÄUSCHPEGELANALYSE IM STADTRAUM / MARSTALLPLATZ
SOUND LEVEL ANALYSIS IN URBAN SPACE / MARSTALLPLATZ

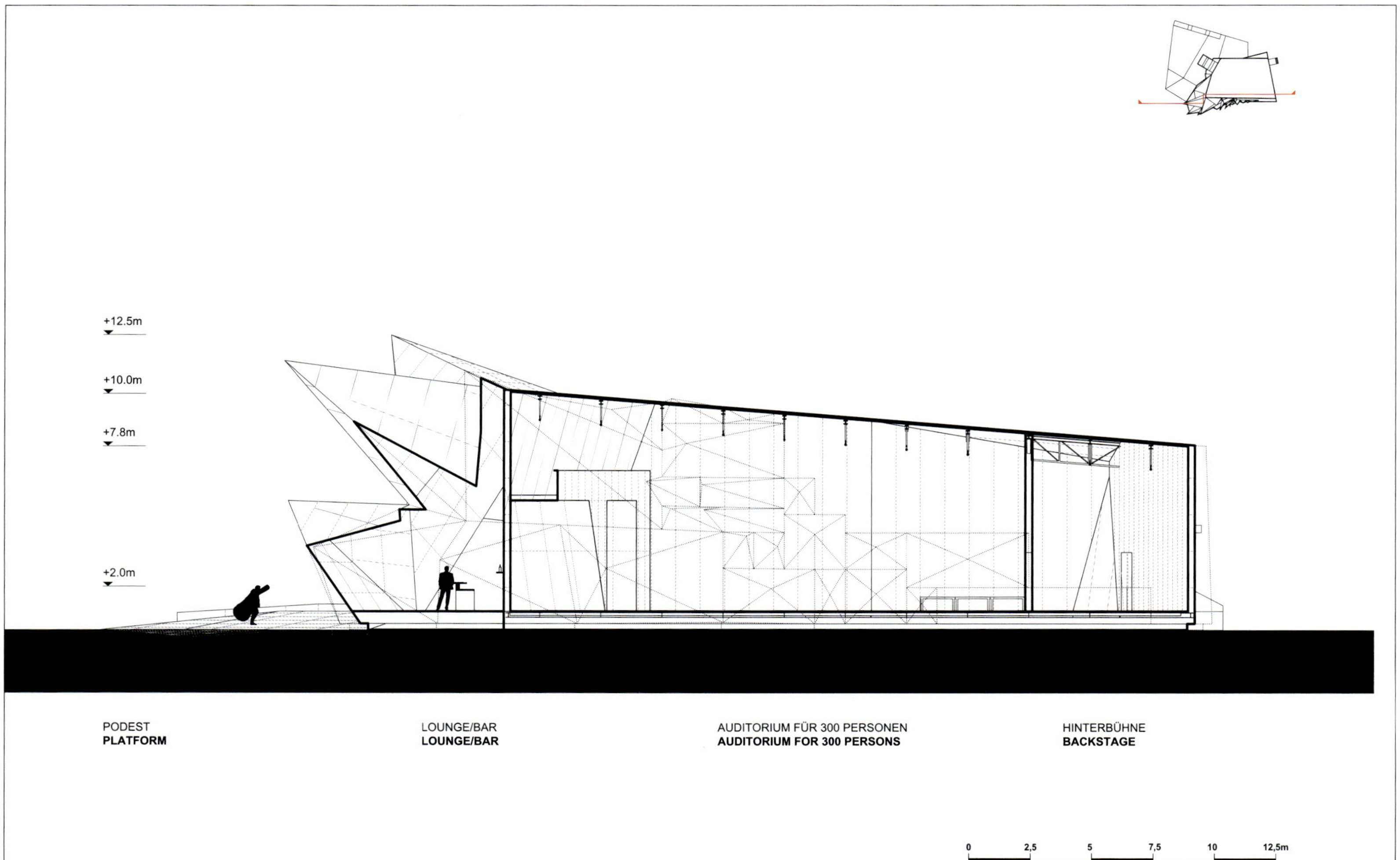

Pavilion 21
SCHNITT / SECTION

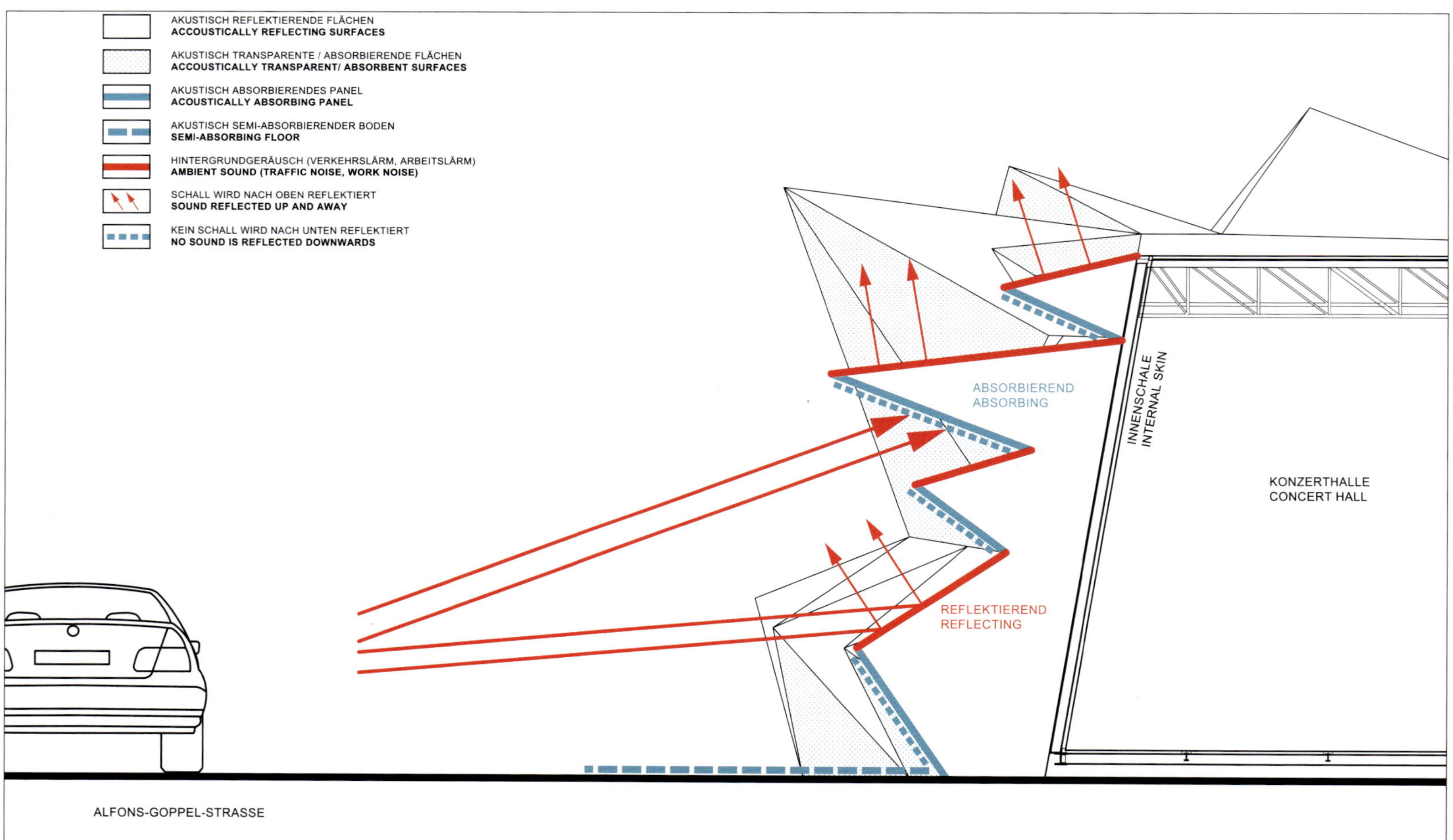

Pavilion 21
AKUSTISCHES VERHALTEN / FASSADENSCHNITT
ACOUSTICAL PROPERTIES FAÇADE / FAÇADE VERTICAL SECTION

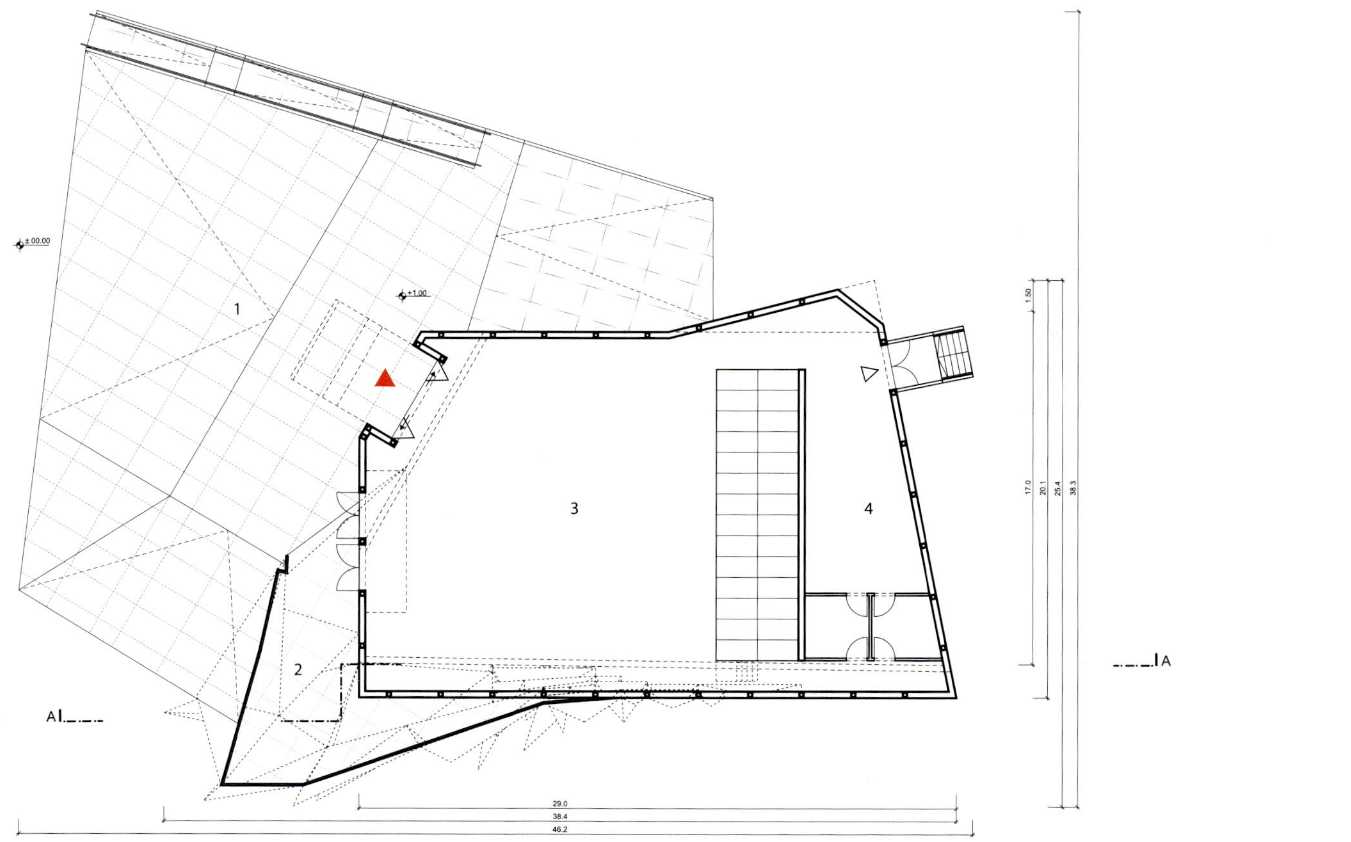

1 PODEST / **PLATFORM**
2 LOUNGE / **BAR**
3 AUDITORIUM FÜR 300 PERSONEN / **AUDITORIUM FOR 300 PERSONS**
4 HINTERBÜHNE / **BACKSTAGE**

Pavilion 21
GRUNDRISS / FLOOR PLAN

HOTO FUDO

This is a building like inside and outside.
The project was planned on the site with Mt. Fuji rising closely in the south and the two sides facing the trunk roads.
This building seems to belong to such nature objects as mountains and clouds. It is made from soft geometry, which will not arise from the figures like quadrangles and circles. By continuously operating innumerable polygon mesh points, we have determined the shape that clears the conditions such as the consistency as shell construction and the undulations that ward off rainwater in spite of its free geometry. The RC shell with cubic surfaces creates such spaces as 530 square meters of seats, 140 square meters of kitchens, and 50 square meters of rest rooms, in such a manner that it envelops and opens them.
This building has no air conditioners. It is open to the air at most seasons, and people have a meal in the air like outside air. The curved acrylic sliding door is closed only during the strong wind and the coldest season. Giving 60 mm thick urethane insulation to the outside of the RC shell and keeping a stable RC temperature secure a stable temperature environment for the building like inside and outside, and also reduce the deformation volume due to the temperature of RC to make the building last longer. For the lighting plan, we have determined such illumination to make people simply feel changes in the evening light and do not make insects gather around the lights. When it rains, rain comes in near windows and doors. In the spaces where rain does not come in, people enjoy the sound of raindrops. When it is foggy, the fog comes into the building. When it snows, it becomes a landscape buried in snow, and birds and animals will visit there. In this place like the middle between nature and art, people eat Hoto rich in natural ingredients.

COMPANY	Takeshi Hosaka Architects
DESIGNER	Takeshi Hosaka
PHOTOGRAPHER	Nacasa&Pertners Inc. / Koji Fujii
CLIENT	NOBORU FURUYA
COUNTRY (DISTRICT)	Japan

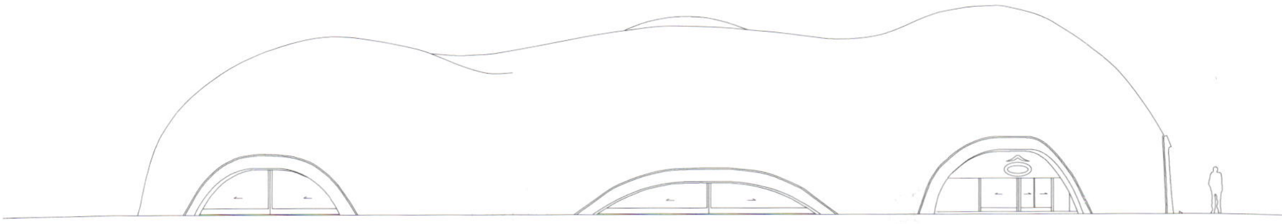

W-ELEVATION S=1:150

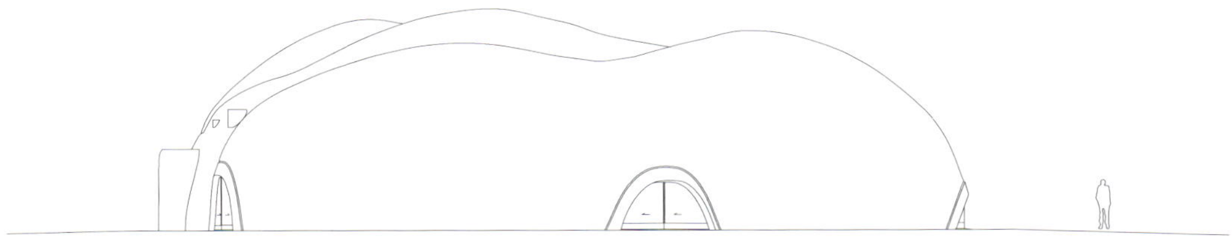

N-ELEVATION S=1:150

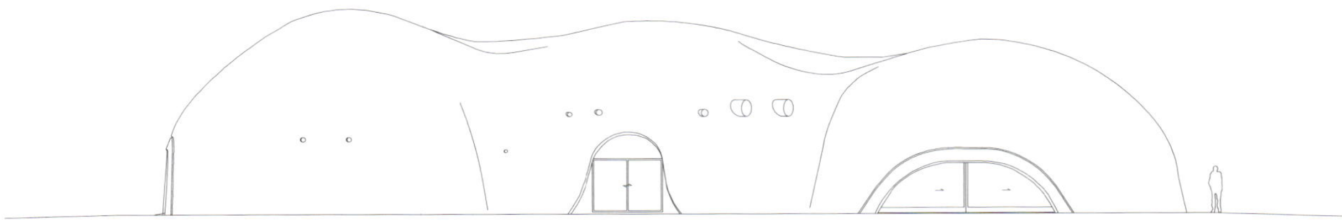

E-ELEVATION S=1:150

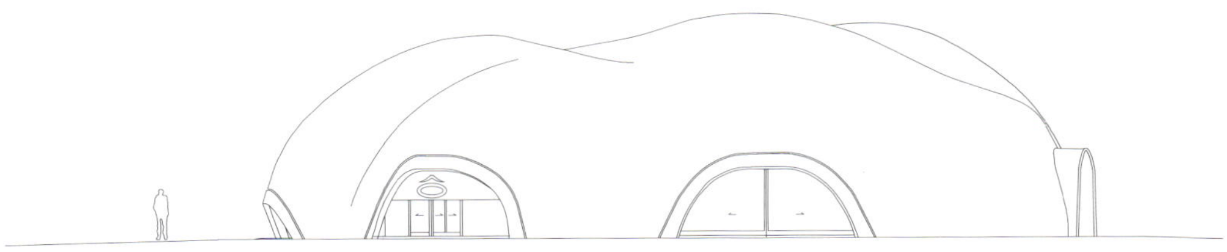

S-ELEVATION S=1:150

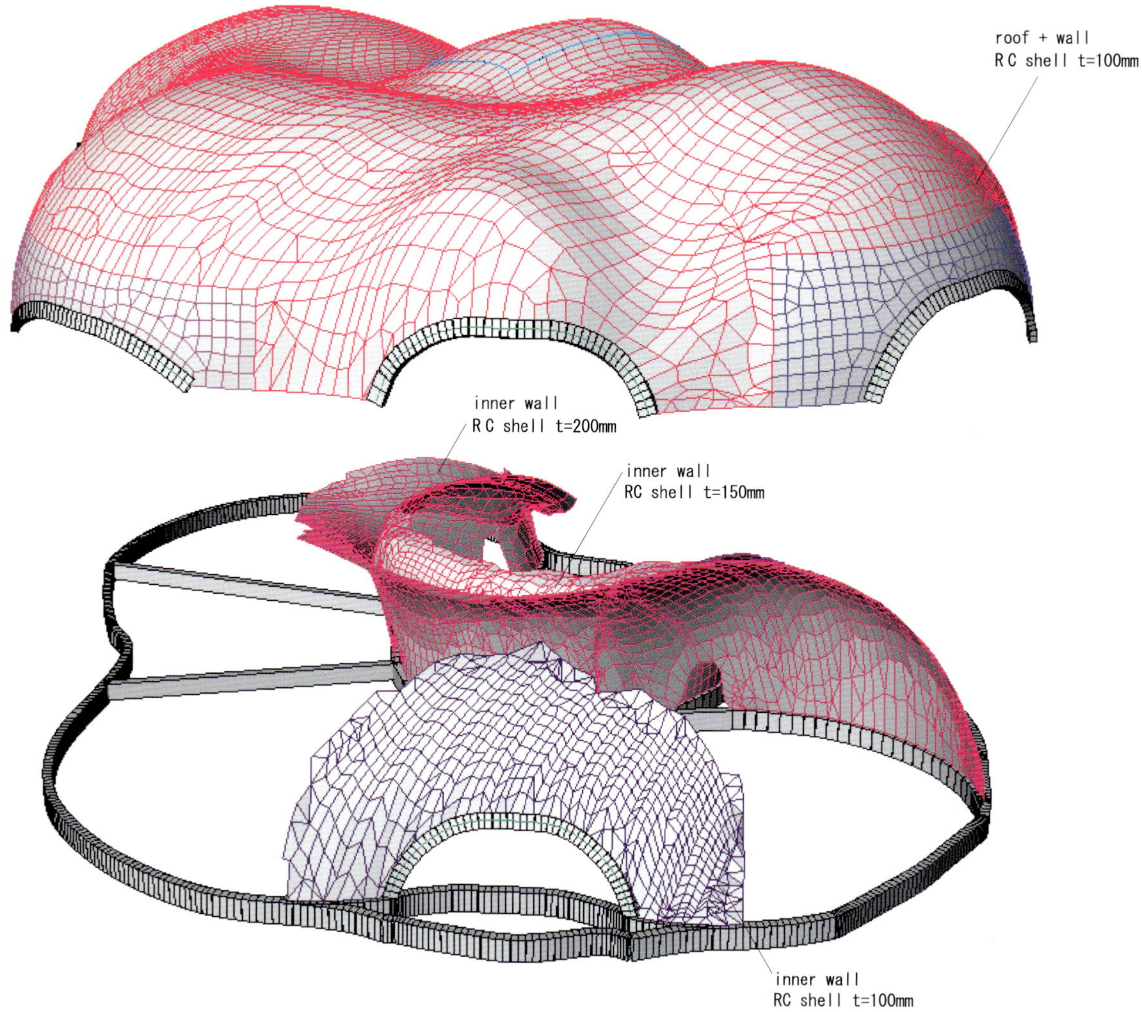
roof + wall
R C shell t=100mm
inner wall
R C shell t=200mm
inner wall
RC shell t=150mm
inner wall
RC shell t=100mm

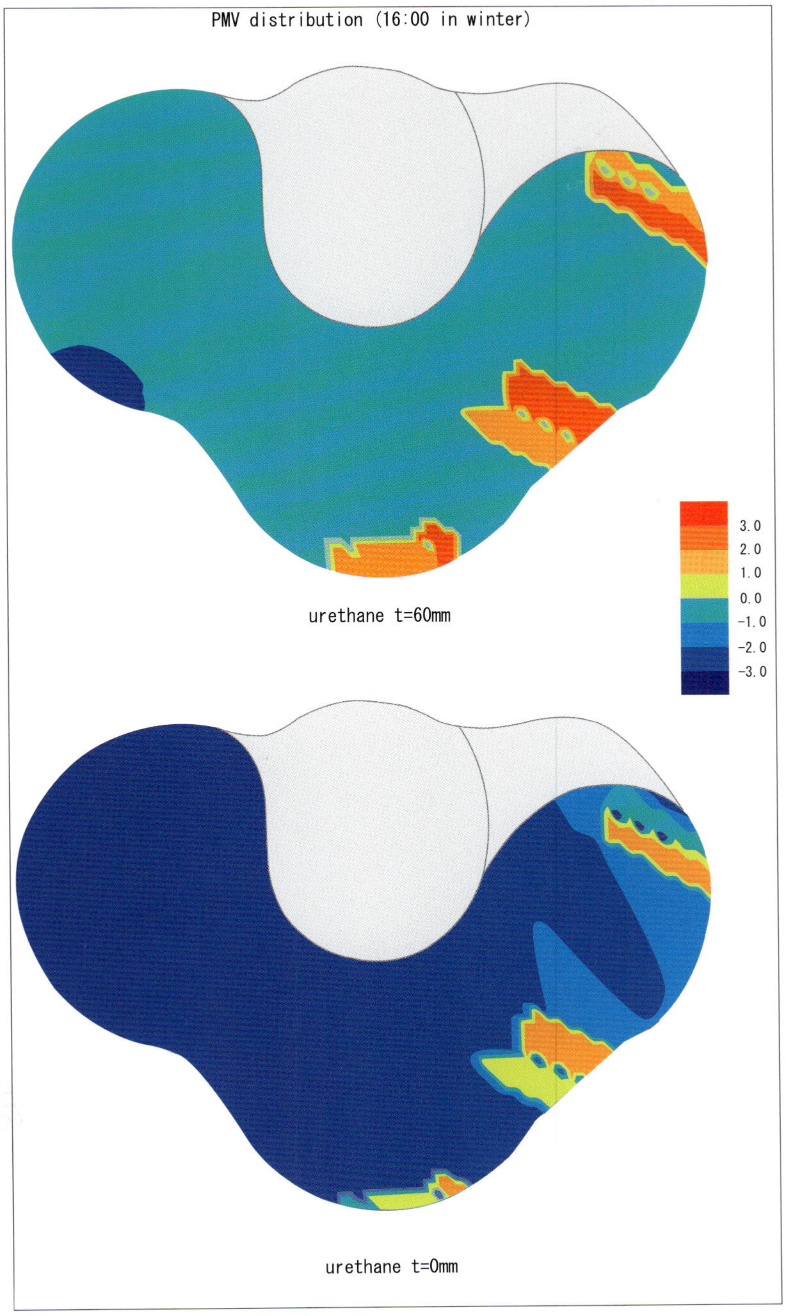
PMV distribution (16:00 in winter)
3.0
2.0
1.0
0.0
-1.0
-2.0
-3.0
urethane t=60mm
urethane t=0mm

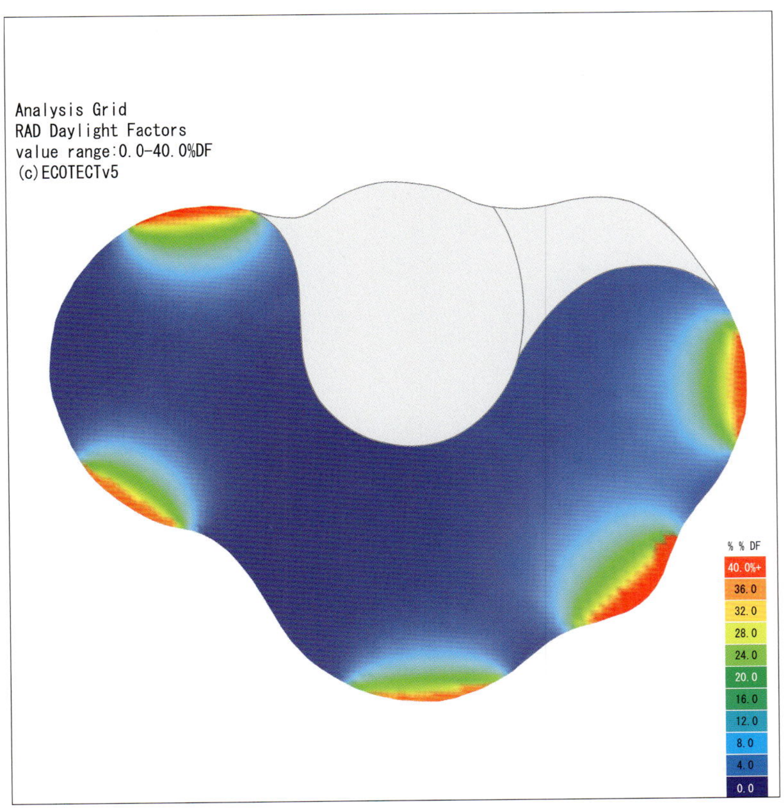
Analysis Grid
RAD Daylight Factors
value range:0.0-40.0%DF
(c)ECOTECTv5
% % DF
40.0%+
36.0
32.0
28.0
24.0
20.0
16.0
12.0
8.0
4.0
0.0

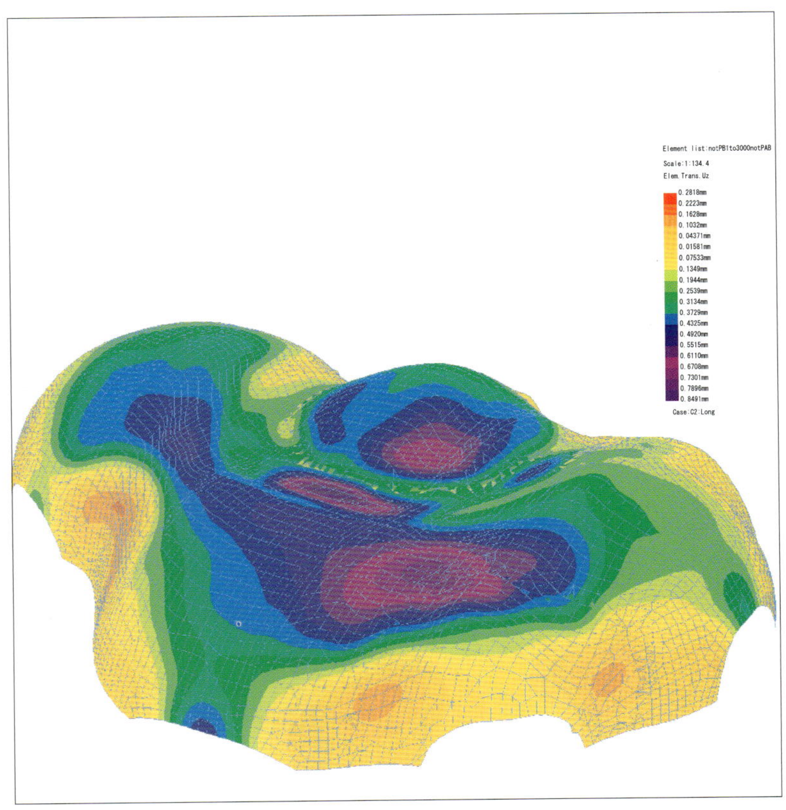

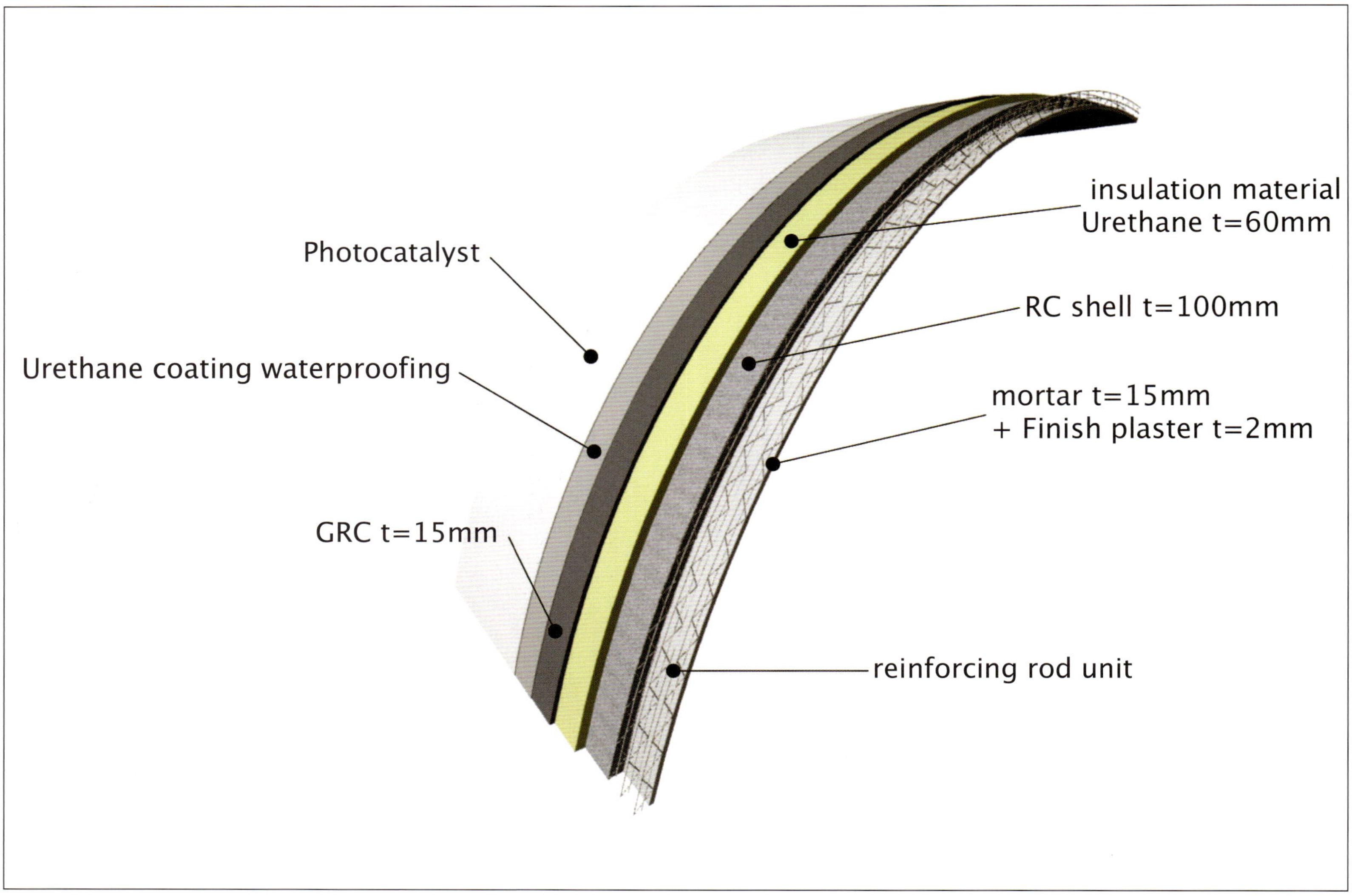

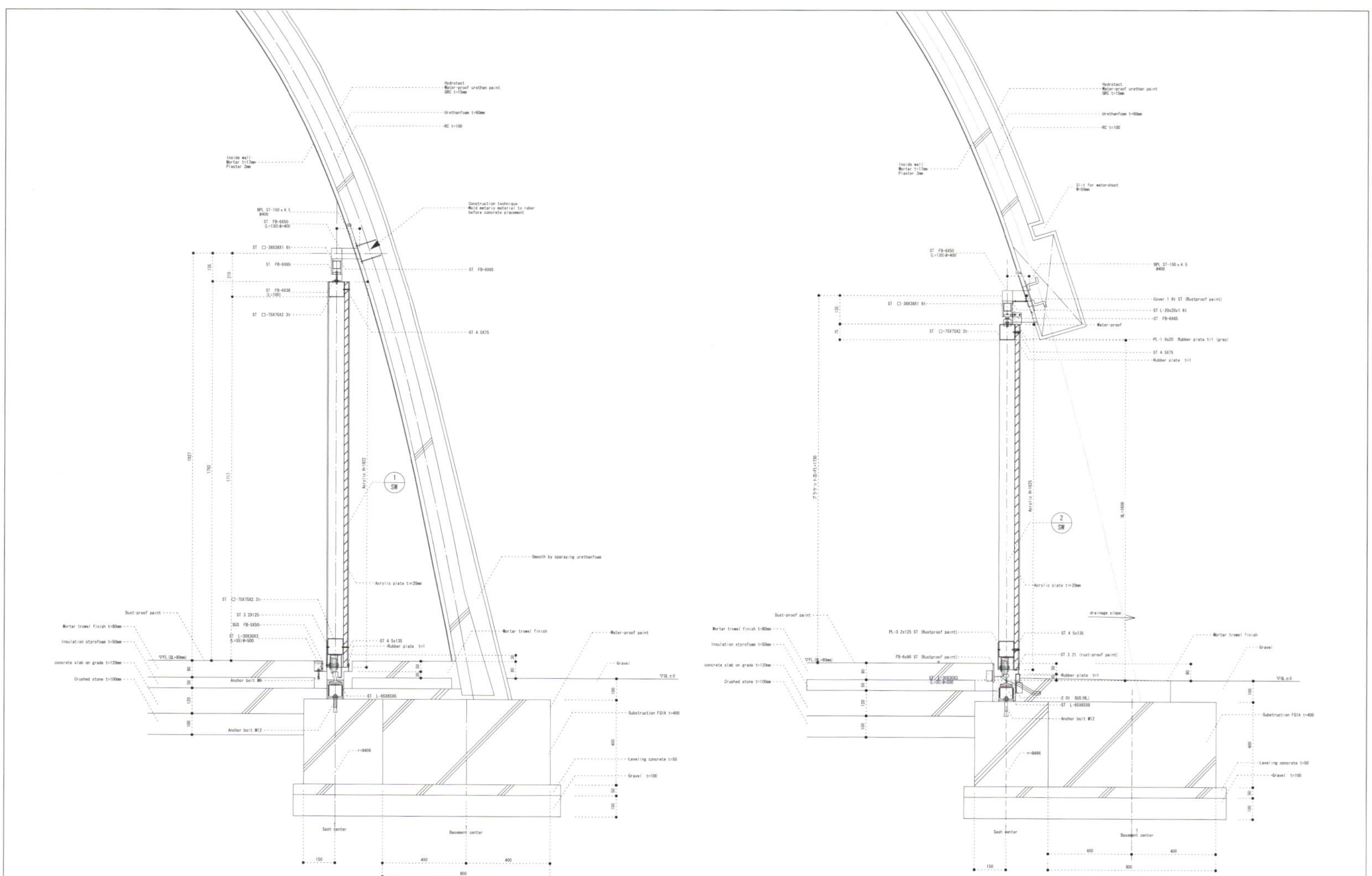

Detail section1 S=1:15

Detail section2 S=1:15

西村造園

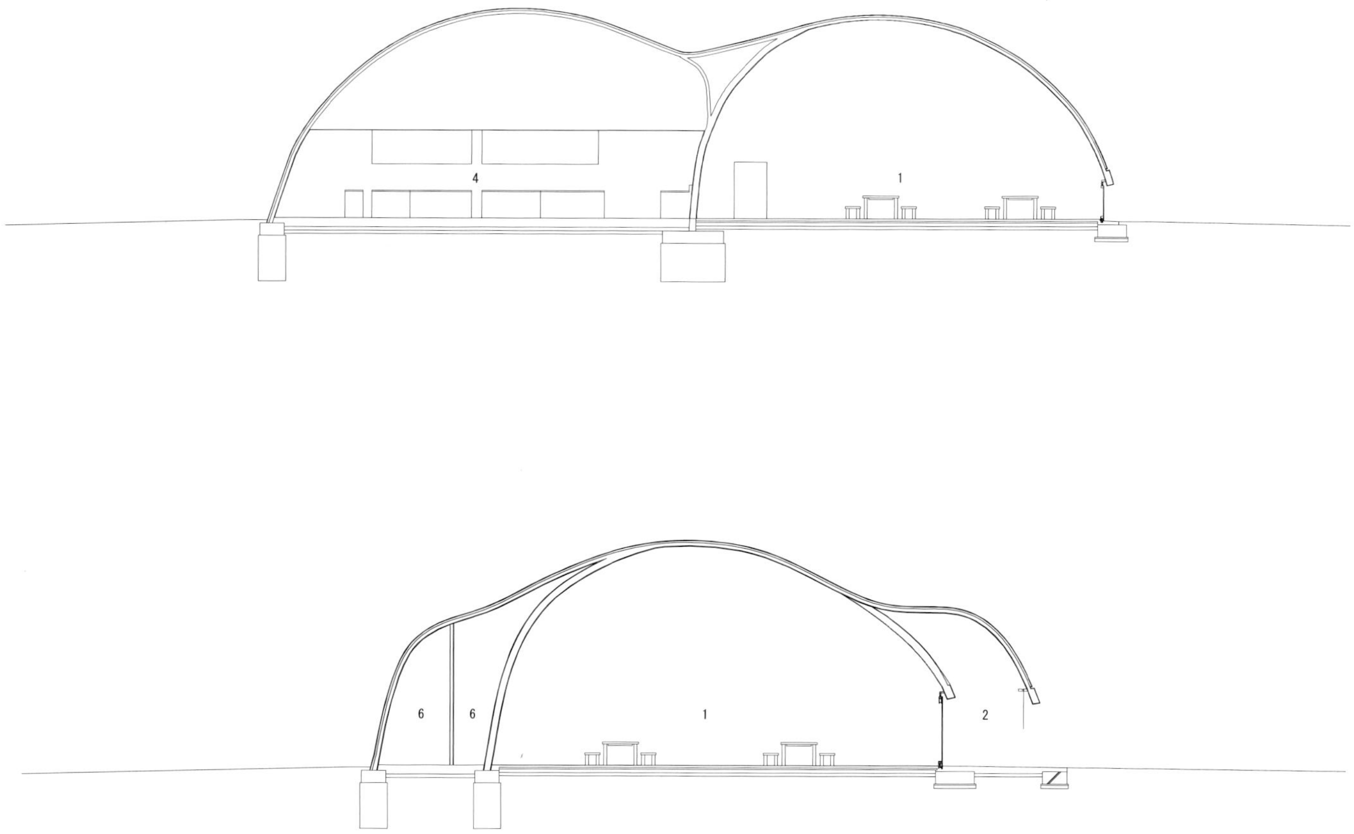

1. table
2. entrance
3. register
4. kitchen
5. pantry
6. wc
7. Parking

Section

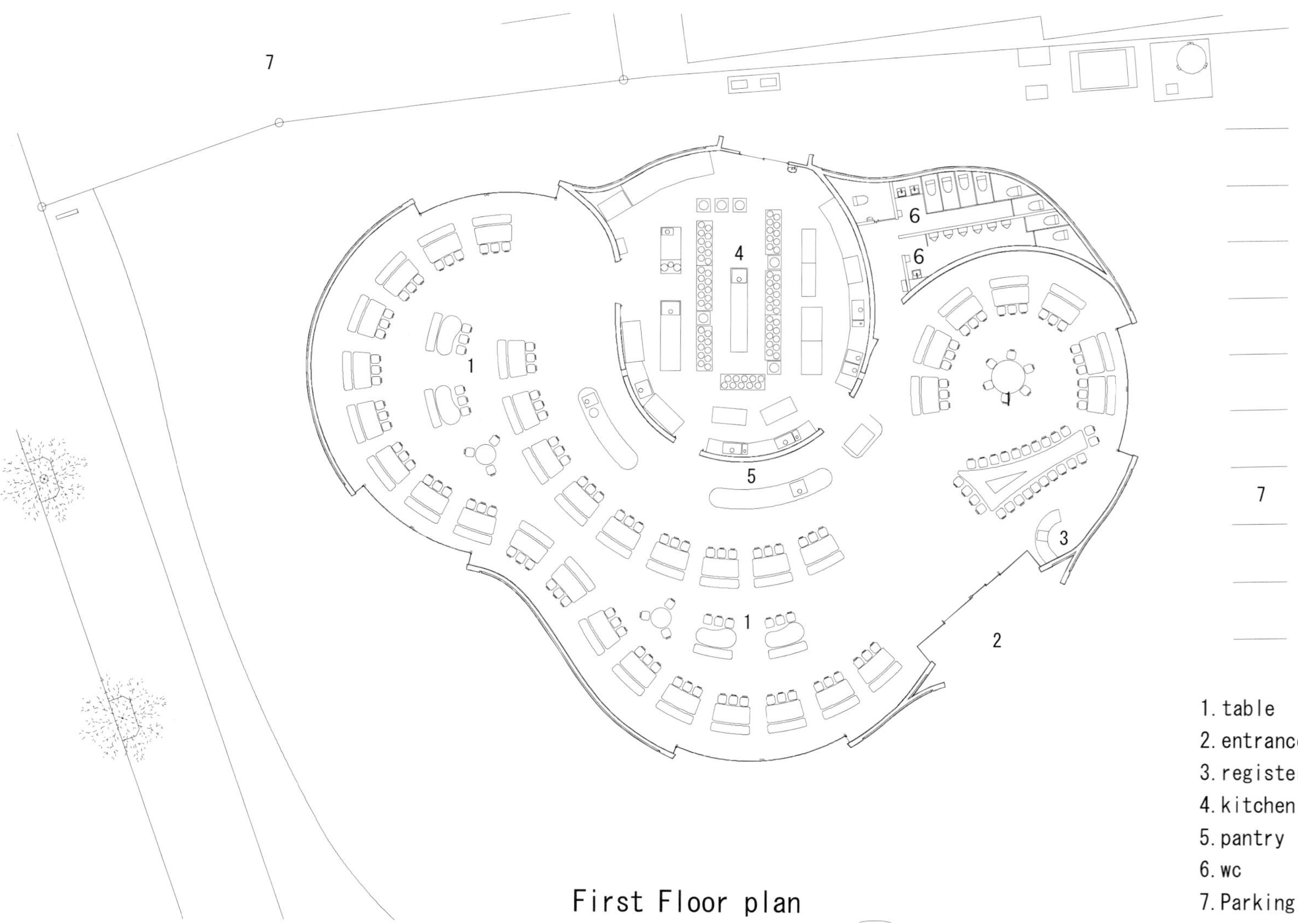

1. table
2. entrance
3. register
4. kitchen
5. pantry
6. wc
7. Parking

First Floor plan

WADI RUM RESORT

In a global competition for a new luxury destination in Wadi Rum, Jordan Oppenheim Architecture + Design's winning proposal, Wadi Resort, provided an ecological sensitive design solution. Slated for completion in 2014 the project is comprised of 47 desert lodges setting forth a future primitive experience.
The design set out to reinterpret the way society deals with surrounding nature by taking full advantage of the mystical valley where desert sand meets desert stone.
The project merges silently with its wondrous setting, exploiting and enhancing the natural beauty of the desert to establish accommodations that are uniquely elemental and luxurious. Dramatically situated, the lodges and villas in their various incarnations are all about a visceral connection to culture and place. The resulting experience is a revolutionary notion of opulence that is intentionally reduced to what is essential.
The structure of the lodges will be carved into the sandstone cliffs, utilizing the existing geological geometries of the rock to devise the form. Other structures are comprised of rammed earth and cement mixed with the local red sand. The minimal yet powerful gestures of the architecture, both built and carved serves to create harmony, and balance while framing and amplifying the surroundings. The interior and exterior are deliberately blurred establishing maximum impact with minimum effort. Inspired by the primordial, Oppenheim used his expertise in sustainable design to create passive means of cross ventilation, taking full advantage of the natural cooling effect of the rocks, and proper positioning allowing the project to minimize energy consumption and maximize comfortable healthy living.
"We have trained and heightened our senses to see, smell, taste, hear, and touch the mystical beauty of Wadi Rum. We tapped the inherent power of the desert through primal and instinctual design moves, informed by the forces, rhythms and patterns of nature— past, present, and future," says Oppenheim about his creative process for the project.
The 80,000-square-foot architectonic form responds directly to the rich regional cues: an evolutionary process that has established, over millennia, a clear and appropriate identity found in the Middle East.

COMPANY	Oppenheim Architecture + Design LLP
DESIGNER	Oppenheim Architecture + Design LLP
PHOTOGRAPHER	Renderings by Luxigon
COUNTRY (DISTRICT)	USA

LOUNGE
PANTRY / STORAGE
HAMMAM
CHANGING ROOM
YOGA / MEDITATION
PROPOSED: 60 M2
N
0 1 2 4 (METERS)

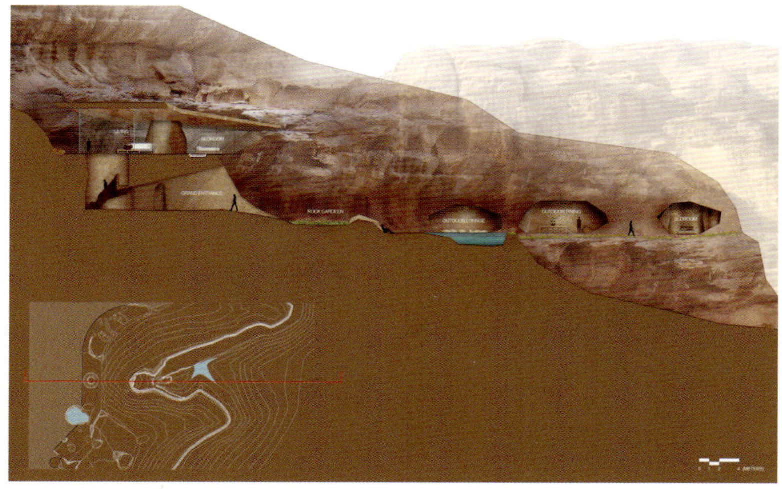

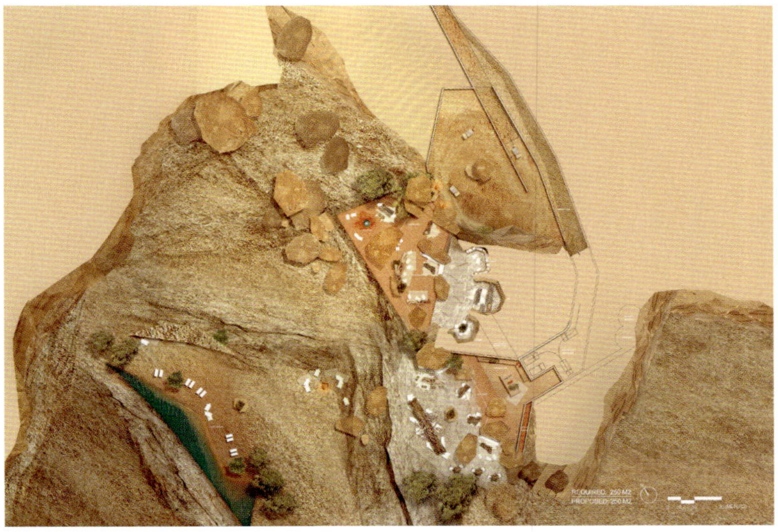

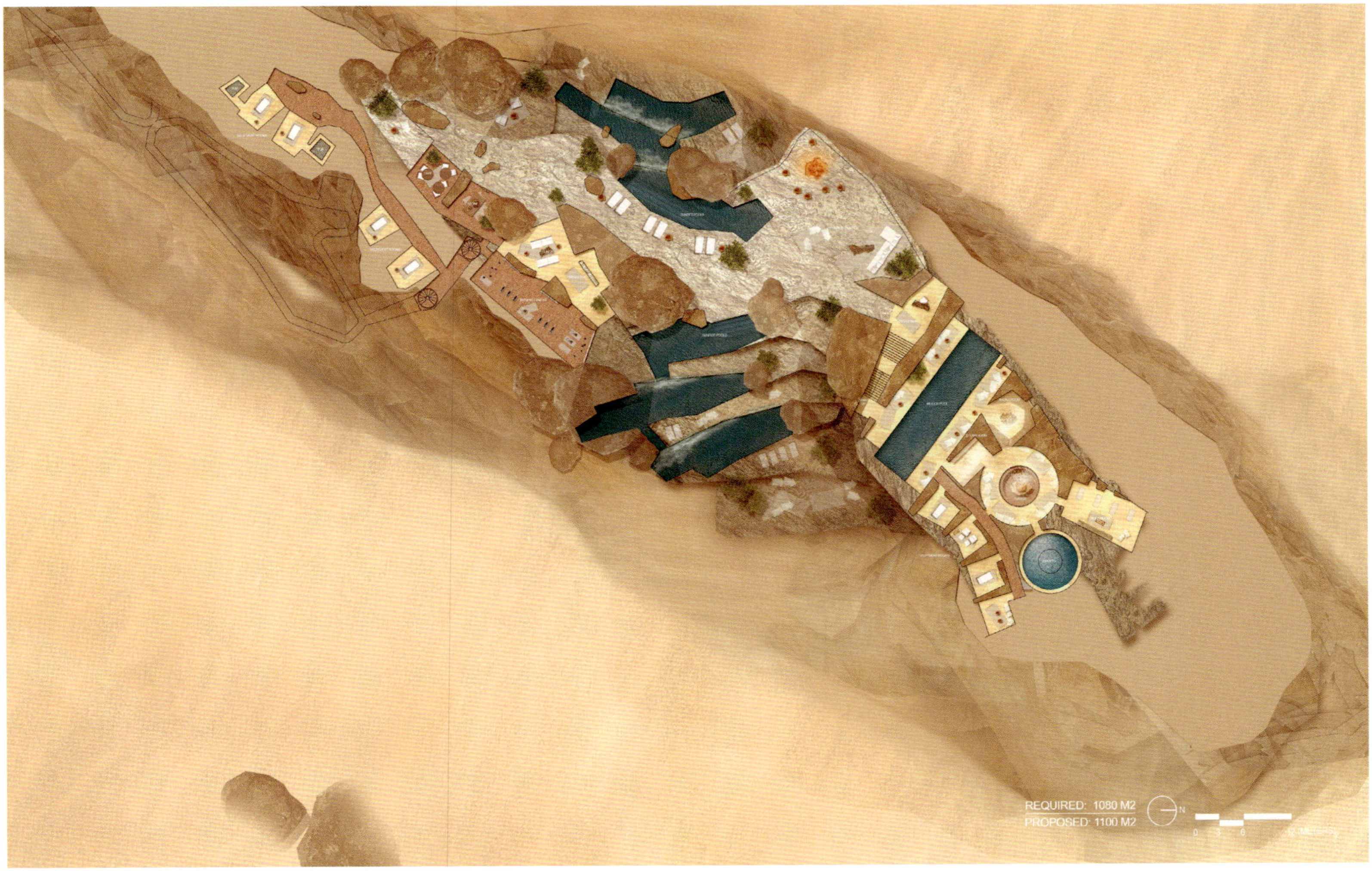
REQUIRED: 1080 M2
PROPOSED: 1100 M2

SILVER CLOUD

The outer skin of the building consists of three-dimensionally deformed steel frames covered with stainless steel or aluminum panels, in order to create a building envelope which will be instantly recognizable even if just seen for seconds out of a moving car.
The shadow created by the cantilever of the building volume of the Automotive Showroom Mall itself provides a pleasant climate in the nearby plaza.
Functional Concept and Circulation
The Silver Cloud is a fluid and continuous museum space, in which the cars, exhibited like art objects, are experienced while walking along the spiral.
The building floor plan is organized in a double loop which forms a large spiral, connecting all public areas of the building. Along the way several resting areas with look-outs are situated. However, visitors can arrange their own tours by using a number of additional ramps and escalators in order to access certain exhibition spaces directly.
The functional and organizational concept allows for a maximum of sellable floor space together with high flexibility. The exhibition areas are conceived as a open free span flexible space, allowing for all kinds of exhibition and circulation concept according to the changing requirements of the car exhibition. All areas are accessible for cars without the need for cargo elevators.

COMPANY	COOP HIMMELB(L)AU
DESIGN PRINCIPAL	Wolf D. Prix
PHOTOGRAPHER	Markus Pillhofer
CLIENT	GB AUTO SAE (Ghabbour), Cairo, Egypt
COUNTRY (DISTRICT)	Austria

WELLNESS ORHIDELIA

The main goal of the building design was to reduce as much as possible its presence in the surroundings. Since the designed wellness centre is vast and in parts demands large inner spaces of big heights, erecting a classically conceived building on the central green plot would fill the last remaining open area within the thermal complex and degrade its spatial quality. The new wellness centre is thus designed closer to a discrete landscape arrangement than a building; however, it still offers a spacious and luxurious interior. The design of the basic elements, the use of materials and colors brings the feeling of connection with nature also to the interior.

Since the building is designed for relaxation and not for sports activities, ensuring a high level of privacy was also an essential part of the design. The diversified spaces enable the visitors to spread through the building and avoid the feeling of being in a crowded space. The same idea leads the design of the slightly unusual flower colored water surfaces, which transform the pools into relaxing baths. The heterogeneous spaces defined with use of different materials and decoration offer numerous scenographic stimuli with a single intention - to evoke a touch of almost forgotten spirit of buildings intended for relaxation from the past, in which the guest was not overwhelmed by excessive information and direct animation, but embraced simply by water, space and light in their full glory.

COMPANY	Enota
PHOTOGRAPHER	Miran Kambič
CLIENT	Terme Olimia
COUNTRY (DISTRICT)	Slovenia

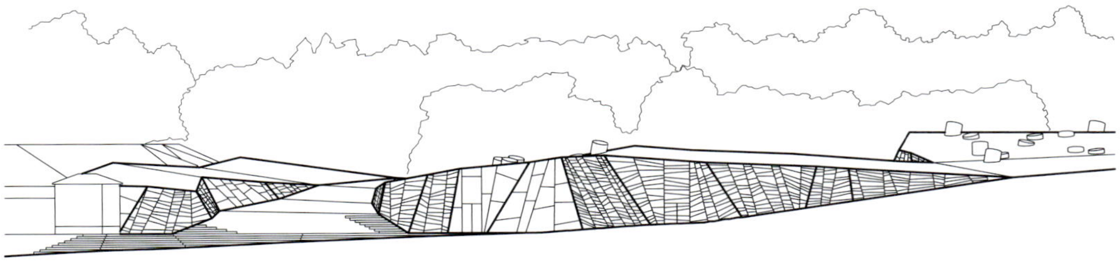

north elevation

05 orhidelia elevations (1:600)

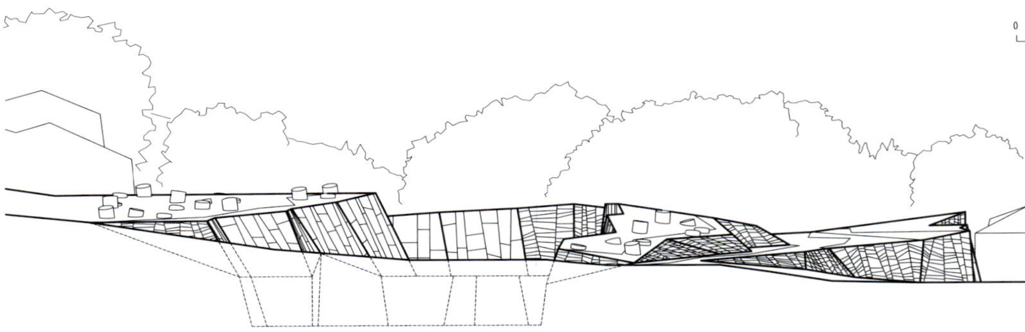

south elevation

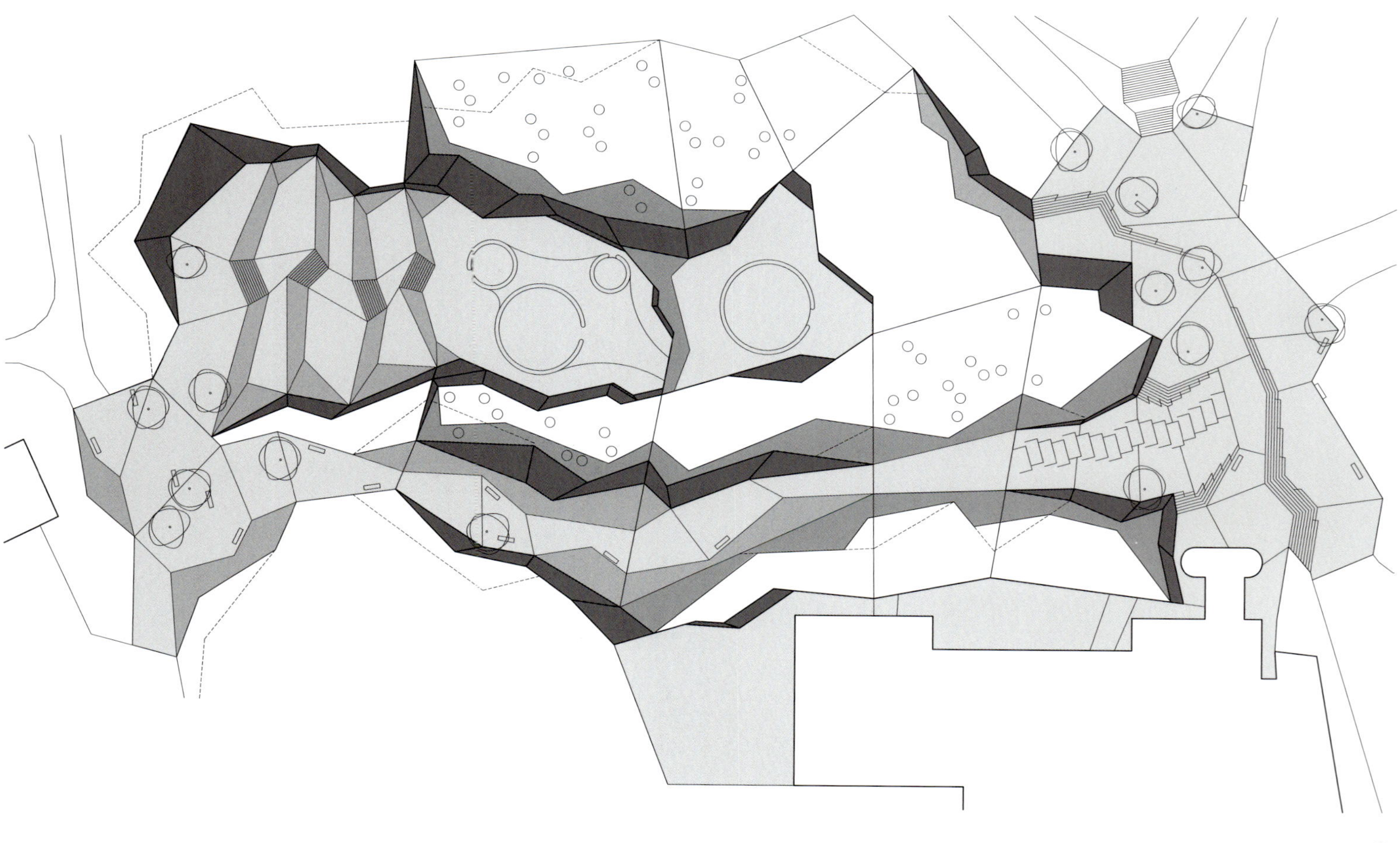

04 orhidelia roof plan (1:600)

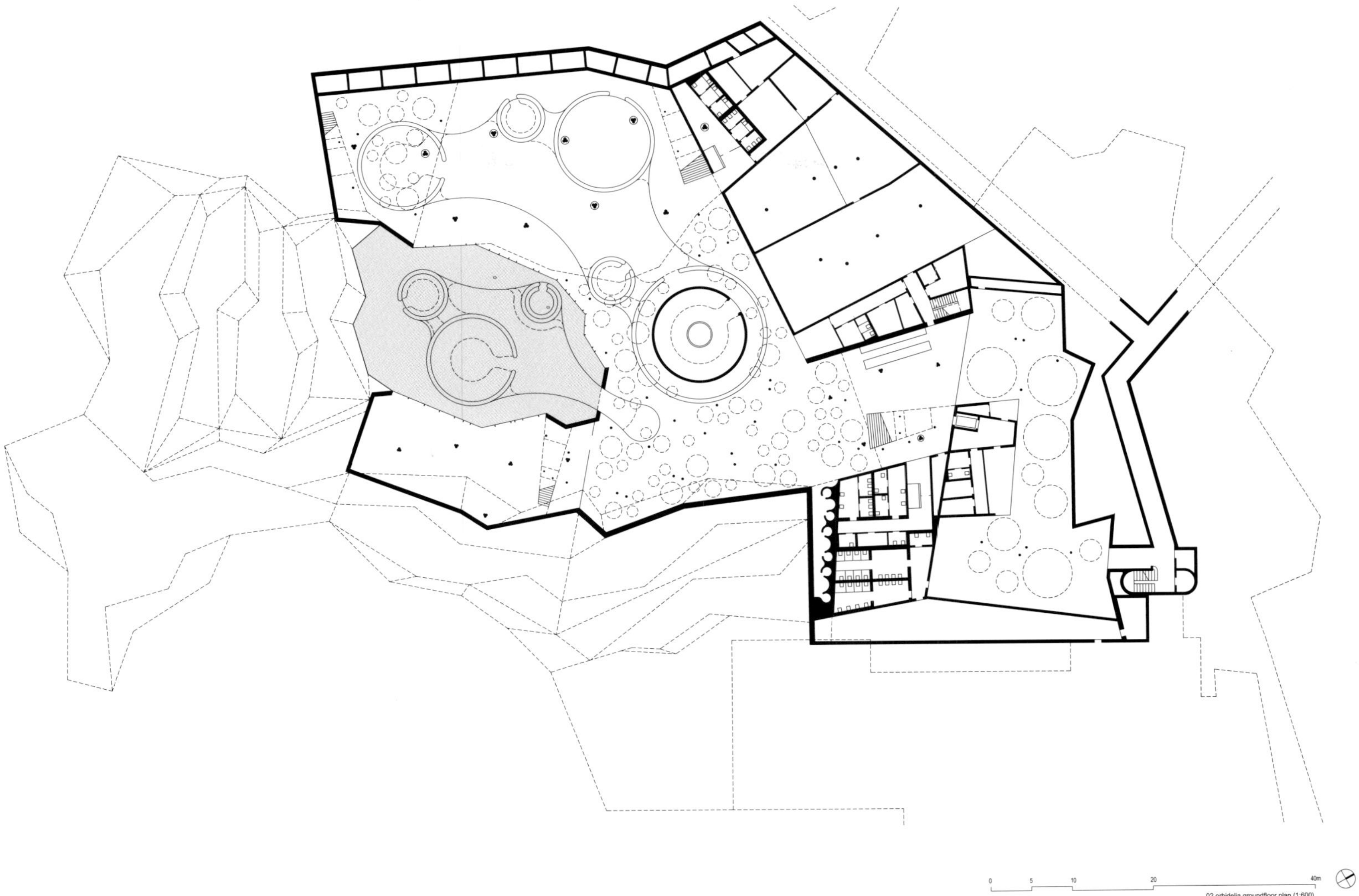

02 orhidelia groundfloor plan (1:600)

03 orhidelia firstfloor plan (1:600)

HOTEL CALDOR

Seedörfl is a small collection of houses, the surrounding landscape is flat. To the northeast the federal highway B16 cuts through the fields. The two-storey folded volume of the building with its projecting snout, bedrooms on the first floor and striking perforated bands along the façade looks like a built logo. The large asphalted approach, turning and parking area and the self check-in facility in the open foyer give the building something of the flair of a motel. Rooms – from a size of only ten square meters – are reduced on a minimum which doesn't feel small. The materials are reduced to a minimum too. The bathroom is screened by glass panes with a sliding door. As a result the red three-dimensional bathroom strip becomes an integral part of the room.
Guests receive their key when they want - on the early morning or late night.

COMPANY	Söhne & Partner Architekten
DESIGNER	Thomas Bärtl, Michael Prodinger, Guido Trampitsch
PHOTOGRAPHER	Severin Wurnig
CLIENT	Martin Reichard
COUNTRY (DISTRICT)	Austria

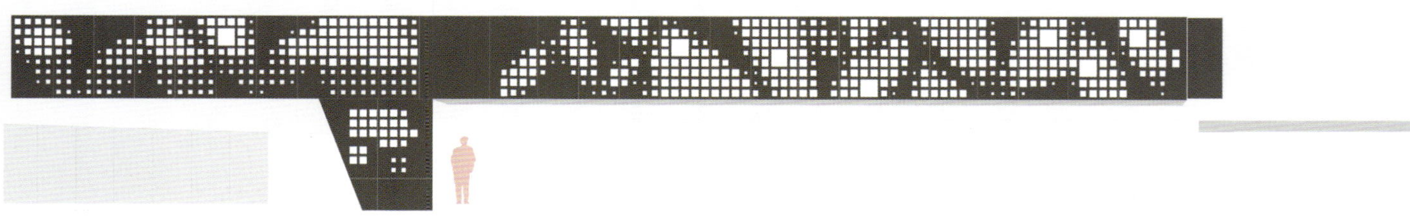

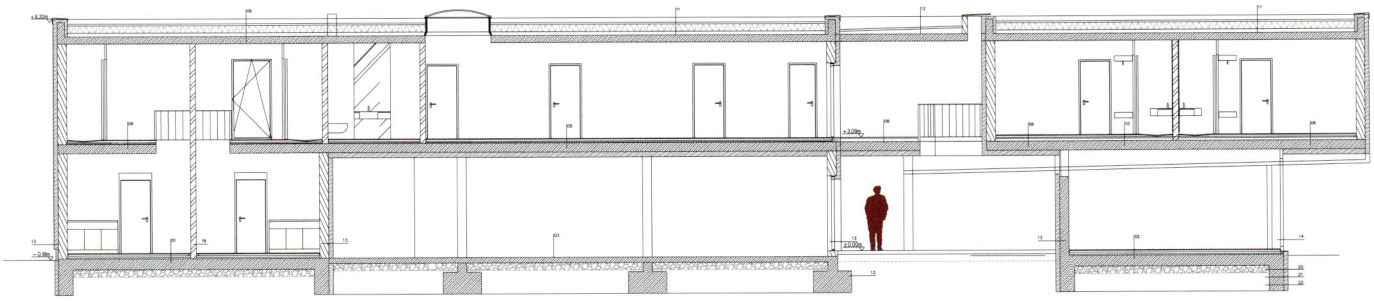

m1:100
section A-A

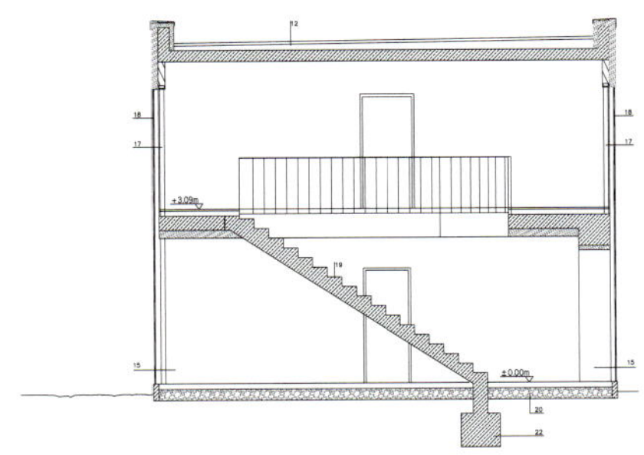

m1:100
section B-B

No.	Thickness	Layer
01	20mm	carpeting
	50mm	screed
		separating layer
	50mm	thermal isulation EPS-W20
	30mm	impact-sound insulation TDP-RT (35/30mm)
		separating layer
	300mm	reinforced concrete
		fleece
	200mm	bed of gravel
02	5mm	synthetic resin stopping
	50mm	screed
		separating layer
	50mm	thermal isulation EPS-W20
	30mm	impact-sound insulation TDP-RT (35/30mm)
		separating layer
	300mm	reinforced concrete
		fleece
	200mm	bed of gravel
03	100mm	reinforced concrete
		fleece
	200mm	bed of gravel
04	20mm	carpeting
	50mm	screed
		separating layer
	50mm	impact-sound insulation TDP-RT (35/30mm)
		separating layer
	250mm	reinforced concrete
	140mm	thermal isulation EPS-W20
	2mm	finishing
05	20mm	carpeting
	50mm	screed
		separating layer
	50mm	impact-sound insulation TDP-RT (35/30mm)
		separating layer
	250mm	reinforced concrete
	140mm	thermal isulation EPS-W20
06	20mm	carpeting
	50mm	screed
		separating layer
	50mm	impact-sound insulation TDP-RT (35/30mm)
		separating layer
	50mm	sand incline
	250mm	reinforced concrete
	140mm	thermal isulation EPS-W20
07	35mm	artificial stone
	140mm	thermal isulation EPS-W20
	250mm	reinforced concrete
		stopping
08	35mm	artificial stone
	85mm	sand incline
		separating layer
	250mm	reinforced concrete
	140mm	thermal isulation EPS-W20
09	20mm	carpeting
	50mm	screed
		separating layer
	50mm	impact-sound insulation TDP-RT (35/30mm)
	250mm	reinforced concrete
		stopping
10	20mm	carpeting
	50mm	screed
		separating layer
	50mm	impact-sound insulation TDP-RT (35/30mm)
		sand incline
	250mm	reinforced concrete
		stopping
11	50mm	gravel incline
		fleece
		separating layer EPDM
	200mm	thermal isulation EPS-W20
		separating layer
		bitumen sealing lane
	80mm	concrete incline
	200mm	reinforced concrete
		stopping
12	50mm	gravel incline
	80mm	concrete incline
	200mm	reinforced concrete
		stopping
13	120mm	thermal isulation EPS-W20
	250mm	brick wall / concrete wall
		stopping
14		thermopane glazing
15	8mm	Max Exterior (façade panel)
	70mm	steel substructure
16	12mm	plasterboard (2xGK)
	30mm	insulation
17		steel substructure
18		Max Exterior (façade panel)
19		staircase: 18stairs (17.1cm/26cm)
20		bed of gravel
21		frost wall
22		foundation

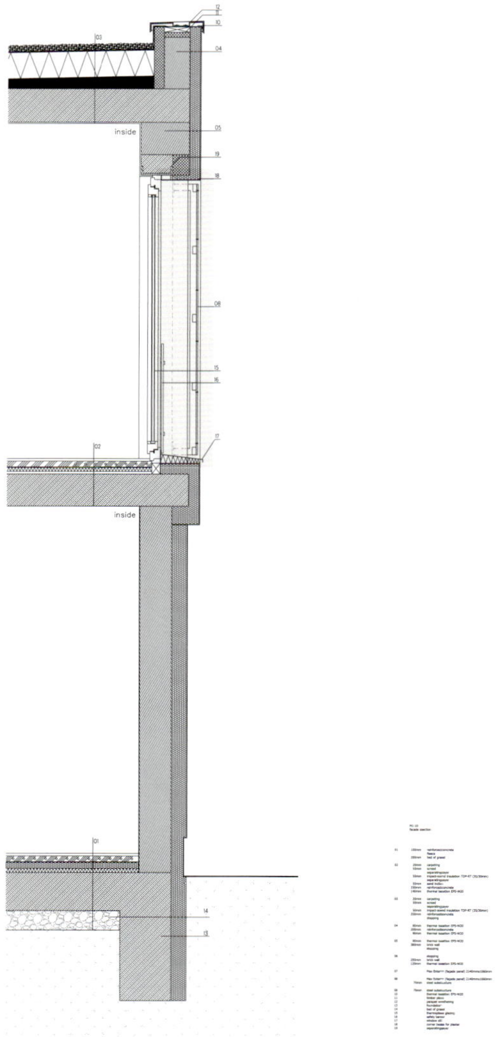
inside
inside

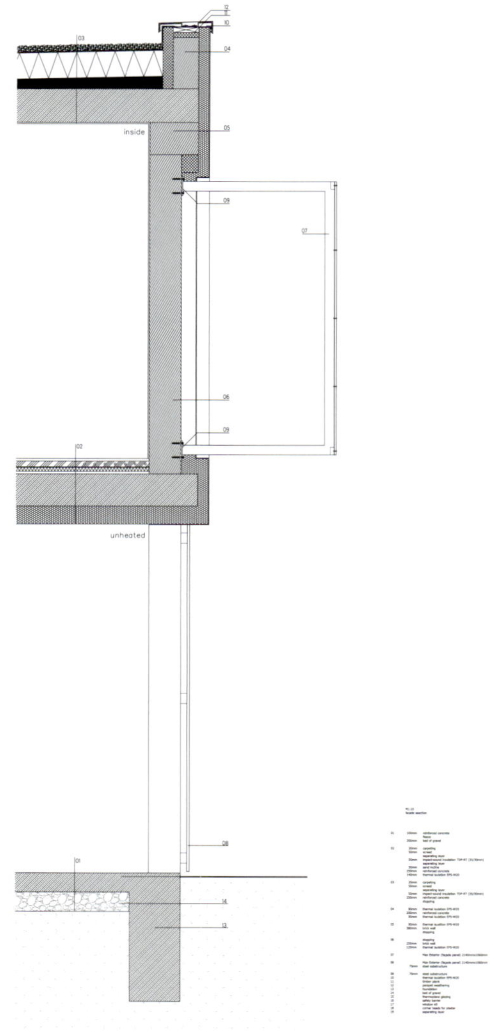
inside
unheated

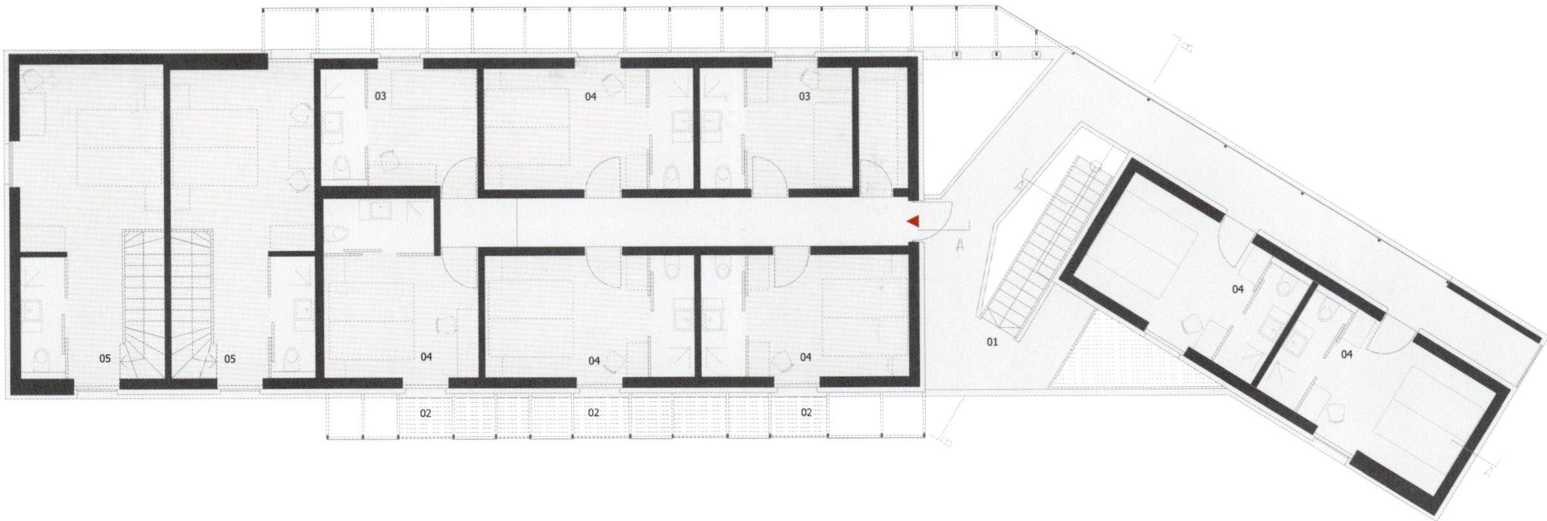

m1:100
first floor

01 acess balcony
02 balcony
03 single room
04 double room
05 maisonette
06 lobby
07 enlargement of area

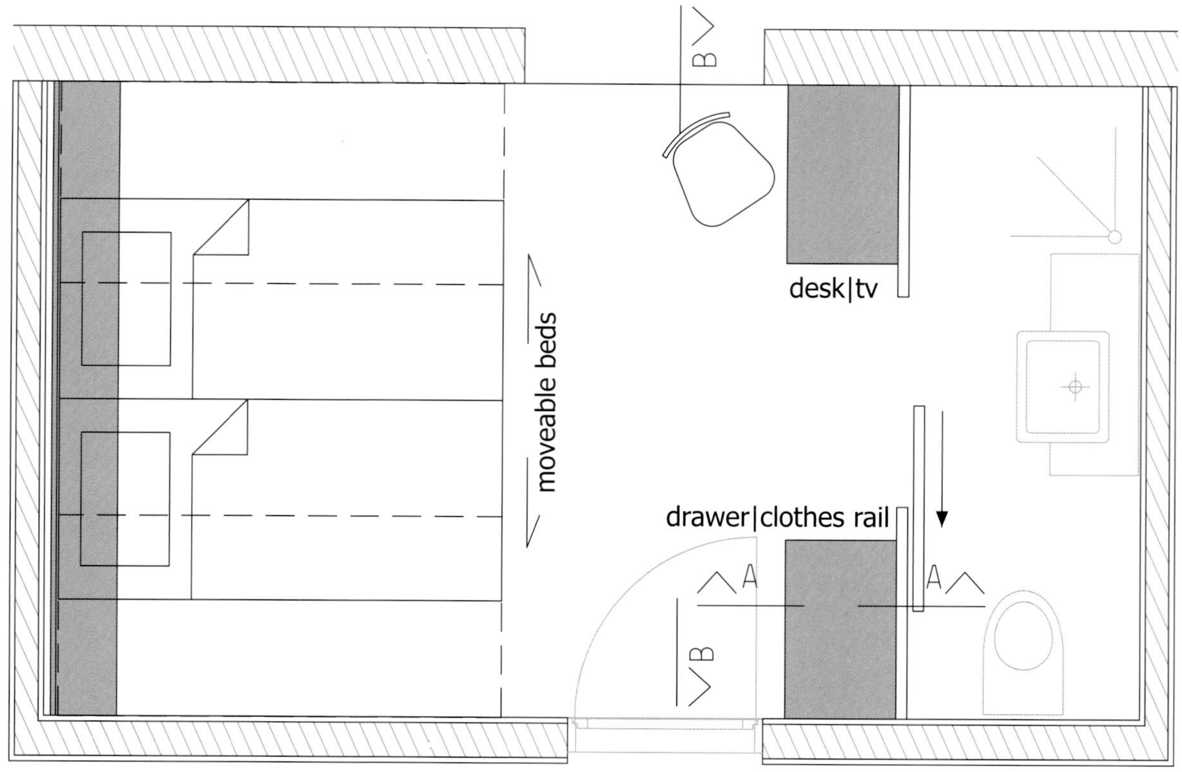

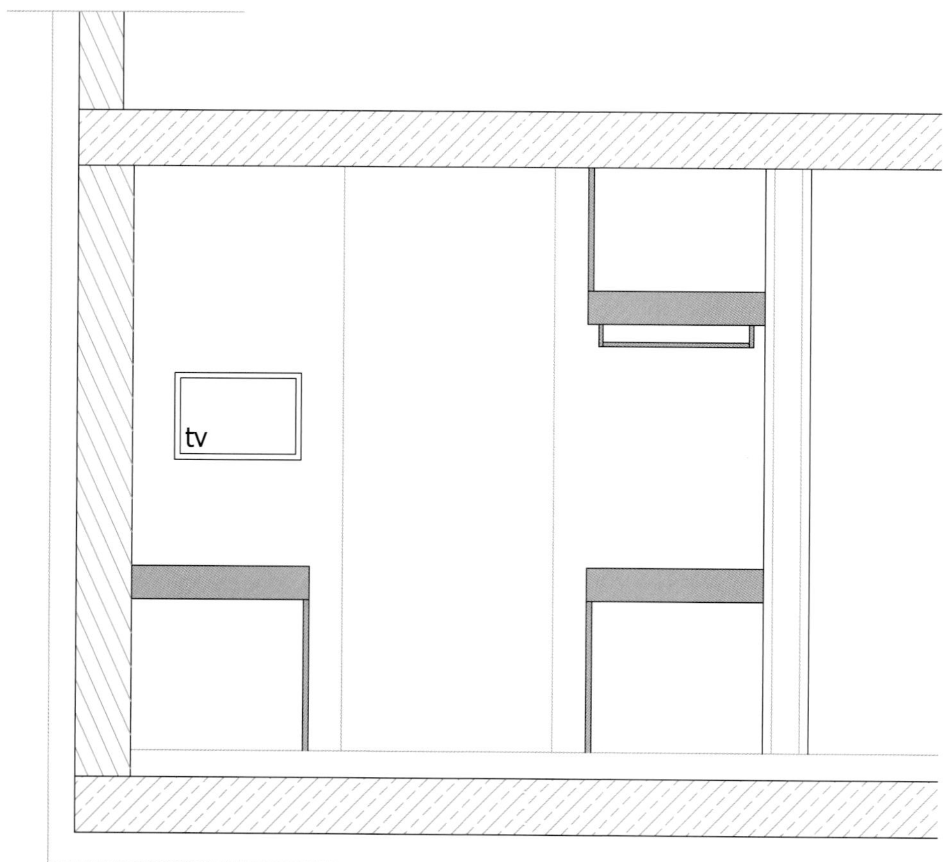

ANSICHT B–B

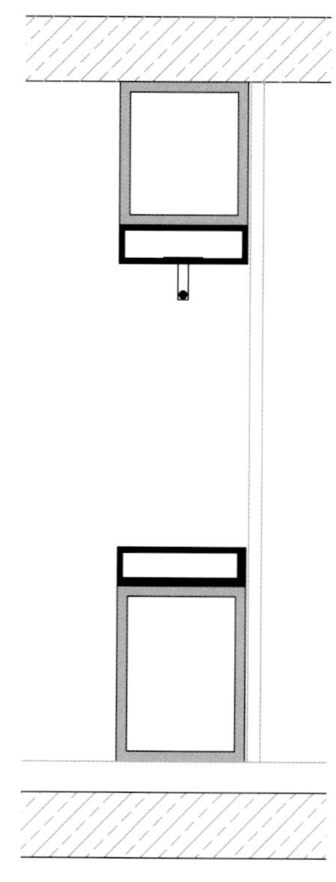

ANSICHT A–A

m1:50
double bedroom

CODE UNIQUE

The facade gives the hotel the name, it is not only an eyecatcher - the implication of the facade structure is a code - a special matrix code to be named - QR Code. Code Unique Hotel is Söhne & Partners concept for a QR Code hotel in Dubai's Studio City. Their concept centers around futurism, creativity, and inspiration. If executed properly the code could allow for all kinds of macro and micro exploration with your mobile device.
Dubai Studio City will be another Mecca of the global illusions industry. It is a logical consequence of Dubai's city history. In this context the strongest expressions for fictions are science fiction movies. And the medium for the fiction trip is the spaceship.
The hotel Söhne & Partners designed is also a medium – a medium for hospitality. It is the inverse of a spaceship; it is a space harbor for business people, actors, and people who want to taste the atmosphere of illusions.

The CODE UNIQUE HOTEL is a place for offering a premium service to all travelers with the best amenities to make the stay of the guests more pleasurable and especially – inspirational.

COMPANY	Söhne & Partner Architekten
DESIGNER	Thomas Bärtl, Michael Prodinger, Guido Trampitsch
PHOTOGRAPHER	miss 3
CLIENT	Ahmed Seddiq Al Mutawaa
COUNTRY (DISTRICT)	Austria

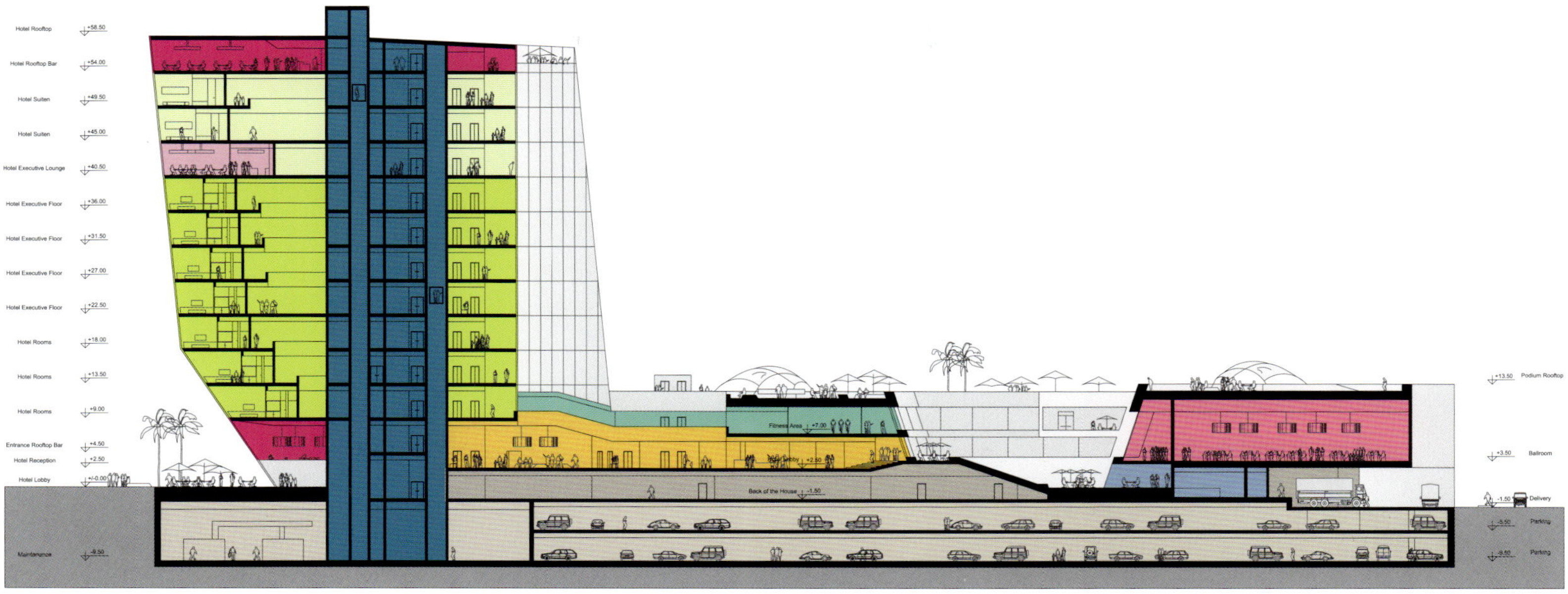
Hotel Rooftop +58.50
Hotel Rooftop Bar +54.00
Hotel Suiten +49.50
Hotel Suiten +45.00
Hotel Executive Lounge +40.50
Hotel Executive Floor +36.00
Hotel Executive Floor +31.50
Hotel Executive Floor +27.00
Hotel Executive Floor +22.50
Hotel Rooms +18.00
Hotel Rooms +13.50
Hotel Rooms +9.00
Entrance Rooftop Bar +4.50
Hotel Reception +2.50
Hotel Lobby +/-0.00
Fitness Area +7.00
+2.50
Back of the House -1.50
+13.50 Podium Rooftop
+3.50 Ballroom
-1.50 Delivery
-5.50 Parking
-9.50 Parking

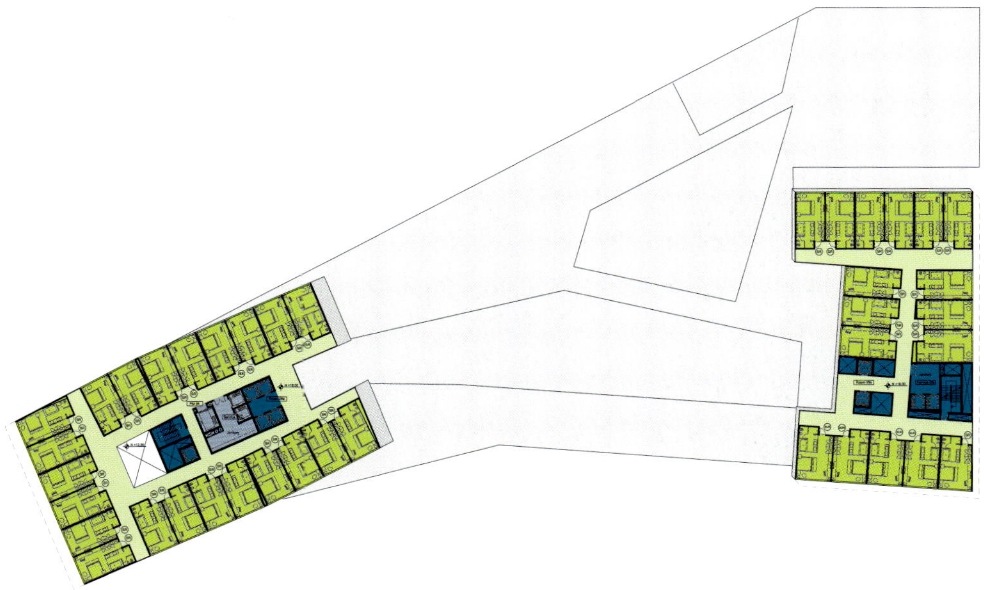

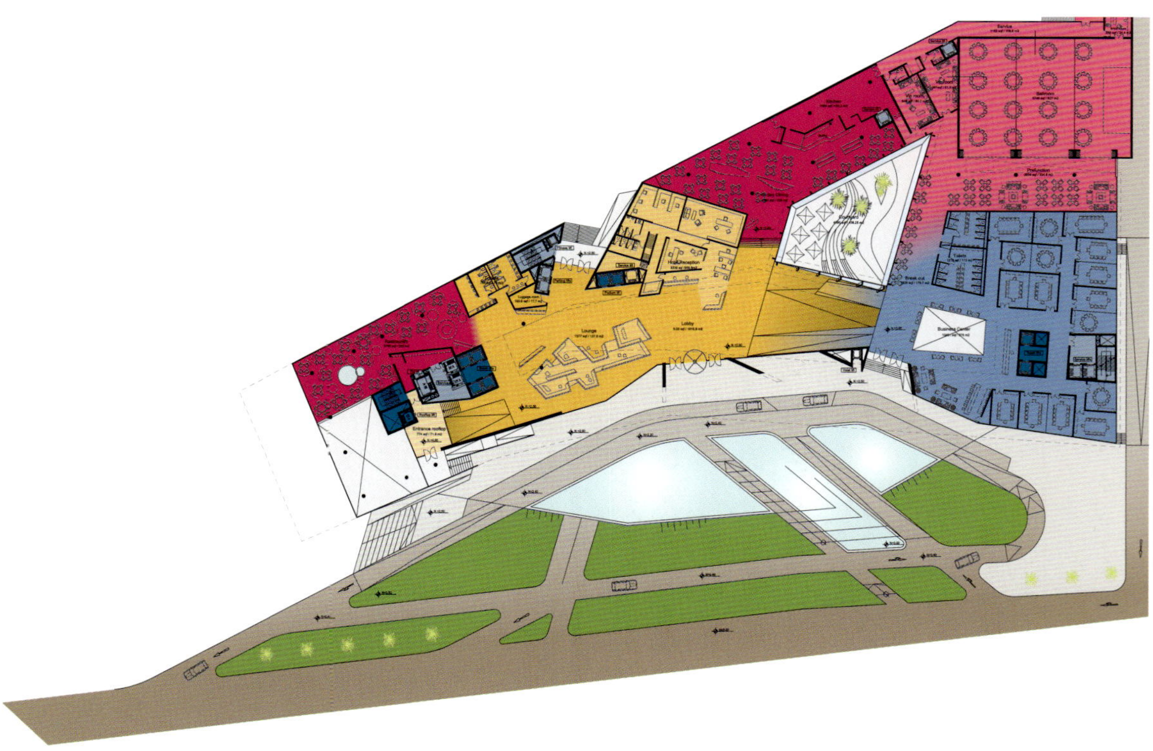

KSS
FM lift

"ROCK IT SUDA"!

Rock It Suda is a name for the pension and it's a concept.
The client is a base guitarist, a member of the amateur rock group named Rock It Suda. On regular basis, they perform live, at the pension.The site has a dry river, and an open view in front, and the other sides are, surrounded by the mountain range.
The 6 ways of capturing the beautiful scenery gave birth to spatial contraction, expansion, and compression, then themes such as Spain, Barbie, Stealth+Ferrari, cave, and Korean traditional house were added.
Play-architecture is born, when giant soft hammock, shaped like tails are attached to hard secured architecture. It is hoped that, the wind and movement made by people playing in the hammock, express the desire that architecture is not secure and unmoving.
Architecture is alive! Moving beyond its limits,also, living in the realm of imaginations.

DESIGNER	MOON HOON
PHOTOGRAPHER	Kim yong Kwan moonhoon yeum seung hoon
CLIENT	Kim Jae-Il
COUNTRY (DISTRICT)	Korea

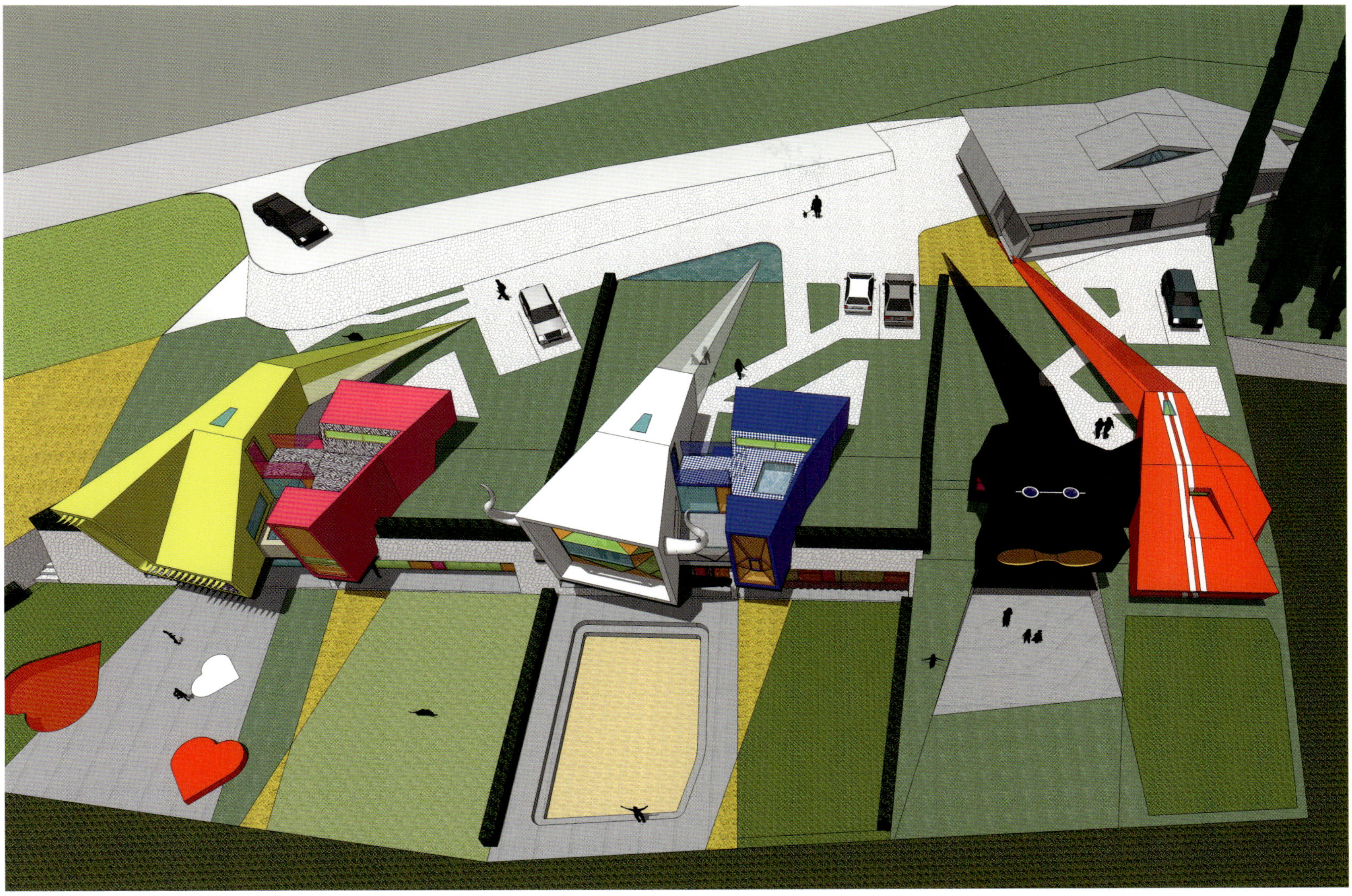

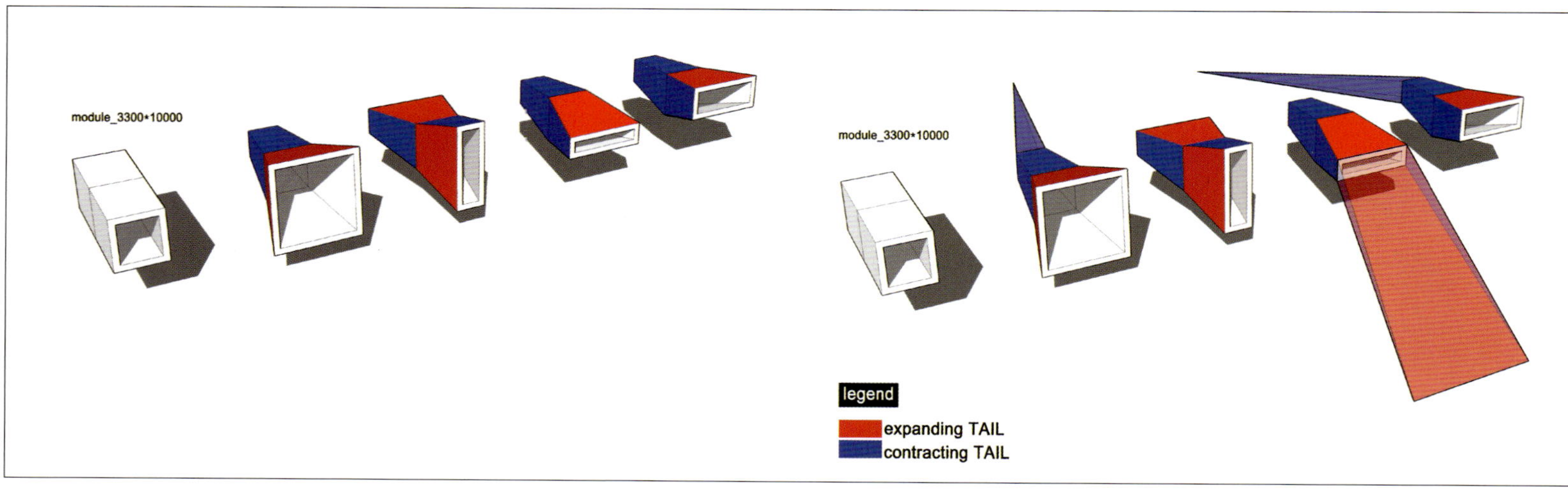
module_3300*10000
module_3300*10000
legend
expanding TAIL
contracting TAIL

legend
expanding VIEW

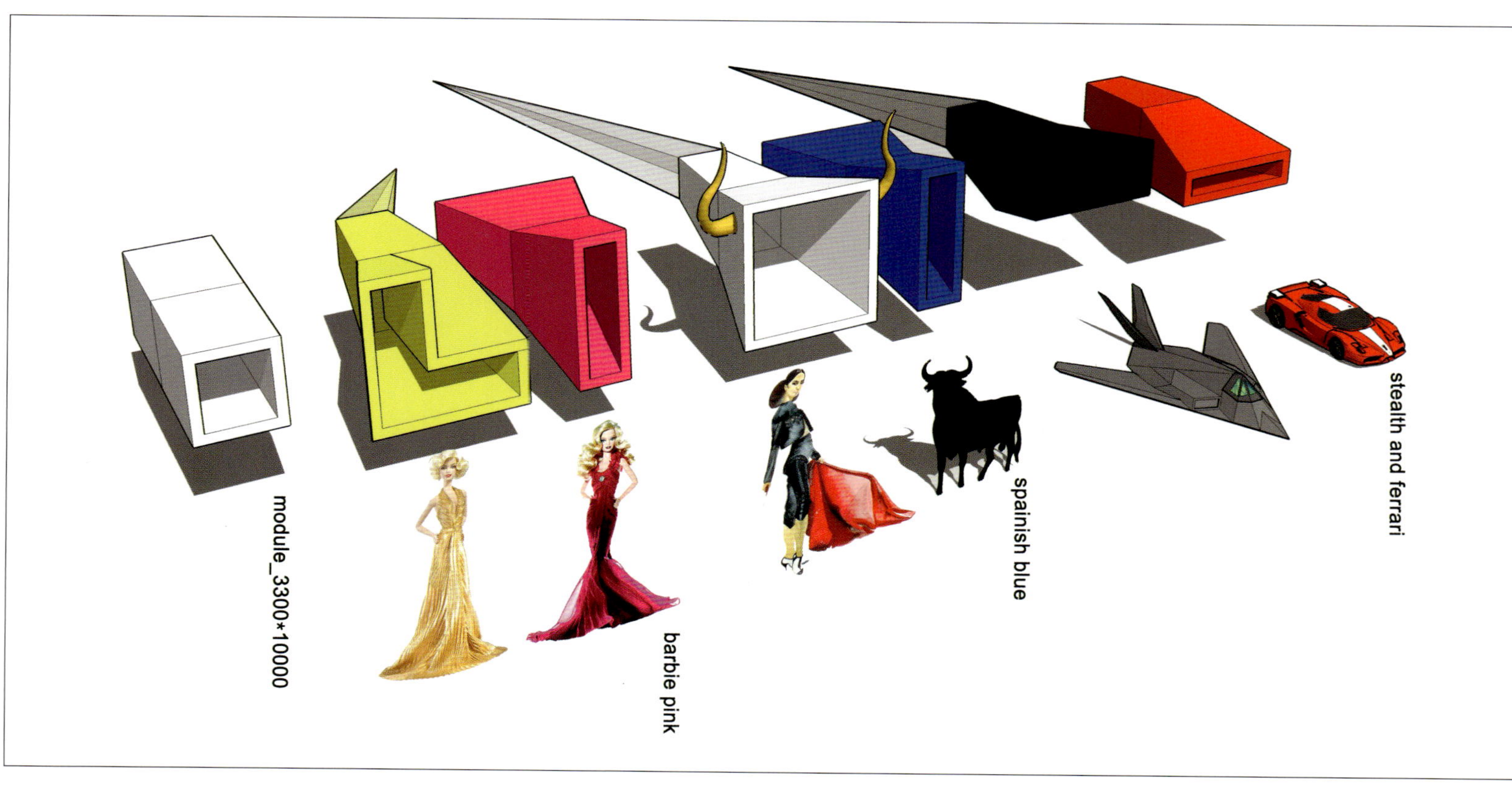
module_3300*10000
barbie pink
spainish blue
stealth and ferrari

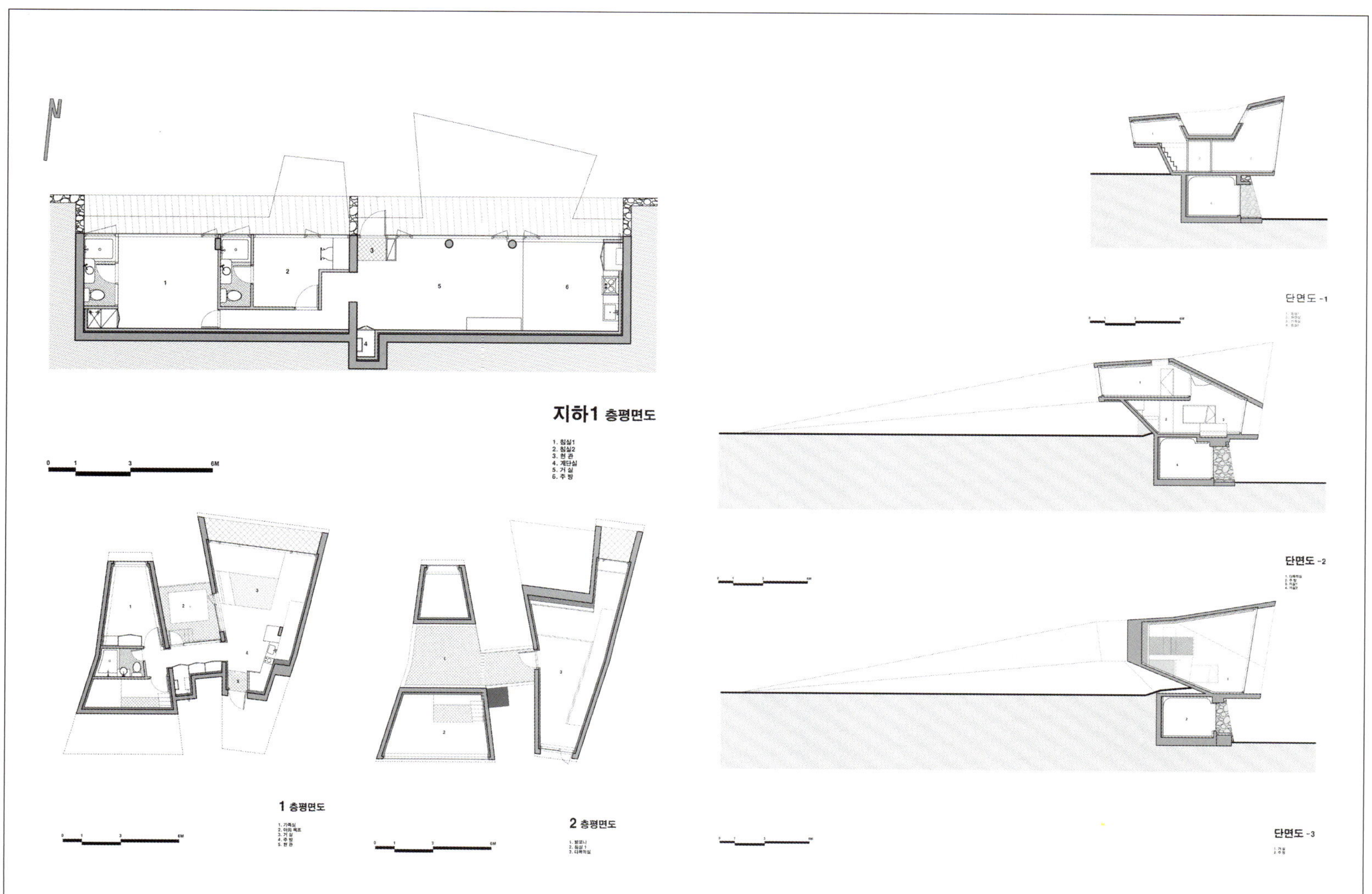
N
지하1 층평면도
1. 침실1
2. 침실2
3. 현 관
4. 계단실
5. 거 실
6. 주 방
0 1 3 6M
1 층평면도
1. 가족실
2. 야외 욕조
3. 거 실
4. 주 방
5. 현 관
0 1 3 6M
2 층평면도
1. 발코니
2. 침실 1
3. 다목적실
단면도 -1
단면도 -2
단면도 -3

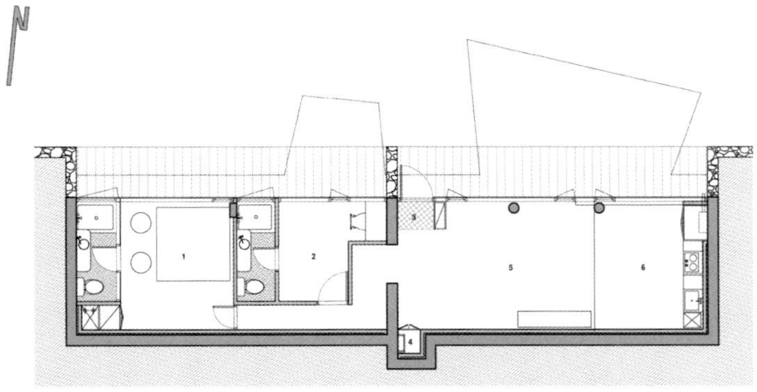

지하1 층평면도

1. 침실1
2. 침실2
3. 현 관
4. 계단실
5. 거 실
6. 주 방

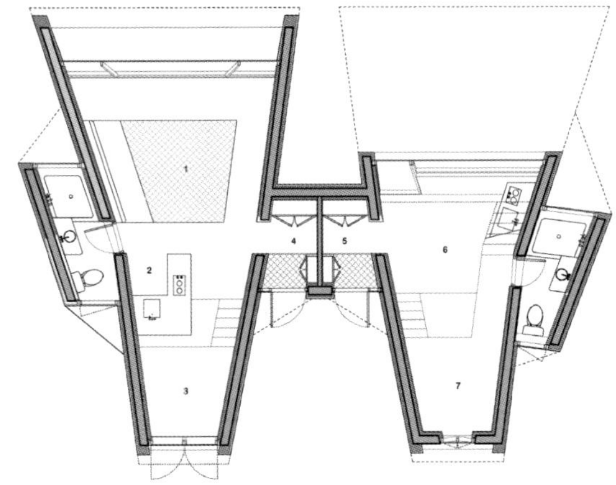

1 층평면도

1. 거 실
2. 주 방
3. 침실1
4. 현 관
5. 현 관
6. 주 방
7. 침실2

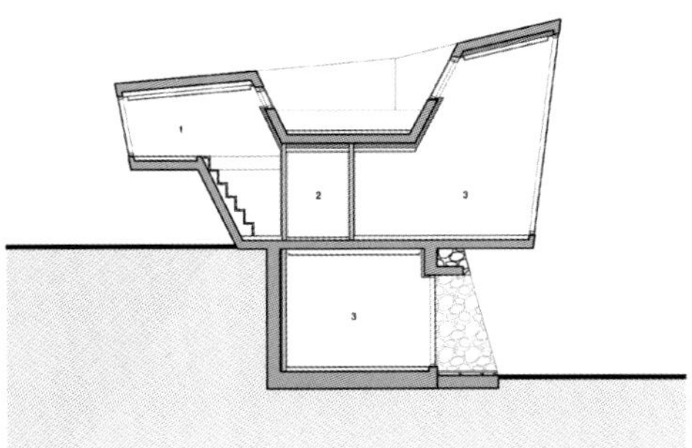

단면도 -1

1. 침실1
2. 화장실
3. 가족실
4. 침실1

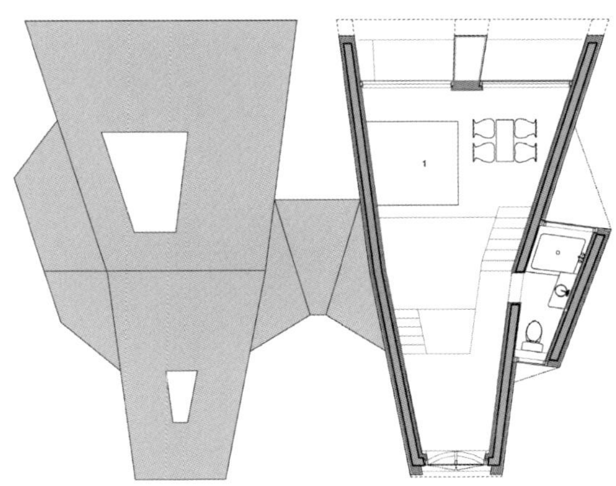

2 층평면도

1. 침실 3

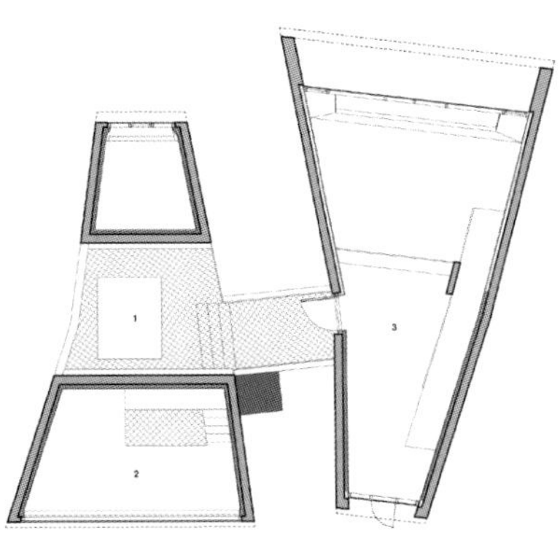

2 층평면도

1. 외부욕조
2. 침실 1
3. 다목적실

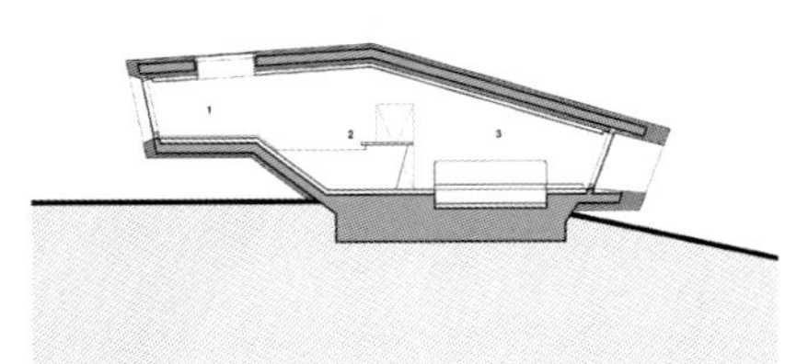

단면도 -1

1. 침 실
2. 주 방
3. 거 실

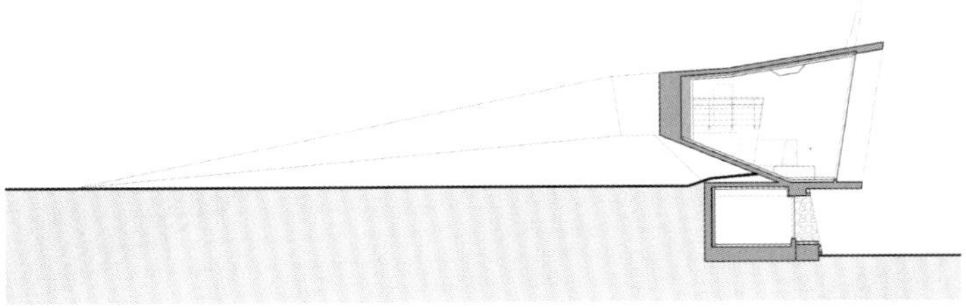

단면도 -3

1. 거 실

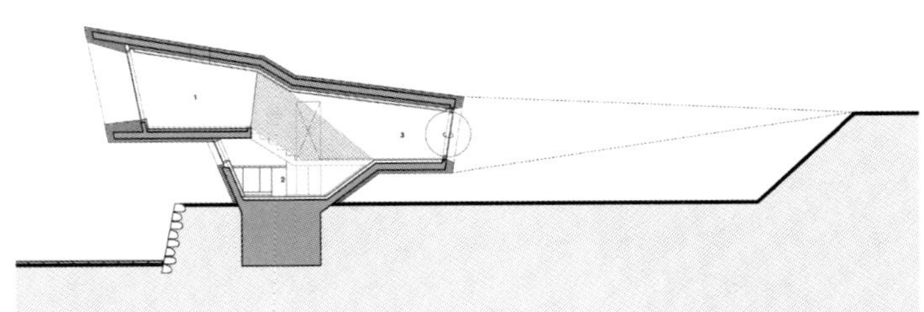

단면도 -2

1. 침실1
2. 주 방
3. 침실2

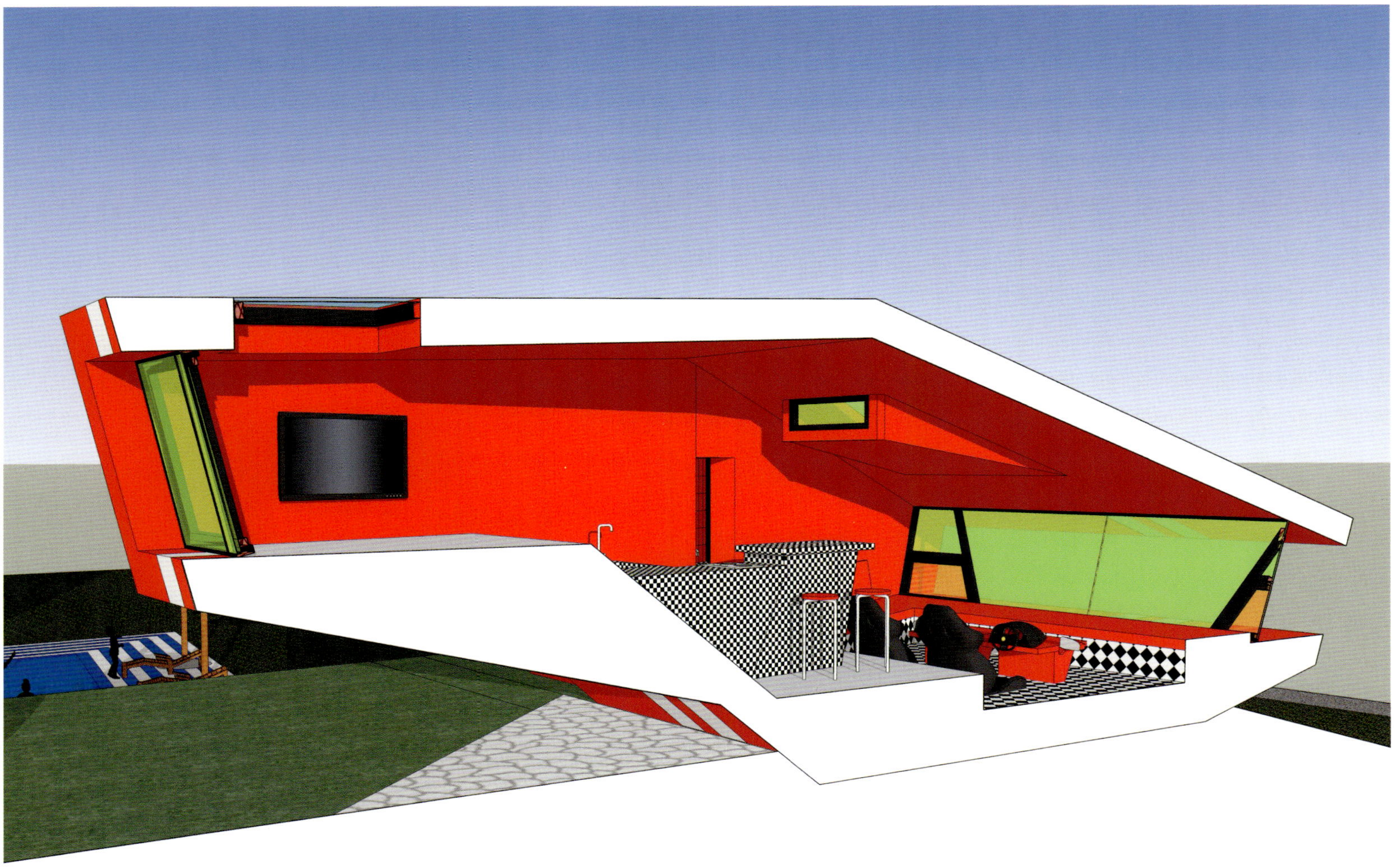

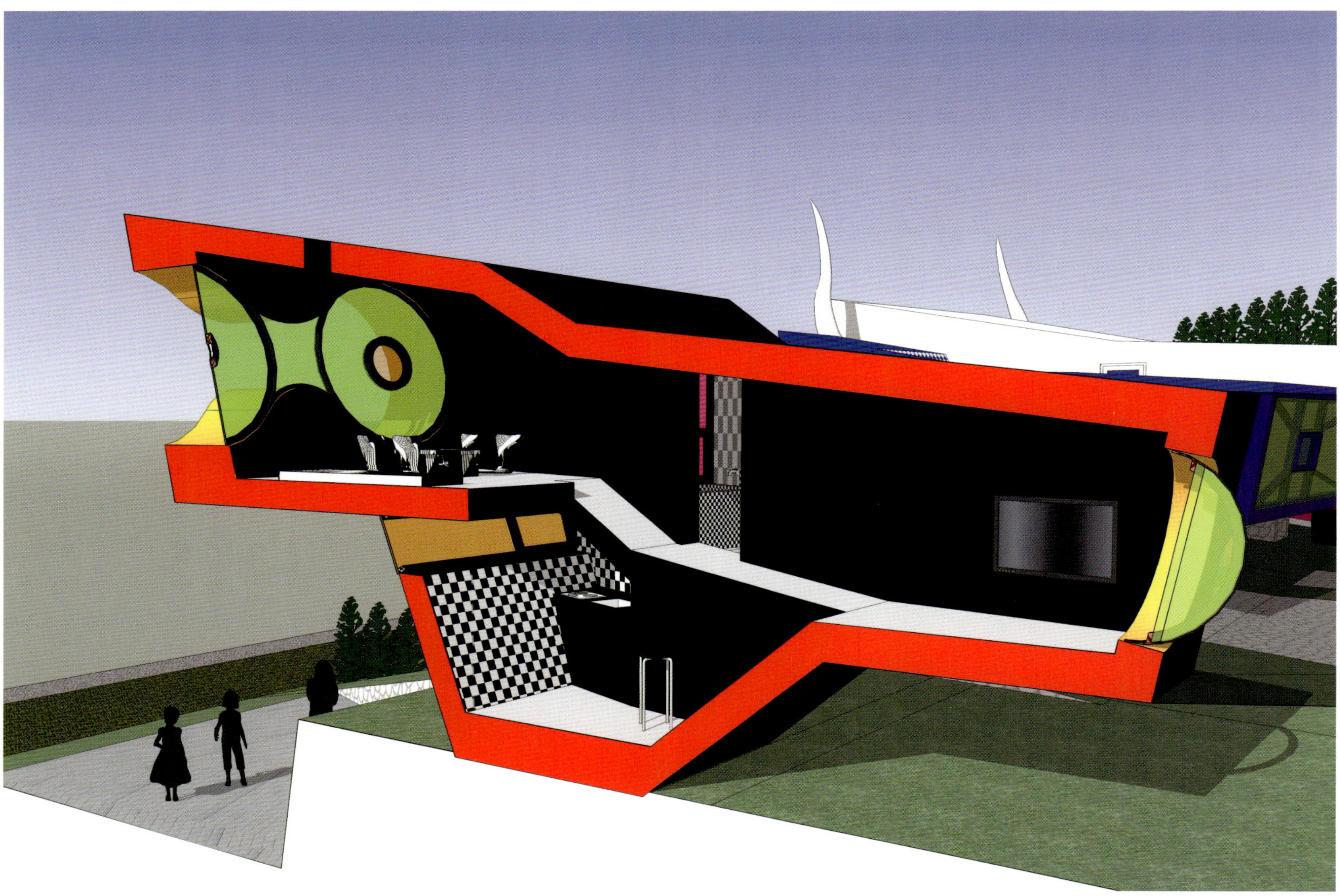

HEADLANDS HOTEL

The Headlands Hotel development proposed an International standard hotel asset that has already attracted major Hotel Brand interest from internationally respected hotel groups. The projected investment and operational outlook for the Headlands Hotel is positive. Regional demand for the Headlands Hotel product has been researched and outlined in government commissioned economic studies that forecast the local and regional direction of the hospitality and tourism sector. An existing local clientele has indicated support for the development headlands hotel that will carry the extensive local character and history into the headland's next phase. The Headland represents a spectacular opportunity for Austinmer to become a landmark of coastal hospitality known for community responsive, environmentally sustainable and commercially viable development along the New South Wales coastal edge.

The unique coastal location of the Headlands, with its close proximity to Sydney Metropolitan area road and rail network, allows visitors easily access the regions pristine natural beauty. The local area is bordered by the a mountainous state owned Royal National Park to the north and west, the South Pacific ocean to the east and the economic activity of Wollongong, the 3rd largest City in New South Wales. The planned development consists of 120 Hotel Rooms, 40 residential Luxury Apartments, Spa Rooms, Public Bar, Restaurant, Café, Ballroom and Corporate Conference facilities, all contained within an allocated floor area of 10,000m^2. The Headlands Hotel proposal builds upon a currently approved Development Proposal by analyzing and realizing the sites full development potential. The currently proposed development size has been calculated and balanced to fulfill brand and operational requirements of recognized hotel groups. This site unique opportunity, coupled with state of the architectural design and a currently assembled specialist development team, offers investors and operators alike an exceptional opportunity to capitalize on this distinctively Australian Coastal Hotel asset.

COMPANY	LAVA
CLIENT	George Dimitrovski
COUNTRY (DISTRICT)	Australia

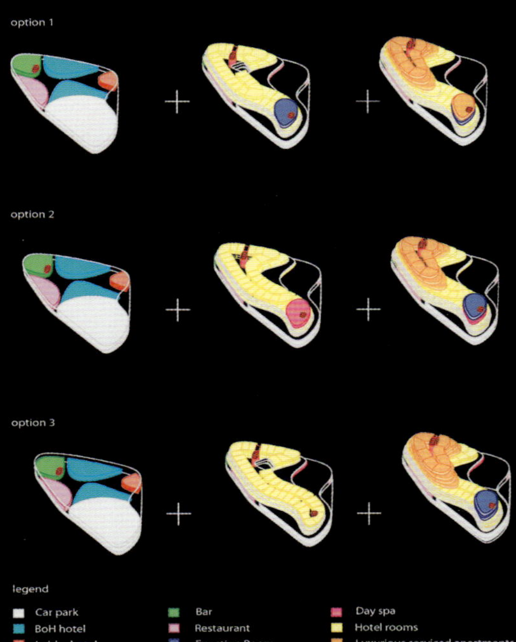
option 1
option 2
option 3
legend
Car park
BoH hotel
Lobby hotel
Bar
Restaurant
Function Room
Day spa
Hotel rooms
Luxurious serviced apartments

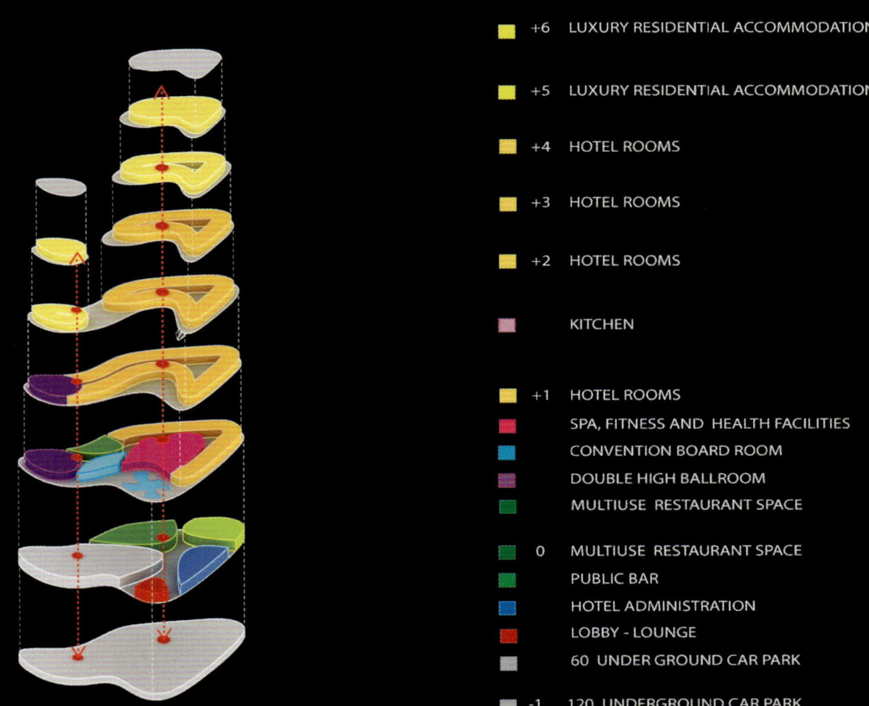
+6 LUXURY RESIDENTIAL ACCOMMODATION
+5 LUXURY RESIDENTIAL ACCOMMODATION
+4 HOTEL ROOMS
+3 HOTEL ROOMS
+2 HOTEL ROOMS
KITCHEN
+1 HOTEL ROOMS
SPA, FITNESS AND HEALTH FACILITIES
CONVENTION BOARD ROOM
DOUBLE HIGH BALLROOM
MULTIUSE RESTAURANT SPACE
0 MULTIUSE RESTAURANT SPACE
PUBLIC BAR
HOTEL ADMINISTRATION
LOBBY - LOUNGE
60 UNDER GROUND CAR PARK
-1 120 UNDERGROUND CAR PARK

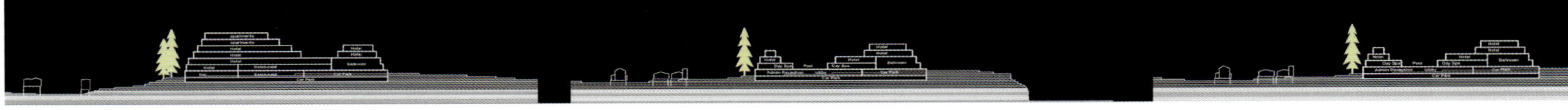

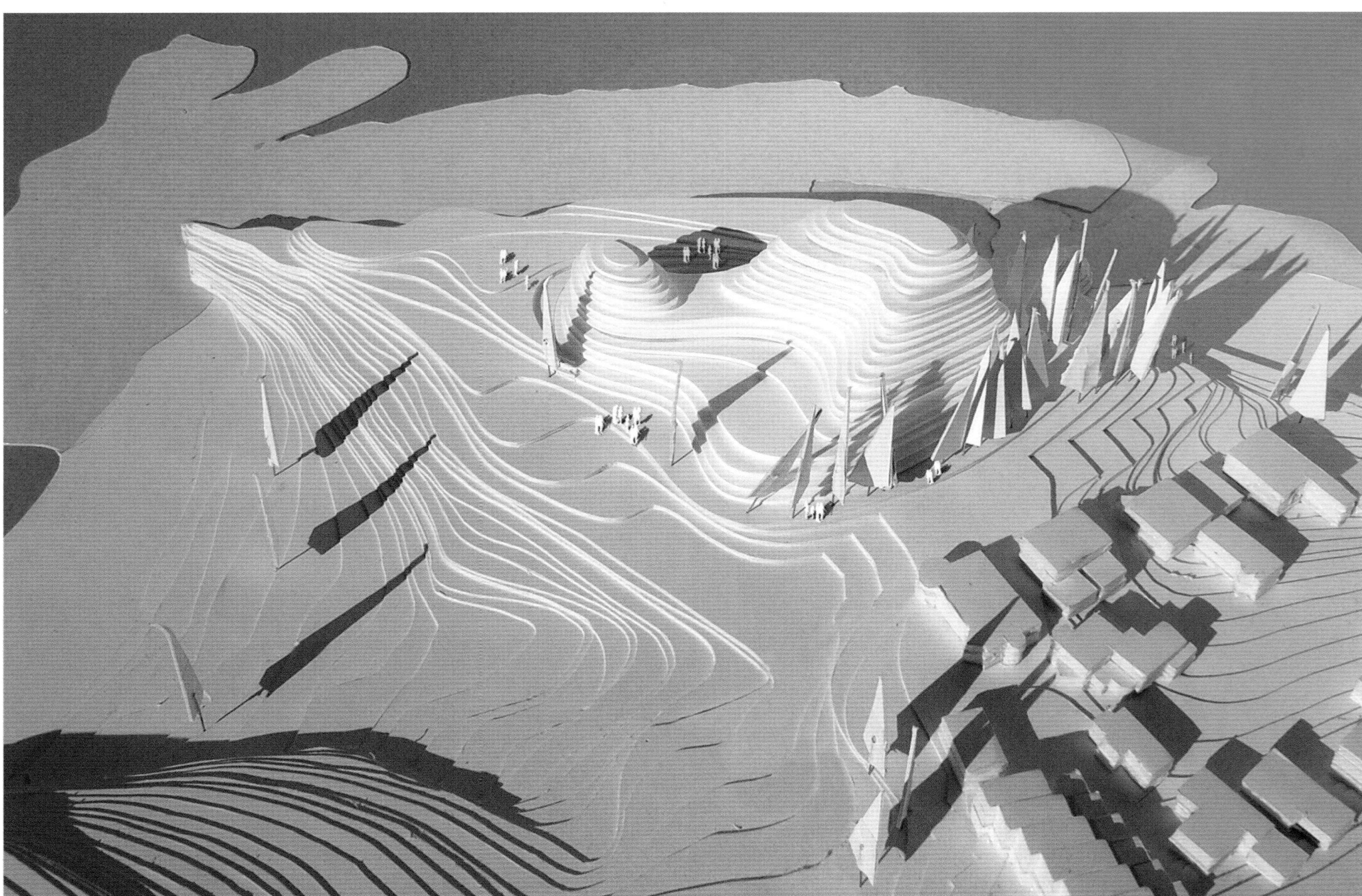

0
50
100
150
200
250

GEM @ TELFORD

G E M: A Glowing Entertainment Magnet,ornamenting the glamorization of entertainment industry and the scarcity of superstars, like the discovery of gem from cutting and polishing of precious stones. The multifaceted surfaces, responsive in different color ambience through different viewing angles, together with sculptural Gem pieces, made up from colored triangular-shaped laminated glass, through spectacular lighting effects,bring out the luster and splendor of the GEM.

PEOPLE . ENTERTAINMENT . COMMUNITY concept begins with discovery: discovery about relationships among people, entertainment and community. Distinctive slanting profile of cinema houses creates dramatic volumetric entrances, allowing an unobstructed and natural lighting foyer environment. High transparency, wisely camouflaged structures, set aside functional requirements, all contribute to the creation of an indoor openness for people gathering and public events, seamlessly link up with the community at the outdoor neighborhood.

COMPANY	AGC Design Ltd.
CREATIVE DIRECTOR	Michael Tsang
DESIGNER	Anthony Ho, Raymond Ho
PHOTOGRAPHER	Brilliance Image Tech
CLIENT	MTR Corporation
COUNTRY (DISTRICT)	Hong Kong China

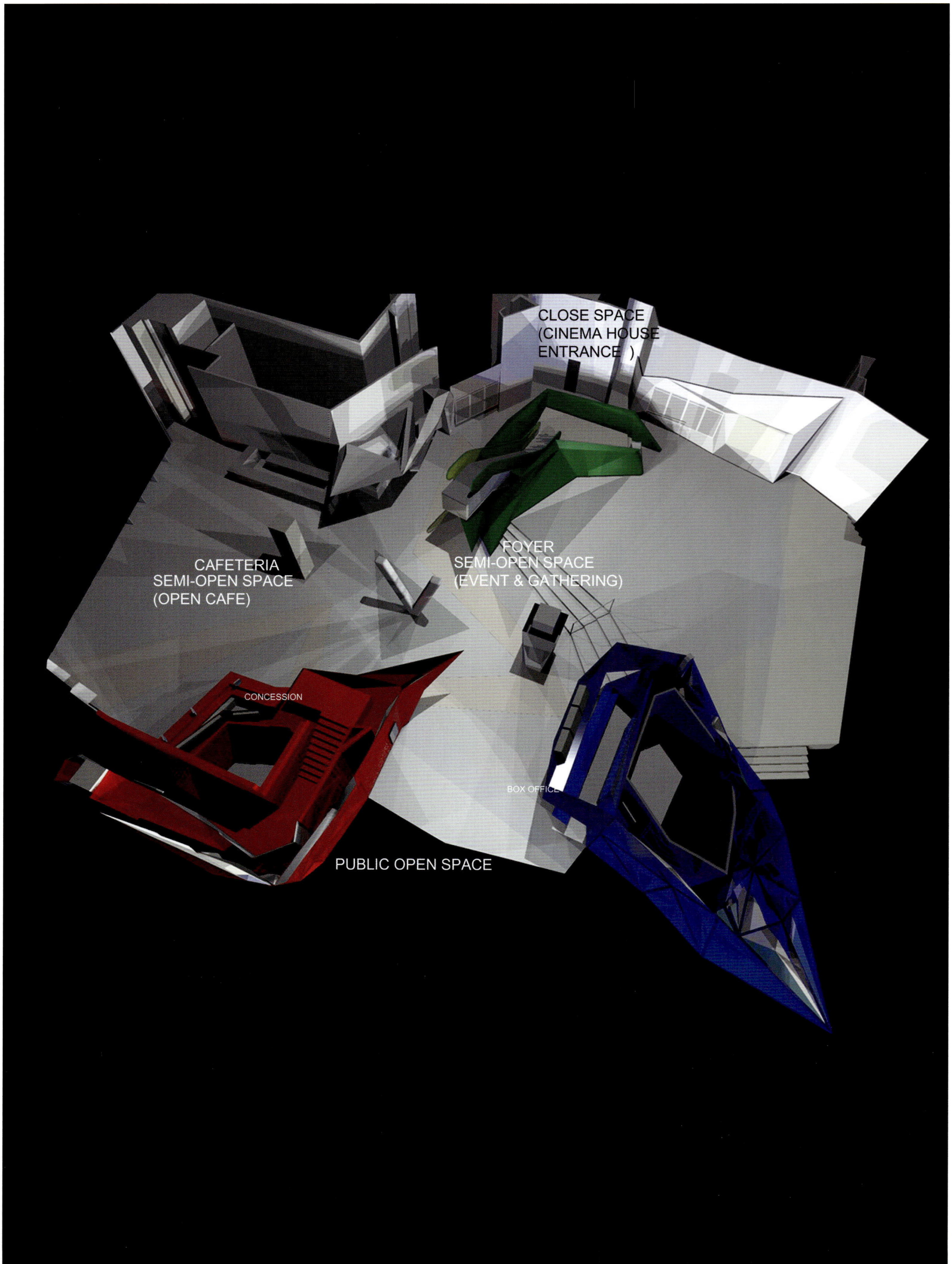
CLOSE SPACE
(CINEMA HOUSE
ENTRANCE)
FOYER
SEMI-OPEN SPACE
(EVENT & GATHERING)
CAFETERIA
SEMI-OPEN SPACE
(OPEN CAFE)
CONCESSION
BOX OFFICE
PUBLIC OPEN SPACE

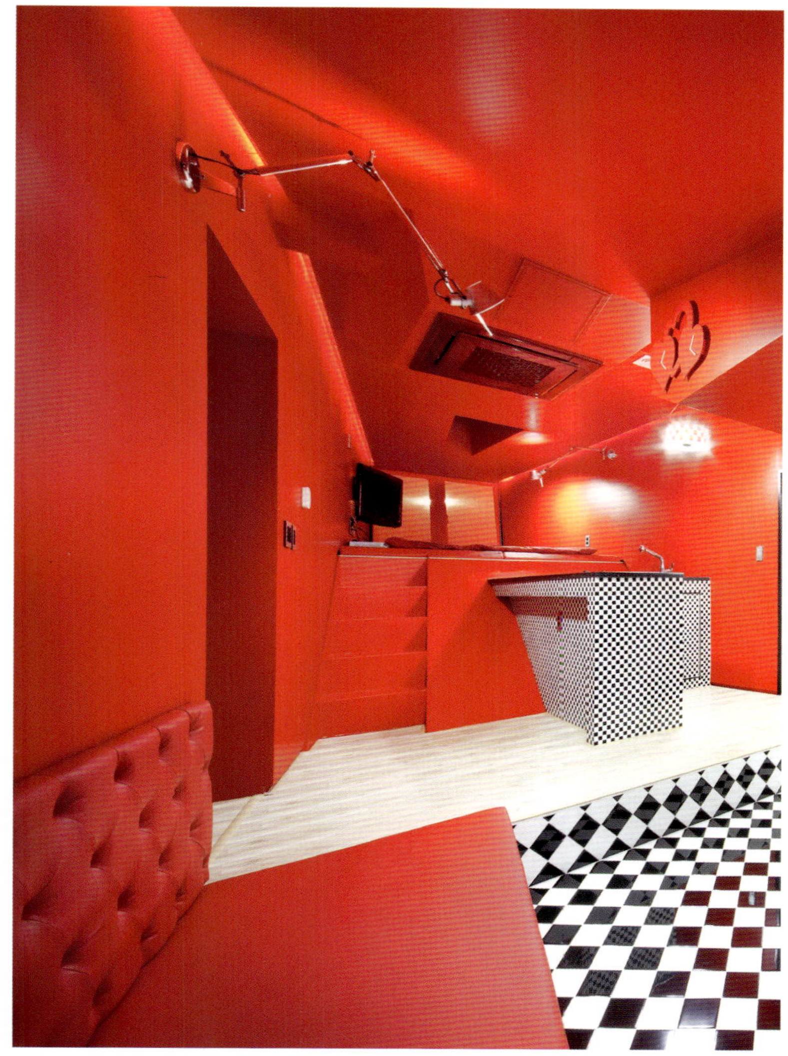

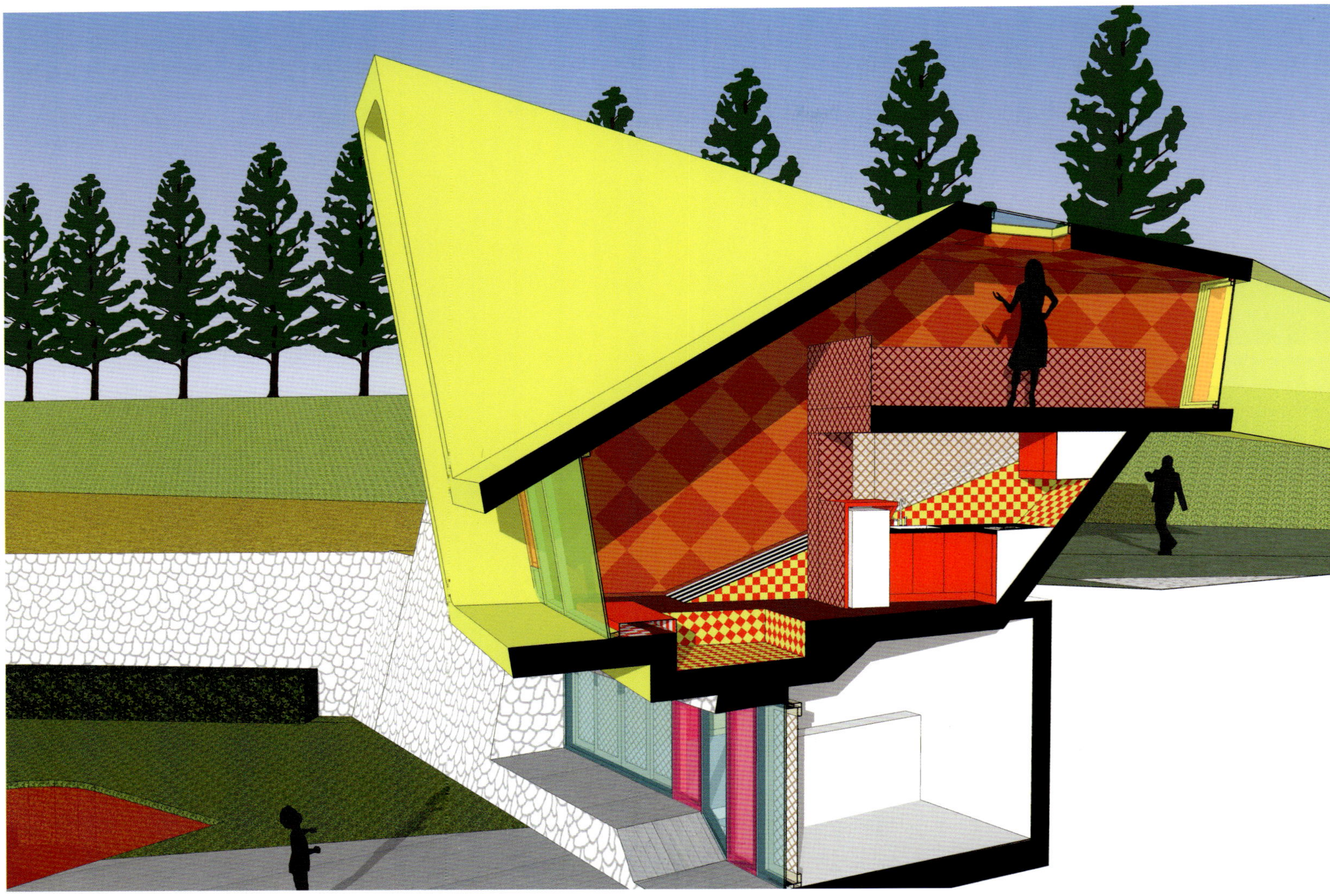

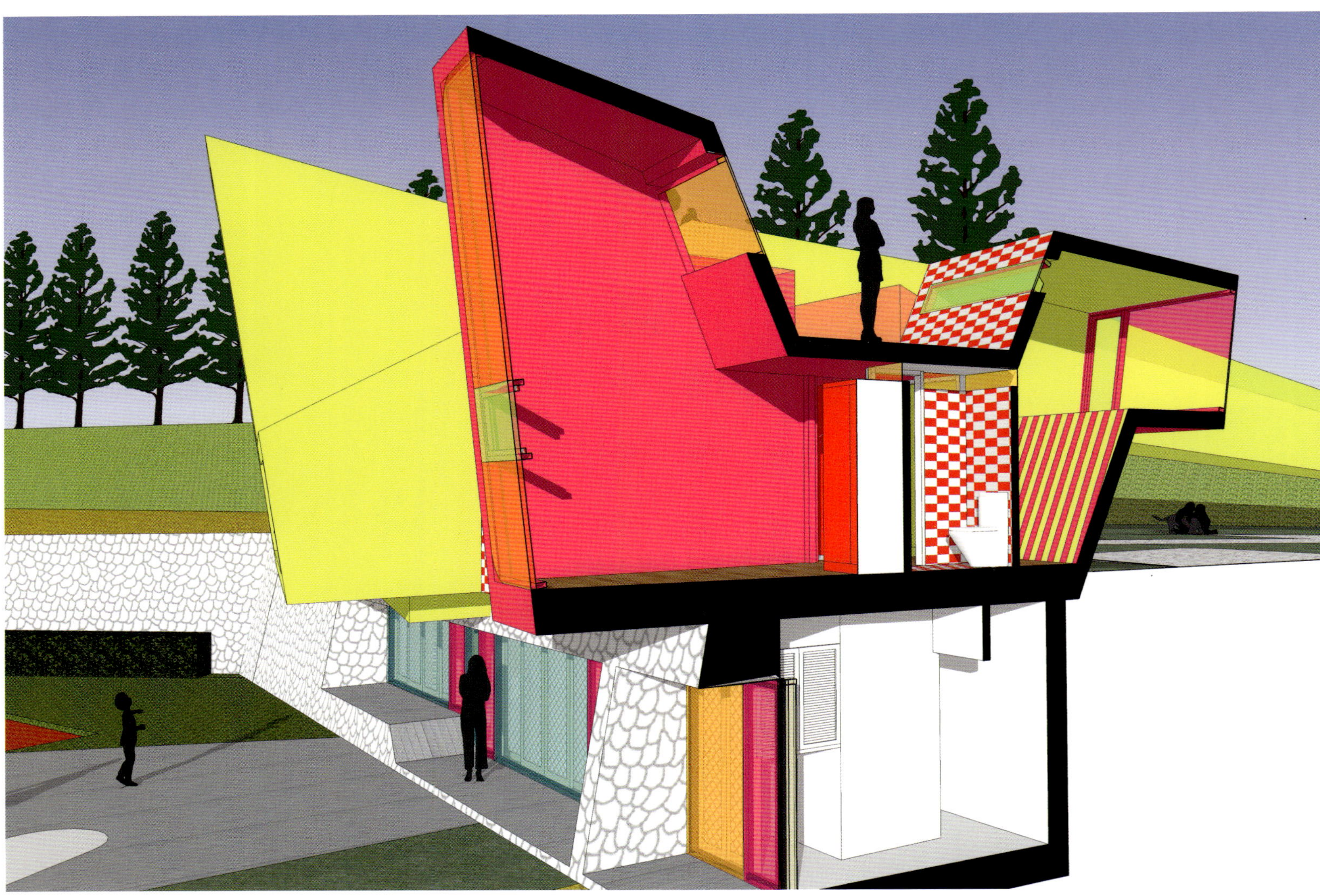

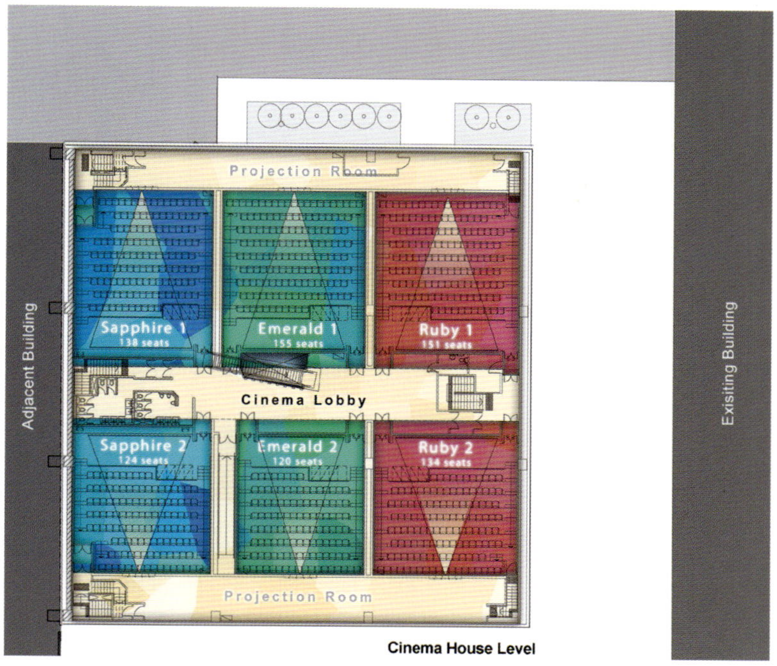
Projection Room
Sapphire 1
138 seats
Emerald 1
155 seats
Ruby 1
151 seats
Cinema Lobby
Sapphire 2
124 seats
Emerald 2
120 seats
Ruby 2
134 seats
Projection Room
Adjacent Building
Exsiting Building
Cinema House Level

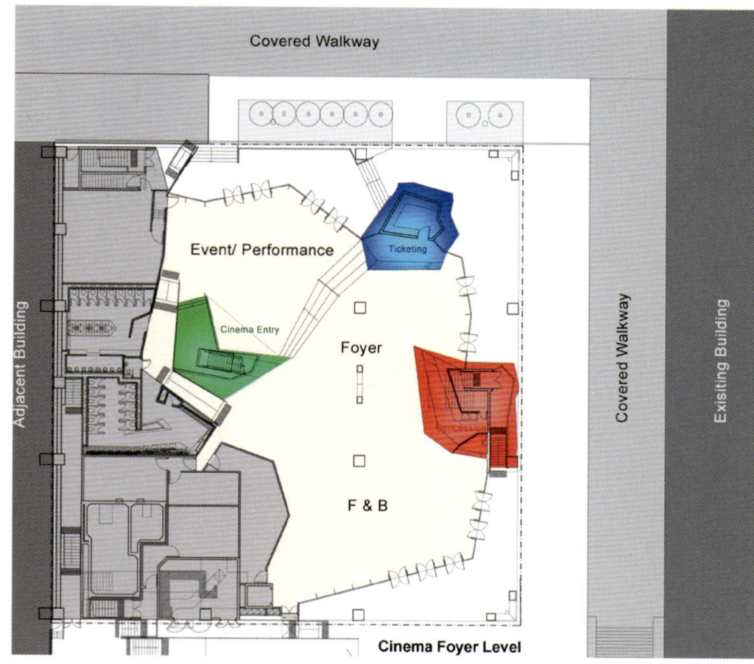
Covered Walkway
Event/ Performance
Ticketing
Cinema Entry
Foyer
F & B
Adjacent Building
Covered Walkway
Exsiting Building
Cinema Foyer Level

House 2
二院

KUGGEN

Kuggen is nestled in among Lindholmen's big office buildings, like a colorful blossom surrounded by gray leaves. As we approach, the triangular forms of the windows emerge. Their design has less to do with appearance than with function: limiting the glazed area to one-quarter of the wall surface keeps the heat in, while the triangular-shaped openings let in the light where it's needed most.
Kuggen strives to be an extremely energy efficient office building. It makes use of green building technology on four different levels: adaptive ventilation, adaptive lighting, interactive heating and cooling systems, and effective daylighting.
The mechanical systems are hidden between the concrete slab and a sealed suspended ceiling in the cellular offices and exposed in the open-plan office spaces, making it easy to change the layout of these areas. The carpeting is glued directly to the slab, thereby benefiting from its thermal mass. The result is a building with a calculated energy consumption under 55 kWh/m^2 annually including all mechanical systems.

Green architecture is about making choices and making compromises. Broadening our tolerance for variations in temperature and humidity generates immediate cost savings. Green architecture is also about social qualities and planning for an uncertain future. We hope the combination of strong form and flexible-use dimensions will give Kuggen great longevity.

COMPANY	Wingårdh Arkitektontor AB
DESIGNER	Wingårdh Arkitektontor AB
PHOTOGRAPHER	Åke E:son Lindman and Wingårdh Arkitektkontor AB
CLIENT	Chalmersfastigheter AB
COUNTRY (DISTRICT)	Sweden

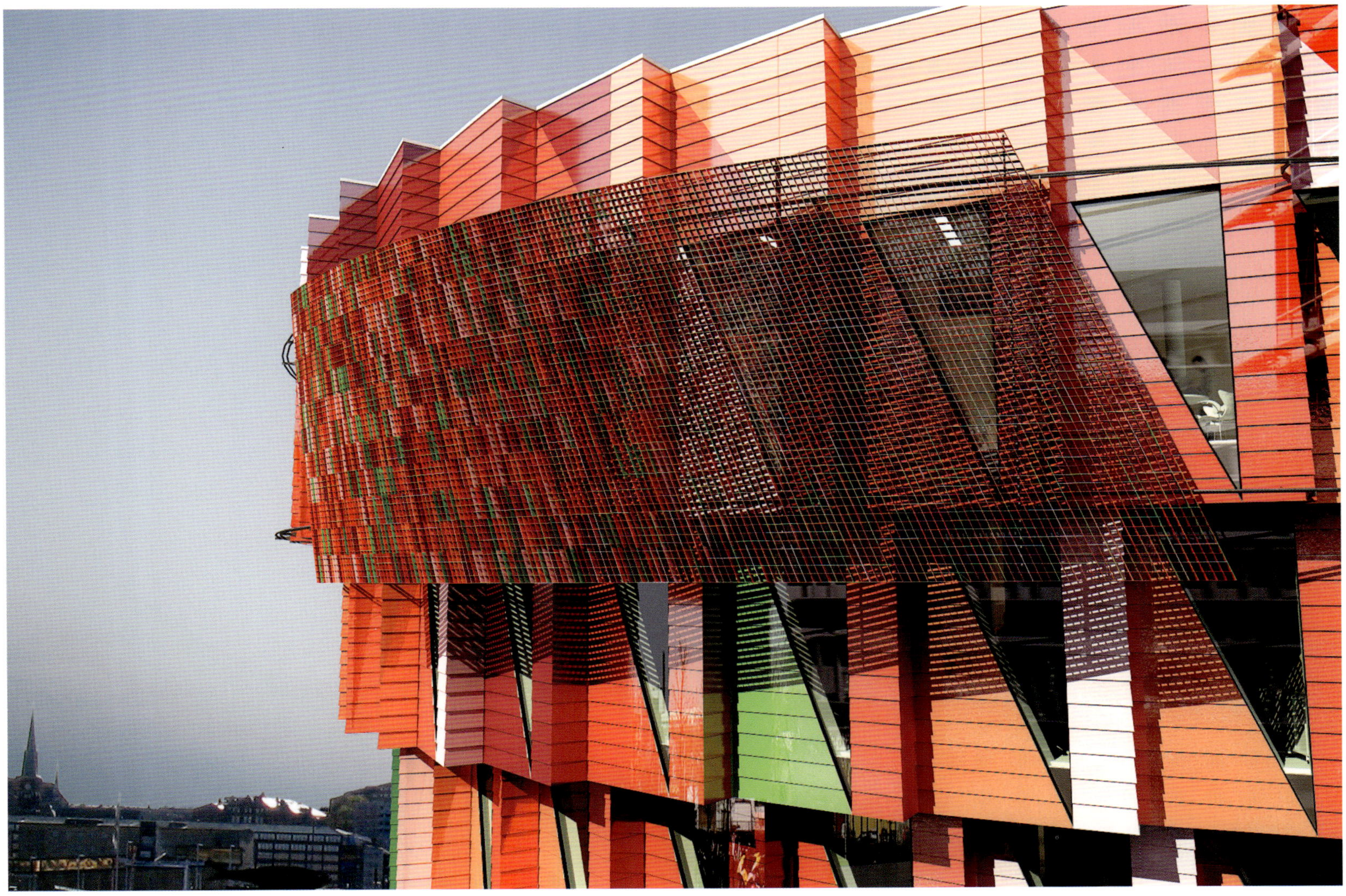

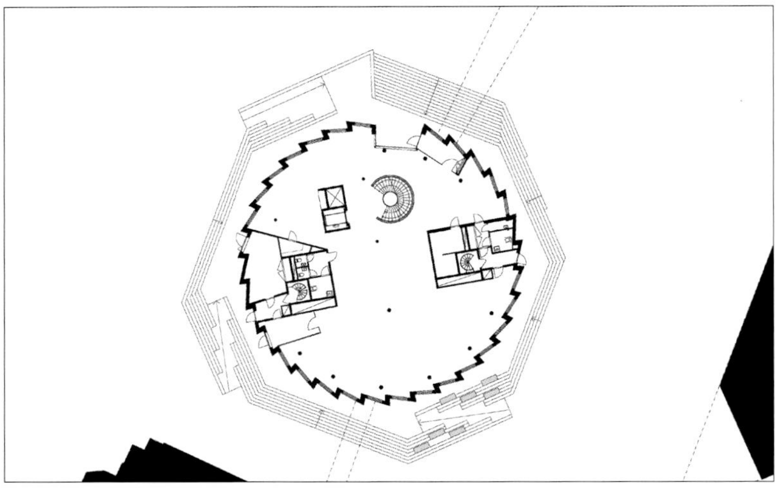

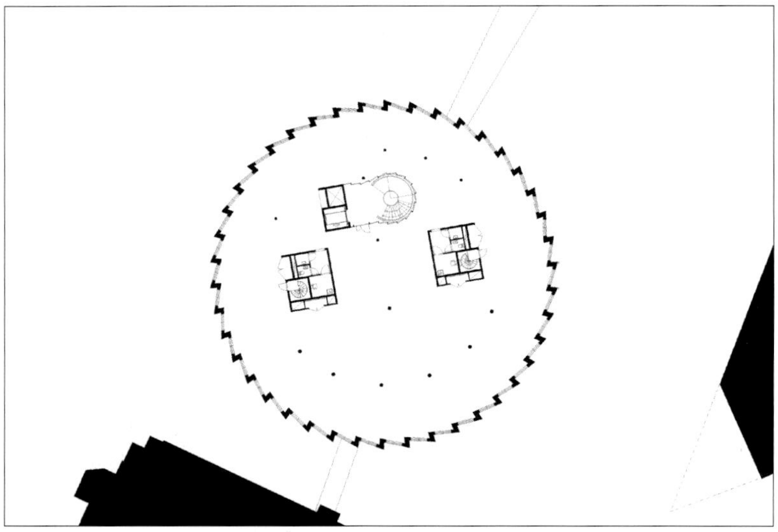

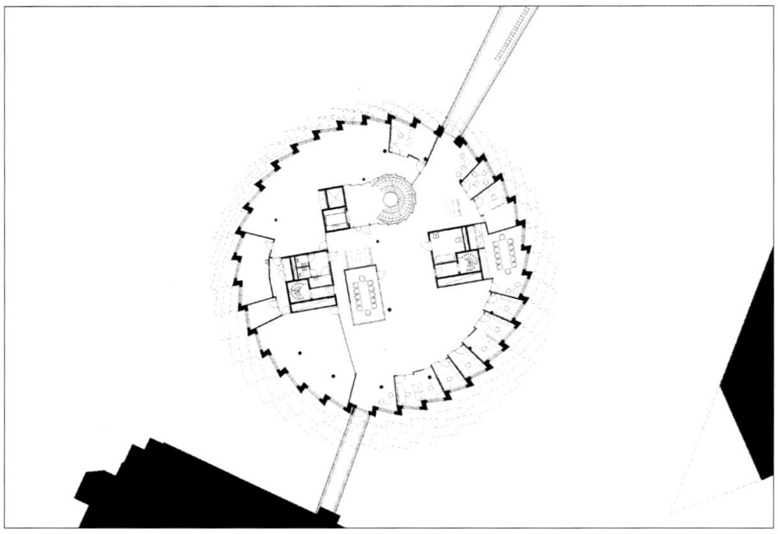

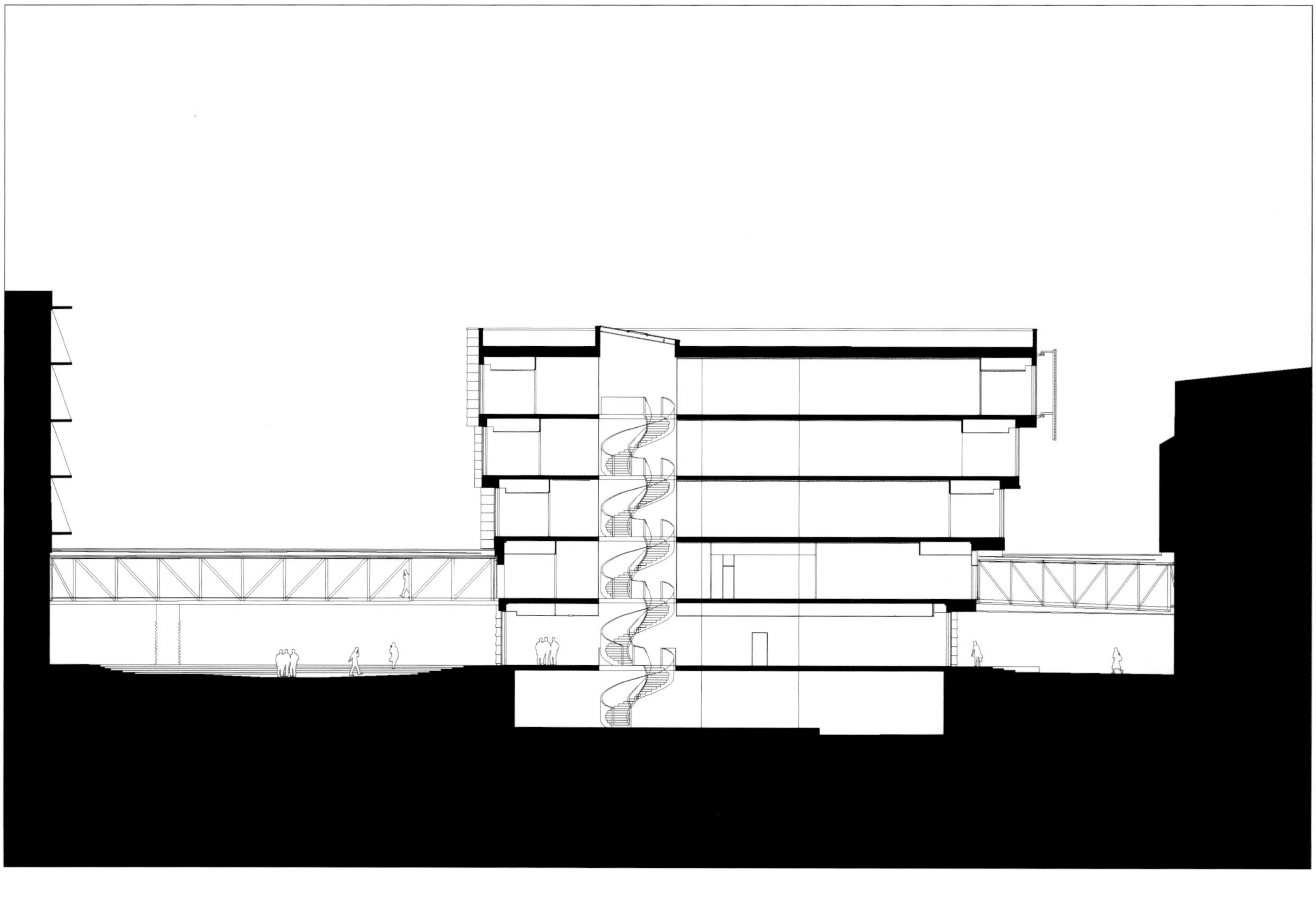

I-WAY

I-WAY is an international first. This exclusive building is entirely dedicated to automobile simulations (simulator technology offering 6 degrees of freedom inspired by the aeronautics industry), providing the public with access for the first time to eighteen machines. Organized around 3 simulation zones (Formula 1, Endurance, Rally/Touring), the complex also includes numerous upscale areas for a global experience: fitness room, alcohol-free bar, bar/ restaurant lounge with terraces, two conference rooms, meeting rooms and offices. Design and construction of I-WAY took 4 years, from an encounter with the project's developer, to the recent opening of the building.

COMPANY	Cyrille Druart Agency
CREATIVE DIRECTOR	Cyrille Druart
DESIGNER	Cyrille Druart
PHOTOGRAPHER	Cyrille Druart
CLIENT	I-vent
COUNTRY (DISTRICT)	France

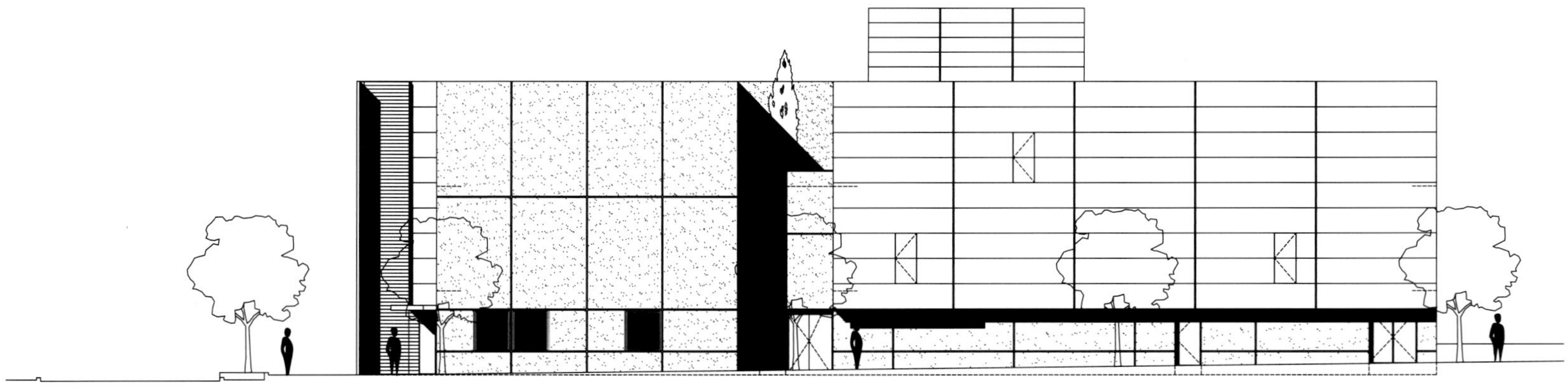

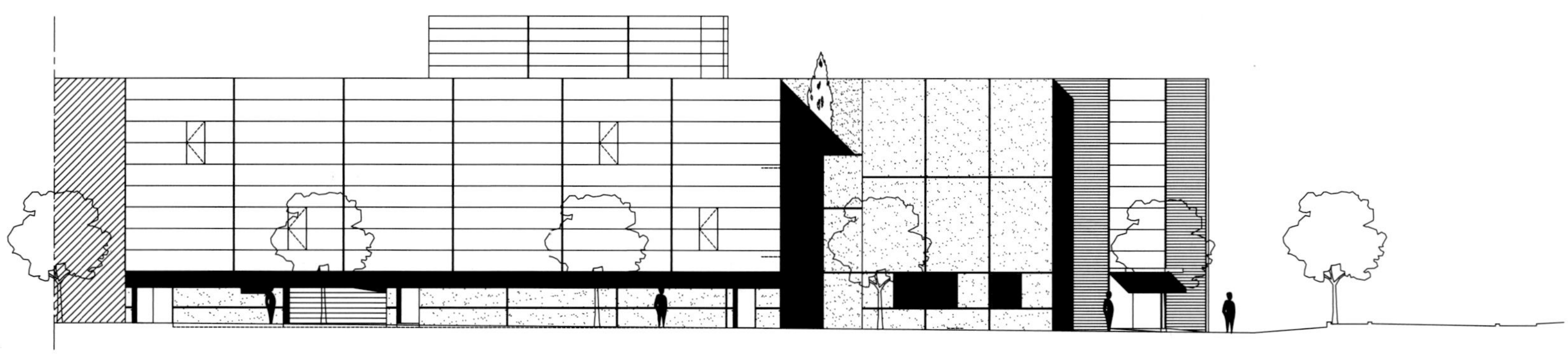

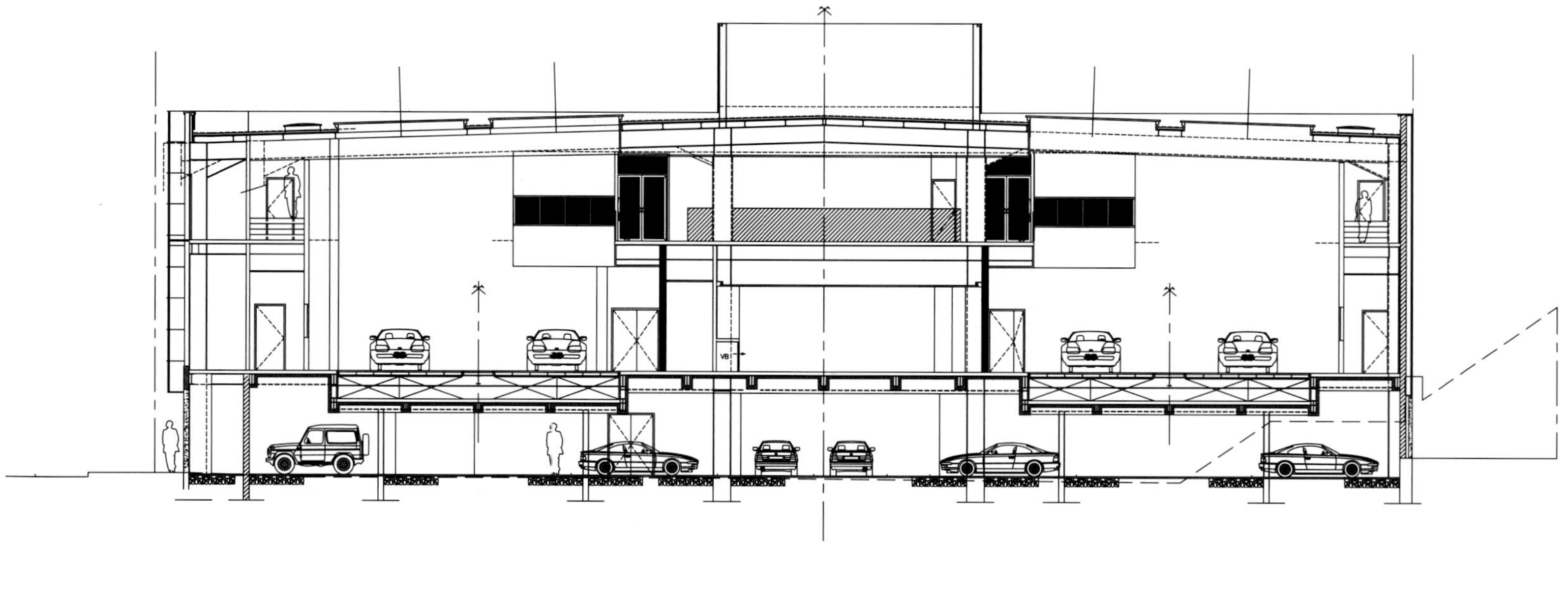

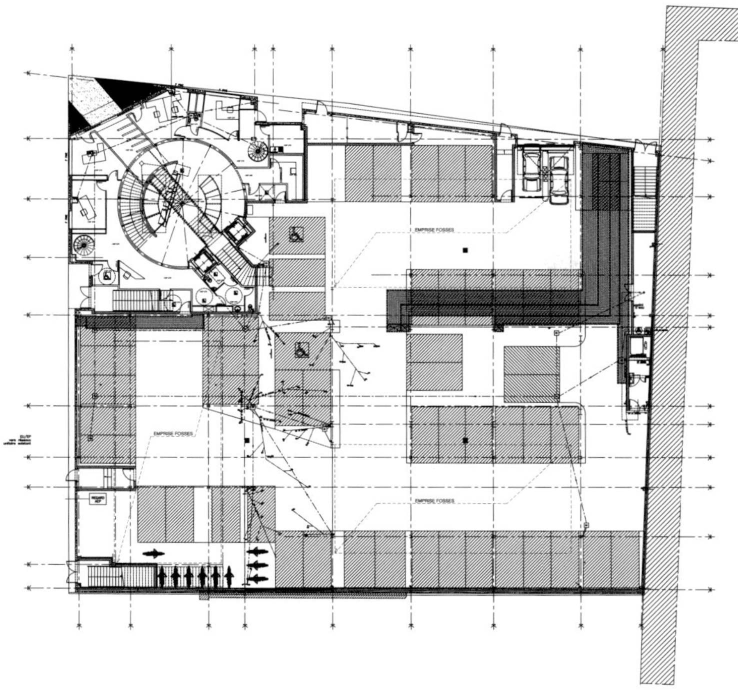

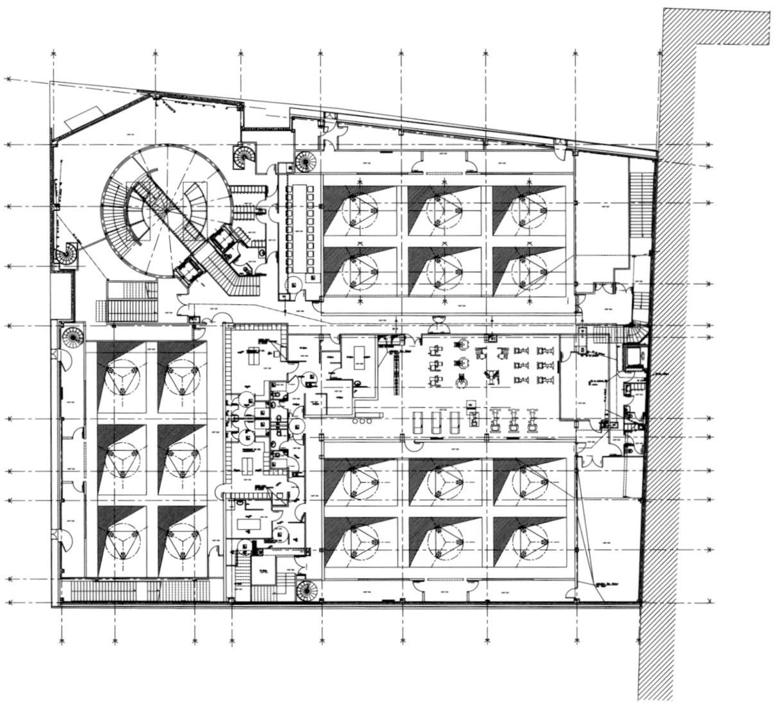

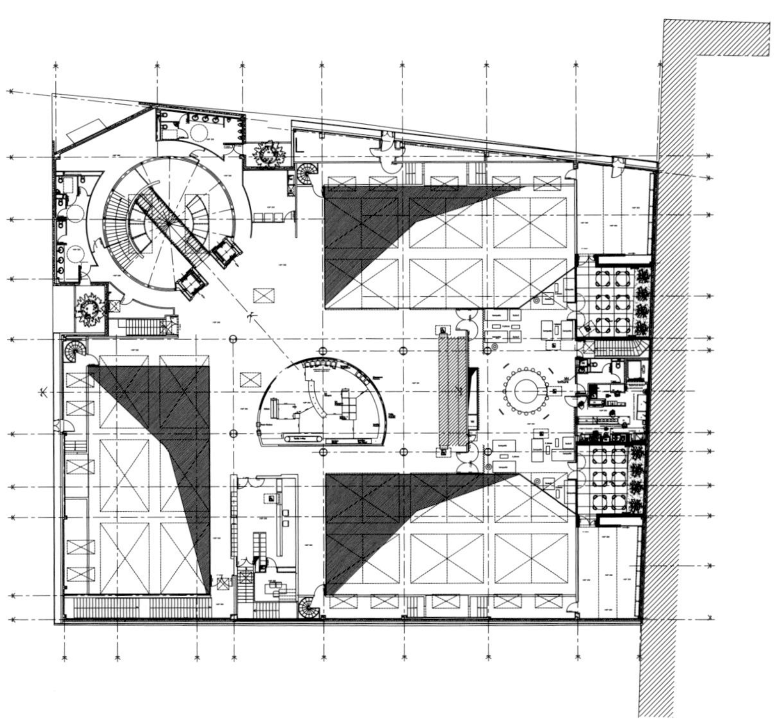

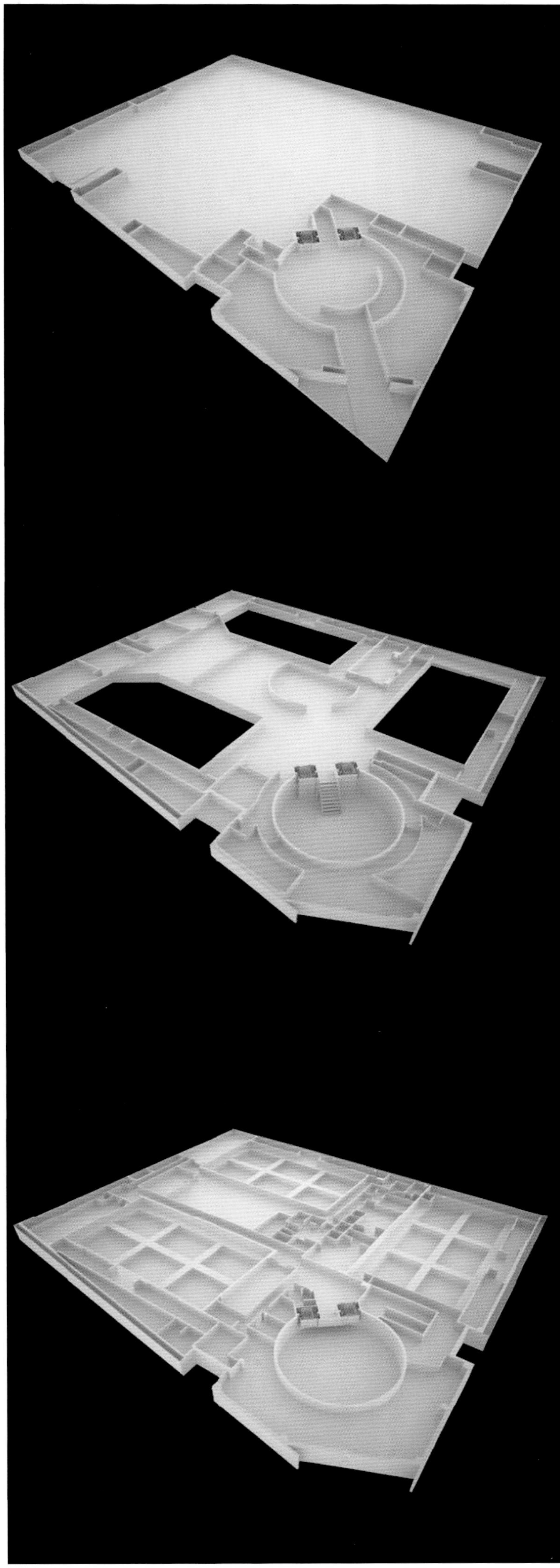

LBBW IMMOBILIEN, HEADQUARTERS

The LBBW headquarters is a forward-looking component of the development of Stuttgart. The zero-energy office building combines high quality public domain life with a resource-optimized workplace.

The innovative office concept is based on the findings of the research project, Office 21 by the Fraunhofer Institute. The traditional, modular building block differs in the proposal in favor of a centralized system.

The building is divided both horizontally and vertically and interconnected via an atrium - the central location and communications heart of the project. The 41,000 square meter zero-energy office building is efficient in both its energy consumption and construction. An adaptive facade system allows light control, shading and energy optimization. The facade consists of circular discs with integrated photovoltaic elements. By moving these elements the appearance of the building changes during different time of day. The energy generating facade moves seamlessly over the structure, articulated at the roof level as a sensuous fifth facade.

COMPANY	LAVA
CLIENT	LBBW Immobilien
COUNTRY (DISTRICT)	Australia

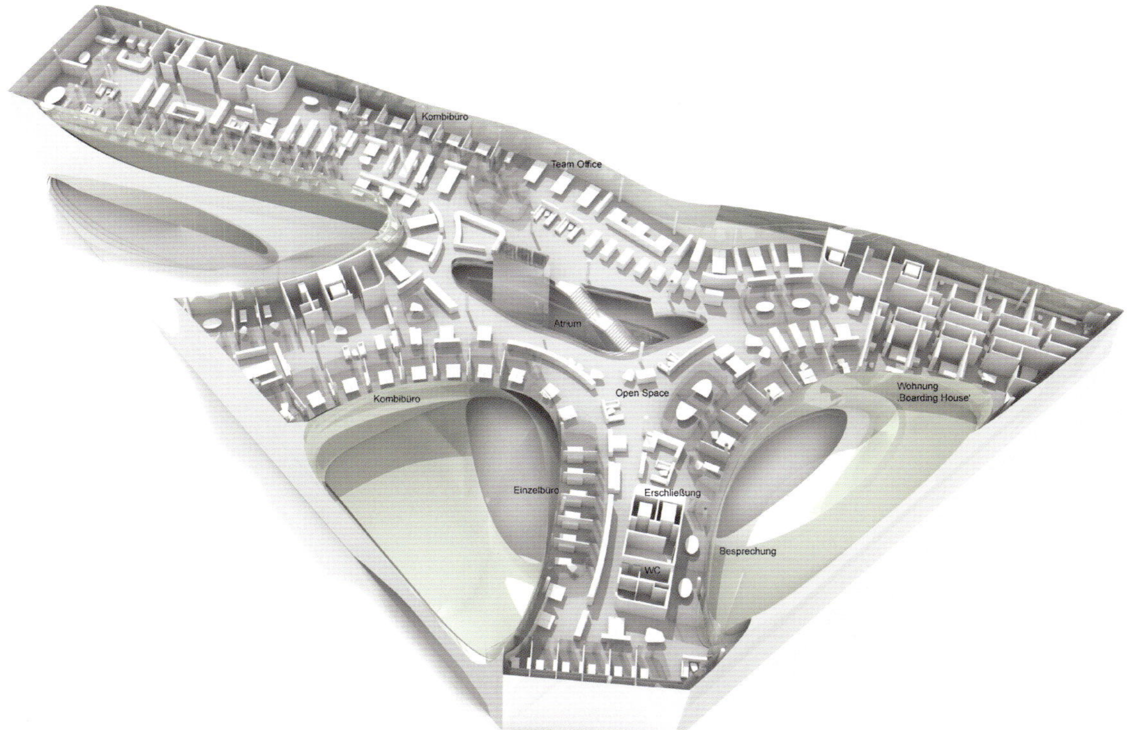
Kombibüro
Team Office
Atrium
Kombibüro
Open Space
Wohnung 'Boarding House'
Einzelbüro
Erschließung
Besprechung
WC

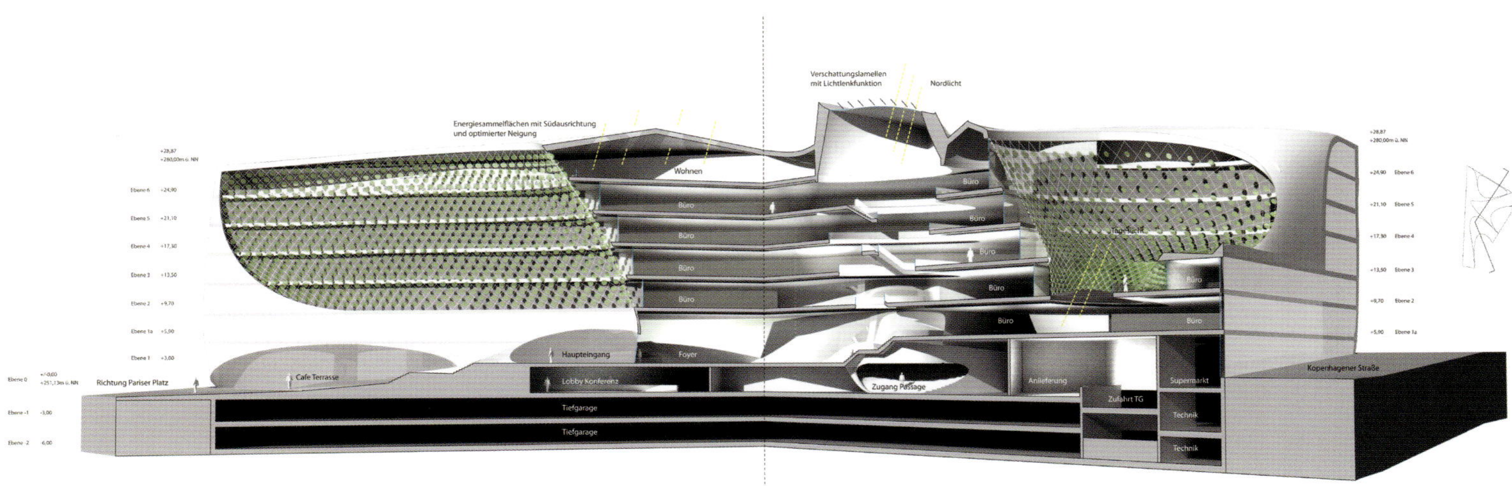
Verschattungslamellen mit Lichtlenkfunktion
Nordlicht
Energiesammelflächen mit Südausrichtung und optimierter Neigung
Wohnen
Büro
Haupteingang
Foyer
Richtung Pariser Platz
Cafe Terrasse
Lobby Konferenz
Zugang Passage
Anlieferung
Zufahrt TG
Supermarkt
Kopenhagener Straße
Tiefgarage
Technik

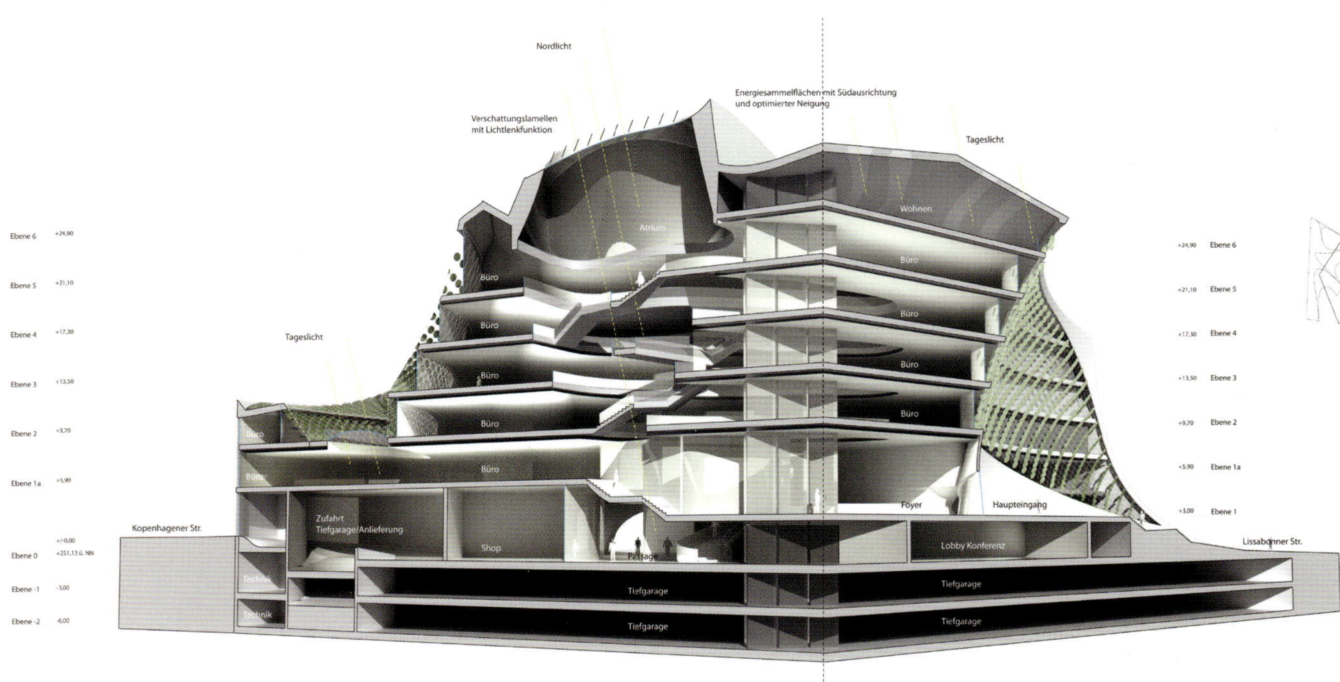
Nordlicht
Energiesammelflächen mit Südausrichtung und optimierter Neigung
Verschattungslamellen mit Lichtlenkfunktion
Tageslicht
Atrium
Wohnen
Büro
Tageslicht
Ebene 6
Ebene 5
Ebene 4
Ebene 3
Ebene 2
Ebene 1a
Ebene 1
Ebene 0
Ebene -1
Ebene -2
Foyer
Haupteingang
Kopenhagener Str.
Zufahrt Tiefgarage/Anlieferung
Shop
Passage
Lobby Konferenz
Lissabonner Str.
Technik
Tiefgarage

SNOWFLAKE TOWER

The tower designers represent a new generation of architects, being responsible as associate architects for world recognized structures such as the Watercube in Beijing and the Mercedes-Benz Museum in Germany.
Just one year ago, they founded LAVA, the Laboratory for Visionary Architecture, a worldwide architectural network, together with architect Alexander Rieck, innovation expert at the Fraunhofer Institute in Stuttgart. Inspired by the geometrical order of a snowflake and the aerodynamics of a Formula 1 racing car, the tower encapsulates speed, fluid dynamics, future technology and natural patterns of organization. Rather than purely mimicking shapes in nature for their elegance and unpredictability, the architects learned from nature's own geometrical orders creating highly efficient structures and intriguing spaces.
The organizational principle of a minimal surface allowed the optimization of the facade/floor area ratio and each apartment in the 59-storey luxury tower has unobstructed ocean views.
The lower levels of the tower, traditionally the most difficult and least attractive area, have been reinterpreted as a series of prestigious wharf apartments, terraced similar to that of cruise ship decks. By widening the base, the tower is anchored into its surrounding water basin similar to the surrounding mangroves and nearby canals. The top Sky villas offer 270 degree views opposite the new cultural district on Saadiyat Island. The Tower Ground Breaking will be at the beginning of 2009, with a completion date around June 2011.

COMPANY	LAVA
CLIENT	Vedera CapitalMarasi
COUNTRY (DISTRICT)	Australia

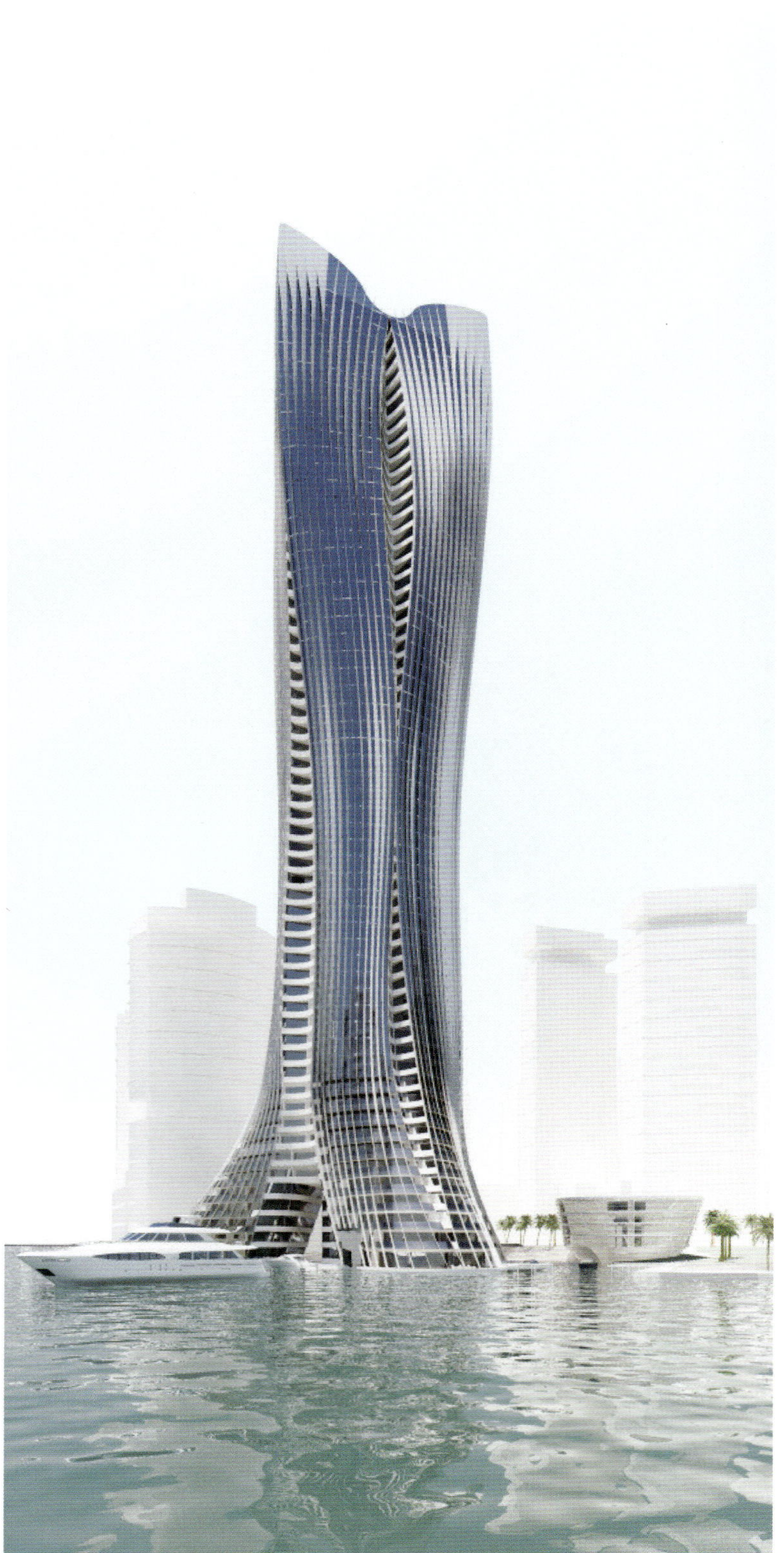

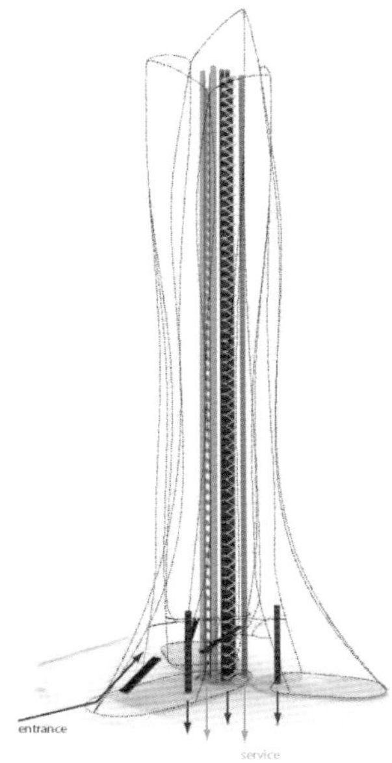

movement *vertical*
core - elevator - staircase

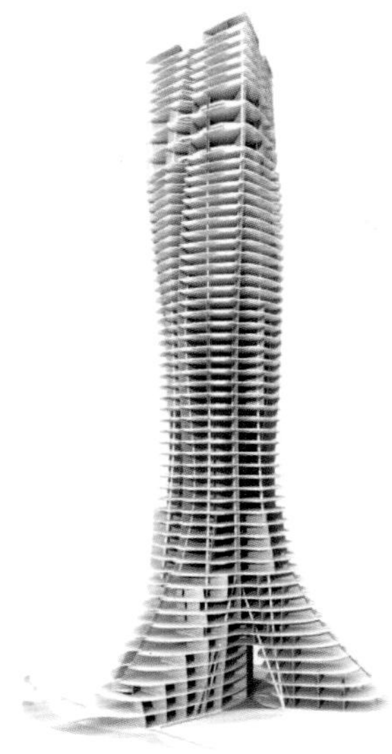

structure *vertical*
columns - core - floorplates

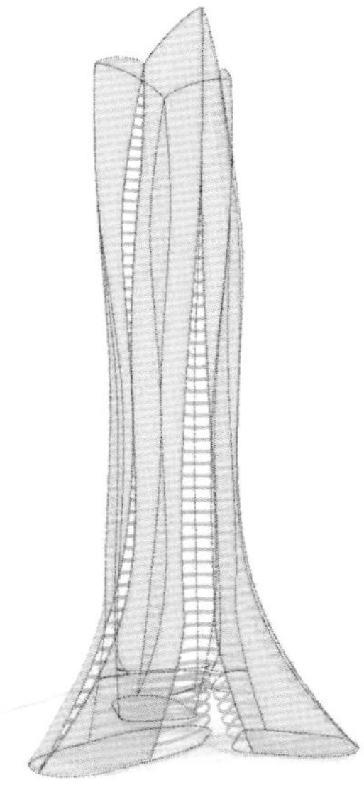

balustrades *horizontal*
balconies

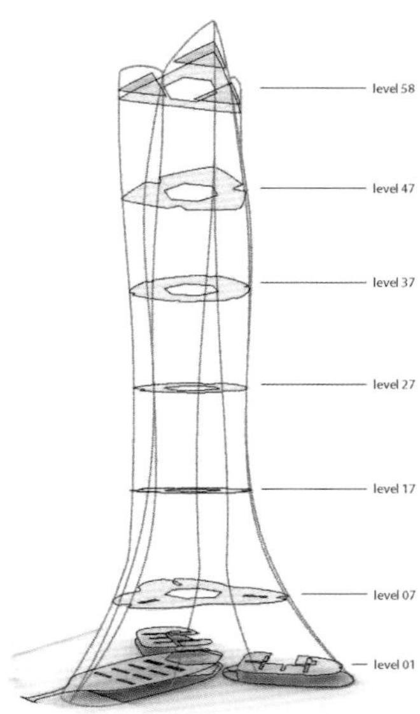

geometry *concept*
design approach

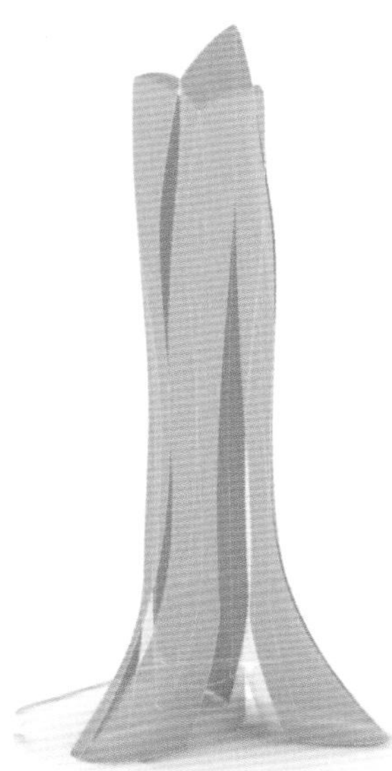

macro *structure*
tower geometry

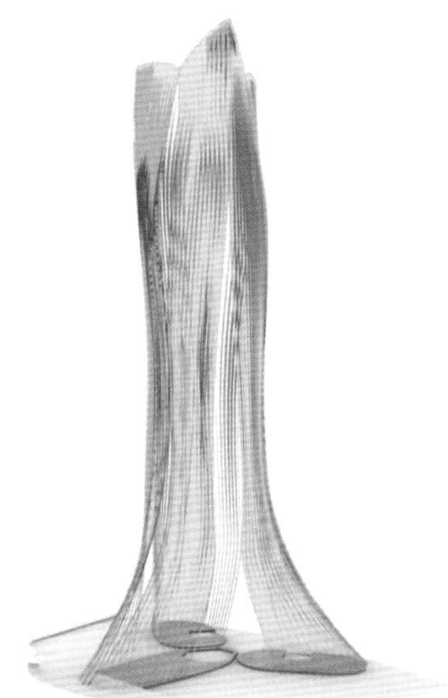

micro *structure*
lamellas - white & silver

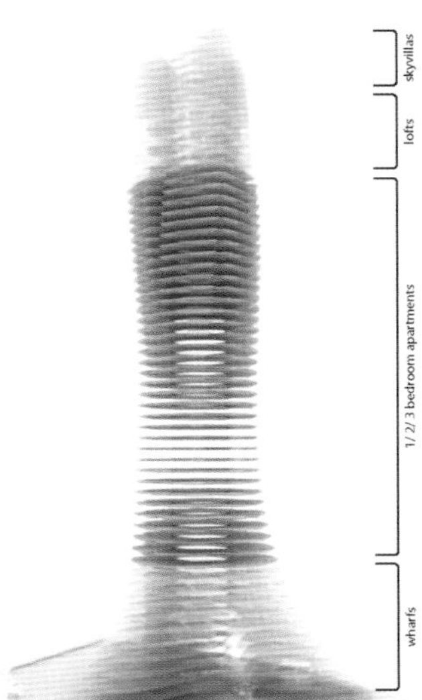

unit mix *apartments*
wharfs - 1/ 2/ 3 bedroom apartments - lofts - skyvillas

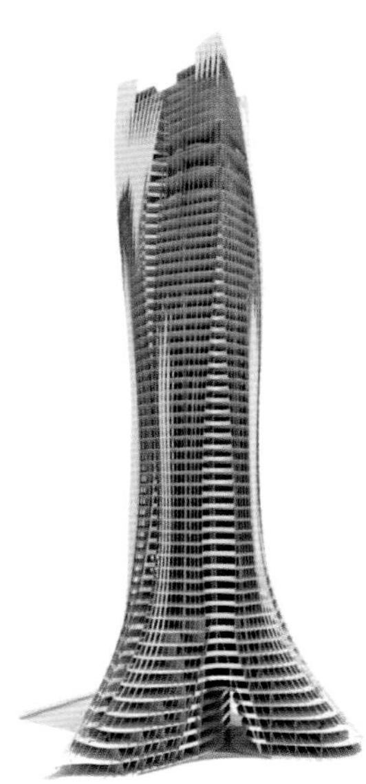

tower *structure*
geometry of tower

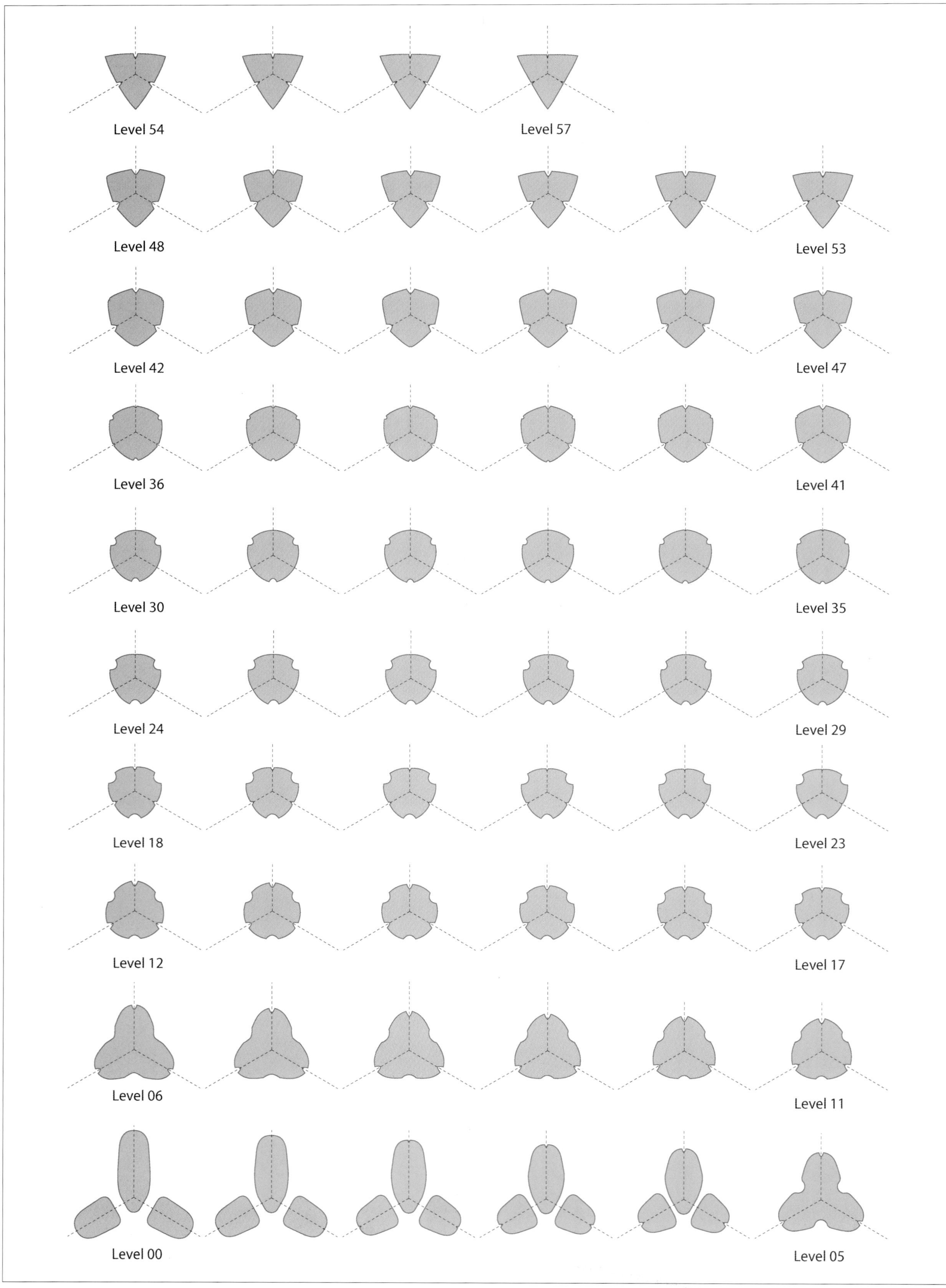
Level 54
Level 57
Level 48
Level 53
Level 42
Level 47
Level 36
Level 41
Level 30
Level 35
Level 24
Level 29
Level 18
Level 23
Level 12
Level 17
Level 06
Level 11
Level 00
Level 05

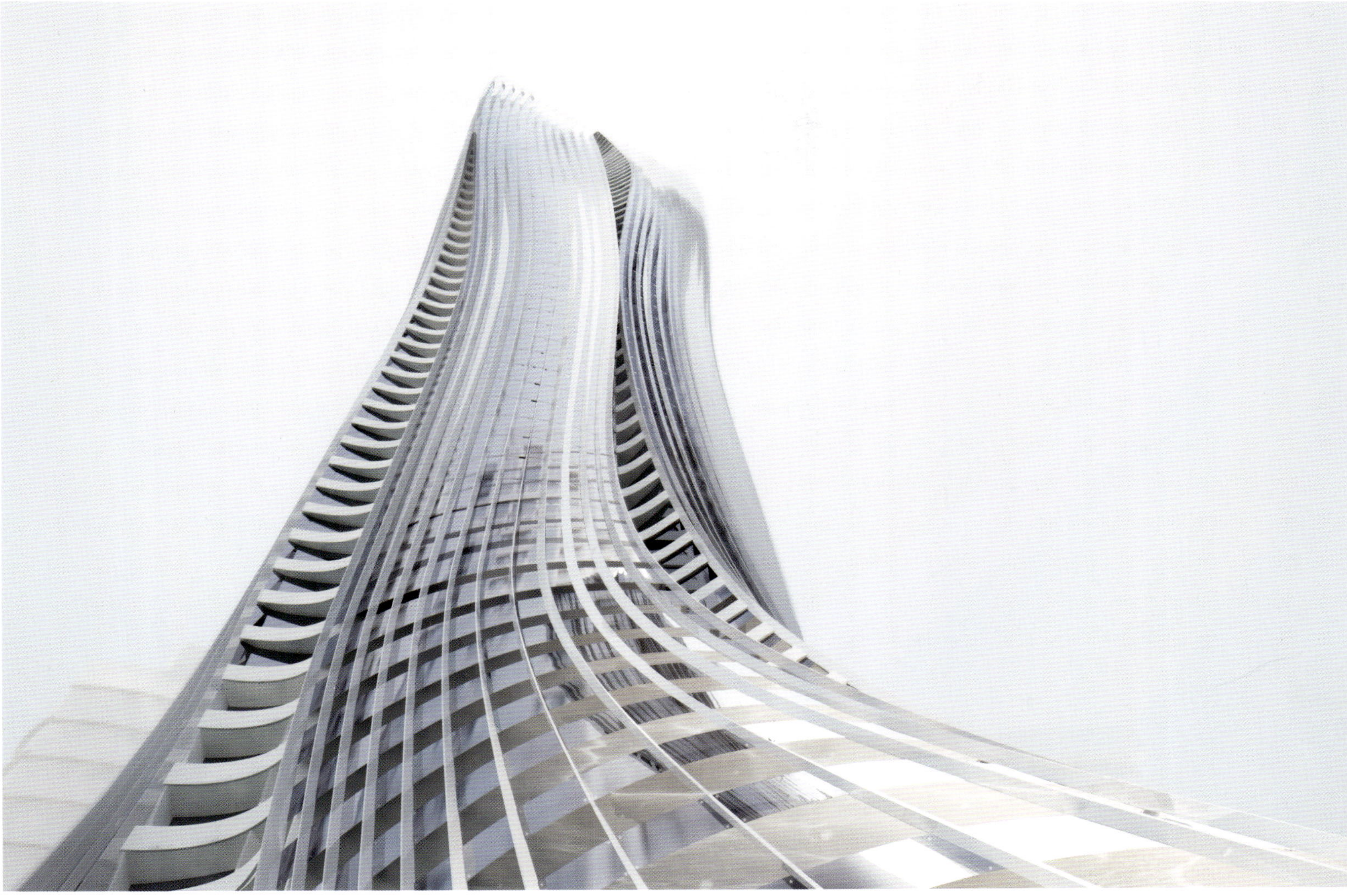

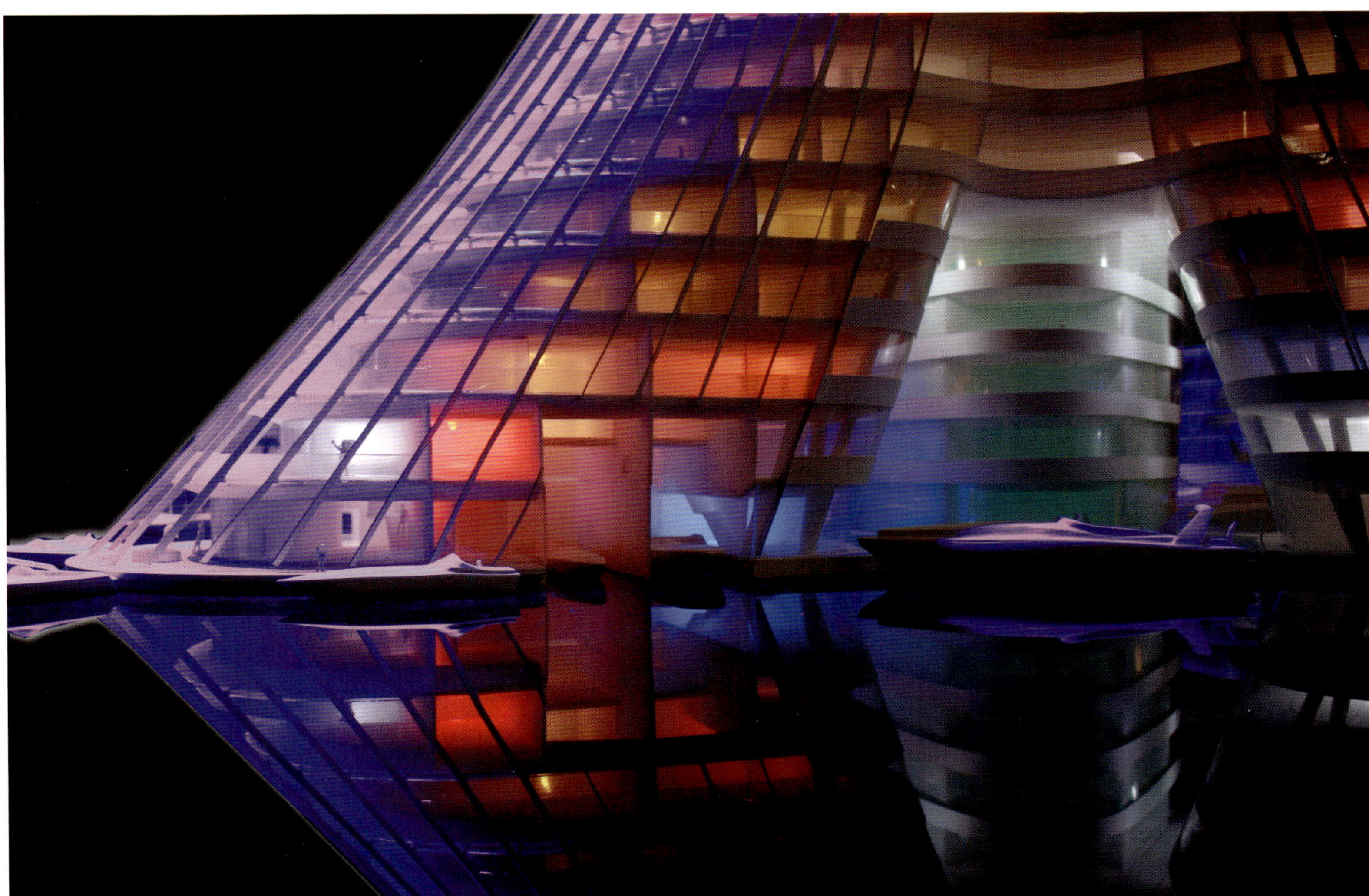

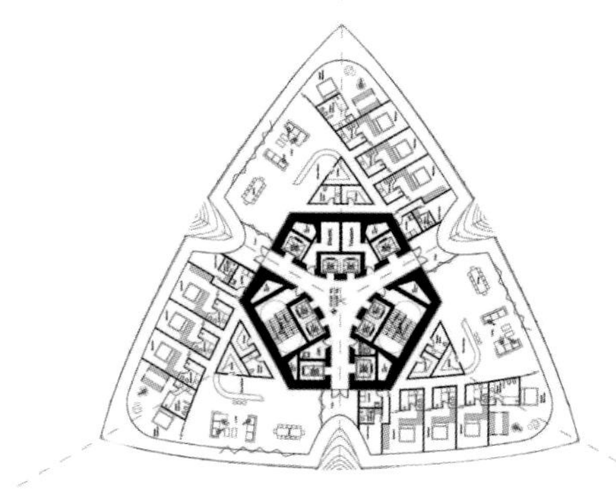

Floor 53

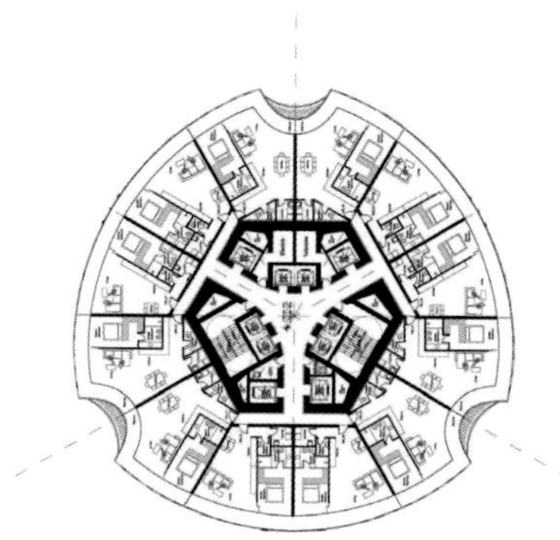

Floor 30

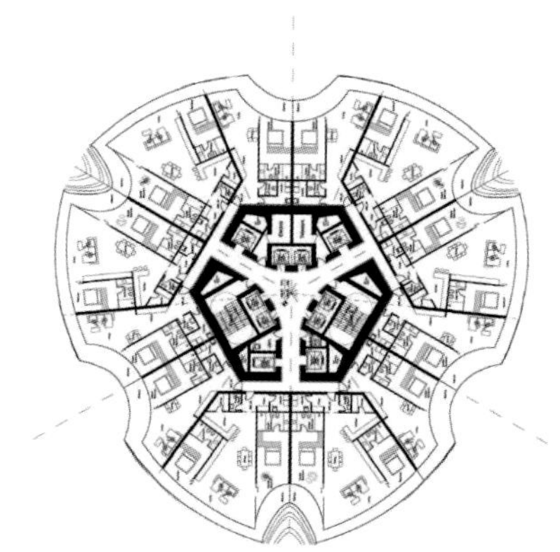

Floor 11

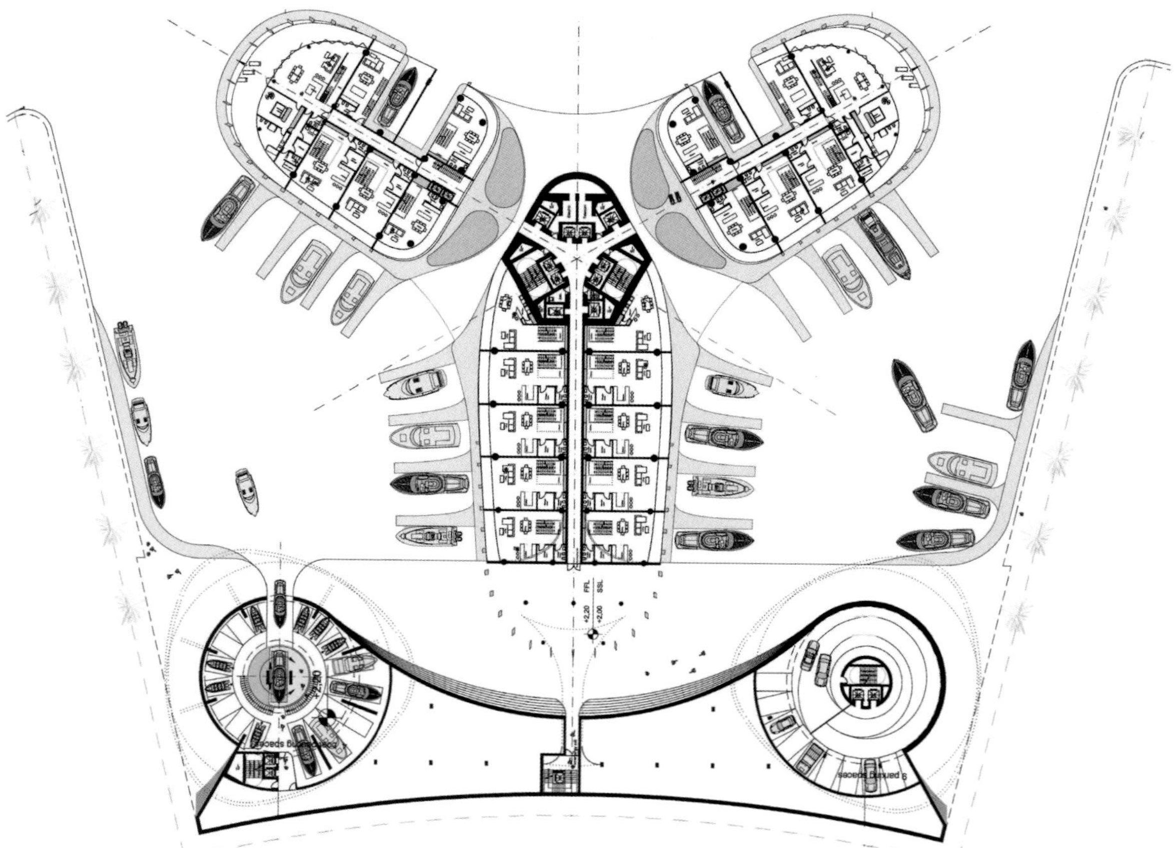

PIXEL IN BEIJING MODELROOM

The concept of Comprehensive Renovation "Pixel"model house. The model house of high-rise residential building with sale center to be in accordance with Skip-Floor Dwelling House's buildings for ten thousand households.
"Pixel" concepts flexibly apply to many parts of interior and exterior decoration. Ceiling filled with paper lighting carry out the impact of the same kind of facilities. Model houses divide into four types of different themes such as "POP".
The Concept of "Pixel" Sales Center in Beijing.
The"pixel" sales center developed overall "cell" concept of "Pixel in Beijing" on the basis of former sales center.
Appearance:
The appearance was formed of many separate tubes accumulated. It is consisting of four kinds of white, light grey, the dark grey and black tubes .To overlapped and accumulates so as to produce bump sense.
Sales center hall:
Sales center hall is a very important part of sales center used as the whole project sale center, including negotiation room, guest rooms and so on. The hall, including entrance hall, seeks to pursue a sense of luxury and dynamic space to match negotiation room.
Interior decoration also developed the cell concept. The wall accumulates different length and gloss wooden cases,400×400 mm^2, to get bump and layer sense. The roof is created by 400×400 mm^2 dropped tubular lightings. Its borders are made of Japanese paper. Then the ground integrate outdoor and indoor, integrate outside landscape to indoor.

COMPANY	SAKO Architects
DESIGNER	SAKO Architects
PHOTOGRAPHER	Misae HIROMATSU
CLIENT	Pixel
COUNTRY (DISTRICT)	Japan

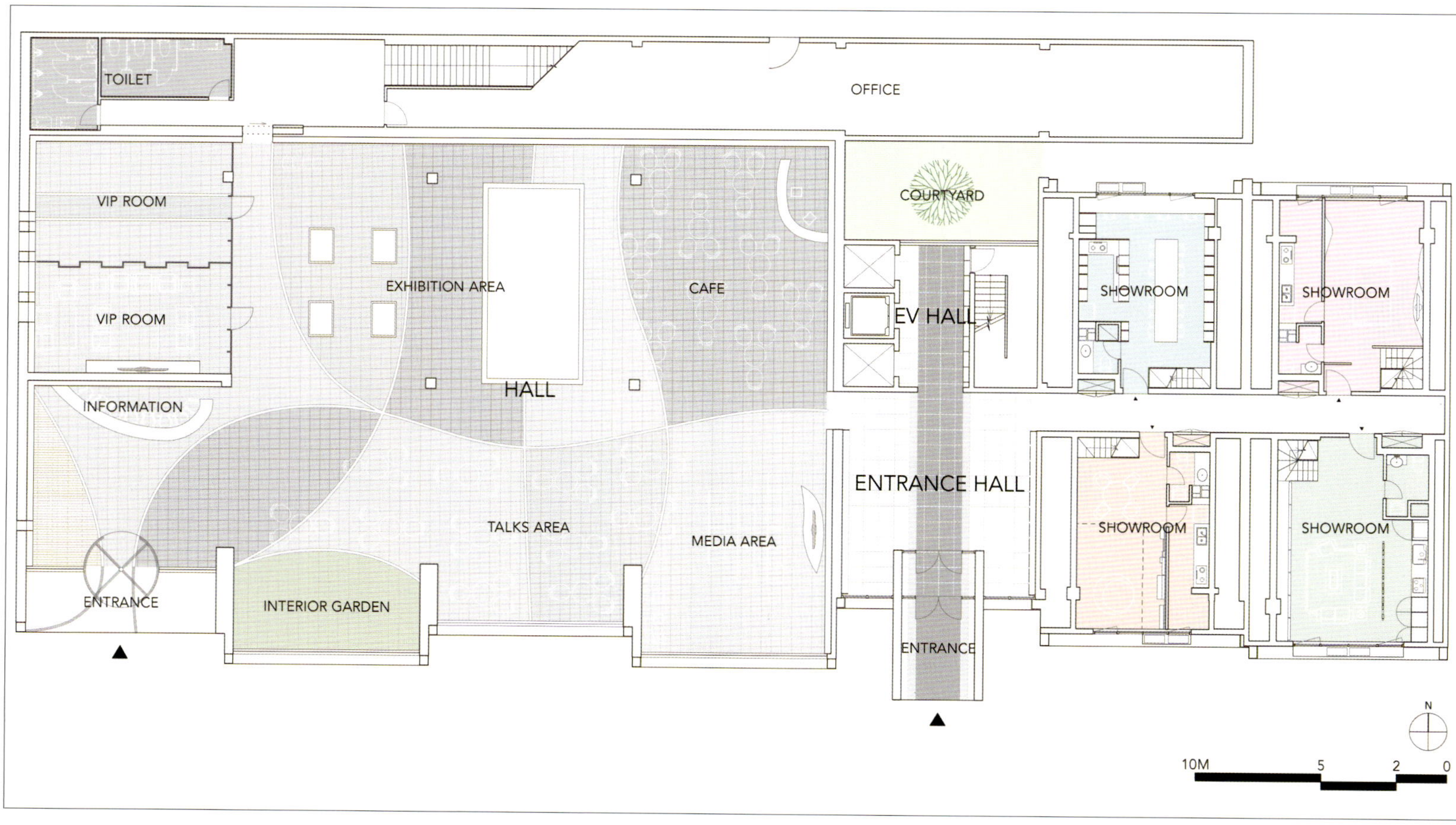
TOILET
OFFICE
VIP ROOM
VIP ROOM
EXHIBITION AREA
CAFE
COURTYARD
EV HALL
SHOWROOM
SHOWROOM
HALL
INFORMATION
ENTRANCE HALL
SHOWROOM
SHOWROOM
TALKS AREA
MEDIA AREA
ENTRANCE
INTERIOR GARDEN
ENTRANCE
N
10M
5
2
0

CUBE TUBE IN JINHUA

This is the office building and dining room. It is located at the entrance of economic development zone. The owner proposed to make the building to be the landmark of this zone, regarding there is a group of crown-like igloo buildings around this area. We chose two minimalist bodies. In the 100 arbor garden decorated like gridding, seated a cube with 32 meters length and width, and a 55 meters long cuboid.

The cube is a 9-floor office building with a central core tube-shaped structure. The owner proposes three design requirements: it must have independent office space, drafty, the midsection must brings in natural light. It is very easy to achieve the first requirement, but the rest two is run in the opposite direction with the shape of the building. As a result, we first designed a cross corridor stretching over the central tube-shaped part; then connected the balcony from east, west, north and south, which resolves the natural lighting and ventilate problems of the central part. The height and the width of the balcony are variegated. Big, medium and small windows freely laid around on the facade, made up a rich and complicated opening of the cube.

The facade of the cube used aluminum veneer with aluminum plate surface color, the facade of the cuboid used glass of transparent, gray and black color. Through the using of random alternate opening and materials that increased the changing of the light, the two pure bodies gained symbol matched with the landmark building.

From the furniture, opening, plane, facade to gardens, all used the element of 550mm square. 550mm is half of the height of railing, this specific element became a kind of link, tightly bend all the related people.

COMPANY	SAKO Architects
DESIGNER	SAKO Architects
COUNTRY (DISTRICT)	Japan

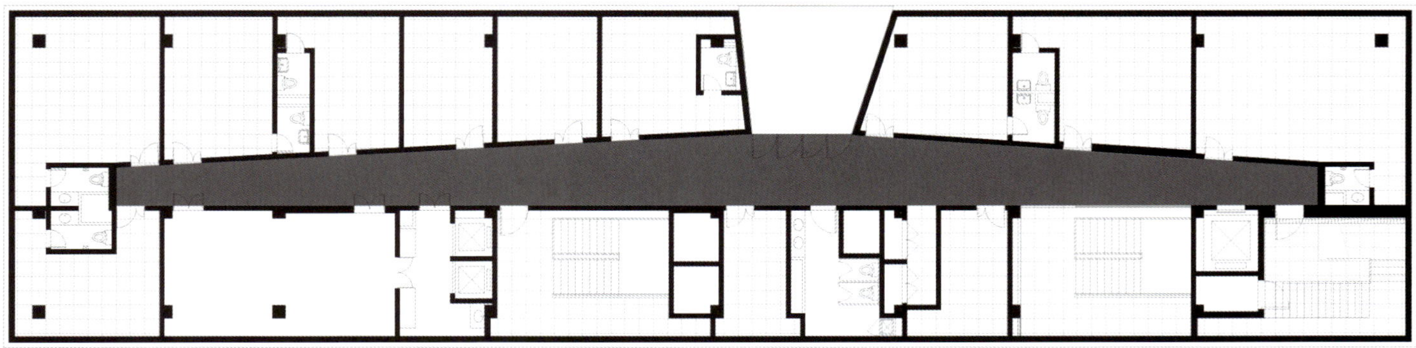

金華キューブチューブ　3F平面図　1/300
CUBE TUBE in Jinhua　3F plan　1/300

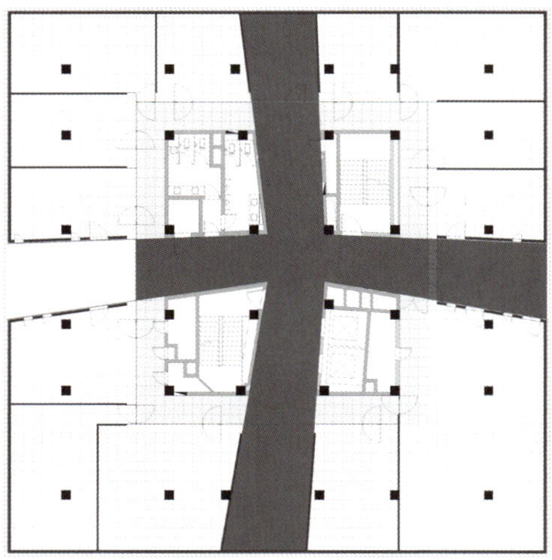

金華キューブチューブ　3F平面図　1/300
CUBE TUBE in Jinhua　3F plan　1/300

金華キューブチューブ　配置図　1/500
CUBE TUBE in Jinhua　Siteplan　1/500

CORNICHE TOWER

Within Abu Dhabi's skyline, the Corniche represents an internationally high standard and state of the art design. The concept follows the original guidelines, simple yet exclusive.

A 'Diamond' design concept is translated into a series of stacked diagonally articulated modules of eight floors each.

The colorful facade of interlocking triangles follows in-depth research that was undertaken to determine optimum surface and material effects associated with the brilliance of diamonds. Different weather situations during night and day are reflected in the building, keeping the external aesthetics animated and responsive when viewed from the public domain.

The Corniche will be immediately recognizable due to its lighting design, both externally and internally. A premium exterior and world class interior place the Corniche well ahead of surrounding buildings. All floors have panoramic views and a glazed facade that allows the user to be in control of climatic conditions.

COMPANY	LAVA
DESIGNER	Wenzel+Wenzel
COUNTRY (DISTRICT)	Germany

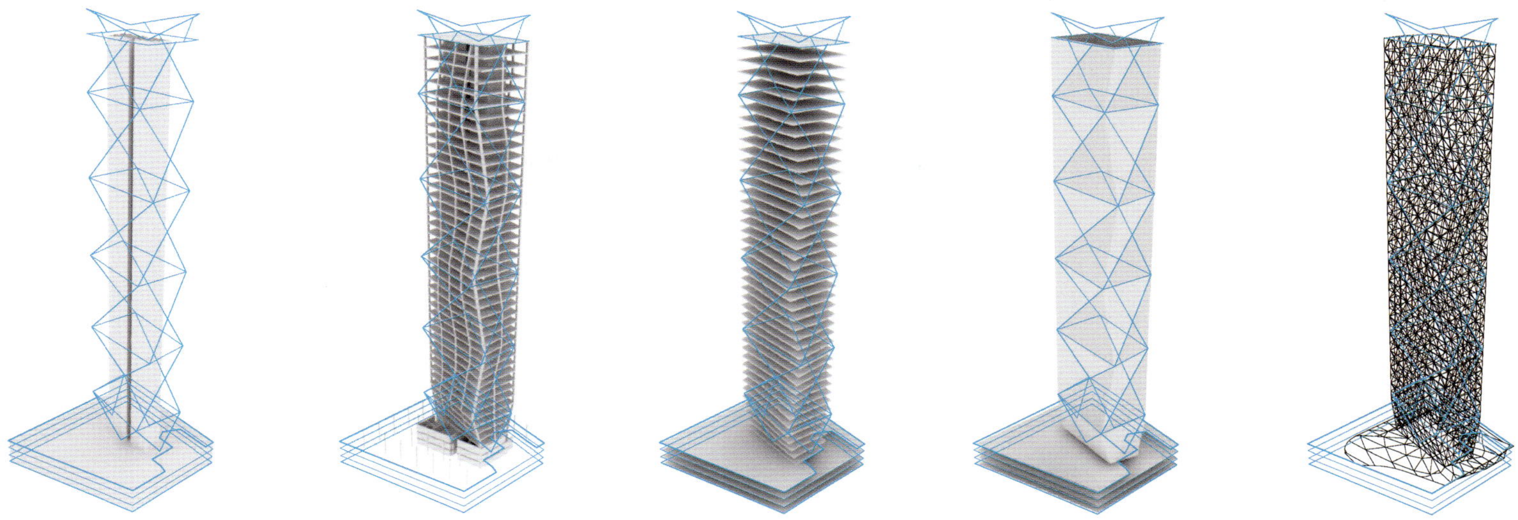

movement vertical
parking - elevator - staircase

structure vertical
columns - core - floorplates

program office slabs
41 level - 2 level lobby/ mezzanine

macro diamond structure
large diagonals

micro structure
small triangulated areas continued into landscape

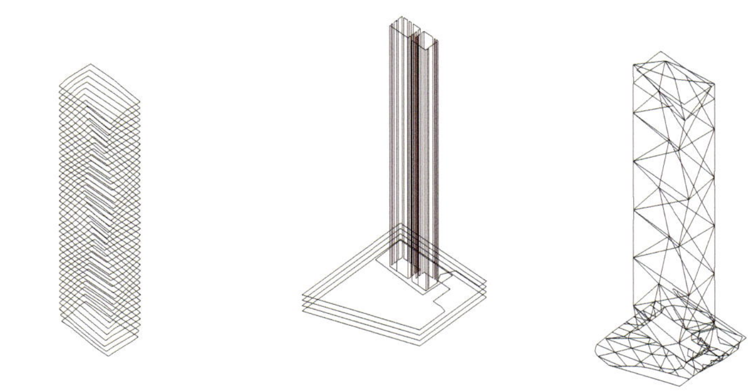

***program** office slabs*
41 level - 2 level lobby/mezzanine

***movement** vertical*
parking - elevator - staircase

***macro** diamond structure*
large diamonds

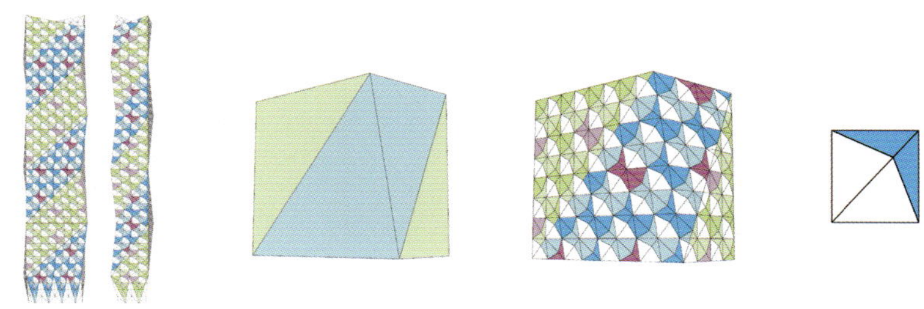

building scale

total facade area
~16965 sqm

modul scale1

8 storeys, 2 main spirals

modul facade area
~3240 sqm = 100%

modul scale 2

- 8 storeys, 2 main spirals
- 6 different colored panels, highly reflective, low degree of transparency
- 1 non-colored glass panel, transparent

glas panels (area)
green light ~564 sqm
green ~420sqm
blue light ~567 sqm = 66.3%
blue ~480sqm
red light ~133sqm
red ~ 130sqm

transparent glas ~1091sqm = 33.7% clear transparency

facade element scale

4 glas elements, in this case 2 blue and two transparent elements

Landscape

The landscape is seen as a fluid continuity of the façade pattern onto the site. The lines of the façade are taken as a radial pattern all the way to the edges.

Different materialisation is applied to echo the colour scheme of the façade. Through the radial pattern a special perspective effect (reference Capitol Hill Michelangelo) is achieved that makes the outside plaza appear larger than it actually is.

Through a vertical differentiation of some parts of the surface the integration of green pockets and technical air exhaust openings for car park are possible.

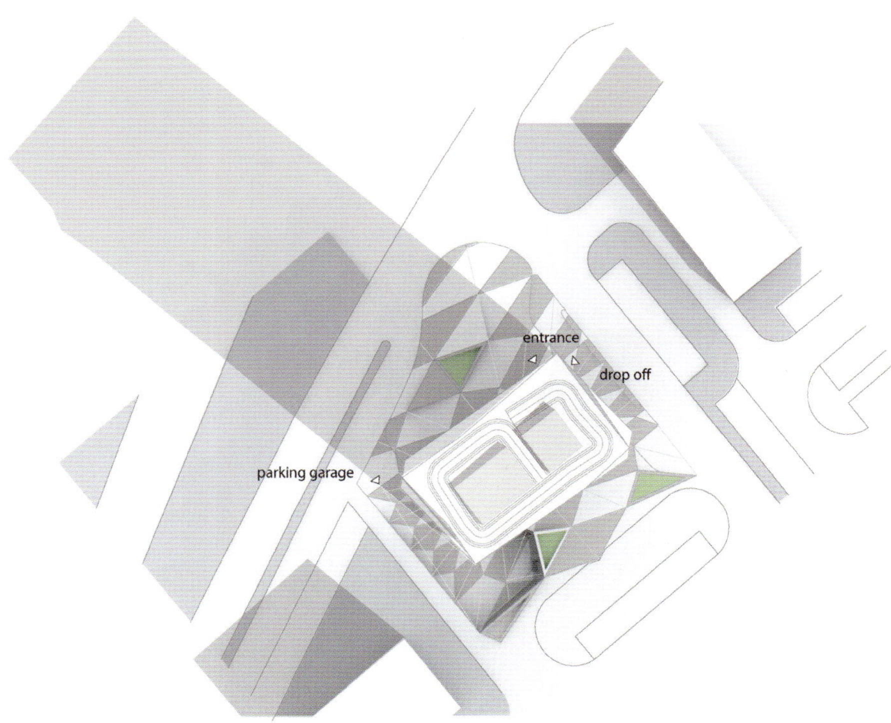

TOWER 123

The business Tower 123 is a design by invitation for the new and tallest building in Zagreb and in Croatia. The solution for the design has made after identifying the shortage of quality public space on the location of the Tower and the surrounding district. The analysis revealed the coexistence of two matrices-one modern and urbane,and the other, the remaining rural architecture which has been absorbed by the city space. It was evident that both matrices lacked quality public space. The principal avenue at the entry to Zagreb has been conceived as the main business area, thus giving to the image of the city a thoroughly new appearance. The business Tower 123 is planned to become the key element of the whole area,with its height of 123m and advanced DIAGRID structure which is a strong, safe and cost-effective diagonal structural concept. A trapezoidal ground plan is without columns which provides for various ground plan possibilities. The interior space of the tower is shared by business and public areas. The ground floor consists of a tall multi level lobby with access from all directions and different levels; the public facilities— a cafe and a restaurant are located at mid height of the Tower and on the top floor,where a belvedere with a 360° sightseeing area and a Museum of Zagreb Urban Development have also been planned. The roof area is reserved for a heliport. The business Tower 123 will be the tallest building in Croatia and in the whole region.

COMPANY	3LHD
DESIGNER	3LHD
COUNTRY (DISTRICT)	Croatia

museum of urban development and belvedere

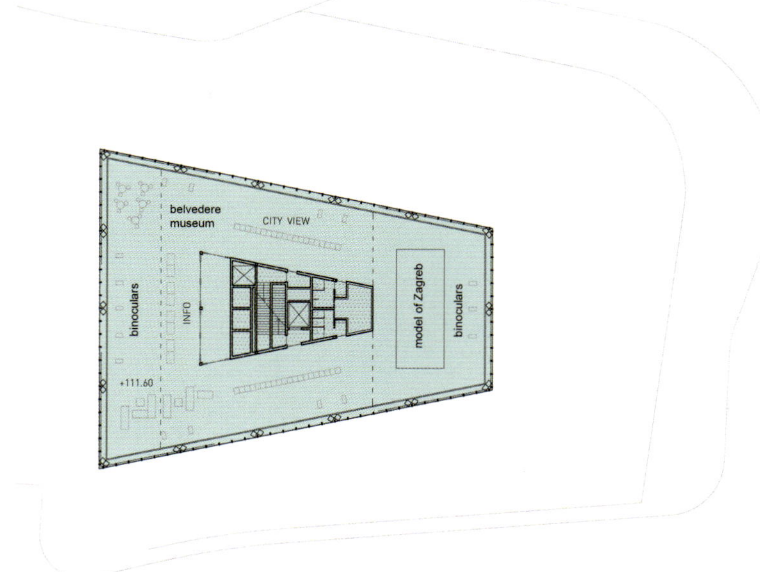

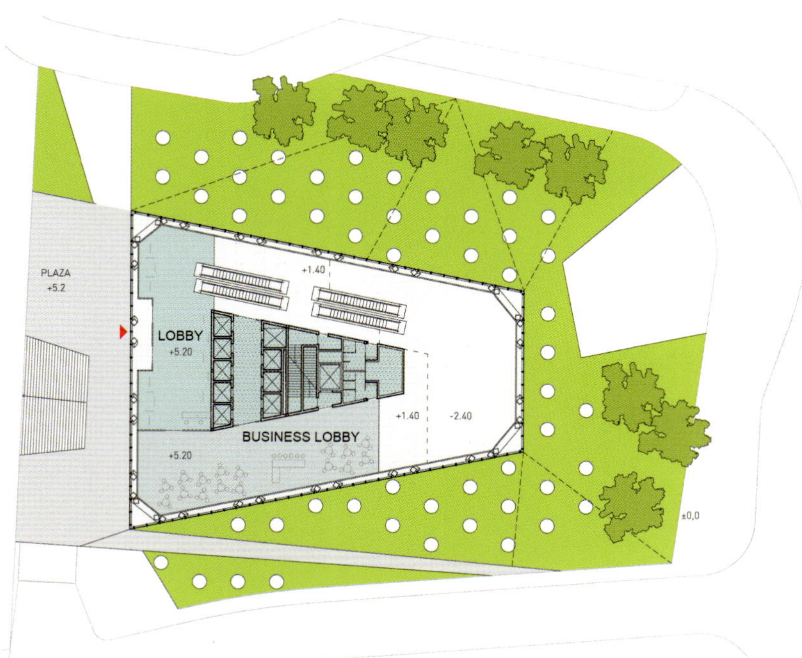

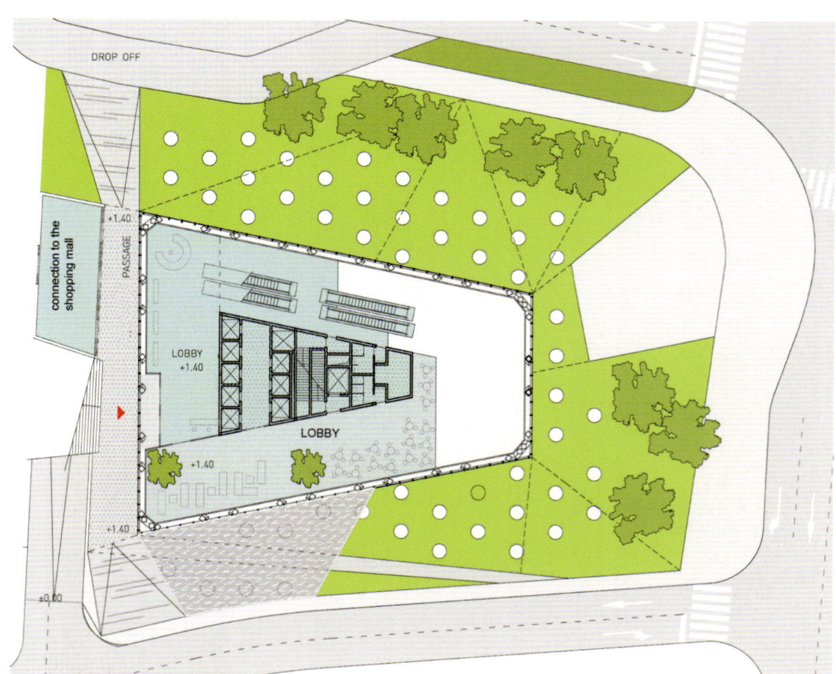

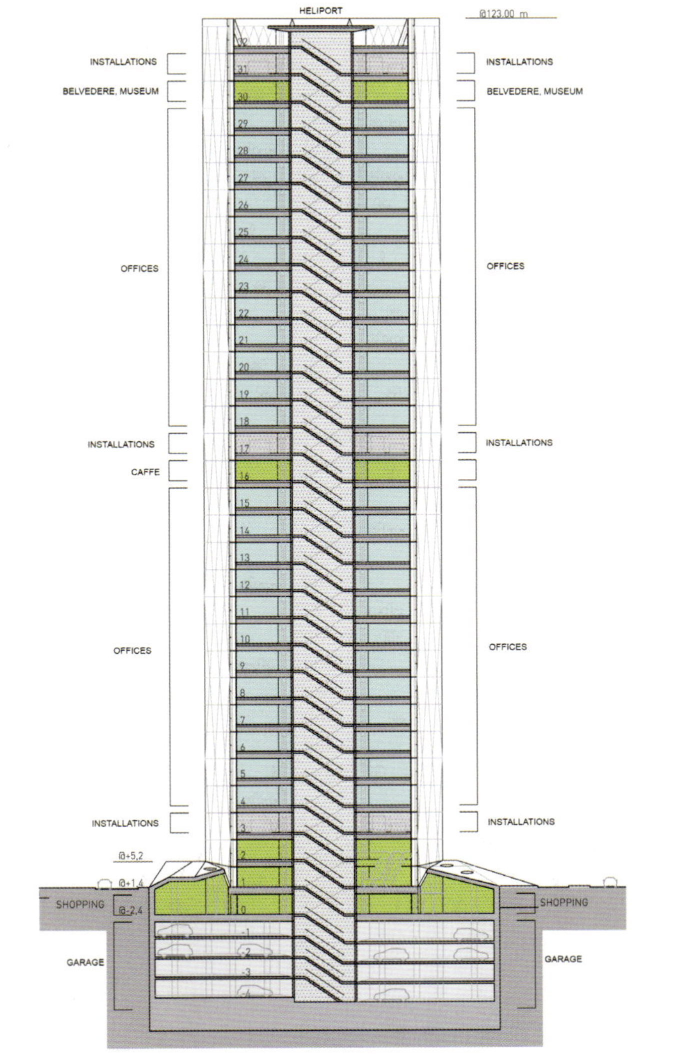
HELIPORT
Ø123.00 m
INSTALLATIONS
BELVEDERE, MUSEUM
OFFICES
INSTALLATIONS
CAFFE
OFFICES
INSTALLATIONS
SHOPPING
GARAGE

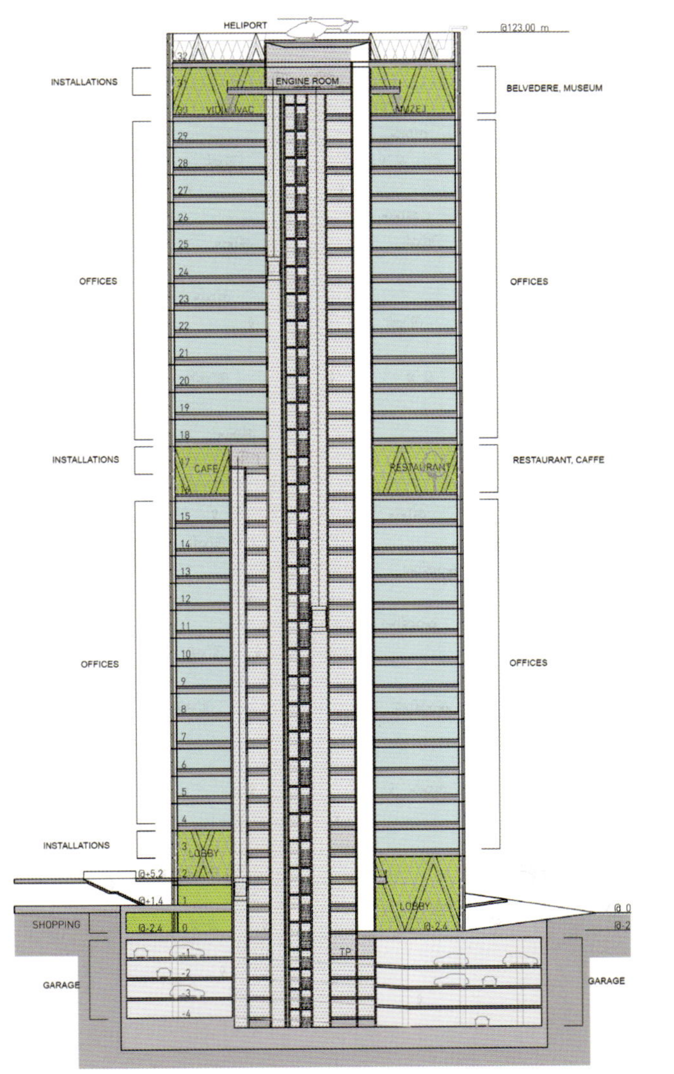
HELIPORT
Ø123.00 m
ENGINE ROOM
INSTALLATIONS
BELVEDERE, MUSEUM
OFFICES
INSTALLATIONS
RESTAURANT, CAFFE
CAFE
RESTAURANT
OFFICES
INSTALLATIONS
LOBBY
SHOPPING
GARAGE

MIRAMARE TOWER CENTRE

The competition program is placed on a crossing of two streets, Miramarska and Bednjanska. It is a point of colliding two urban city concepts: north part with classical city blocks of the Zagreb's lower city enclosed by the railway and the south part primarily along the Vukovarska Street, outlined with modernistic dominant character of mostly public and social buildings. Concept of awarded project stems from forming a unified structure that will reconcile the surrounding urban matrix and meet the program requirements. Solution with two interacting volumes, the tower with 20 floors and the lower part of the 5 floors, united the planned goals and achieve high quality relations with the neighboring buildings. Interspaces between two volumes - semi opened atrium, connect the inner area of the business centre with the surrounding public space.

In the underground 2 floors are a garage for 400 vehicles, a ground floor space is a main access to the centre, with public commercial facilities and cafe. Higher floors are reserved for business users, while the highest floor offers a unique view of the panorama of Zagreb. Simple and at the same time very attractive effect of designing the facade by pulling the glass modules in and out, gave the building of business centre Miramare unique recognition and special value.

COMPANY	3LHD
DESIGNER	3LHD
COUNTRY (DISTRICT)	Croatia

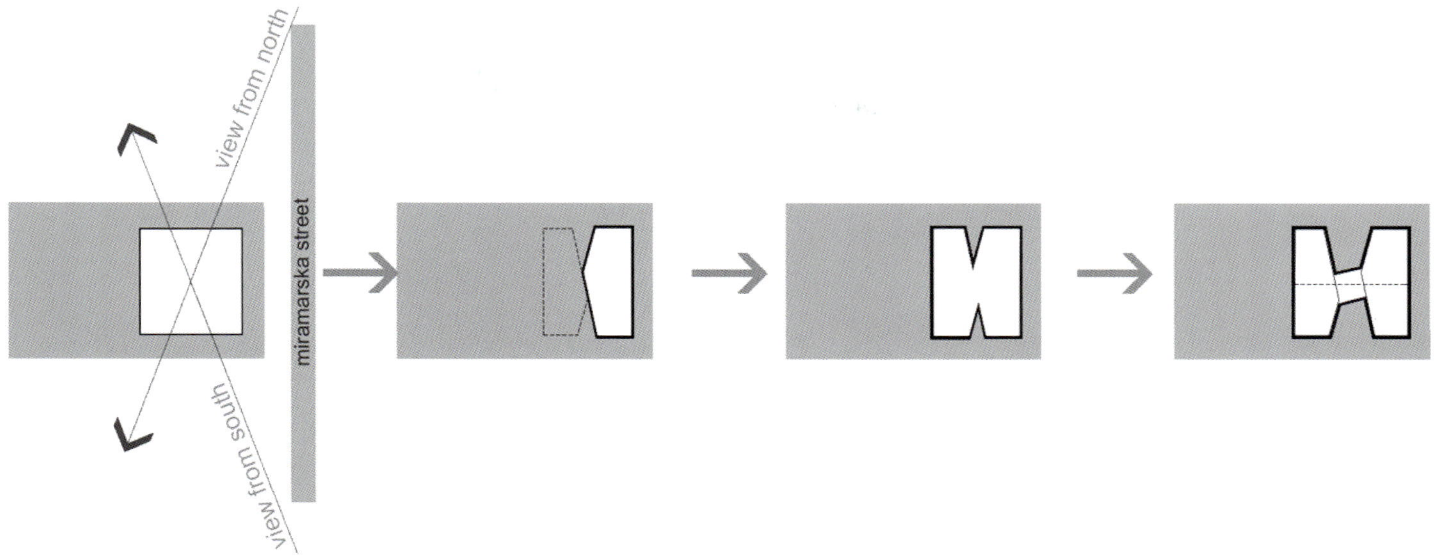
view from north
miramarska street
view from south

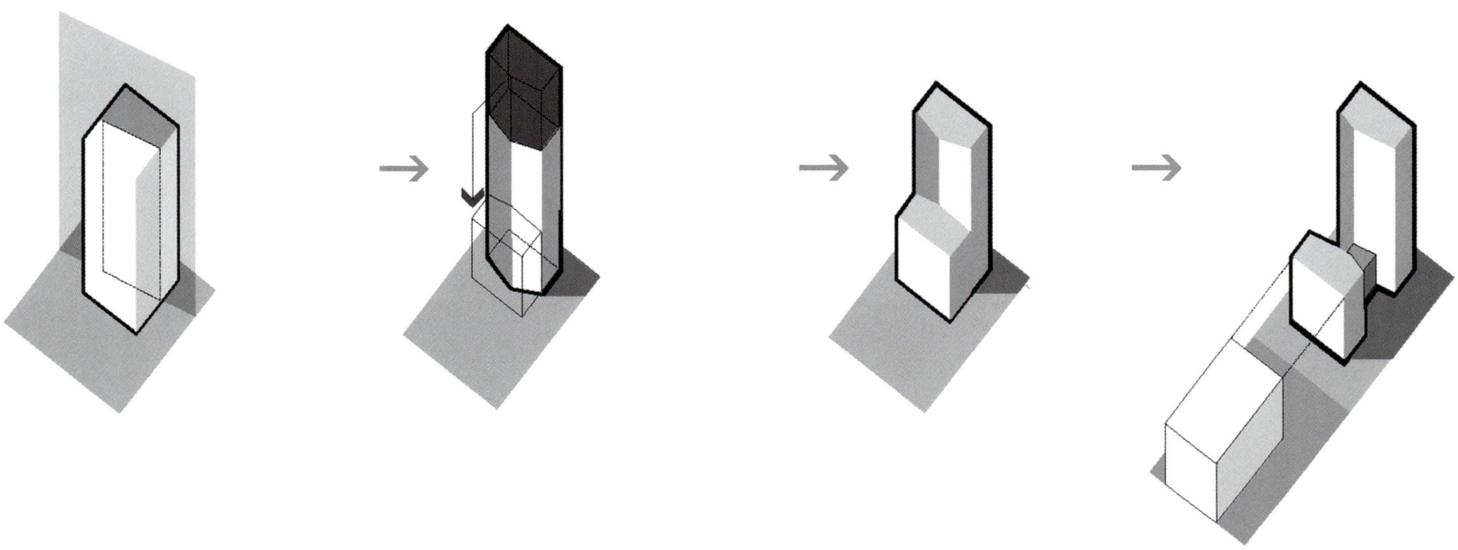

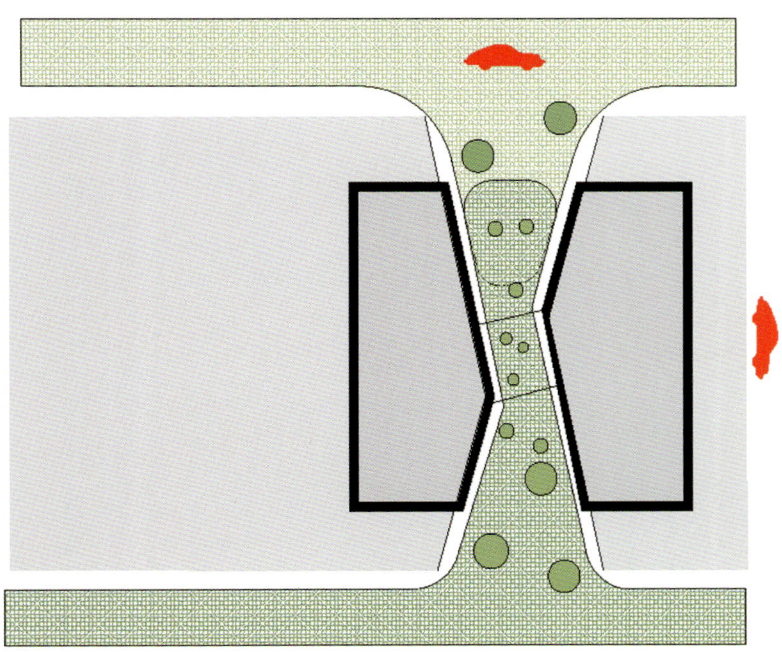

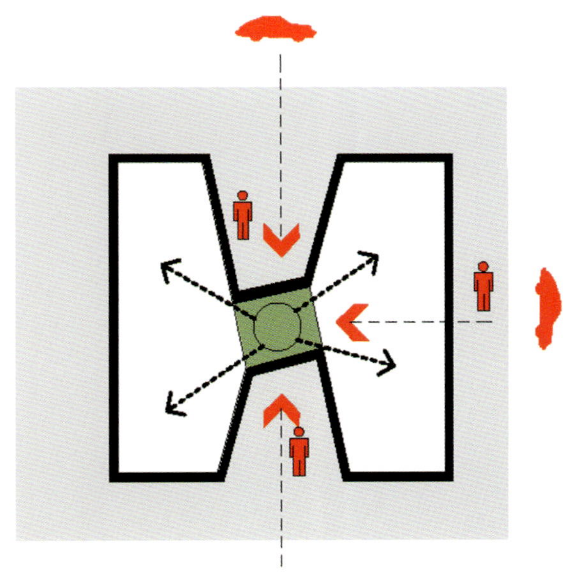

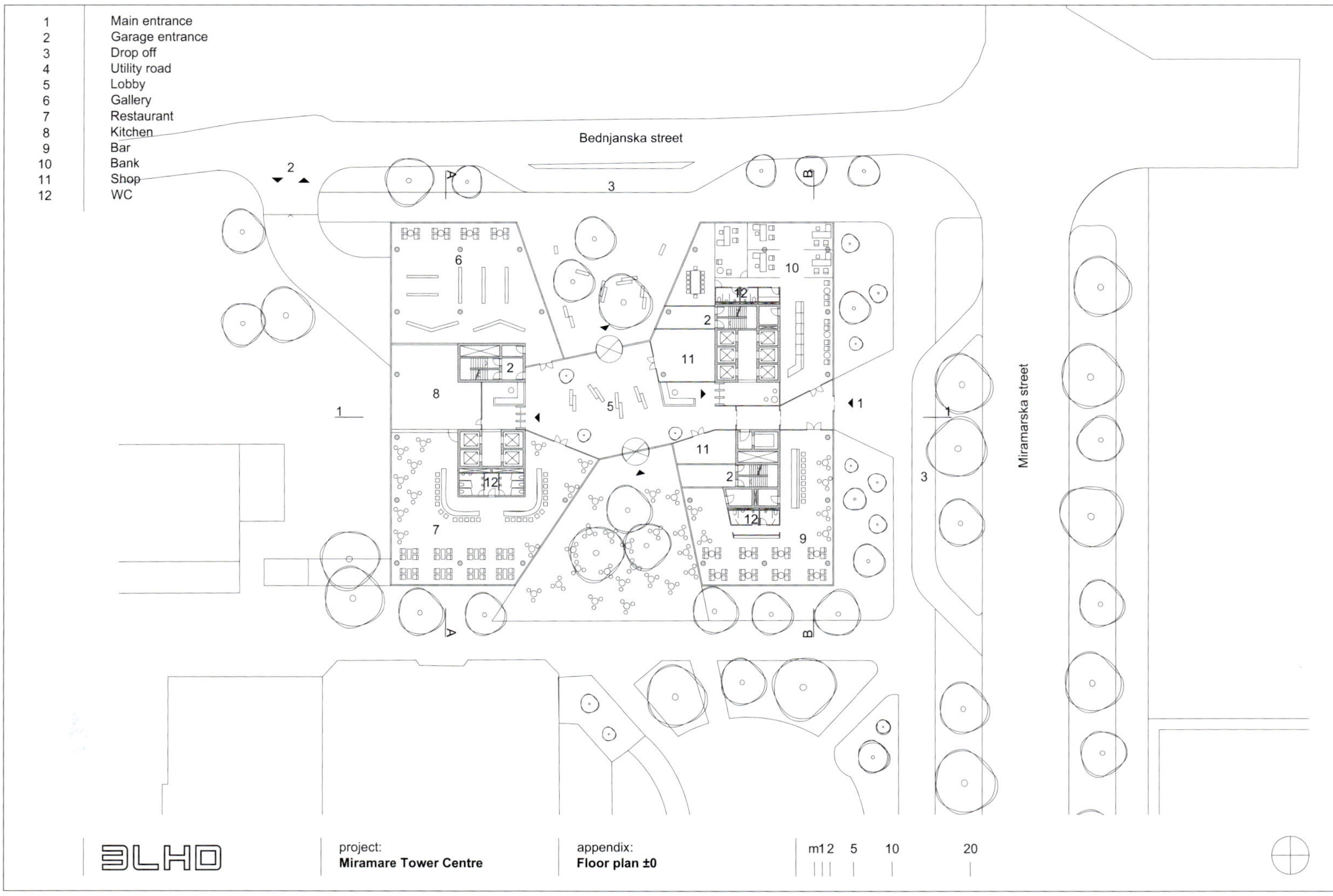
1 Main entrance
2 Garage entrance
3 Drop off
4 Utility road
5 Lobby
6 Gallery
7 Restaurant
8 Kitchen
9 Bar
10 Bank
11 Shop
12 WC
Bednjanska street
Miramarska street
3LHD
project:
Miramare Tower Centre
appendix:
Floor plan ±0
m1 2 5 10 20

PRISM CONTEMPORARY ART I PLASTIC SENSATIONS

Prism is a new three-story contemporary art gallery located at the heart of the Sunset Strip in West Hollywood. The mission of the gallery is to become a cornerstone of artistic experimentation, carving a new niche for the arts in Southern California. Alongside the exhibition space, the gallery also houses a bookstore with a curated selection of texts and products.

While PATTERNS' involvement was limited to the envelope and interior, this project presented the possibility of true material innovation: to be the first facade in the nation to be constructed entirely out of a resin-based composite polycarbonate.

The project's legal status as a renovation of an existing structure placed unique restrictions upon the scope of work and the inflections within the facade's surface. An existing steel column grid left from a previous renovation predetermined floor-to-floor heights, and areas of existing stucco exterior walls from the original building provided opportunities for playful exchanges and guided the development of the design.

The gallery envelope is designed to create subtle sensations by inducing a physical and optical dynamism that both challenges and enhances the pedestrian movement along the iconic Sunset Strip. Its formal logic is the outcome of a productive negotiation between the ordering structural grid of the existing building and the intense vitality of the context. Almost theatrically, the facade surfaces appear to lift up and then down, dramatically opening the interior while suspending its mass over the strip and projecting a sense of weightiness for pedestrian and vehicular traffic approaching from the west. Deeply inspired by the supple forms, streamlined detailing and plastic finishes of automotive design, the facade has a dual aesthetic performance associated with plastic materiality and responsive to its lively context: it behaves as a reflectively glossy surface during the day and as a viscously translucent skin when lit from inside at night.

As part of our collaboration with 3Form, a series of full-scale prototypes was developed and fabricated as an essential part of the design process. These prototypes were used to test various conditions affecting performance and aesthetics, cost and construction: from the limits of structure and its connections to mullions and polycarbonate panels, to issues pertaining to waterproofing and the behavior of a glossy translucent surface, to the examination of custom assembly details and connections that support and seal the finished facade.

The material solution for the facade involves 3/8-inch resin-based polycarbonate panels, which are color dyed and extruded in a single pull. Color and translucence are entirely design controlled. Panels were heat-formed over medium-density fiberboard (MDF) molds. All waterproofing and thermal expansion and contraction are taken up by hardware at the face of the panels, freeing the facade from any substrate or interior wall.

COMPANY	PATTERNS
DESIGNER	PATTERNS
PHOTOGRAPHER	Joshua White Courtesy of PATTERNS
COUNTRY (DISTRICT)	U.S.A.

8746 SUNSET

DEXTER
SUNDAYS 9PM
SUNSET TOWERS

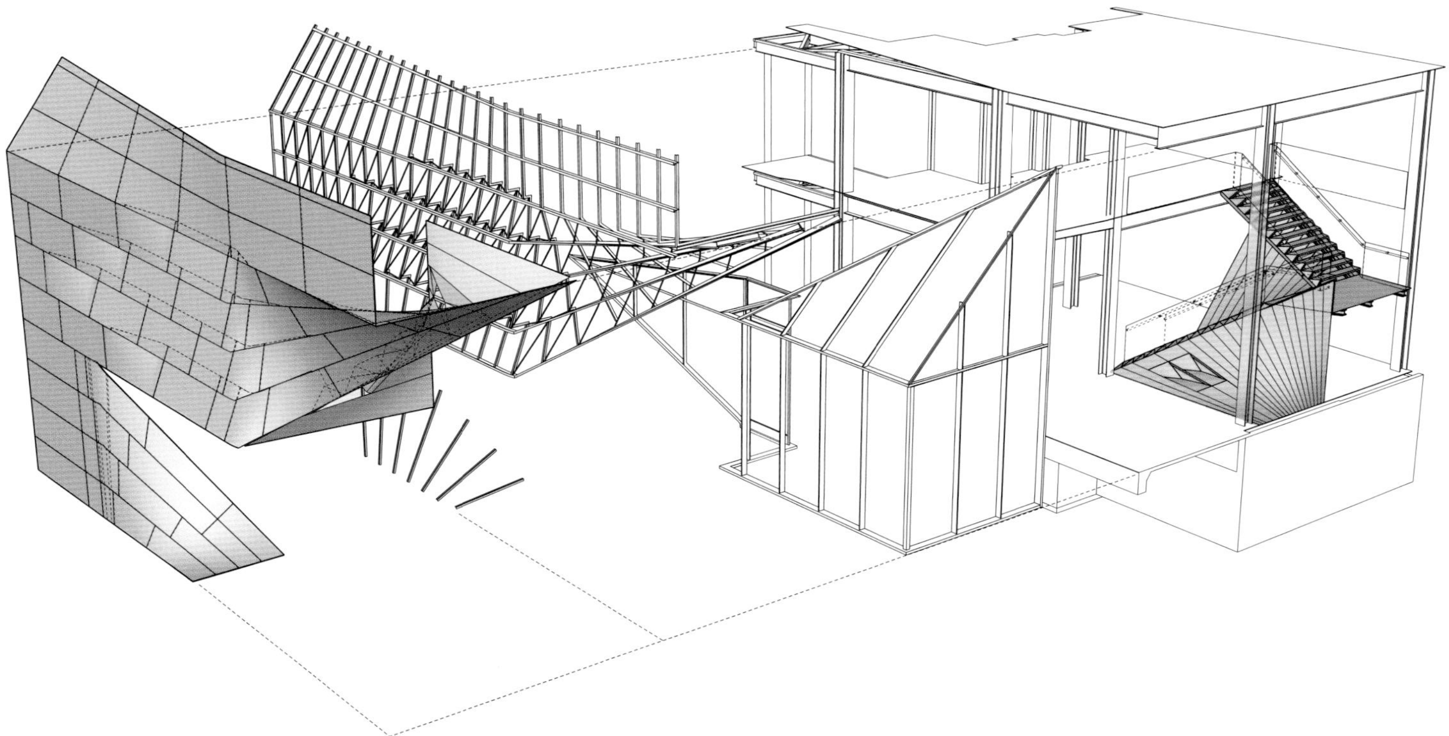

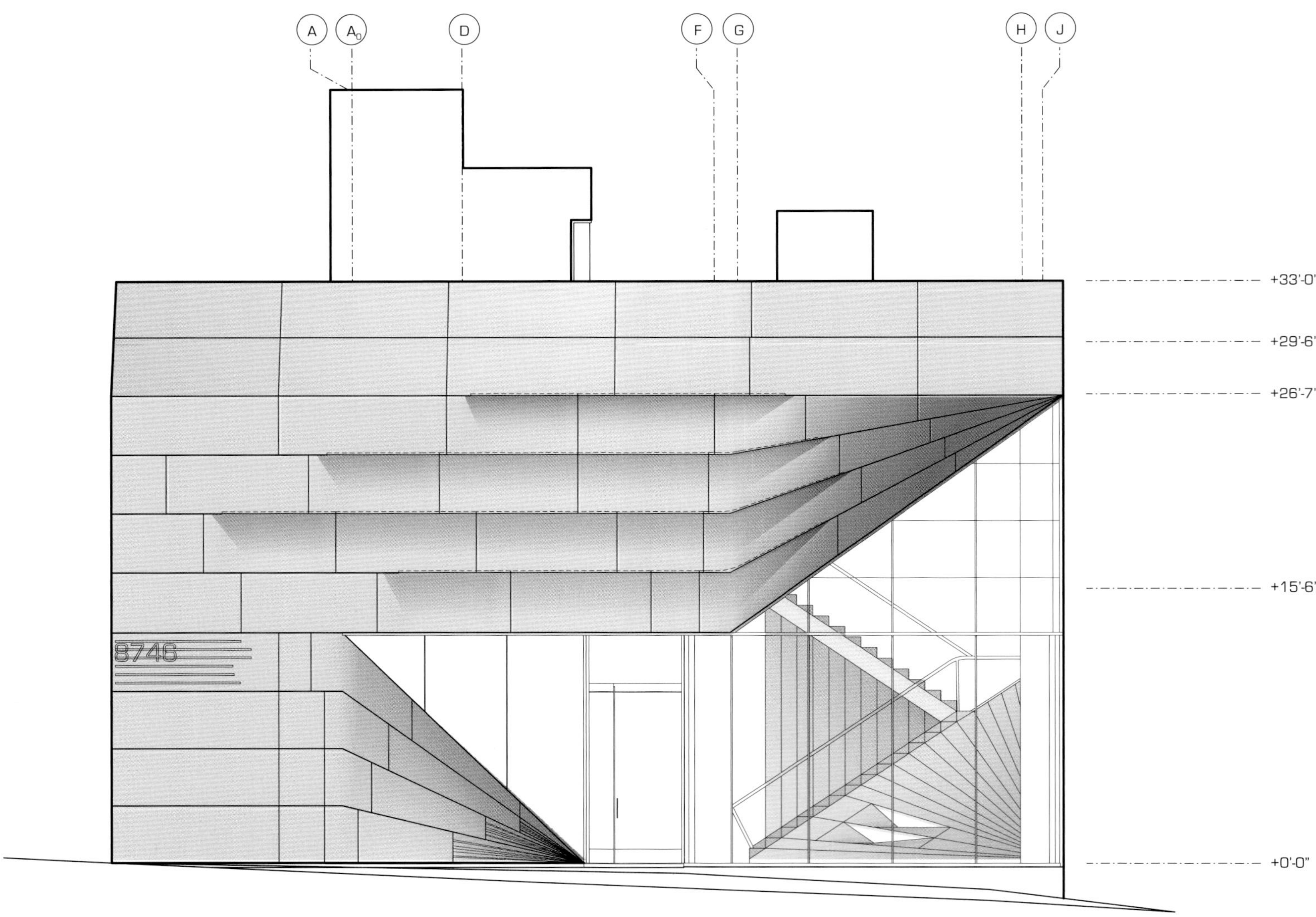
A
A0
D
F
G
H
J
+33'-0"
+29'-6"
+26'-7"
+15'-6"
+0'-0"
8746

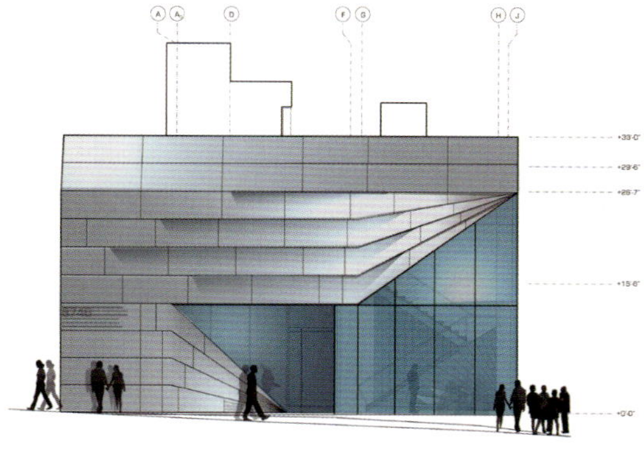

Gallery.1_

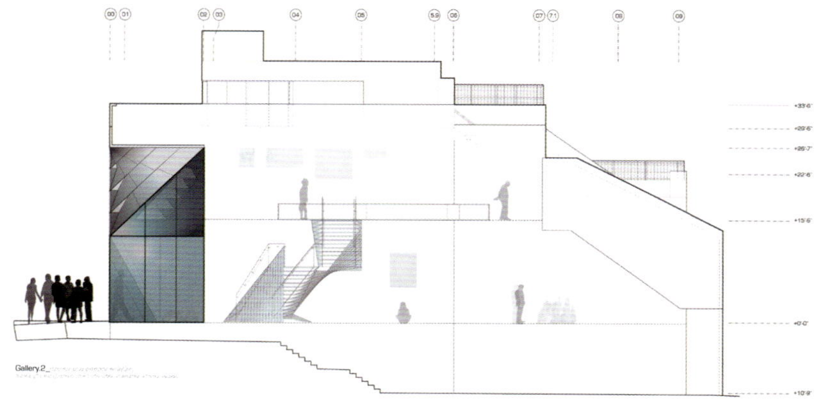

Gallery.2_

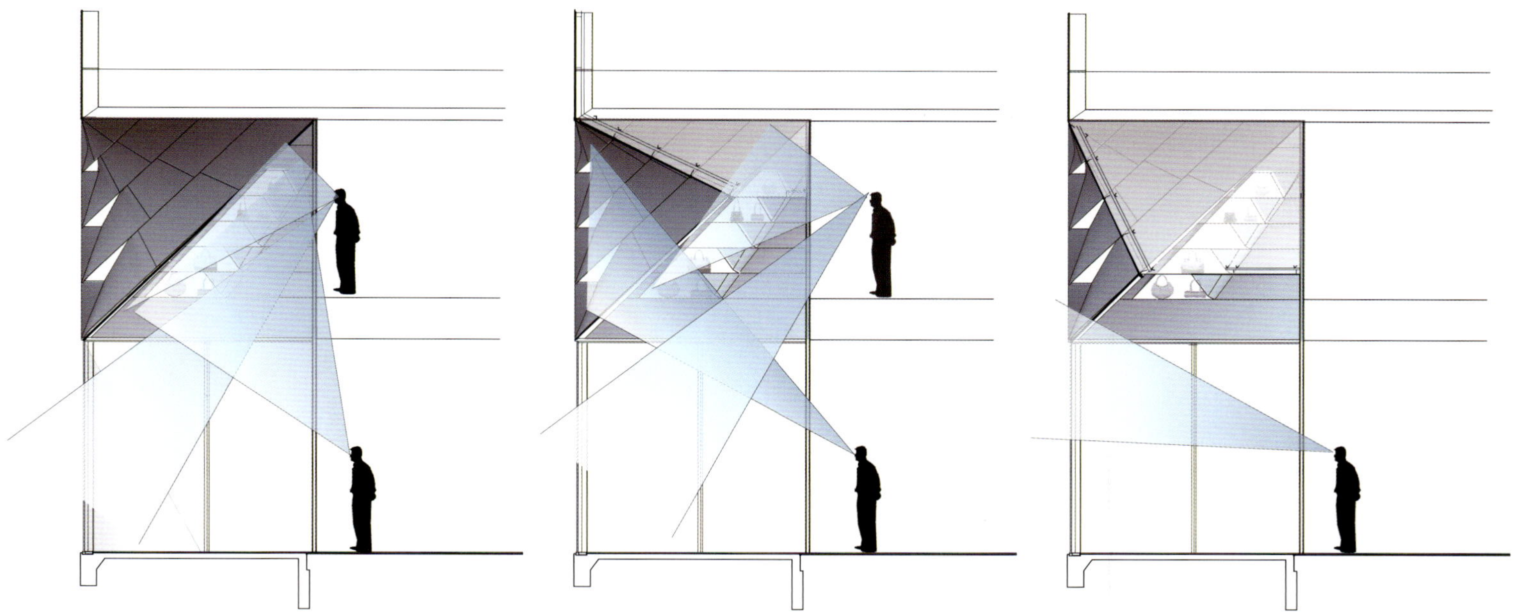

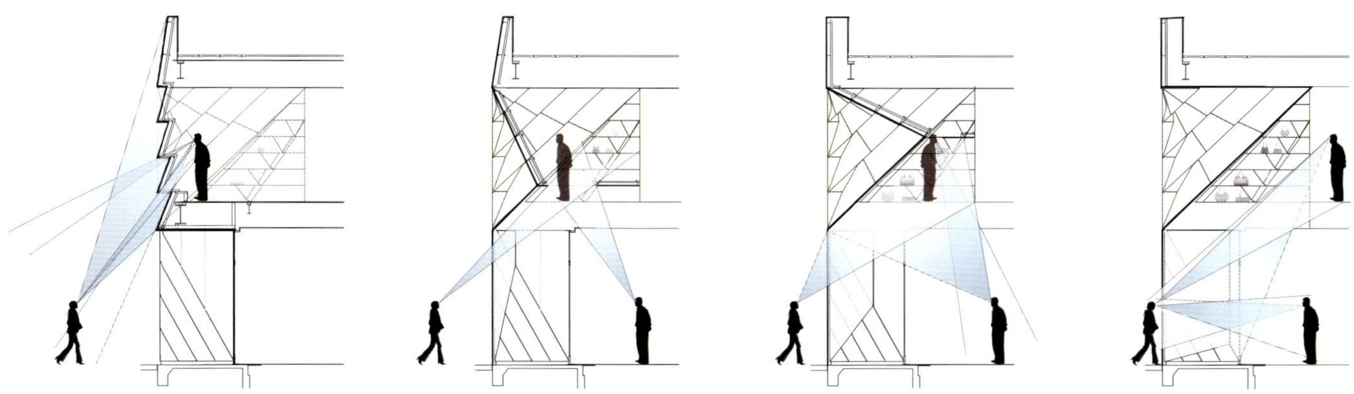

b.1_ b.2_ b.3_ b.4_

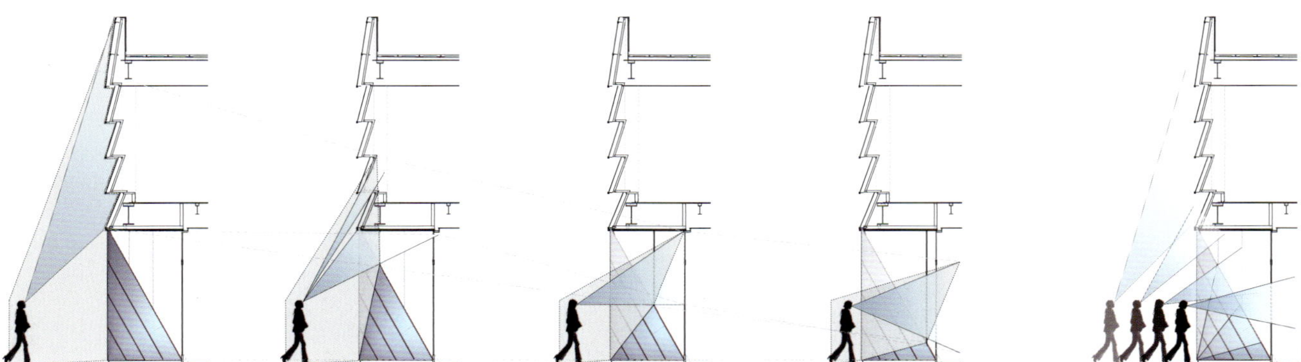

A.1_ A.2_ A.3_ A.4_ A.5_

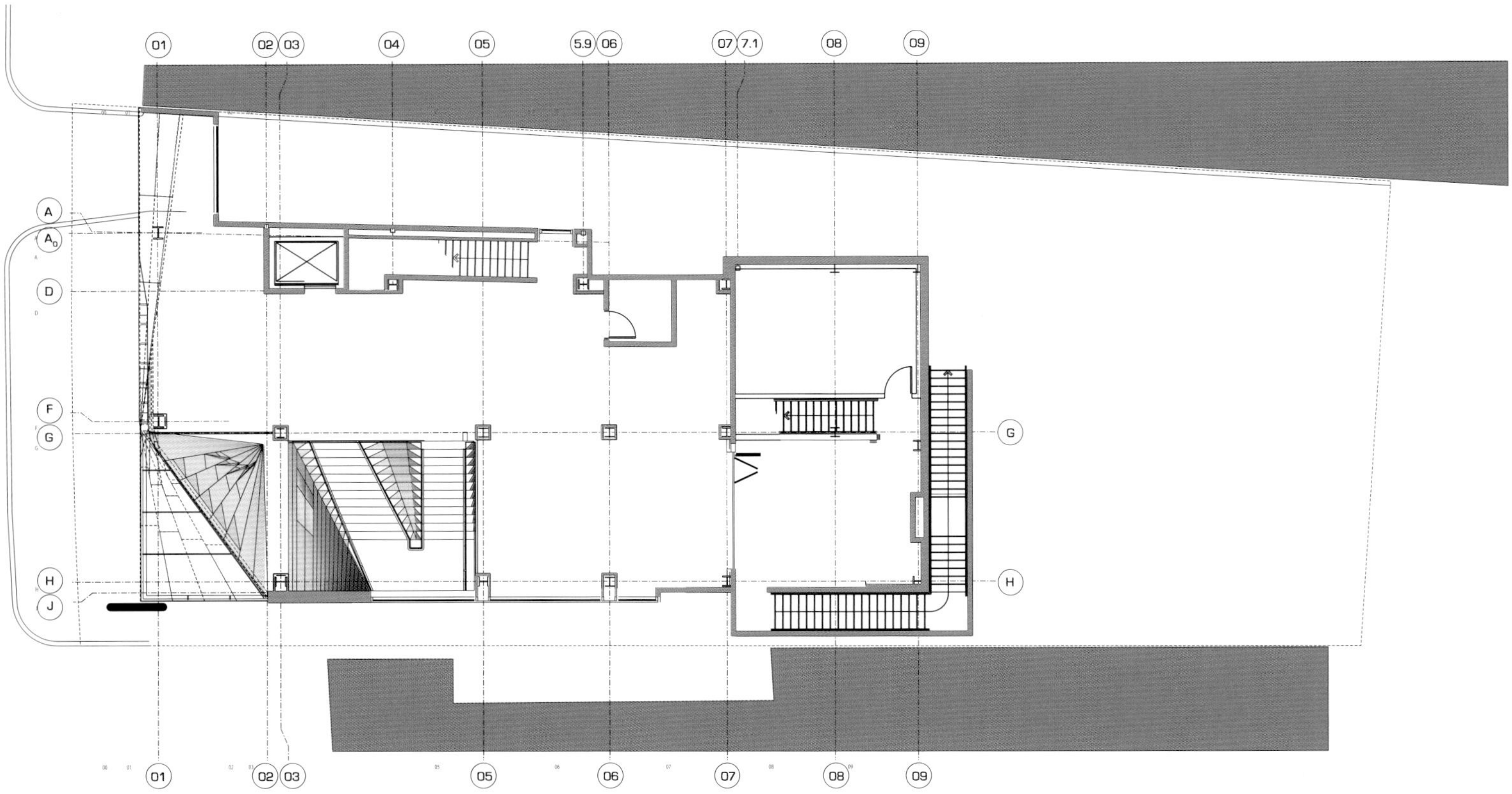
01
02
03
04
05
5.9
06
07
7.1
08
09
A
A0
D
F
G
H
J

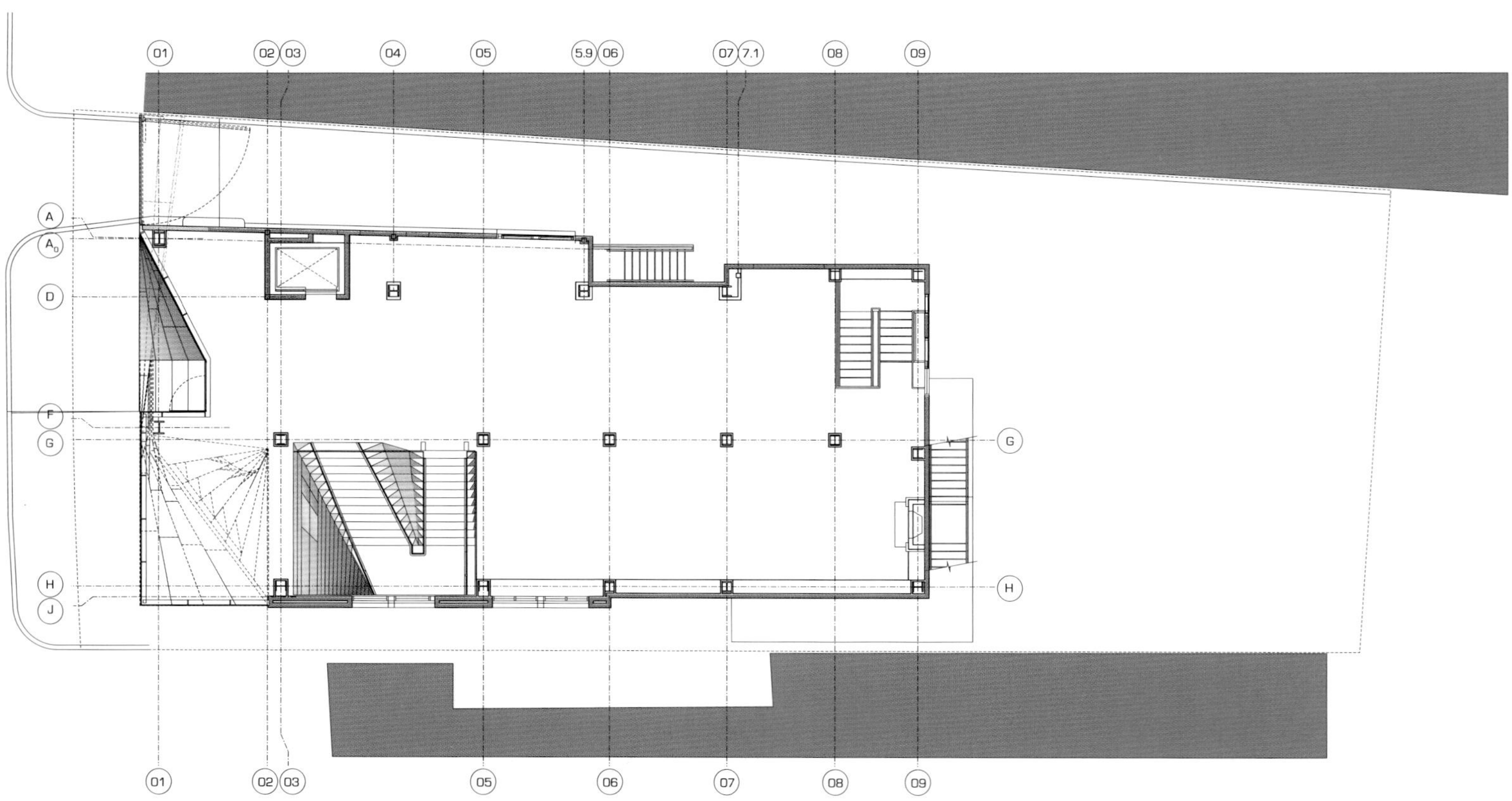
01
02
03
04
05
5.9
06
07
7.1
08
09
A
A0
D
F
G
H
J

BIONIC TOWER

Concept

The tower proposes a naturally occurring system of structural organization that generates a building embodying efficiencies found within natural structures and architecture. The proposed facade also envisions an intelligent automation of surface to address pragmatic issues such as ventilation, solar access and water collection.

In the same natural envisions organic regeneration, the building proposes a natural system of organic structure and organization.

Structure and ornament

There is a unity between structure, space and architectural expression, similar to cathedrals, and any natural system.

Learning from nature and advanced computing enables us to conceive structures of incredible lightness, efficiency and elegance. The intelligence of the smallest unit results in the intelligence of the overall system.

By parametric modeling of a behavioral logic the system is constantly optimized. The whole is greater than the sum of its parts. New materials and technologies enable adaptability, responsiveness, environmental awareness and strength.

Instead of an array of individual elements the building behaves like an organism or ecosystem. The building systems and skin are controlled and react to external influences like air pressure, temperature, humidity, air pollution and solar radiation.

Intelligence of the System Architecture of the future is not about the shape but about the intelligence of the system. No building skin today approaches the performance of the biological world.

The traditional curtain wall facade is passive, lacking the power to adjust to the fluctuating external environment.

It should be able to intervene actively in the buildings struggle to maintain its internal stability.

Architecture has to perform as an ecosystem within the organic tissue of the city.

COMPANY	LAVA
COUNTRY (DISTRICT)	Australia

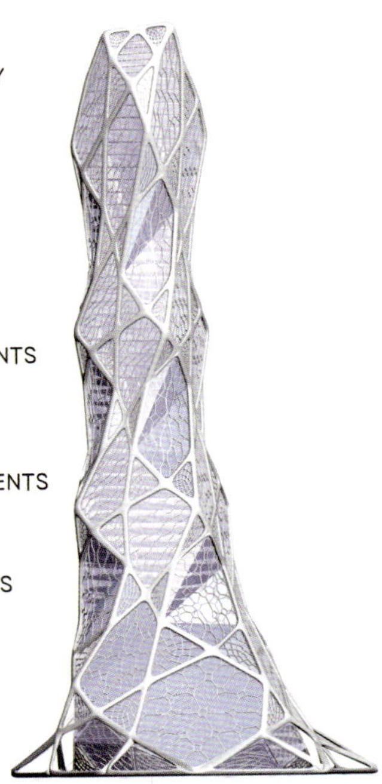
SKYLOBBY
HIGHRISE APPARTMENTS
MIDRISE APPARTMENTS
LOWRISE APPARTMENTS
LOBBY

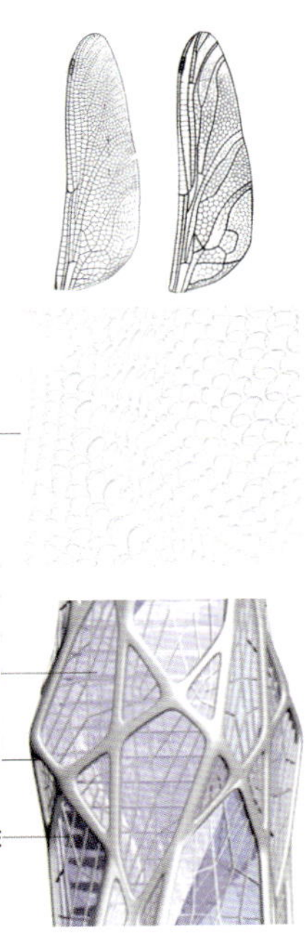
SHADING SYSTEM
INTELLIGENT SKIN
STRUCTURAL FRAME
ORGANIC SUBSTRUCTURE

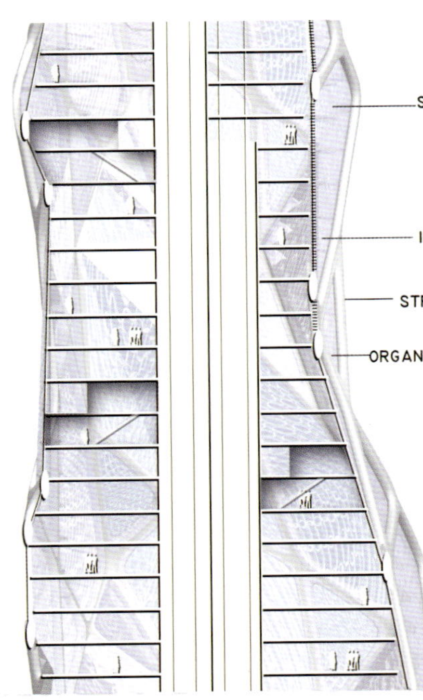
SHADING SYSTEM
INTELLIGENT SKIN
STRUCTURAL FRAME
ORGANIC SUBSTRUCTURE

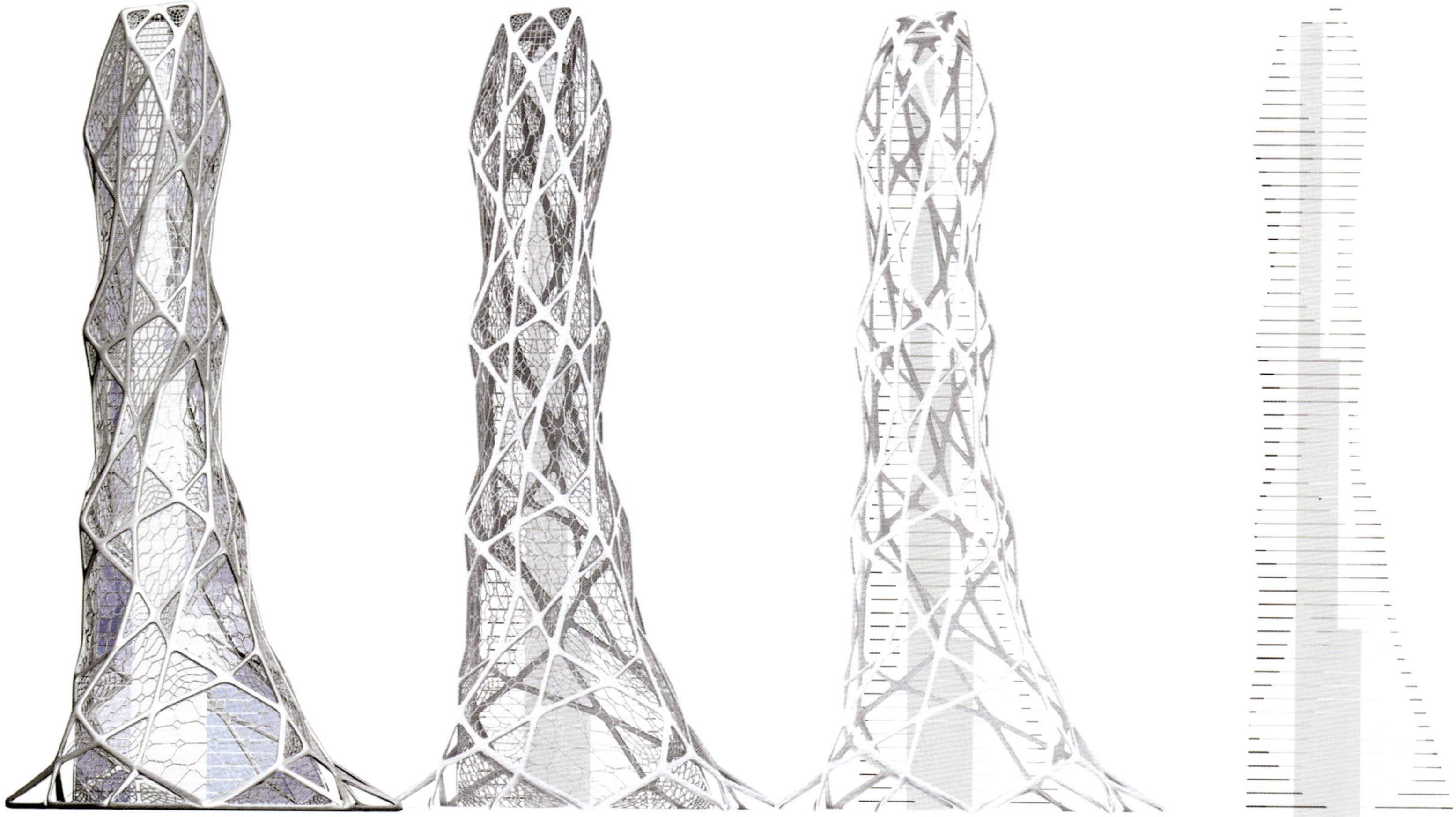

BUILDING SKIN | SUBSTRUCTURE | EXOSKELETON STRUCTURE | SLABS AND CORE

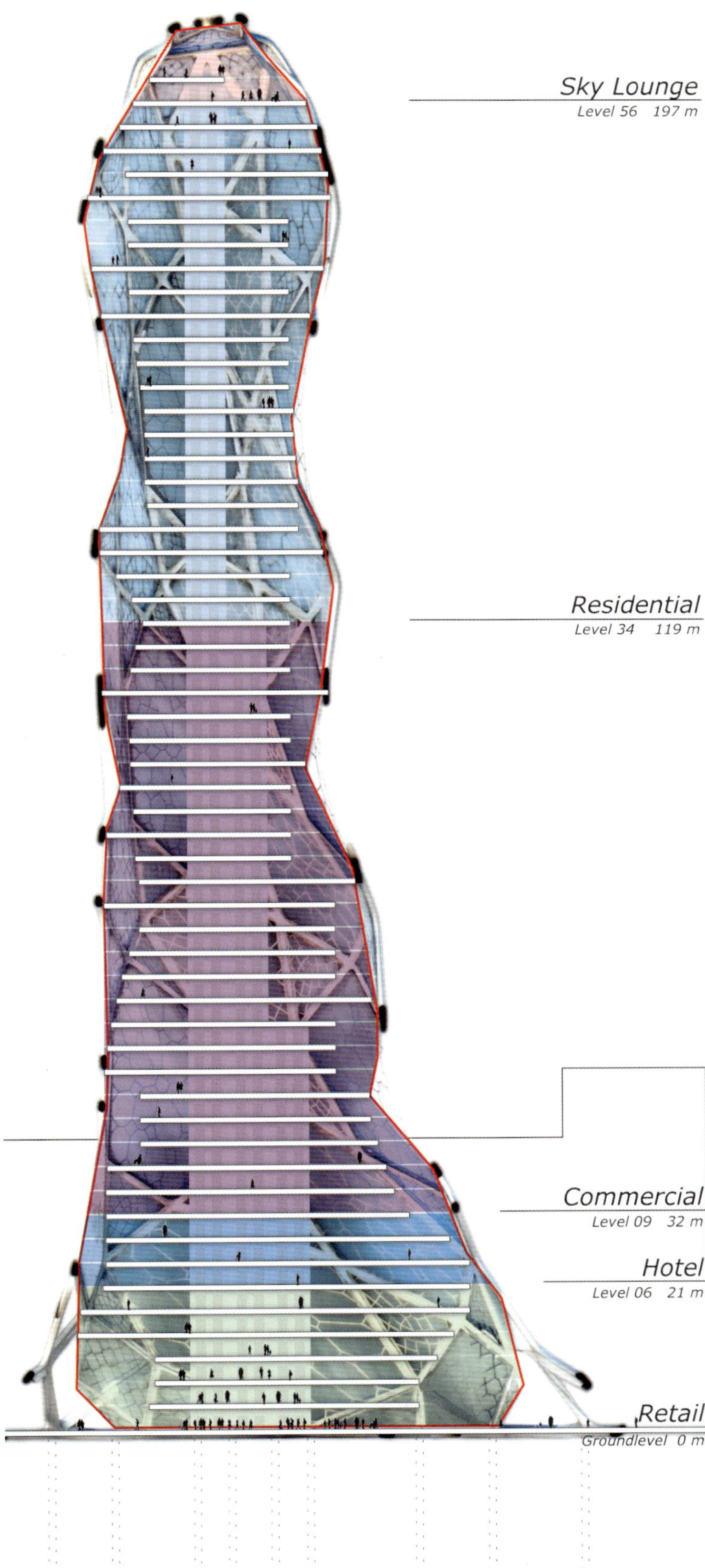
Sky Lounge
Level 56 197 m
Residential
Level 34 119 m
Commercial
Level 09 32 m
Hotel
Level 06 21 m
Retail
Groundlevel 0 m

VILLAGE CENTER - CENTER PARCS

In May 2010 a fourth French Center Parcs resort was created in the Harcholins woods, close to Sarrebourg, after a provisional contract between Pierre & Vacances, Center Parcs France, the Moselle's General Council and the Lorraine Regional Council. This project stands out through an architecture where wood predominates, both in the structural elements and the facade coverings.
Located towards the lower part of the site, at the edge of a spruce and larch wood, the buildings fade into the vegetation.
AQUAMUNDO, water, earth, air and light: the great Aquamundo hall hosts 5,000m² worth of water games and submersed beaches in dense tropical vegetation.
The project's main challenge consists in inserting, within the landscape, the large superstructures that are necessary to the trees' growth. The plant, in the shape of a trefoil cross, is covered with a set of centrings made of glued-laminated timber with stainless steel angle braces. Its cover is an inflatable transparent multilayered TEXLON-type membrane. Three vaults, spanning 35 meters and varying in height from 13 to 16 meters, shape this building. These superstructures rest upon a solid mineral base measuring 5 to 7 meters high, which encloses the swimming-pools. This base, which forms a green wall on the outside, also hosts the fluids necessary to the building's energy-saving efficiency.
THE GREENHOUSE: it is first and foremost the resort's winter garden. Its concept stems from the site's history and from the inside-outside space status and tropical feel of the greenhouse. The Greenhouse is covered with a very light wood structure which rests upon a lattice of randomly inclined posts so as to imitate the rhythm of spruce and larch trunks swaying wildly during a storm which previously left its mark on this site. The very light glued-laminated timber structure allows reaching heights of 12m. It is made of composite posts (steel pipes covered on their outside by a glued-laminated timber facing) planted according to a 7.5m by 10.0m grid, and of glued-laminated timber beams running lengthways along the building, under which glued-laminated trusses are suspended every 1.25m. The geometrical disposition of the roofing elements allows for the integration of North facing sheds.
This resort is a pilot project for the partnership with WWF-France and applies the official THPE (Very High Energy Efficiency) certification standards. It was awarded the NF Bâtiments Tertiaires Démarches HQE certification (High Quality Environmental standard for Service industry buildings) and is included in Center Parcs's own environmental management system which has been used and validated since 1999 by the international ISO 14001 certification. All efficiency requirements in terms of materials, energy, isolation and building site management have been reached. The 600m² wood-fuelled boiler room covers at least 90% of the building's energy needs in terms of heating and hot water, and wood is supplied from the local area. The savings in CO_2 therefore reach 2,900 tons/year. Natural ventilation is optimal and allows saving 250 MWh/year in electricity. The outside swimming pools' water is stored in protective buffer canvasses during the night, making intensive re-heating unnecessary, which represents another annual saving of 1,200 MWh. Finally, the implementation of "reverse osmosis" allows reusing 60% of filtered water, which amounts to 20,000 m³ per year.

COMPANY	Art'Ur Architectes
CREATIVE DIRECTOR	Philippe Pascal and Muriel Teynier
DESIGNER	Philippe Pascal and Muriel Teynier
PHOTOGRAPHER	Florent Michel / 11h45
CLIENT	Pierre et Vacances Company / Center Parcs France
COUNTRY (DISTRICT)	France

Centre Village Center Parcs Domaine des Trois Forêts - Coupe transversale sur la Grande Serre - Echelle 1/500

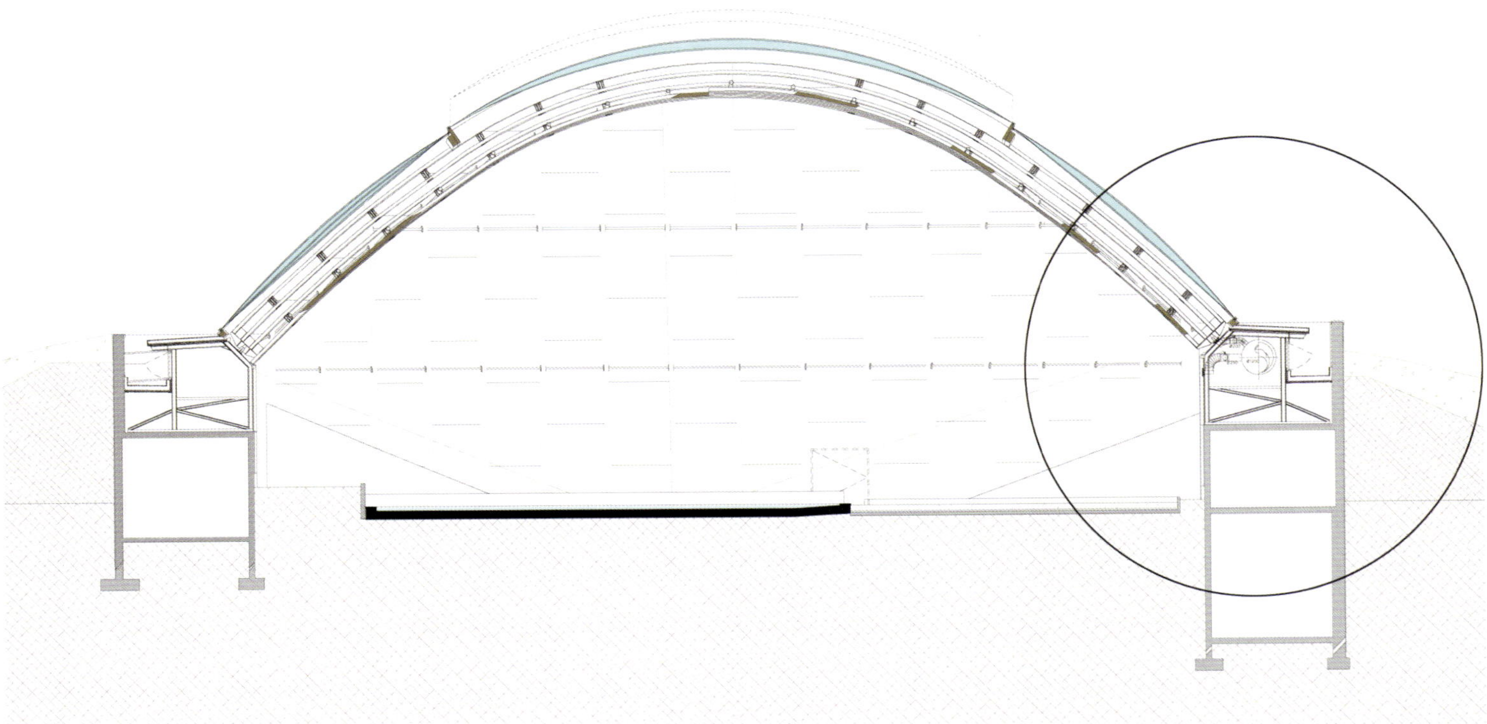

Centre Village Center Parcs Domaine des Trois Forêts - Coupe sur Aquamundo - échelle 1/200

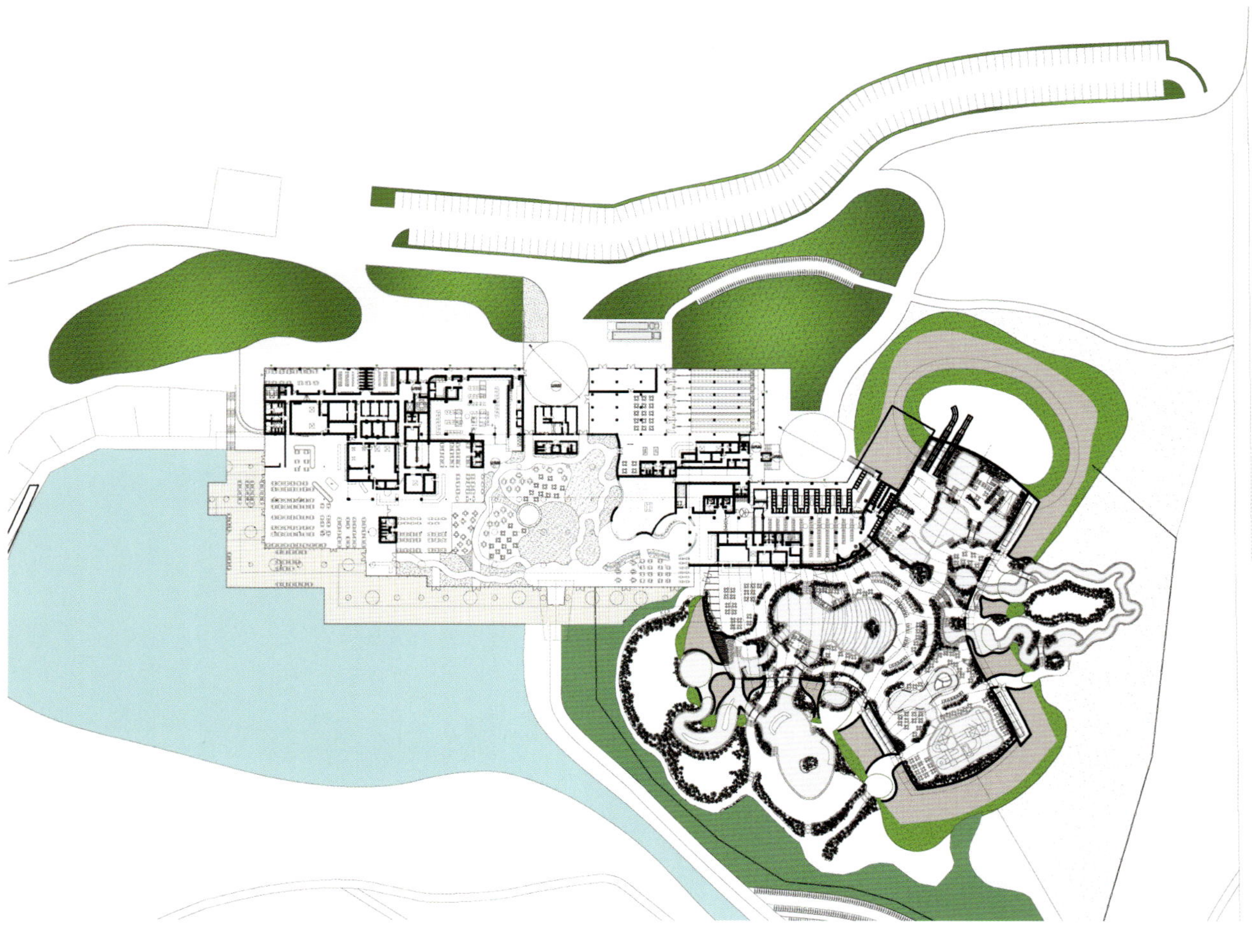

Centre Village Center Parcs Domaine des Trois Forêts - Plan Niveau 0 - Echelle 1/1500

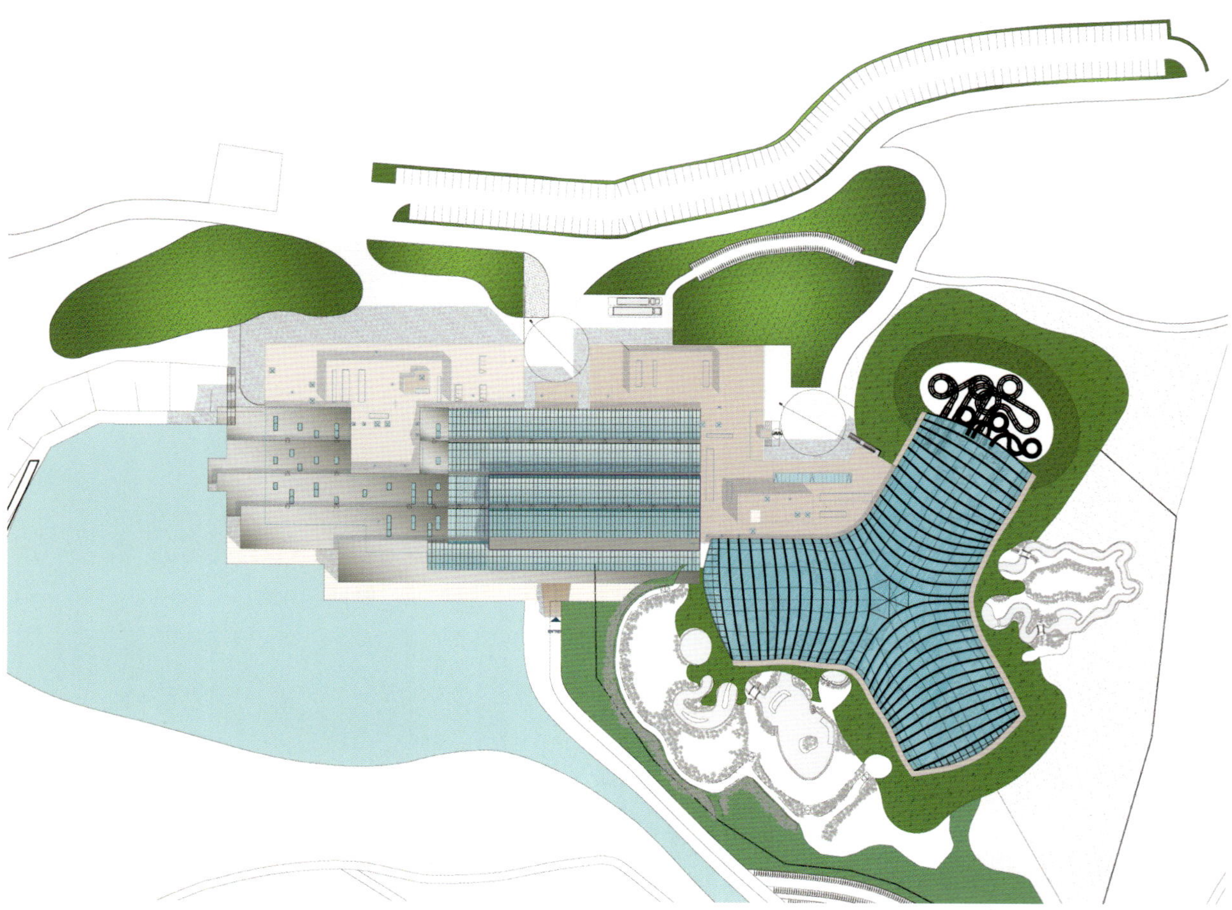

Centre Village Center Parcs Domaine des Trois Forêts - Plan de toiture - Echelle 1/1500

YELLOW TREEHOUSE RESTAURANT

The concept is driven by the "enchanted" site which is raised above an open meadow and meandering stream on the edge of the woods.

The tree-house concept is reminiscent of childhood dreams and playtime, fairy stories of enchantment and imagination. It's inspired through many forms found in nature -the chrysalis/cocoon protecting the emerging butterfly/moth, perhaps an onion/garlic clove form hung out to dry. It is also seen as a lantern, a beacon at night that simply glows yet during the day it might be a semi camouflaged growth, or a tree fort that provides an outlook and that offers refuge. The plan form also has loose similarities to a sea shell with the open ends spiralling to the center. It's the treehouse we all dreamed of as children but could only do as an adult fantasy. Access is via a 60m tree-top "accessible" walkway –an adventure in itself.

The selected site and tree had to meet a myriad of functional requirements -18 seated people and waiting staff in relative comfort complete with a bar; gaining correct camera angles with associated light qualities for filming the adverts, web cam and stills, have unobstructed views into the valley and entrance to the site and structural soundness. The final selected tree is one of the larger trees on the site and sits above a steep part of the site which accentuates the tree's height. Kitchen/catering facilities and toilets are at ground level.

The Architectural component embodies a simple oval form wrapped "organically" around the trunk and structurally tied at top and bottom, with a circular plan that is split apart on the axis with the rear floor portion raised. This allows the approach from the rear via a playful tree-top walkway experience, slipping inside the exposed face of the pod and being enchanted by the juxtaposition of being in an enclosed space that is also quite "open" and permeable to the treetop views. There is also a "Juliet" deck opposite the entrance that looks down the valley.

The scale and form of the tree-house creates a memorable statement without dominating it's setting.

While its natural "organic" form sits comfortably, the rhythm of the various materials retains its strong architectural statement. The verticality of the fins mimics the verticality of the redwoods and enable the building to naturally "blend" into its setting, as though it was a natural growth.

COMPANY	Pacific Environments NZ Ltd Architects
CREATIVE DIRECTOR	Pete Eising
DESIGNER	Pete Eising, Lucy Gauntlett
PHOTOGRAPHER	Lucy Gauntlett
CLIENT	Yellow Pages Group
COUNTRY (DISTRICT)	New Zealand

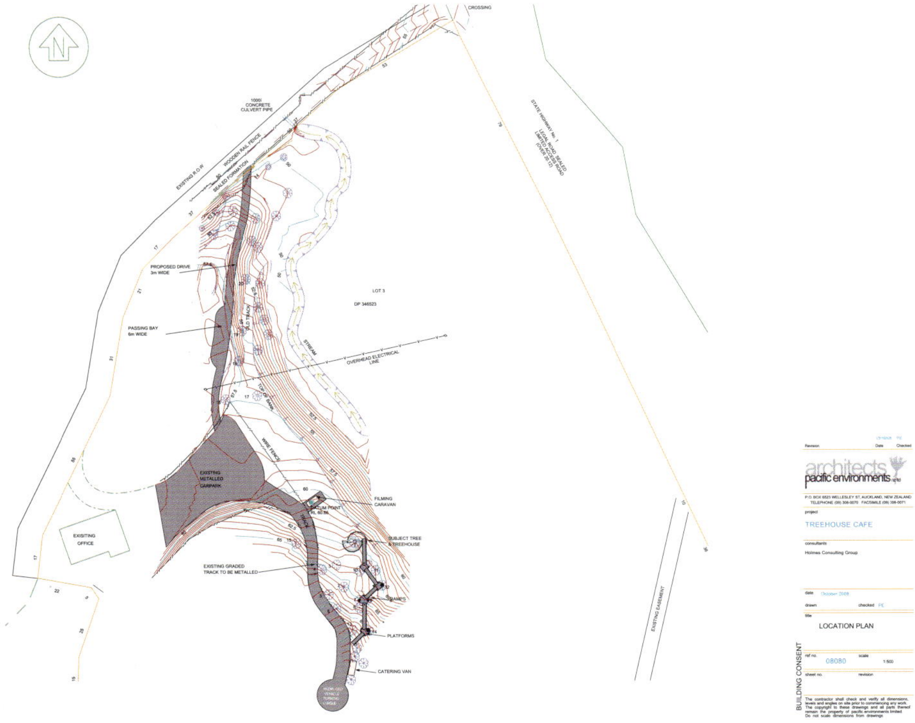
architects pacific environments
TREEHOUSE CAFE
Holmes Consulting Group
LOCATION PLAN
08080
BUILDING CONSENT
EXISTING OFFICE
PROPOSED DRIVE
PASSING BAY
EXISTING METALLED CARPARK
SUBJECT TREE & TREEHOUSE
PLATFORMS
CATERING VAN

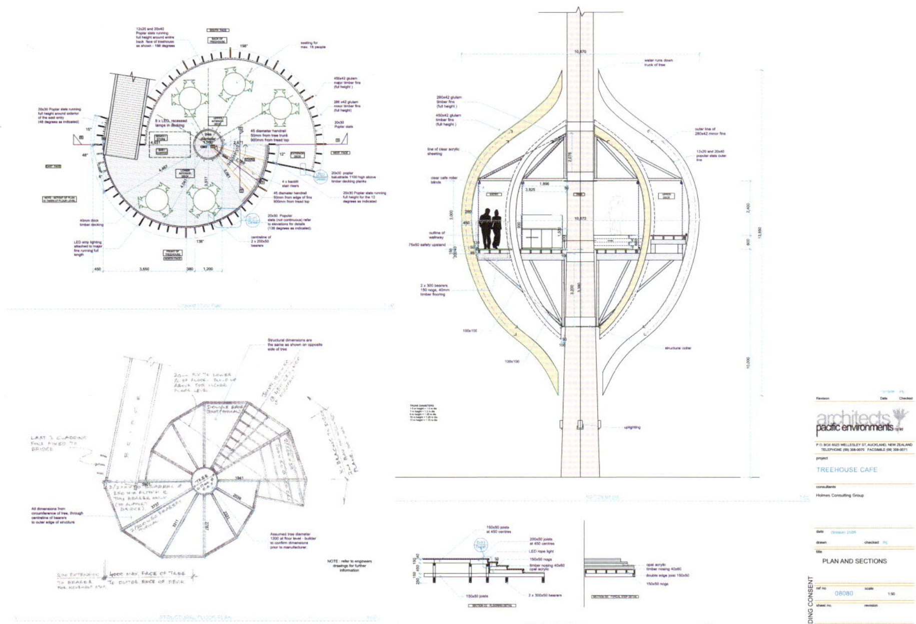
architects pacific environments
TREEHOUSE CAFE
Holmes Consulting Group
PLAN AND SECTIONS
08080
BUILDING CONSENT

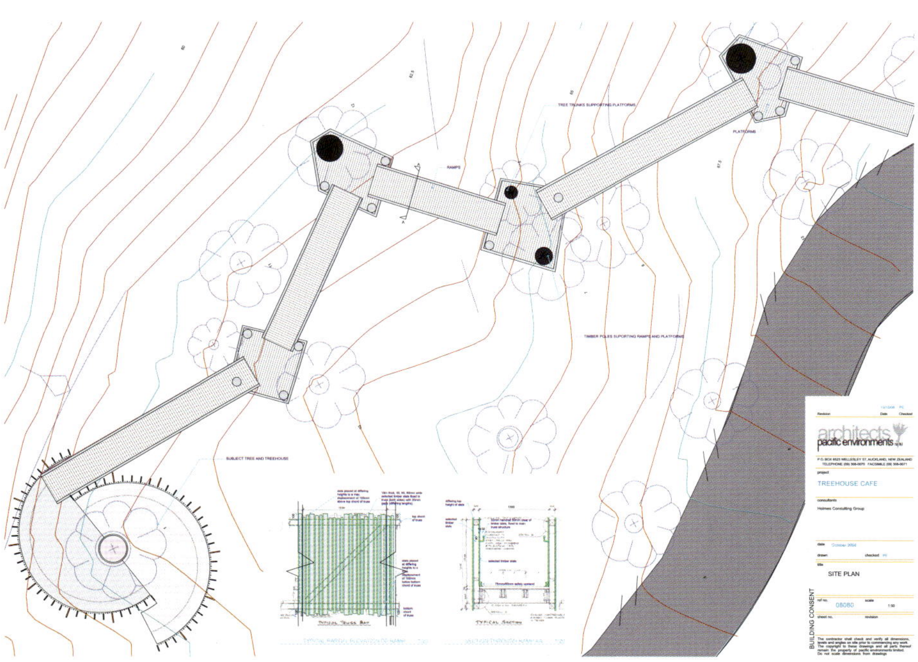
architects pacific environments
TREEHOUSE CAFE
Holmes Consulting Group
SITE PLAN
08080
BUILDING CONSENT

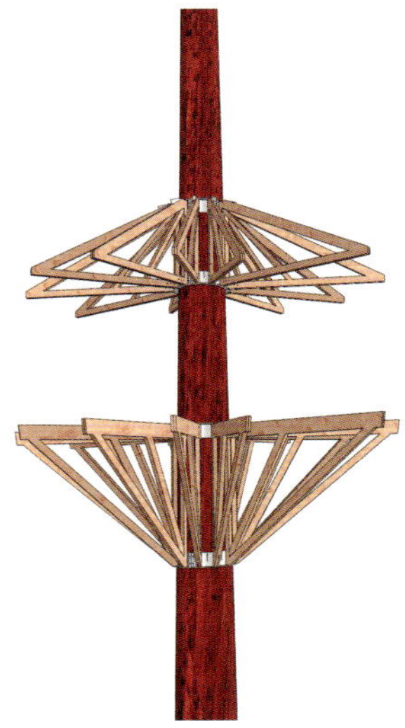

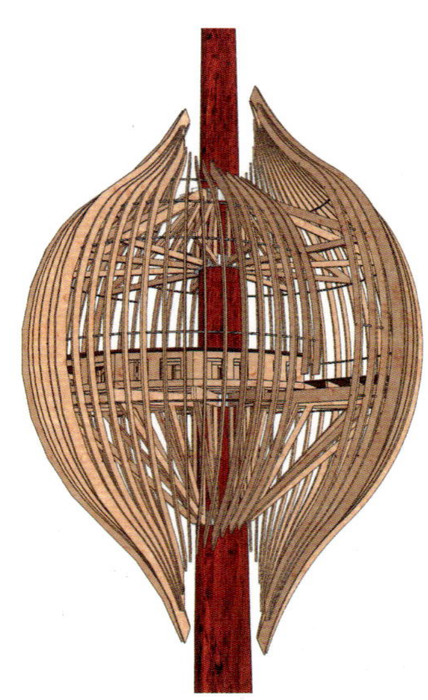

MASDAR PLAZA, OASIS OF THE FUTURE

The future well-being of cities around the globe depends on mankind's ability to develop and integrate sustainable technology.
Masdar City is the city of the future; positioned at the forefront of integrating sustainable technology into modern architectural design. Rome, Athens, Florence; most great historical cities have had the plaza, forum, or square at their epicenter – where the life, values, ideals, and vision of the population evolved. Equally, the centre of Masdar must be an iconic beacon that attracts global attention to sustainable technology. We see Masdar Plaza as "The Oasis of the Future": a living, breathing, active, adaptive environment; stimulated by the social interaction of people, and spotlighting the use and benefits of sustainable technology. Hence, our design proposal focuses on the delivery of three key issues:

1. Performance – to demonstrate the use and benefits of sustainable technology in a modern, dynamic, iconic architectural environment.
2. Activation – to activate or operate the sustainable technology in accordance with the functional needs of this environment, 24 hours a day, and 365 days of the year.
3. Interaction – to encourage and stimulate a social dynamic where the life, values, ideals, and vision of the population of Masdar evolve.

The "Oasis of the Future" is conceived as an open spatial experience, whereby all features; whether hotel, conference, shopping, or leisure, offer the highest quality of indoor and outdoor comfort and interaction. As in the case of an oasis, the Plaza is the social epicenter of Masdar; opening 24-hour access to all public facilities. Interactive, heat sensitive technology activates low intensity lighting in response to pedestrian traffic and mobile phone usage. The Plaza is able to change into an outdoor cinema for international events and national celebrations. Buildings' surrounding the Plaza form gorges, evoking mystical comparisons with the Grand Canyon and the entrance to Petra.
The "Oasis of the Future" demonstrates sustainable technology in a user-friendly architectural environment– flexible use of space, outdoor and indoor comfort, and optimum performance.
The user experience is the heart of the "Oasis of the Future".
By analyzing the potential pedestrian flows throughout the Plaza and surrounding facilities, the design seeks to accentuate this 'loop' of indoor and outdoor user experiences. This 'loop' marries the lowest possible energy expenditure to the highest levels of user comfort in correlation to pedestrian flows.

COMPANY	LAVA
CLIENT	Masdar Future Energy Company
COUNTRY (DISTRICT)	Australia

section 02

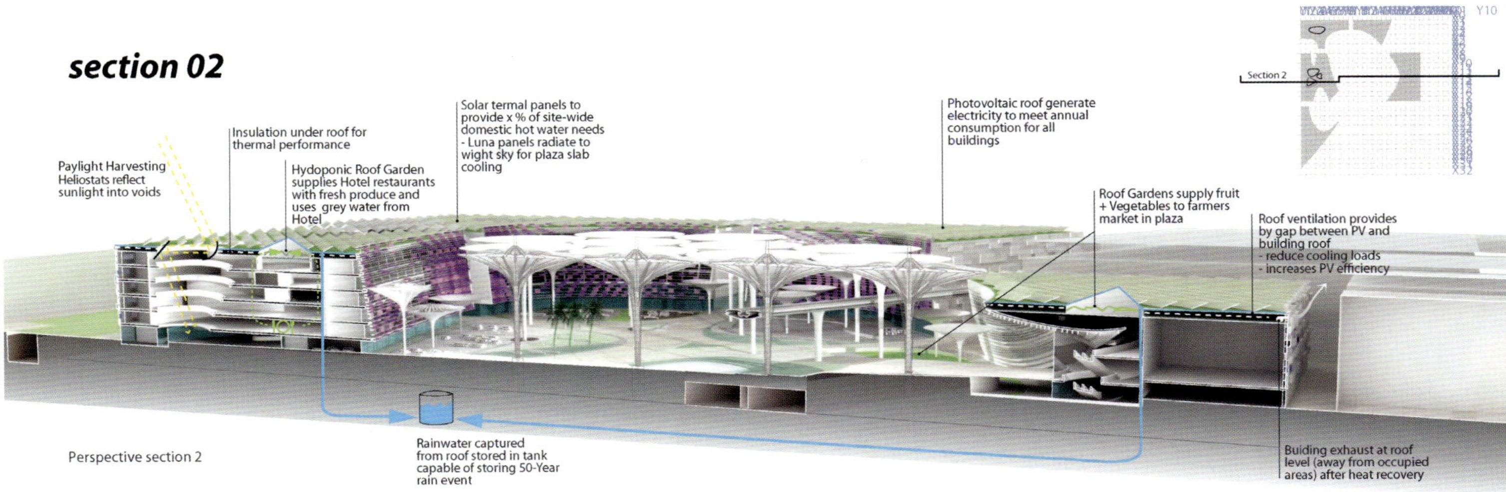

Perspective section 2

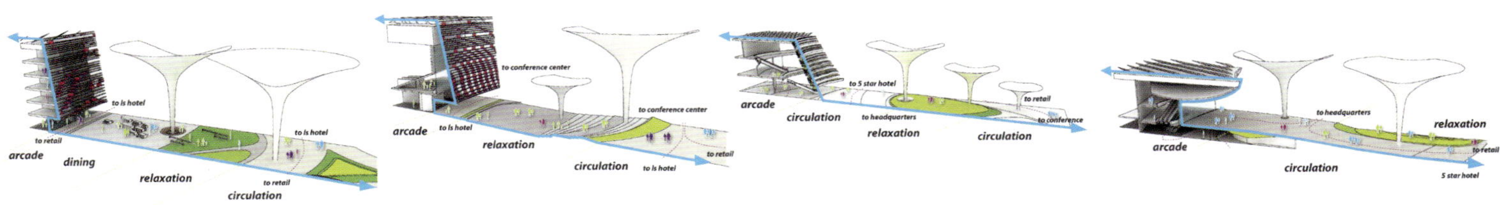

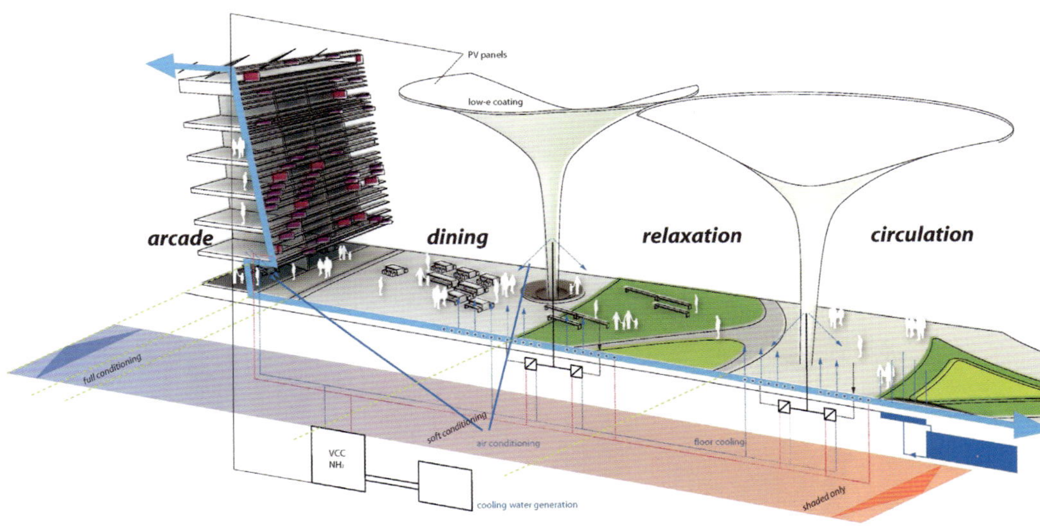

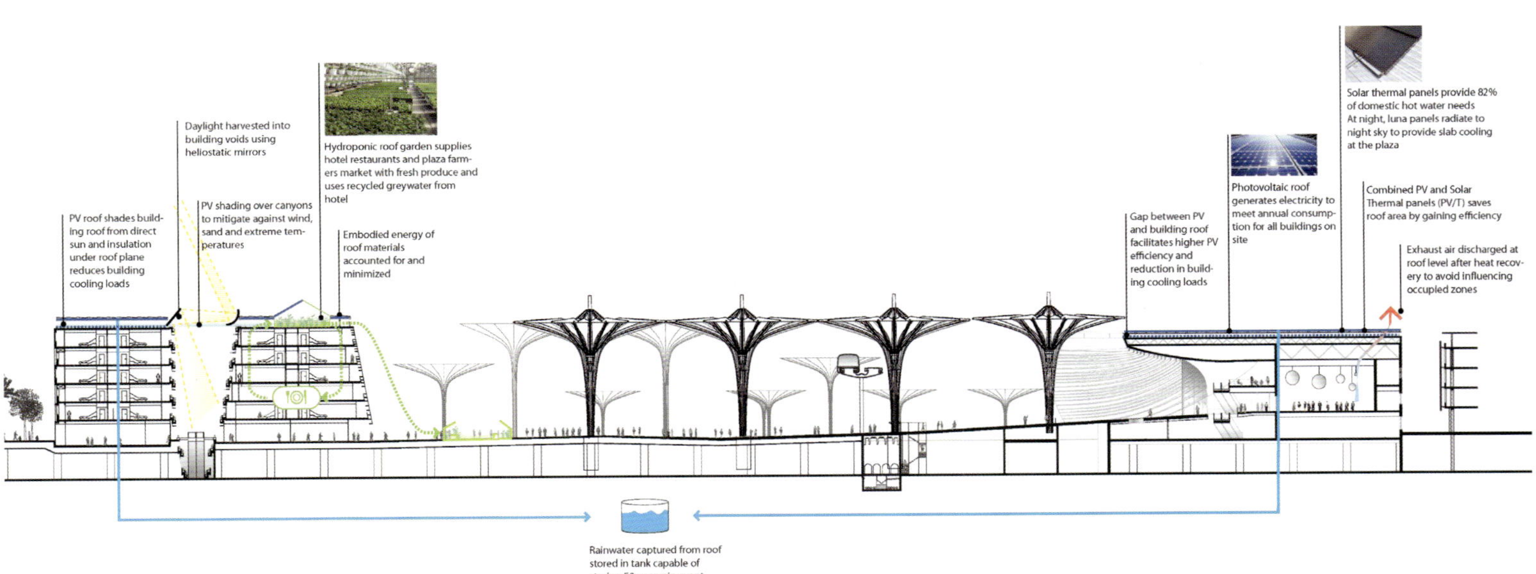

MONDE D'EAU RESORT AND THEMEPARK

Worldwide tourist destinations have common features. The customer searches for beauty, adventure, and hospitality. In order to give a destination a unique character, it is necessary to provide a local identity within the self-contained resort. Local art, colors, vegetation and fauna would ideally guide the design of this location. Current luxury definitions will be shifted in the future from exclusive items towards wellness and longevity of the body and mind, creating a rediscovery of our deep bond with nature. Green will be the new gold.

A lifestyle of health and sustainability will replace the need for consumption. Current tourist attractions consume excessive amounts of energy and natural resources.

The goal here is to develop a sustainable resort, setting new standards for energy efficient tourism. Constructed on Zero Emission principles characterized by zero carbon and zero waste, the resort will simultaneously maintain the highest quality of life and luxury.

Relying on renewable energy sources, this development will promote social responsibility and the protection of the natural environment.

Implementing intelligent building technologies such as interactive shading devices, natural day lighting and ventilation systems, as well as the use of locally sourced materials, ensures that these targets will be met.

COMPANY	LAVA
COUNTRY (DISTRICT)	Australia

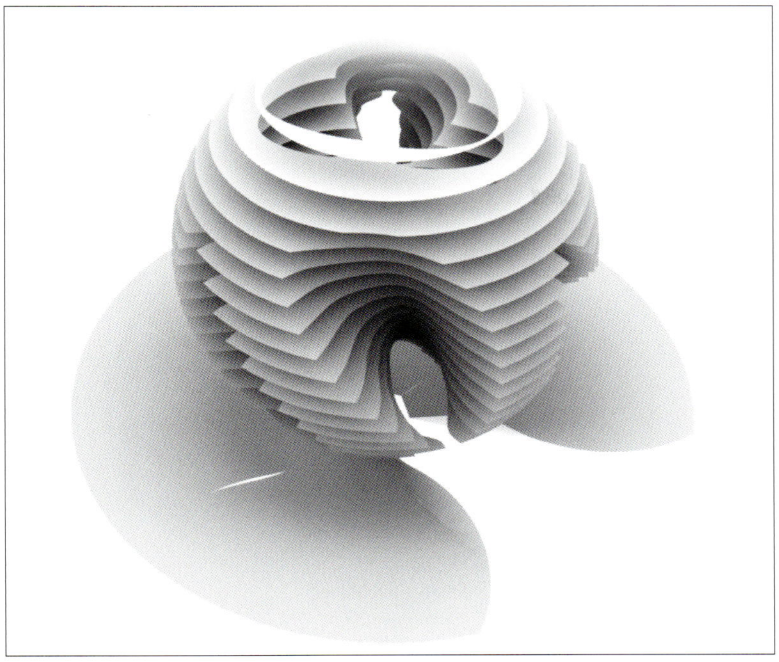

LITTLE ONE-ROOM HOUSE WITH A CURVE

Little shop of 41m² in Nagoya city.
The site has an elongated shape with a width of about 9m and a depth of 20m.
While the front road is relatively wide, with a sidewalk, one might get a feeling of oppression due to the small size of the site surrounded by shops and houses that are 2 to 3 stories.
The required elements were spaces for parking 2 cars, a space for drying laundry, and a space for the shop.
The building has to stand at the back of the site since the frontage is not of sufficient width to permit a K-turn and the front portion is occupied by the parking area.
One can seldom escape from such approaches when the building is a shop with parking spaces.
A good example of this would be the convenient store two lots from the site.
I was afraid that the shop would disappear in the area because the area of 41m² is too small when compared with the neighboring houses.
That is why I started thinking of how to make it an eye catching building for passersby and drivers.
I placed the main space at the most remote part of the site, while the entrance was on the opposite, street-facing side.
The building transverses the site in a gentle manner and so residual exterior spaces are created.
These residual spaces became a garden, the drying space, and the parking area, and all of them complete the beauty shop as a whole.
The shop has the continuous style of a studio apartment and you can see the totality of the interior from the entrance.
Yet you are able to see some spaces not visible from the entrance, as you walk into the back, because of the building's curve.
The shape of the building is something like the volume of the entrance door stretched, and the section at the entrance is only the size of the door. However, the section becomes larger both vertically and horizontally, as one walks into the back, and becomes subtly smaller again at the end.
The volume of the curve was determined by a study to maintain the overall balance of the continuous interior space on its very edge.
I analyzed the degree of curvature to balance two factors: the ability to see throughout all of the continuous space; and the sequence of gradual changes as one walks in.
At the same time, I tried to create 3 distinctive zones out of one room by changing the density of the openings.
The first is the entrance space. With the largest opening on the wall, one can feel the openness and the proximity to the outside regardless of its small space, almost the same size as that of the door.
The second is the cutting space in the middle.
The light rhythmically streams into the space from the 5 small side windows with a view of the garden.
The third is the shampoo space in the back.
This space is the one most filled with natural light from the building's skylight.
You can look up at the sky from the shampoo basin. You will be attracted by and would like to walk in when you see the brightest, innermost curving space from the entrance.
I am thinking of how I can create something like a new environment by layering the various degrees of light in this gently connected space.

COMPANY	Studio Velocity
DESIGNER	Studio Velocity
PHOTOGRAPHER	Kentaro Kurihara
CLIENT	Synthetic Hair Design
COUNTRY (DISTRICT)	Japan

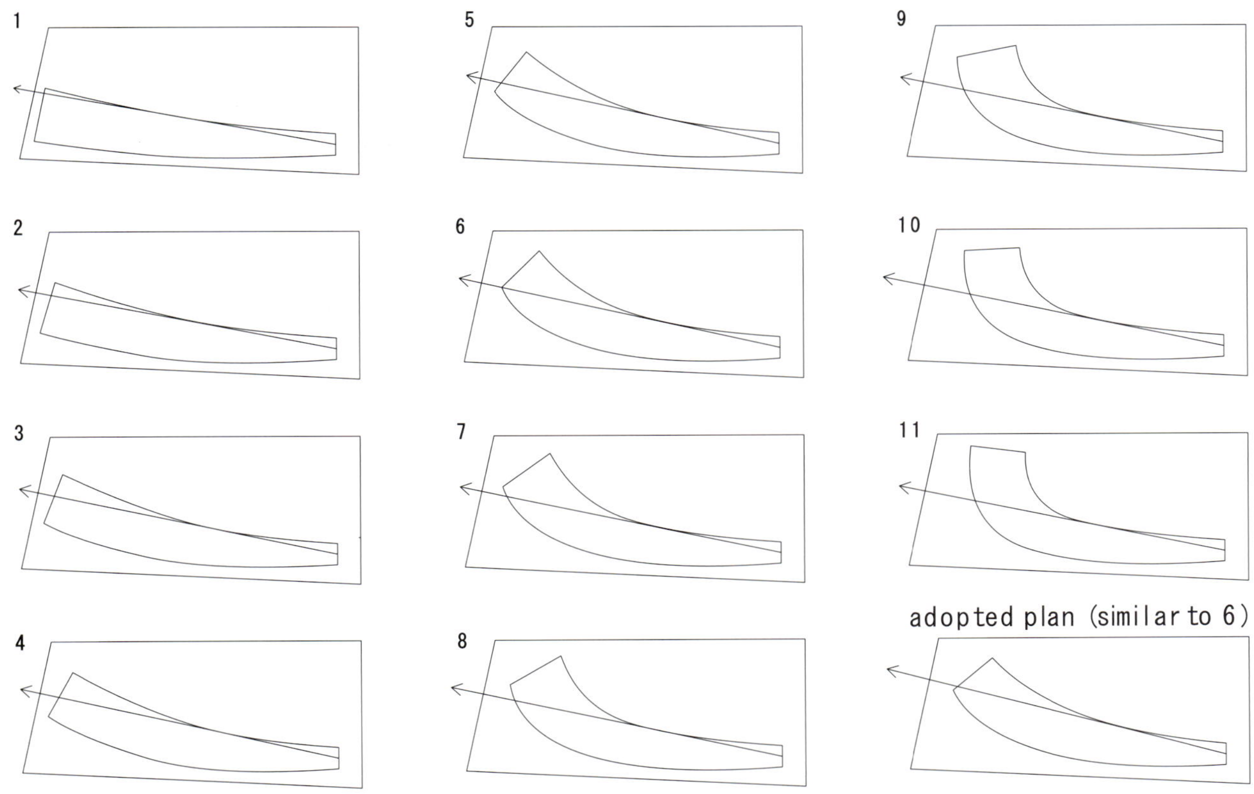

curvature of adopted plan has both space 1 and 11

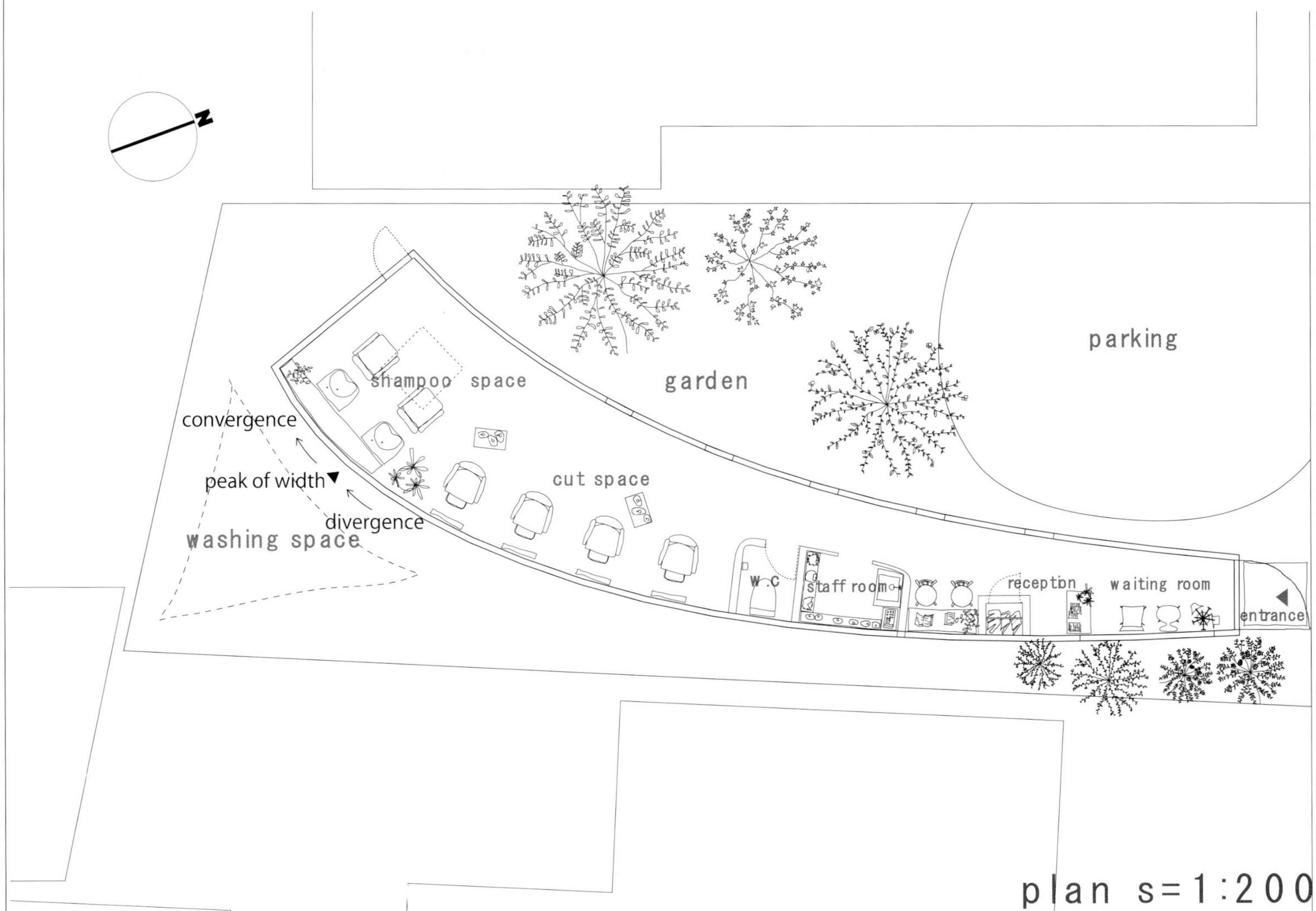

plan s=1:200

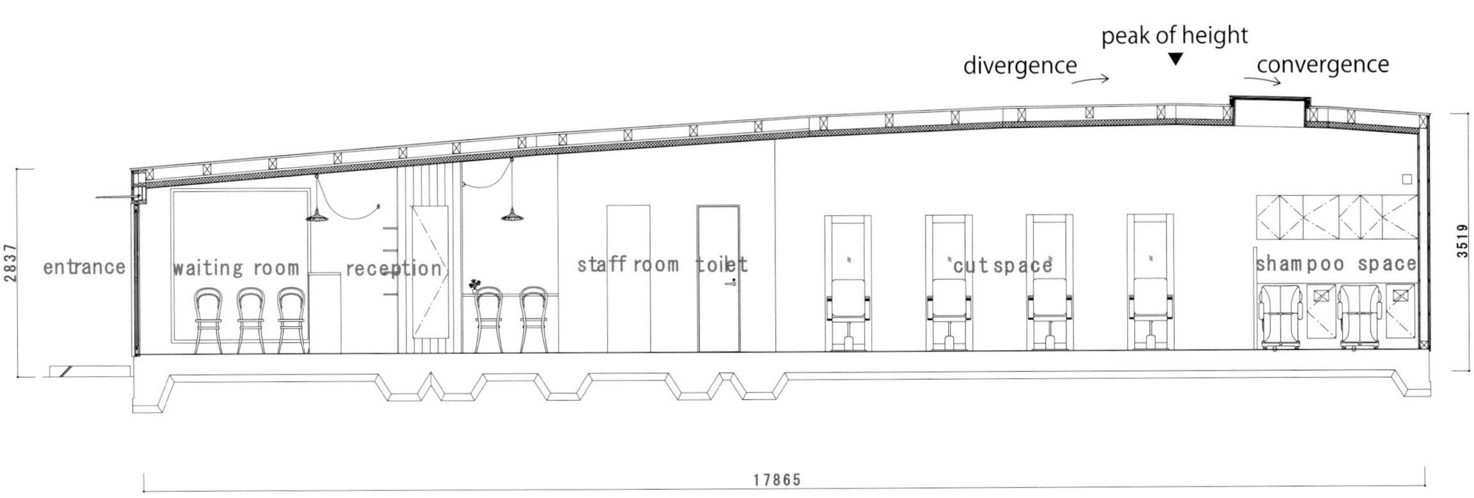

section s=1:150

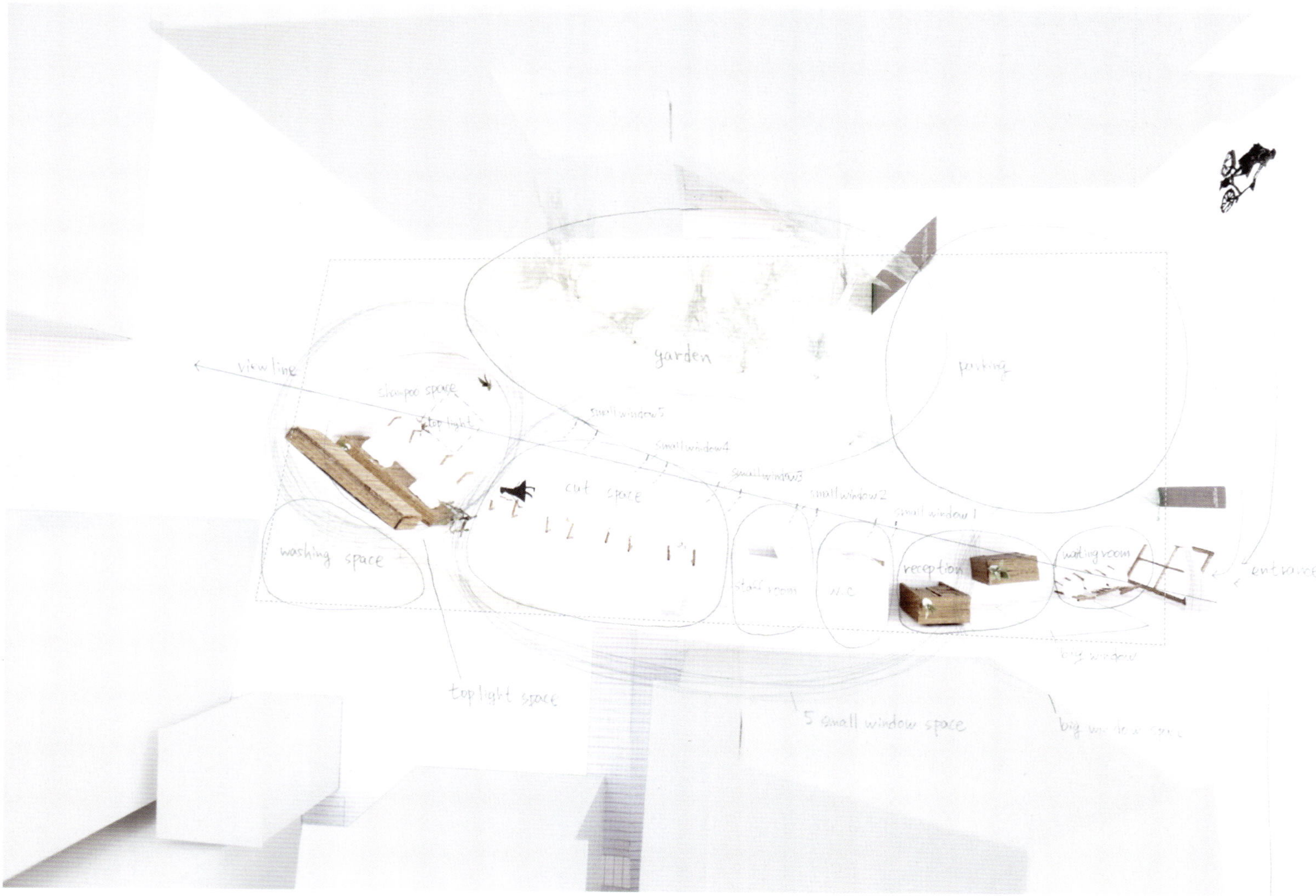
view line
garden
parking
cut space
washing space
staff room
W.C
reception
entrance
top light space
5 small window space

PUBLIC CULTURE SPACE

HONGODAI CHRIST CHURCH SCHOOL & NURSERY

It is a complex of church school (2nd floor) and nursery (1st floor) administered by Protestant Christ church. The premises are located at a greenery area in Yokohama city surrounded by fields, parks and hills in the neighborhood. It has been planned in the open space. Such places for children to stay are mixed into forest with rich natural environment.

Drawn continued line in the forest in a spiral manner mixes buildings with the forest and indoor part with outdoor part as if they were stirred by hands, simultaneously creating individual classrooms and open spaces as well. The continued line runs through the forest while avoiding and surrounding trees. It is a building with new mixture of indoor and outdoor parts.

We've selected wooden construction as a place for children from infant to senior in high school to stay. Making wooden building of wood framework, wood floor and wood sash to be clear and light, we've realized a transparent wooden construction. In a simple grid building, steel frames are adopted to five courtyards to bear earthquake load. Since pillars of solid steel of 110 square are fit between wooden pillar and sash, their existence is successfully eliminated without any sense of discomfort while they are exposed without being hidden. Glass sliding door is equipped at the interface between indoor and outdoor area. Light falls and spreads into the building through the trees and winds from the forest run through the building. It is possible for children to vividly spend their time both at indoor space where they feel as if they were in the forest and at outdoor area where they also feel as if they belong to the building. School children go to each class room after holding morning service in the hall at second floor. They take classes in sunlight falling through the trees and read books in the forest. Children in nursery freely run around from indoor to outdoor while taking a nap with comfort brought by forest wind.

The building has been built by trying to figure out a new concept for building establishments in forests. I hope not a building excessively managed artificially but such easygoing building defined to lie between natural and artificial will be a good place for children to stay.

COMPANY	Takeshi Hosaka Architects
DESIGNER	Takeshi Hosaka
PHOTOGRAPHER	MASAO NISHIKAWA
CLIENT	HIROSHI IKEDA / HONGODAI CHRIST CHUCH
COUNTRY (DISTRICT)	Japan

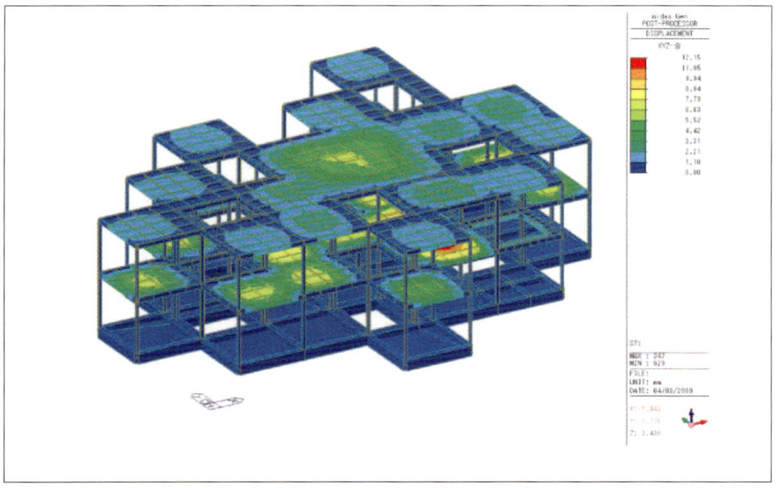

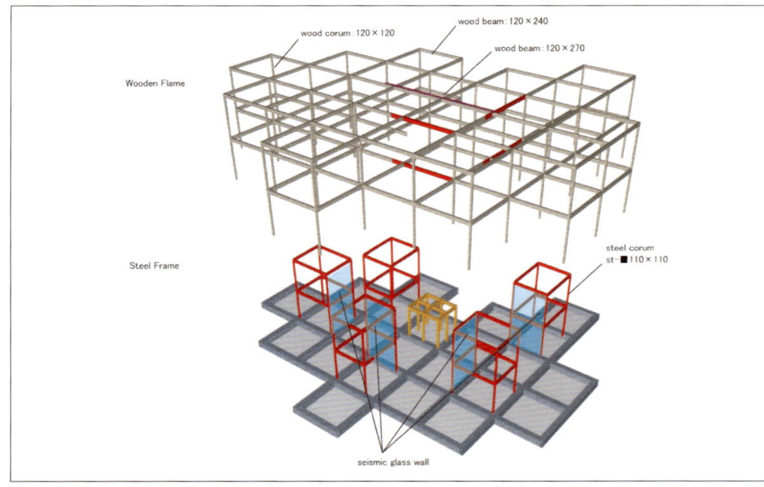

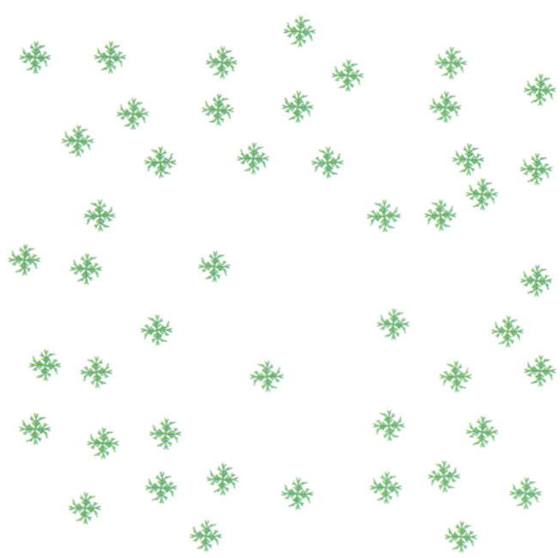

forest

The line drawn with one stroke runs through the forest , looking like steared by a hand.

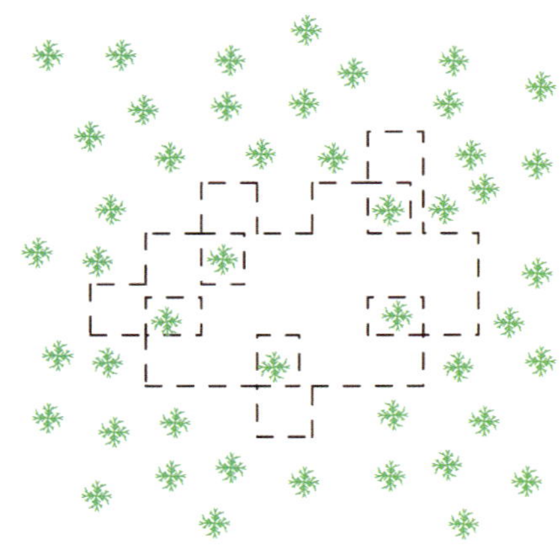

develop to the wooden grid architecture

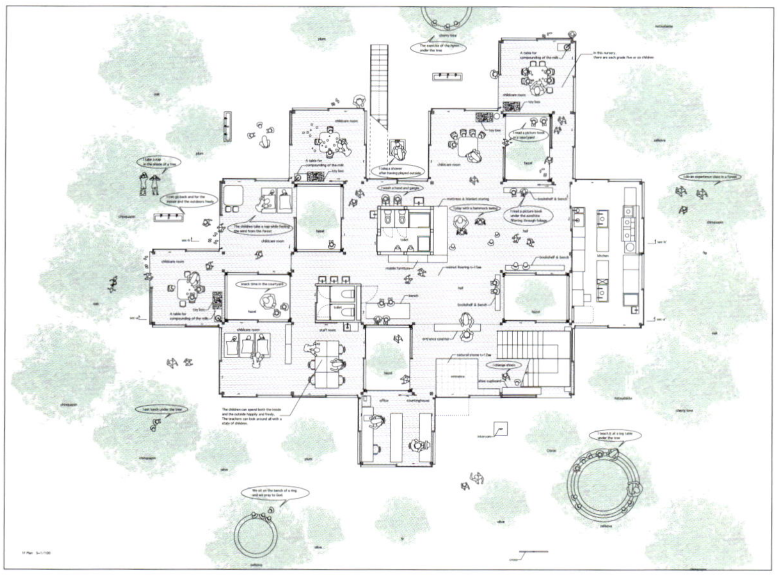

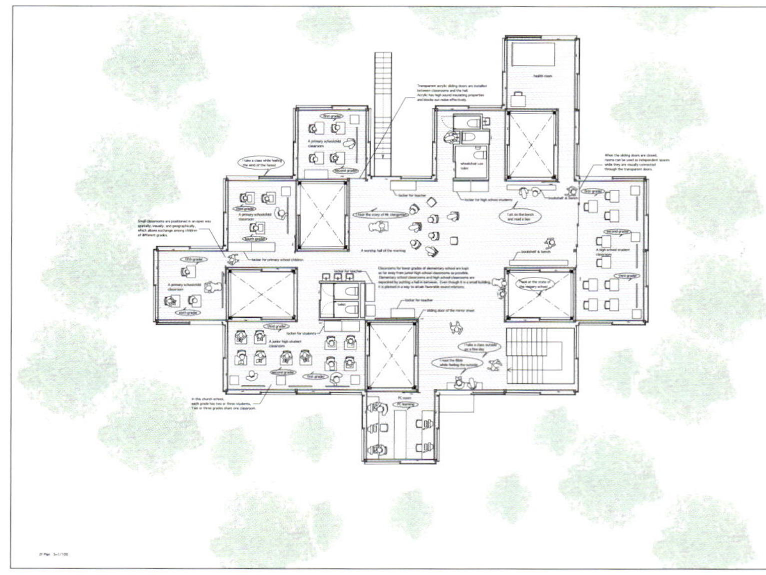

"JOSEPHINE BAKER" GROUP OF SCHOOLS

The 'Josephine Baker' group of schools recently completed in La Courneuve manages to fit into the difficult context of the 'Cité des 4000' neighbourhood, on a site marked by the painful memory of the demolition of the 'Ravel' and 'Presov' longitudinal blocks of flats. However, it is also capable of opening up inside itself, creating a different landscape, a different place, a utopia.

The requirement to refrain from constructing closed volumes based on the rectangle that is a feature of the plot of land, combined with the constraints in terms of density and height, has enabled Dominique Coulon to question the separation of the primary and nursery schools in the brief. His proposal therefore sketches out a unitary organisation, deployed with virtuoso skill in the three dimensions of the space between two poles linked by a system of ramps.

Thus the nursery school classrooms are pushed to the east, on a floor cantilevered above the entrance, and the primary school classrooms occupy areas to the west overlooking interstitial gardens. The older children's playground merges into the area reserved for the younger children, which already contains the shared canteen, while the sports areas have been placed on the roof of the other block, which contains the library shared by the two schools.

The corridors change shape and expand in front of the classroom doors and receive abundant natural light from the zenith, as if it's better to define themselves as areas for decompression before taking a deep breath and plunging into the work areas. Lastly, the canopy of the playground thrusts out well beyond the ramp that leads up to the rooftop sports areas.

This play of compression and expansion, giving an organic feeling to the concrete structure, is further accentuated by use of the colour orange. It covers the floors and occasionally spills over onto the walls and ceilings, rendering the slightest ray of sunshine incandescent and lighting up the roof area.

The use of natural products – such as linoleum on the floors, and wood for the door and window frames – and the attention paid even to the smallest details contribute to making the building an almost luxurious place, a place hailed enthusiastically at its inauguration by a population of parents and pupils who are keen to turn the page of the demolitions and look resolutely to the future.

COMPANY	Dominique Coulon et associés
DESIGNER	Dominique Coulon et associés
PHOTOGRAPHER	Eugeni Pons, Olivier Nicollas, Delphine George
CLIENT	City of LA COURNEUVE
COUNTRY (DISTRICT)	France

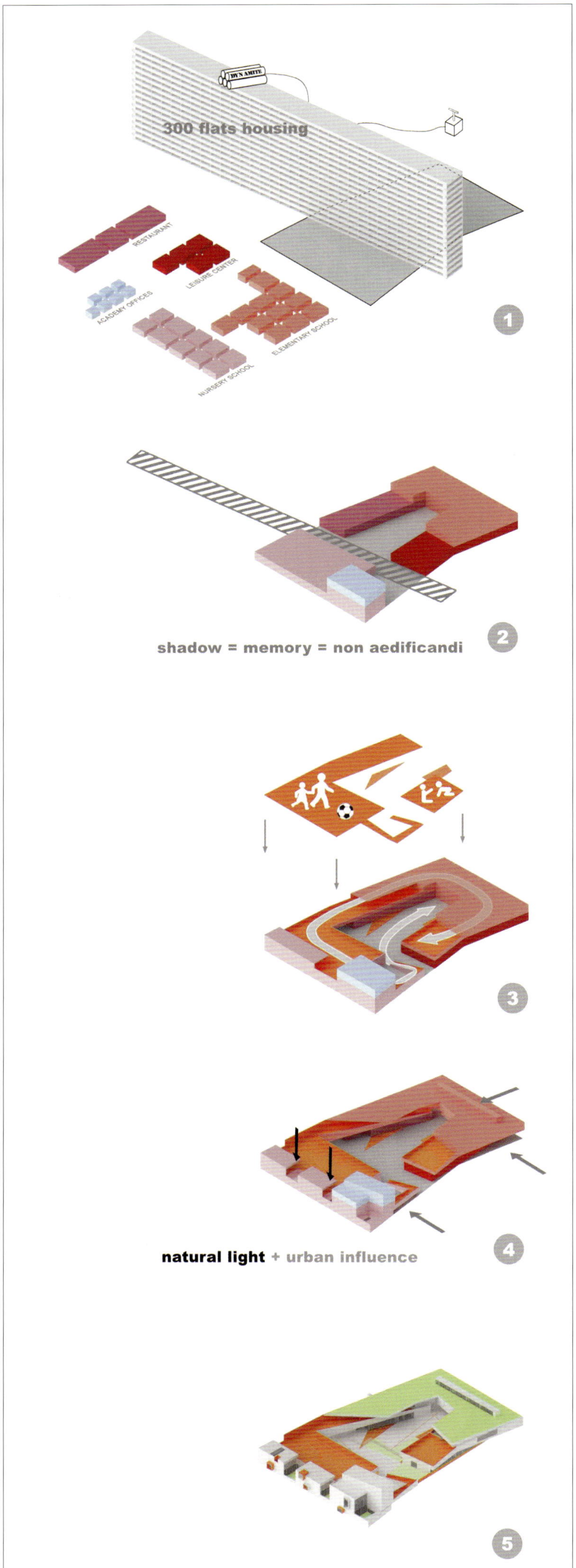
300 flats housing
RESTAURANT
LEISURE CENTER
ACADEMY OFFICES
ELEMENTARY SCHOOL
NURSERY SCHOOL
1
shadow = memory = non aedificandi
2
3
natural light + urban influence
4
5

GROUPE SCOLAIRE JOSEPHINE BAKER à LA COURNEUVE
Dominique Coulon et associés
Plan du 2ème étage
INSPECTION ACADEMIQUE 3.01
GROUPE SCOLAIRE JOSEPHINE BAKER à LA COURNEUVE
Dominique Coulon et associés
Plan du 1er étage
SALLE DE CLASSE ELEMENTAIRE 2.01
PREAU 2.02
AIRE D'EVOLUTION 2.03
SALLE DE CLASSE MATERNELLE 2.04
SALLE MULTIMEDIA 2.05
SALLE DE MOTRICITE 2.06
SALLE DE REPOS 2.07
SALLE DES MAITRES 2.08
GROUPE SCOLAIRE JOSEPHINE BAKER à LA COURNEUVE
Dominique Coulon et associés
Plan du rez-de-chaussée
SALLE DE CLASSE ELEMENTAIRE 1.01
BIBLIOTHEQUE 1.02
SALLE INFORMATIQUE 1.03
DIRECTION 1.04
SALLE DES MAITRES 1.05
SALLE D'ACTIVITES CLSH 1.06
BUREAU ANIMATEURS 1.07
INFIRMERIE 1.08
LOGE GARDIEN 1.09
DIRECTION 1.10
RESTAURANT MATERNELLE 1.11
RESTAURANT ELEMENTAIRE 1.12

CHAPEL OF ST.LAWRENCE

The Vantaa Parish Union held an open architectural competition in the spring of 2003 for the design of a new chapel in the vicinity of the historic Church of St. Lawrence. The area has been classified as a nationally important cultural environment. The winning entry, out of 194 proposals, was "Polku" ("Path") by Avanto Architects.

The old stone church with its bell tower remain the dominant features in the landscape. The new chapel ties together different aspects of the area without emphasizing itself. The chapel connects with the graveyard, leaving the old buildings their own boundaries and territories untouched. It delineates the northern boundary of the graveyard and hides the service yard behind its back. The chapel has been divided into smaller parts to adapt to the scale of the surroundings. The stacked stone walls of the cemetery are echoed in the design – a series of three chapels of different sizes are nested within orthogonal masonry walls. A new bell tower in a corner of the chapel completes the composition and leads the eye skyward.

The building uses similar materials as the old structures in the area. The massiveness of the load bearing solid masonry walls balances changes in temperature and moisture. The lightly plastered and whitewashed walls are a bright, tranquil background for the events taking place in the chapel spaces. Apart from the walls, the building has a steel structure. The partition walls are in-situ cast white concrete and the roof is of patinated copper, like the roof of the church. The patina in all copper surfaces in the chapel has been added by hand. The ceilings and the glazed walls toward the graveyard in the chapels are covered with a patinated copper mesh; it functions as a screen between the outside and the spaces of the chapel. The mesh also decreases heat loads from sunshine. The low stone walls flank the small gardens and courtyards use stone extracted from the site. The floors of public spaces are of slate.

The lifespan target for the chapel is two hundred years. The main structure will certifiably last that long and the natural materials used will age with dignity. A lifespan simulation was used as an aide for the design. An important factor in choosing the materials was locality in addition to longevity, and on-site building and an emphasis on craft were distinct features of the whole project. These ways of working ground the building in its surroundings and display the traces of handcraft.

COMPANY	Avanto Architects Ltd
DESIGNER	Avanto Architects Ltd / Ville Hara and Anu Puustinen, Architects SAFA
PHOTOGRAPHER	Kuvio, Minna Hopia Tuomas Uusheimo
CLIENT	Vantaa Parish Union
COUNTRY (DISTRICT)	Finland

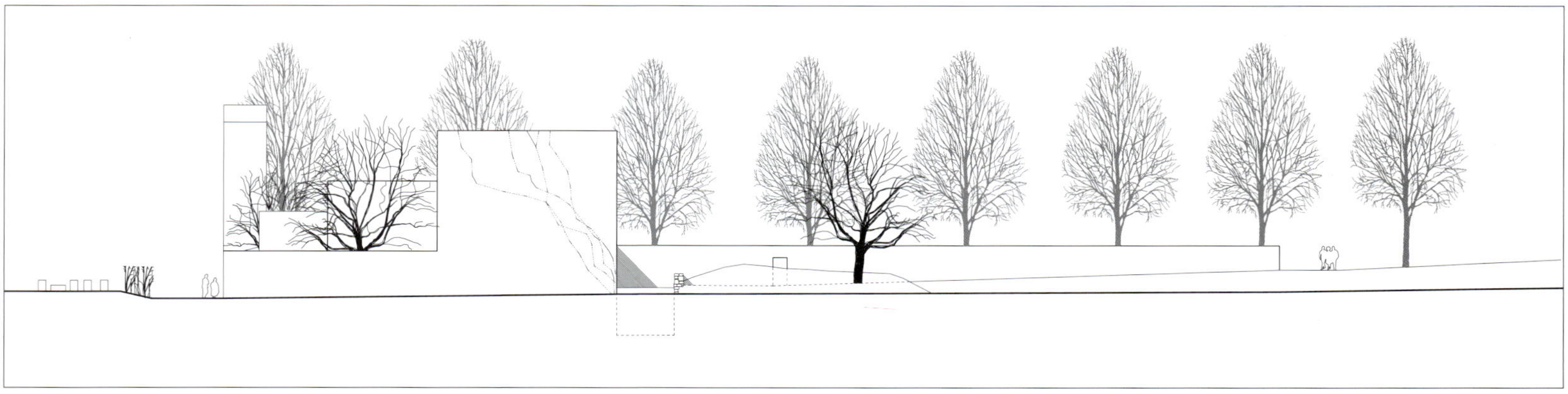
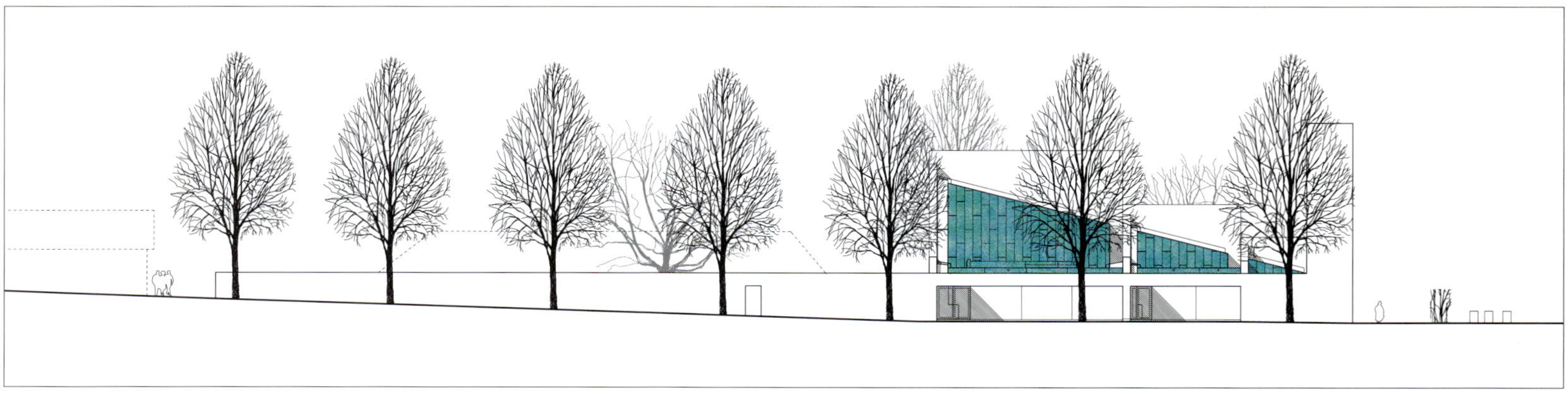
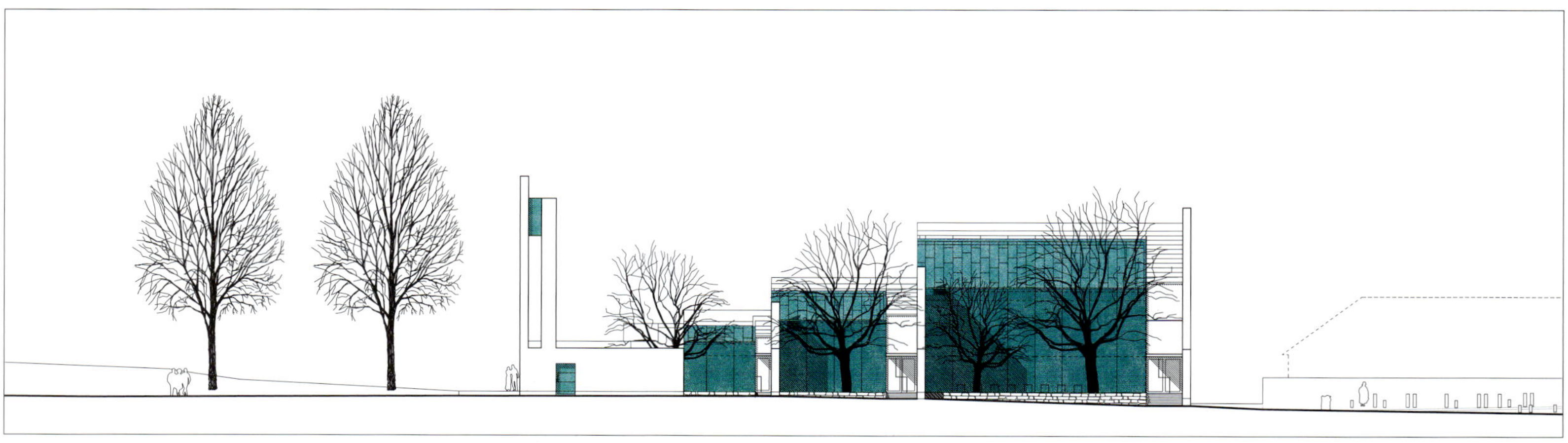
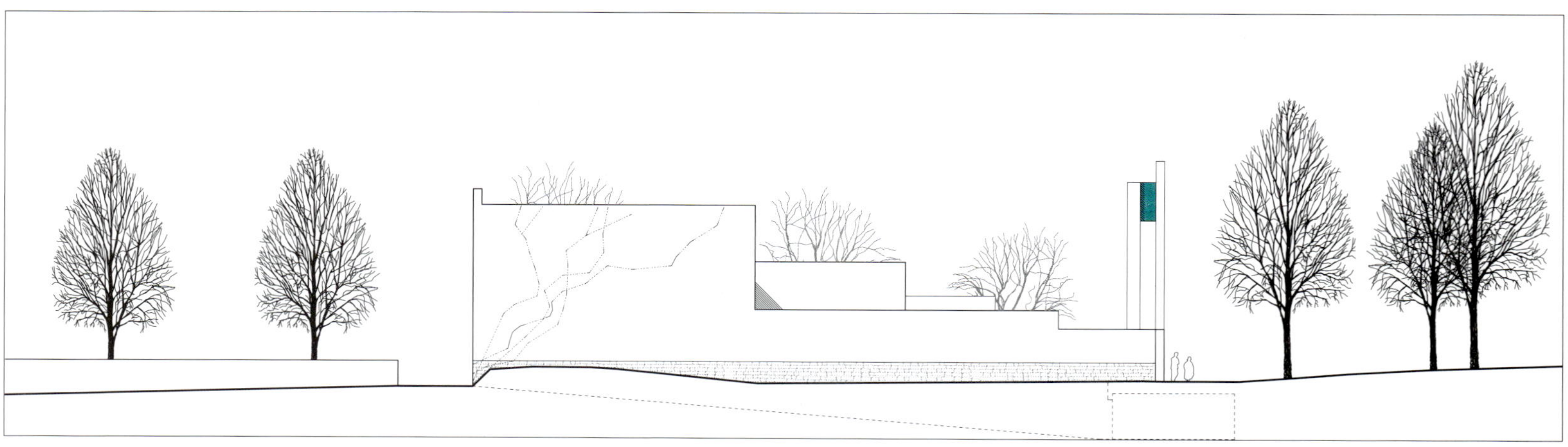
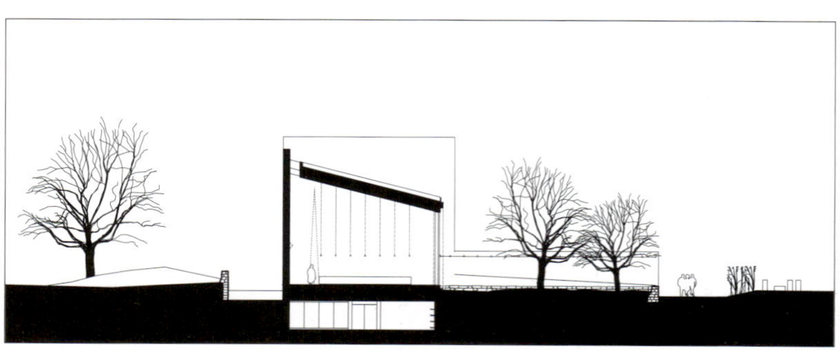
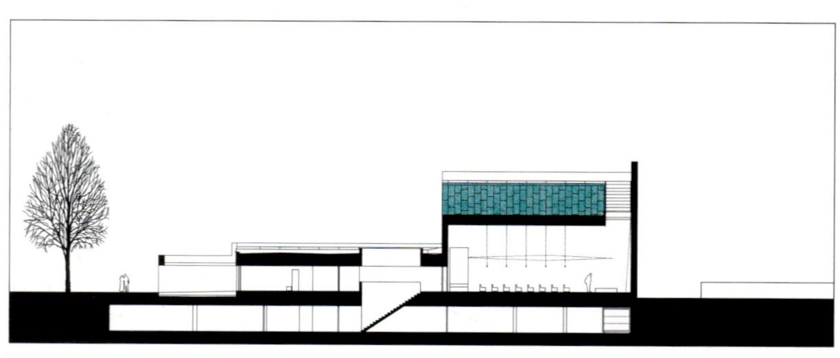

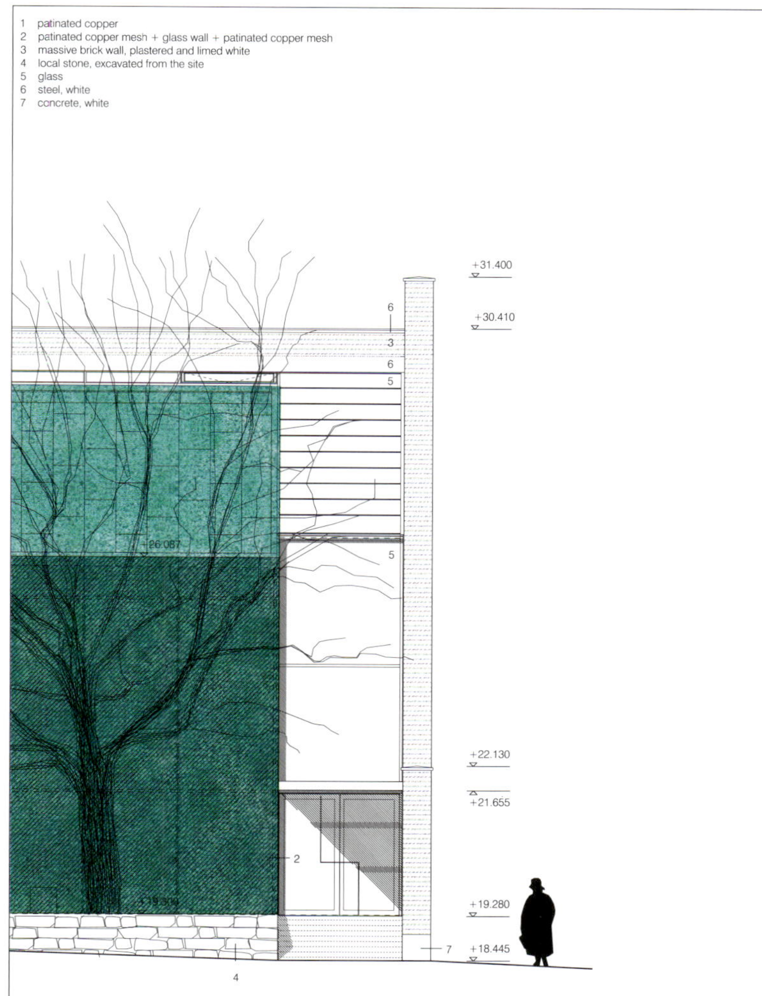

FACADE PROJECTION 1:100

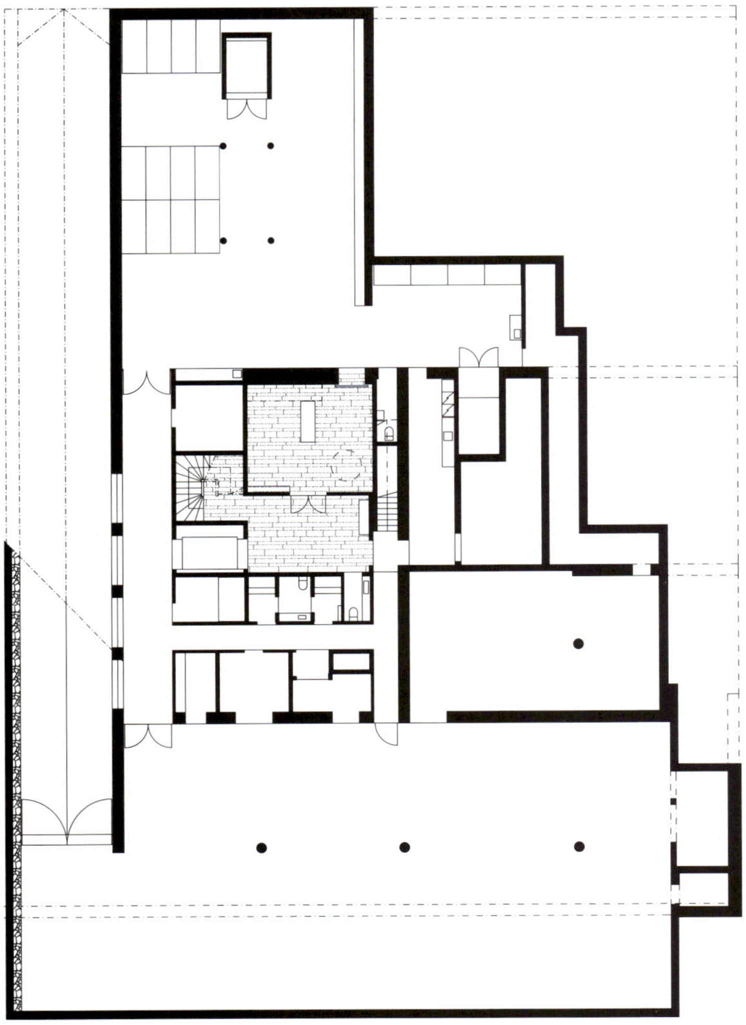

ISO SALI
STORA SALEN

ALMONTE THEATRE IN HUELVA

The building is located in the site of an old winery. It has the challenge of integrating the existing old buildings, declared as cultural interest, and being part of a cultural complex of a total of three buildings and a common space. This space turns into the main place of the town and an important meeting area. It's an opportunity to work on light, material and space. The path chosen to work on these concepts, is the contrast. Contrast between outside and inside, between old and new, including a monumental scale and human scale, and the journey as the thread that sews and explains the intervention. A large area covered with large proportions and controlled height works as a high threshold. A monumental scale lobby welcomes the visitor showing the scale of a public building.

COMPANY	Donaire Arquitectos
DESIGNER	Juan Pedro Donaire Barbero
PHOTOGRAPHER	Fernando Alda
COUNTRY (DISTRICT)	Sevilla

alzado principal

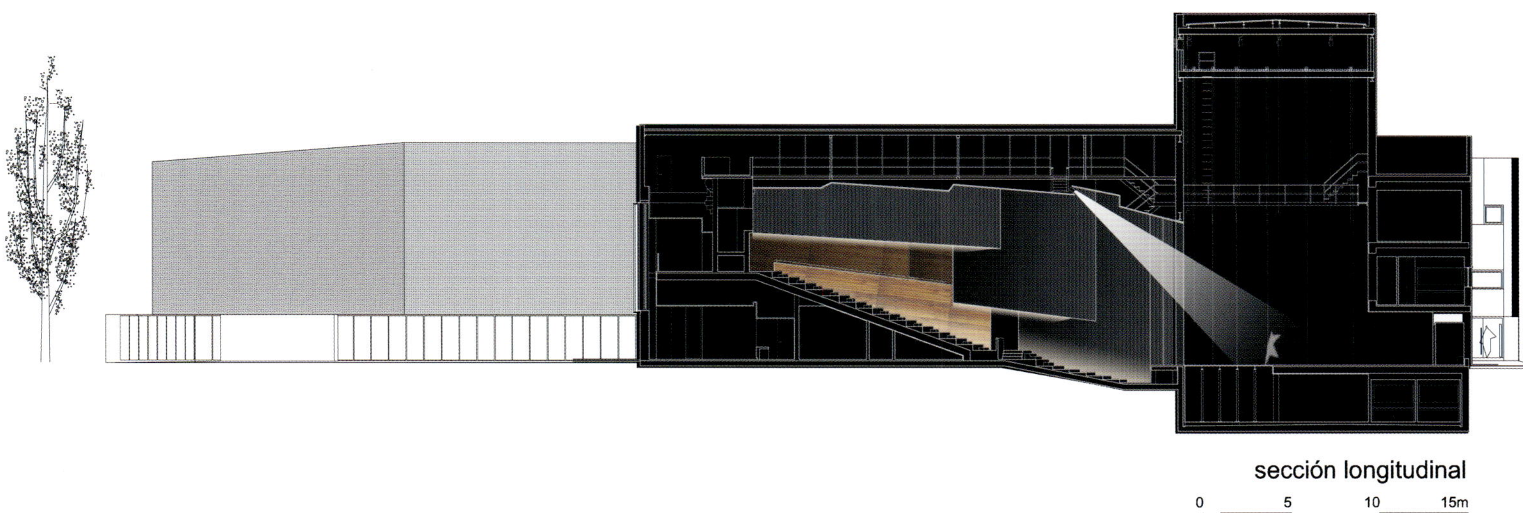

sección longitudinal

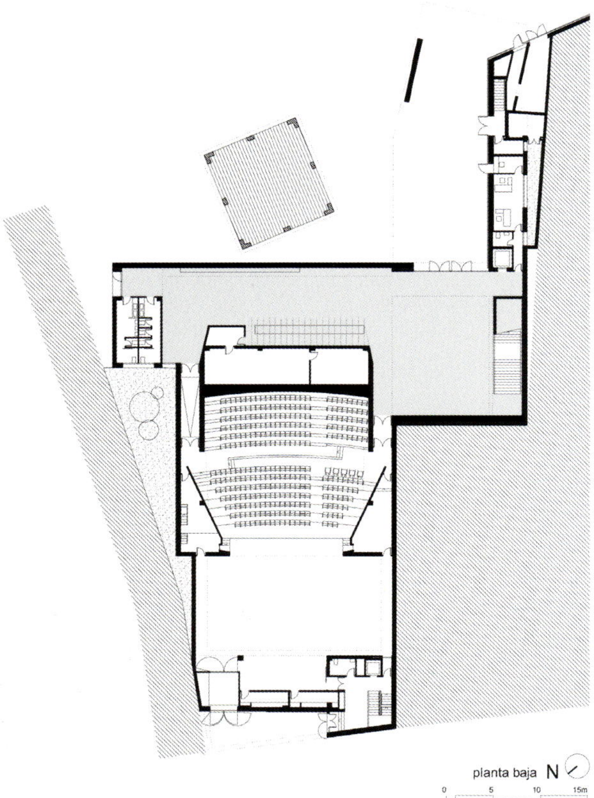
planta baja N
0 5 10 15m

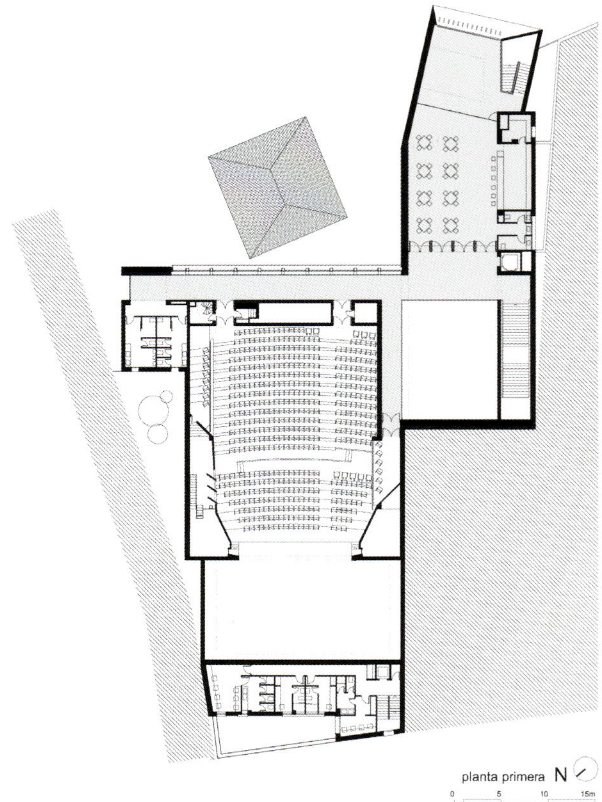
planta primera N
0 5 10 15m

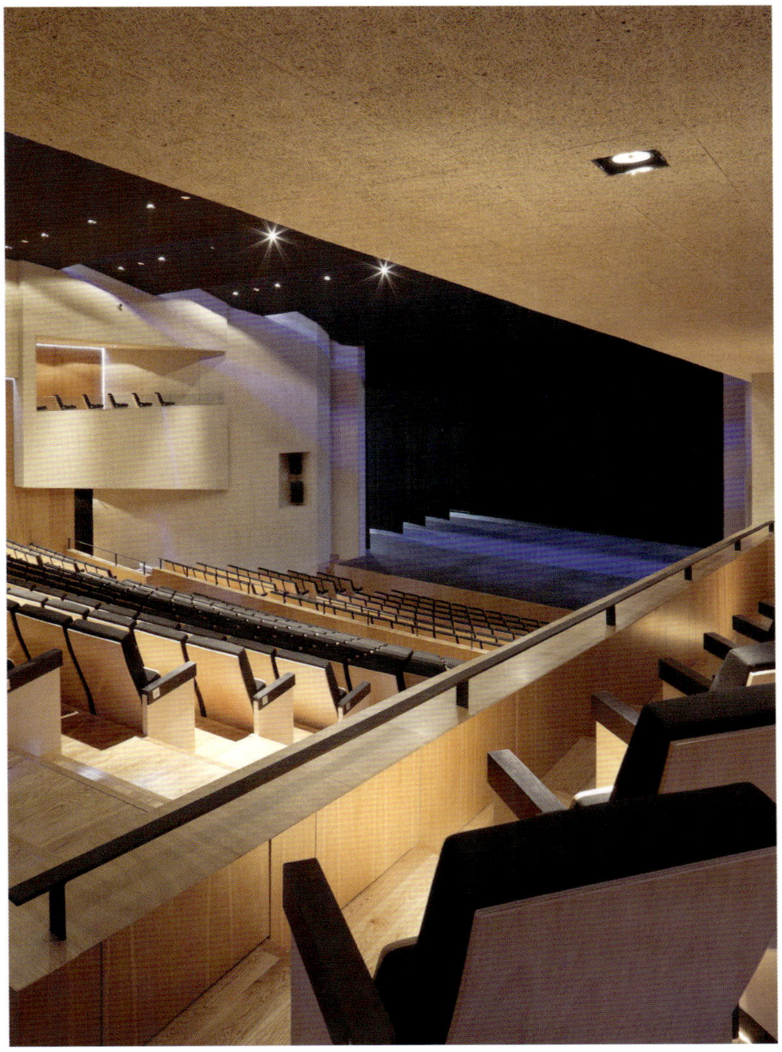

ACCESO A SALA

SOCIAL KINDER GARDENS

THE PUBLIC BUILDING

The public building must not only fulfill their role as urban equipment, but also as a collective element that dignifies the living, therefore it must play a role beyond their specialty, it must create a social space, educational and dignity of life - a building as a symbol of a changing society and a democratic society more egalitarian.

URBAN POSITION , THE BUILDING THAT LOOKS AT THE CITY.

Different ways of implement the building were studied; finally decided to develop an implementation to build a clear front, defined and generous toward the city which in turn will maximize the function. The capacity of optimizing these functional infrastructure leads to degeneration into a landscaped green areas and fun for the sector, compacting the program it was looked to make the greatest possible public space.

Therefore the project is composed by a container building, that joins in the same element, the four parts of the program.

The project plans the re-composition of the place through the manipulation of base level as a unifying element of the urban piece, a platform that rises from 0.00 level to operate the pool, because the area has serious problems of water table as it is filled area. This image is presented as an artificial topography capable of promoting events that congested the location of new activities, enriching the city with a new centrality.

The architectural design is planned, positioned and dimensioned based on their relevance and ability to enhance as much empty space in the block. In this sense its design allows for complete autonomy, it is also an excuse to become a trigger project for a process of reorganization of the sector where it is located.

THE BUILDING

It is planned as a container of curtain walling (lattice metal) mounted on a base as a balcony, which is located in the four programs, like boxes inside the container, each one with a different skin type, whether or stacking program differentiating each thematic box.

The facade of the container is metal laser cut designs alluding to the four programs.

It can only generate an access to four different entrances to buildings (boxes), making each one independent.

COMPANY	Mazzanti Arquitectos
DESIGNER	Mazzanti Arquitectos
PHOTOGRAPHER	Aereas Fotos Rudolf Iwaan Baan LOW Rodrigo Davila
CLIENT	Secretaria de Integración Social
COUNTRY (DISTRICT)	Colombia

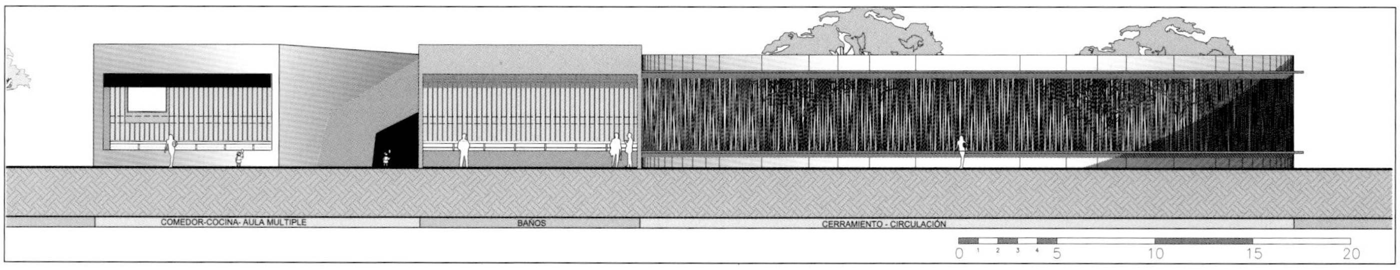
COMEDOR-COCINA- AULA MULTIPLE
BAÑOS
CERRAMIENTO - CIRCULACIÓN
0 1 2 3 4 5 10 15 20

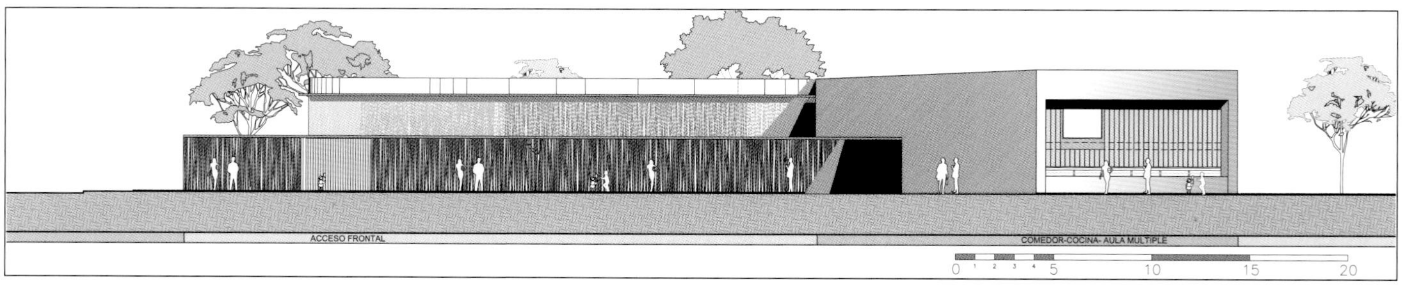
ACCESO FRONTAL
COMEDOR-COCINA- AULA MULTIPLE
0 1 2 3 4 5 10 15 20

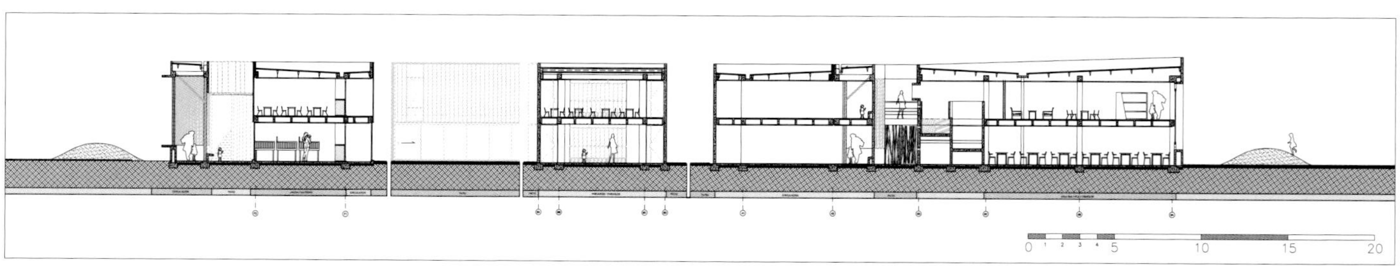
0 1 2 3 4 5 10 15 20

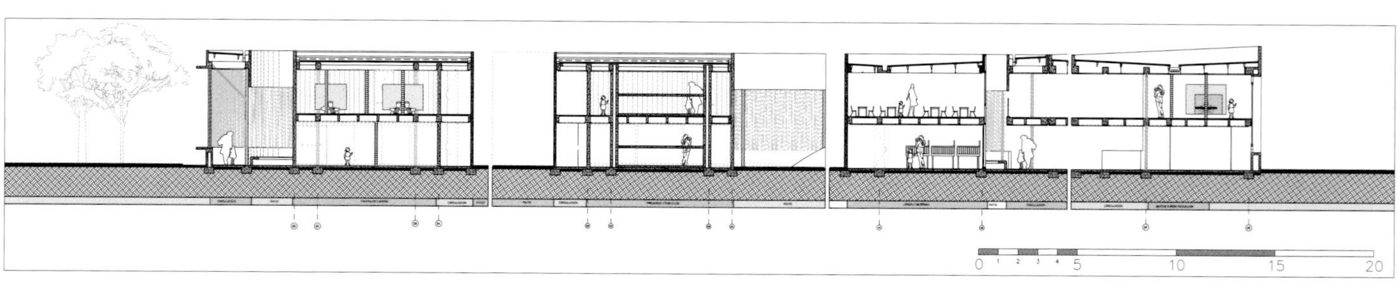
0 1 2 3 4 5 10 15 20

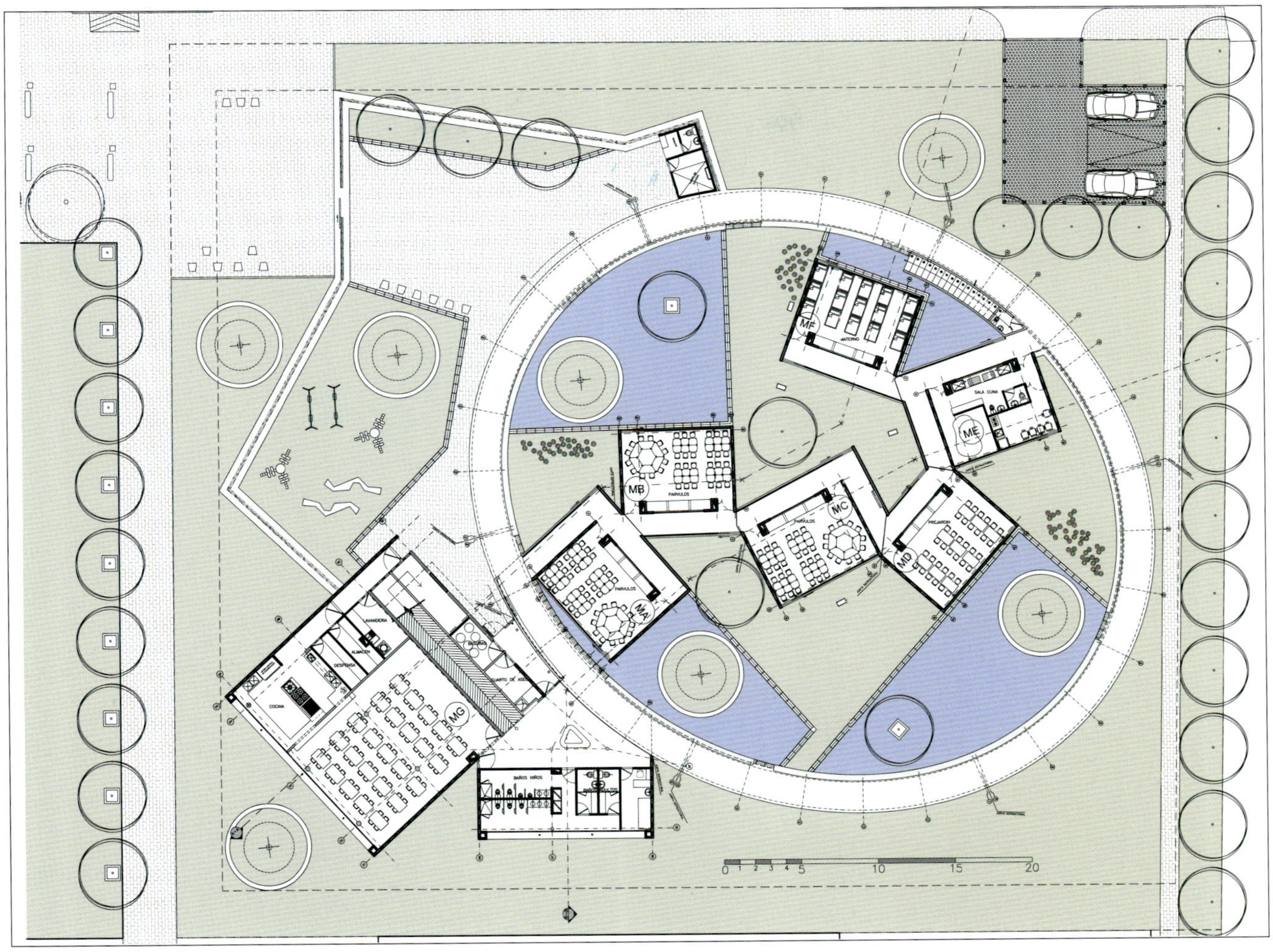
MF
ME
MB
MC
MD
MA
MG
0 1 2 3 4 5 10 15 20

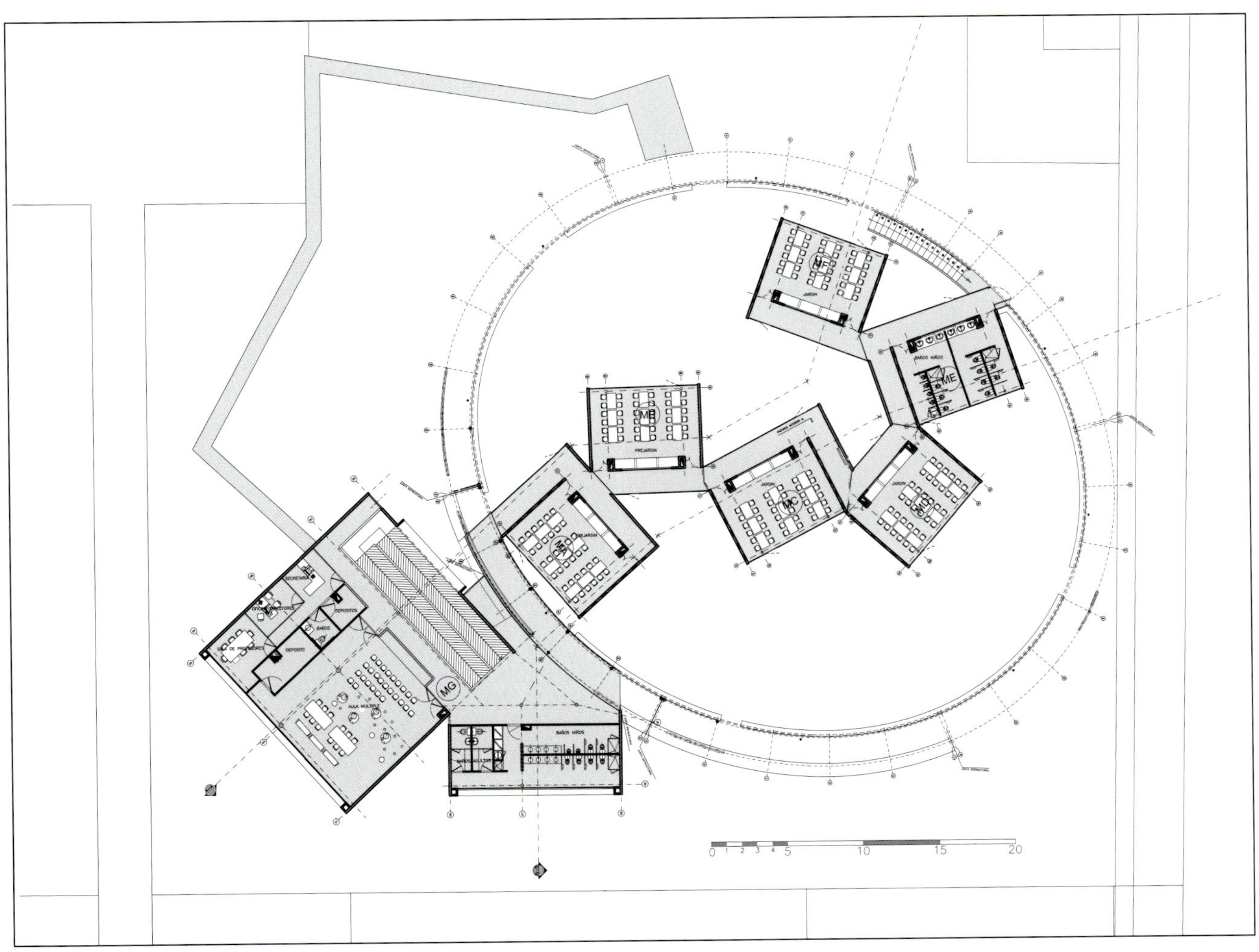
ME
MG
0 1 2 3 4 5 10 15 20

TELLUS NURSERY SCHOOL

On the border between a former urban/industrial development and a small forest where new housing is being developed, this nursery school mediates between different contexts and scales. A semi enclosed entrance courtyard constitutes a first exterior space for parents and children meeting and leaving. The organic layout encourages movement as space becomes continuous and creates both exterior and interior rooms of challenging shapes. Windows are freely placed at different heights and allow for light and views to be adapted also to the scale of children, which further the relation between the interior and the exterior play ground and the wooded hill.

Together with the client and the pedagogues' inspiration from the Reggio Emilia school, a new way to organize the interior was developed. The result is a rather unorthodox plan, where instead of a complete "flat" for each group of children, there will be a large common interior plaza where the six groups can interact around different activities, playing and learning projects. This main space is complemented with separate atelier spaces for water projects and art, as well as small secluded group rooms for rest and quiet activities.

The facade panel, made of 50x50mm sawn wood, filters direct sunlight into the nursery school and create hidden windows that underscores the curved interior and exterior spaces. The building complies with the highest standards for environmentally friendly and long term sound construction.

COMPANY	THAM & VIDEGÅRD ARKITEKTER
DESIGNER	THAM & VIDEGÅRD ARKITEKTER
PHOTOGRAPHER	Åke E:son Lindman/ Martin Videgård
CLIENT	Vasakronan AB.
COUNTRY (DISTRICT)	Sweden

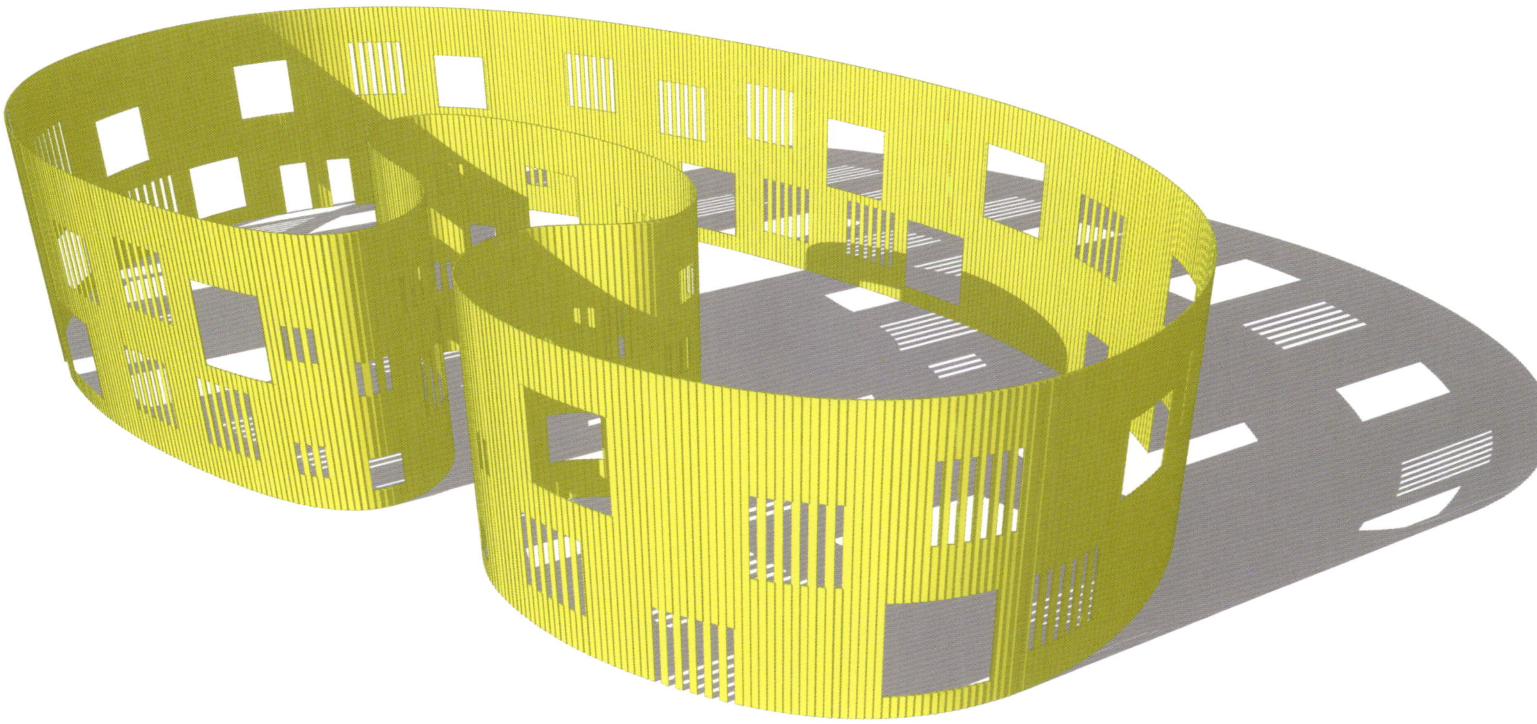

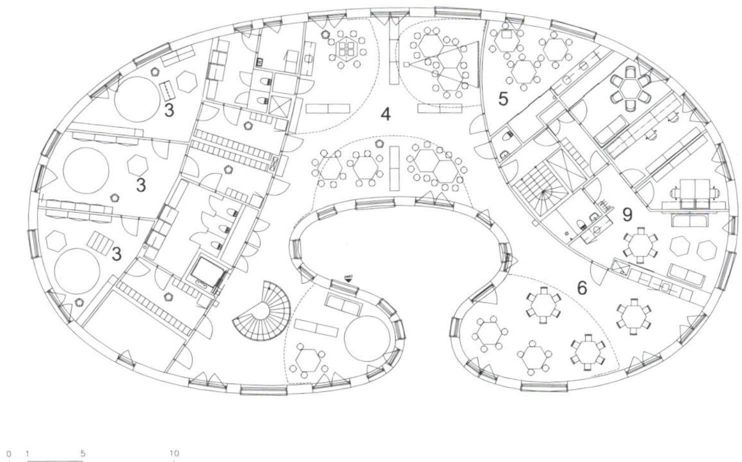

LEVEL 2

2 CLOAK ROOM
3 GROUP ROOM
4 COMMON SPACE
5 ATELIER
6 CANTEEN / ATELIER
9 OFFICE / ADMIN.

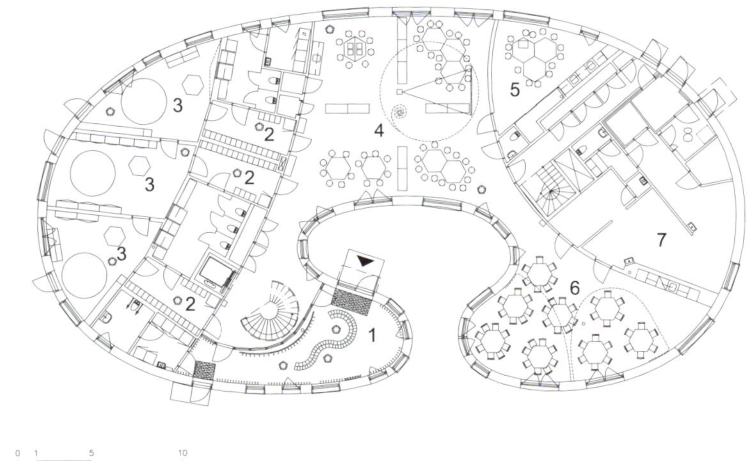

LEVEL 1 - ENTRANCE

1 ENTRANCE
2 CLOAK ROOM
3 GROUP ROOM
4 COMMON SPACE
5 ATELIER
6 CANTEEN / ATELIER
7 KITCHEN
8 LOADING

LUCINAHAVEN - DAY CARE CENTRE, TAULOV

Like a flower with the seed grains in the centre surrounded by the petals we have logically arranged the common room of the institution to be a central area with access from group rooms as well as service centre. In this way all functions are closely connected to the common room and to each other; at the same time this arrangement reflects our architectural interpretation of the diagram of functions. The arrangement is not only functional, but also symbolic: community is a central point in the spirit and design of the day care centre.

As mentioned, the use of hexagons is meant to create recognition. In combination with the use of different colors a strong identity inside each hexagon will arise.

We all know the usual names as "blue room" or "yellow group" from other institutions. These names are almost worn down, however, they express a need among children (and adults) for a community or their own identity in the institution: I am a sunflower. I am a crumb. I am from the blue room…

We have chosen to strengthen the community and identity by means of the arrangement of rooms and use of colors in the building. Materials used for facades and roof support our wish of creating variation and diversity along with recognition. They are individual parts of the unified whole. In some way you may consider the hexagons to be related. They are members of the same family but are just as unique as each member of a family. In this way we have obtained a more balanced architectural picture and the possibility to work with more educational and challenging arrangement designs.

COMPANY	CEBRA a/s, arkitekter maa
PHOTOGRAPHER	CEBRA
CLIENT	The municipality of Fredericia
COUNTRY (DISTRICT)	Denmark

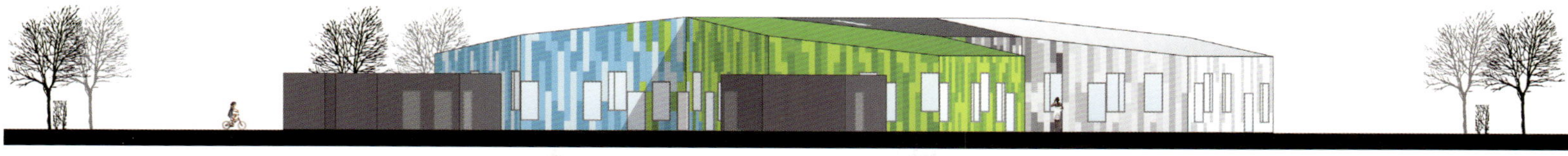

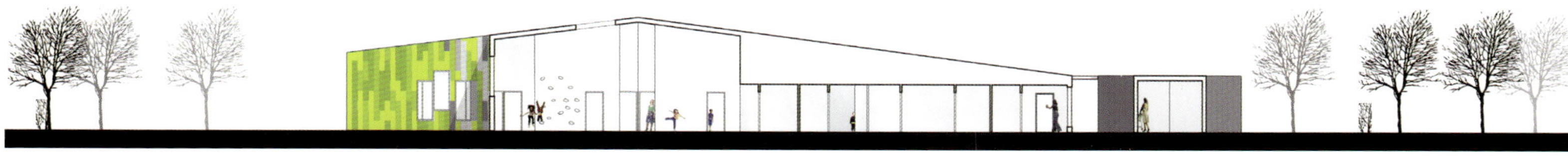

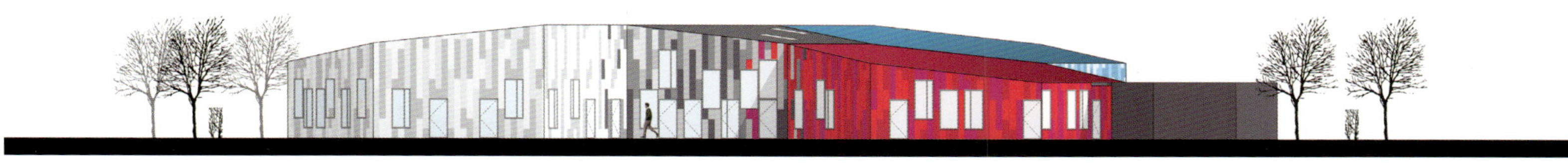

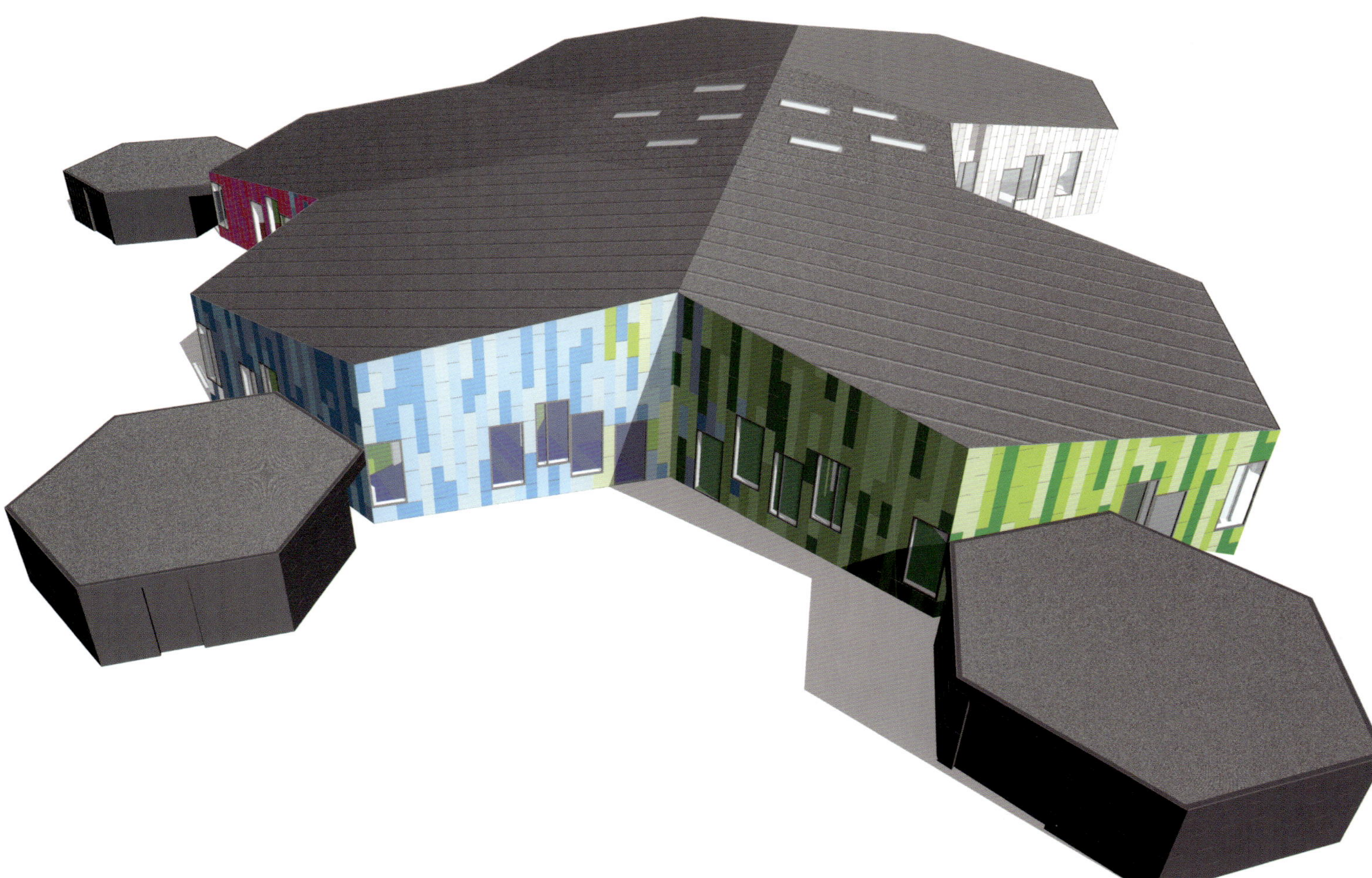

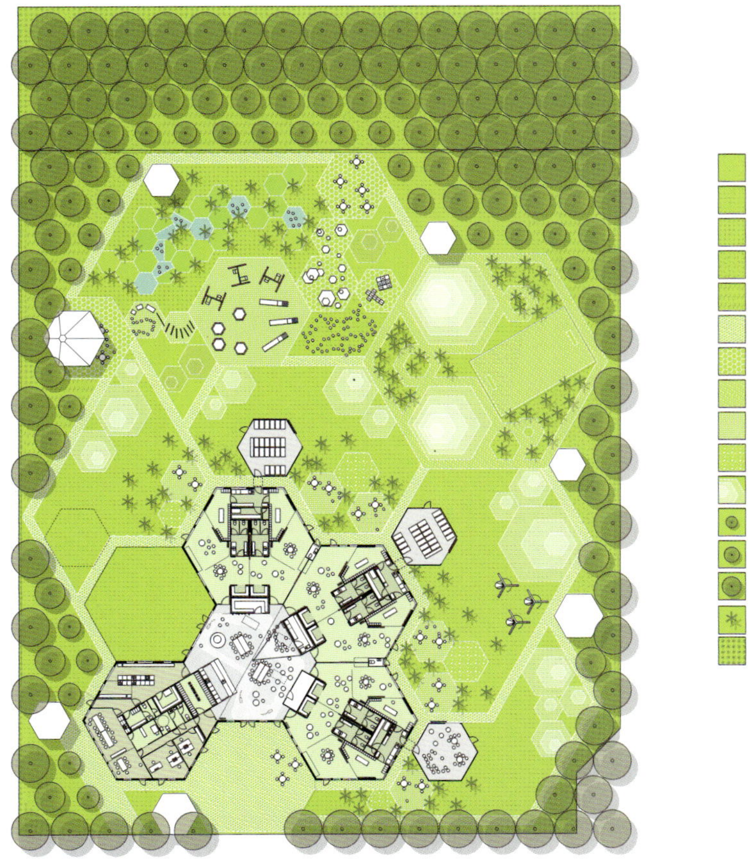

OSLO INTERNATIONAL SCHOOL

Oslo International School is a private school with about 500 children from more than 50 different nations, divided into kindergarten, reception, primary and secondary school.
The school is based on a traditional use of classrooms combined with special facilities for advanced studies. The primary goal of the building project is to upgrade existing areas, replace temporary structures and establish new educational areas for specific needs.
The project is divided into 3 phases to make possible continuous use of the school during the construction period.
The existing structure from the 1960s was worn down, but had obvious architectonic qualities. The organization on one level gives easy orientation, good natural lighting and a close contact to the outdoors.
The modular structure is flexible to programmatic changes. The new structure gently transforms the easy organization within a limited budget, and tries to keep the inherent qualities. The new mechanical systems are placed on the roof.
Phase 1 is established as pavilions within existing atrium. They include science laboratories, library and a main "square". The main entrance, as a result of the addition, is moved to the west side of the building.
The architecture is developed as a new vocabulary of soft and organic forms, softening dense spatial relationships between new and old areas. At the same time these new areas contain special programs framed by the rectilinear structure of the old. Daylight fills the rooms from narrow slits from floor to ceiling combined with circular roof lights.
Phase 2 is a separate pavilion for the smallest children. It houses 10 classrooms in addition to offices. The common areas get daylight from the atrium. Sizes of rooms are flexible, and can be changed according to number of children on each level.
Phase 3, under planning, will house new areas for drama, music and physical education. Parts of the areas will be open at night.
Materials:
Organically shaped walls are clad with specially milled wooden paneling in convex and concave shape, treated with clear tar. Inside, the wooden walls are whitewashed. Phase 2 has a facade covered with fiber cement boards in 10 different colors. Outside materials are also used on the inside of outside walls.
With reference to the qualities of the old structure, the new buildings are organized around three new atria suited for play and recreation for the different groups of children.
The existing atrium is established as the quiet garden with white gravel, benches and greenery suited for quiet play and conversations. Two large existing oaks are preserved.
The atrium in phase two has a rubber floor suited for play for the smallest children. The open school yard towards the west is planned for ball play.

COMPANY	Jarmund / Vigsnæs AS Architects MNAL
DESIGNER	Jarmund / Vigsnæs AS Architects MNAL
PHOTOGRAPHER	Ivan Brodey
CLIENT	Oslo International School
COUNTRY (DISTRICT)	Norway

FLOR DEL CAMPO SCHOOL

This project is proposed as the sequence and relationship of four configurations named the "Rings".

Each is defined by a perimeter of two levels with different thicknesses and gardens with activities. The relationship between the four rings, the way they are articulated with the solar geometry and its connectivity strategy, define a central and interstitial area connected with one and each of them.

Rings (Program and Function)

a. Core Ring (Integrated Resource Center)

Located in south-eastern side of the site and forming the school's access. This group program, is the most public of all, containing general services, and can work independently.

b. Pre-school education ring In the first floor, its perimeter hosts classrooms of grade 0 and the playroom, and in the second floor classrooms in grade 1. Administrative areas are distributed in the ring's first and second floor.

c. Basic Education Elementary Ring Located on the Western side, is in contact with Preschool,the elementary education and the middle school rings. The classroom programs, workshops and the required services are located in its perimeter and throughout the two floors.

d. Basic Middle and Secondary Education Ring Located in the extreme southwest of the site. In its perimeter classroom, workshops and required services are located in its perimeter, encouraged by a yard of activities with colorful Guayacanes.

Articulating the four rings, the connectors act as binding and intersection zones between them. These are covered and double height spaces, allowing communication, relaxation and dispersion of students and teachers.

The project has a membrane that controls: light, environment and access. This membrane is the exterior and interior facade of the patios and the interstitial space.

The four rings are positioned leaving a public and pedestrian perimeter circuit, allowing the students and inhabitants to completely surround the school. Rather than one isolated school, it aims to develop an urban project that promotes new sectored centers with the existing school's library, the athletic fields and the outdoor auditorium as support for neighborhood activities.

COMPANY	Mazzanti Arquitectos
DESIGNER	GIANCARLO MAZZANTI FELIPE MESA
PHOTOGRAPHER	Cristobal Palma
CLIENT	FONADE
COUNTRY (DISTRICT)	Colombia

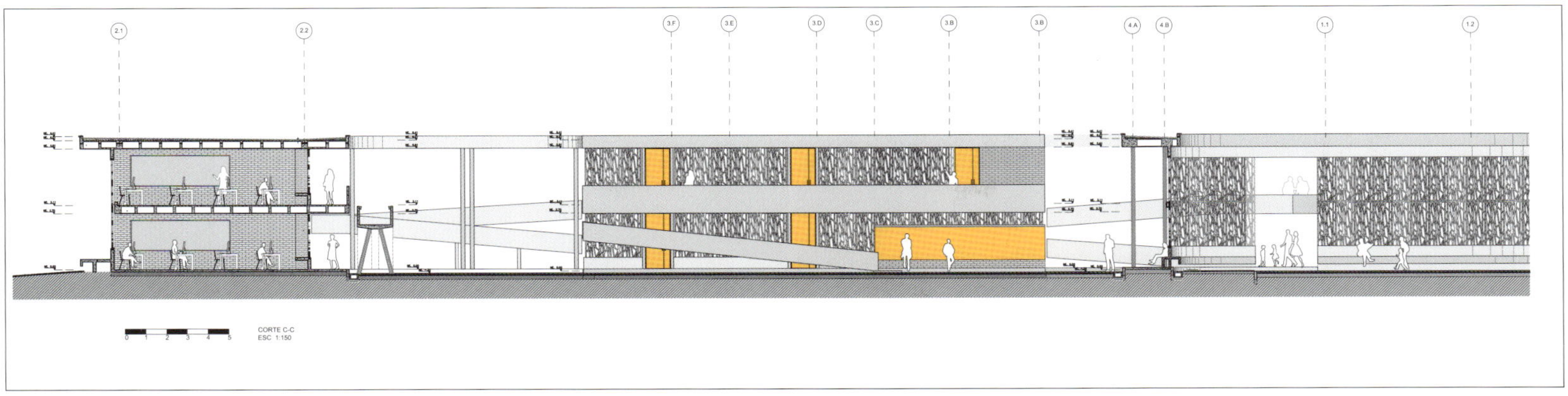
CORTE C-C
ESC. 1:150

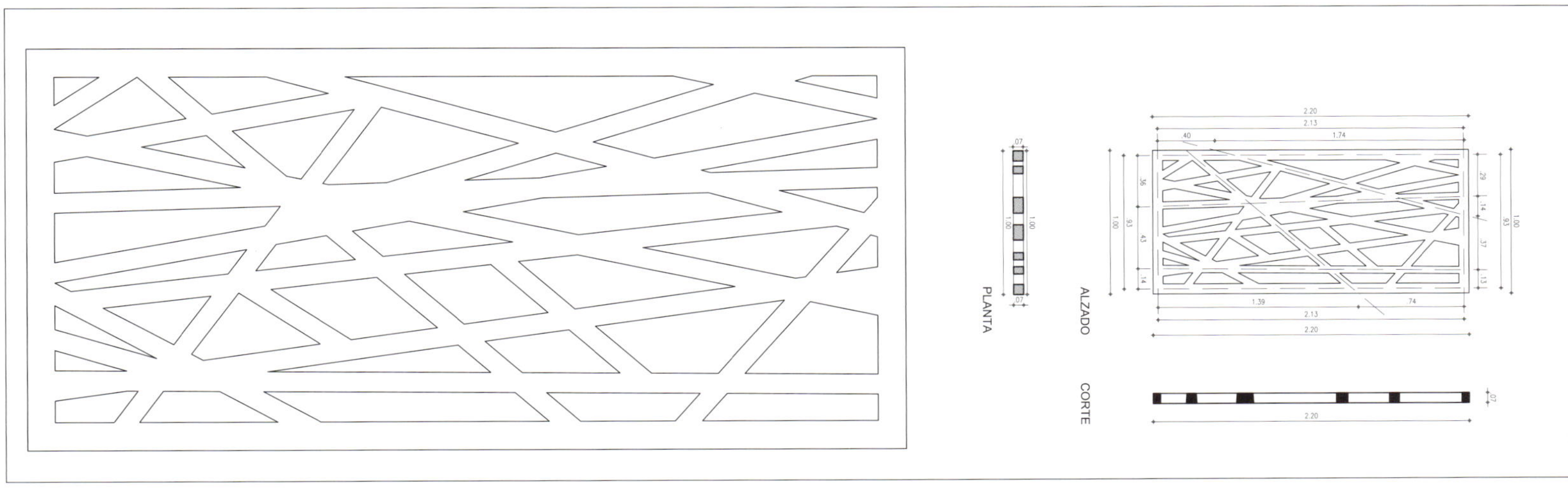
PLANTA
ALZADO
CORTE
2.20
2.13
1.74
1.39
.74

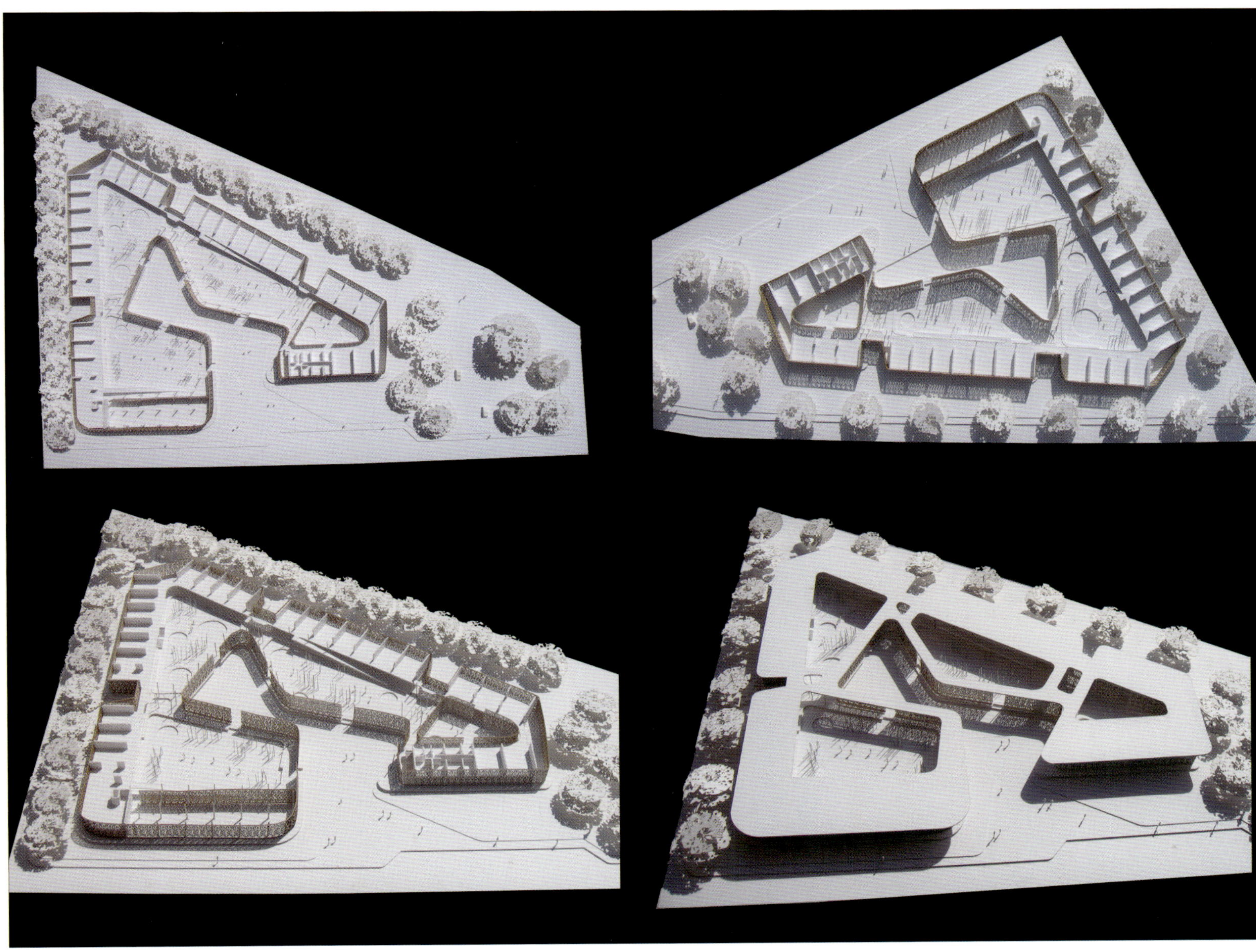

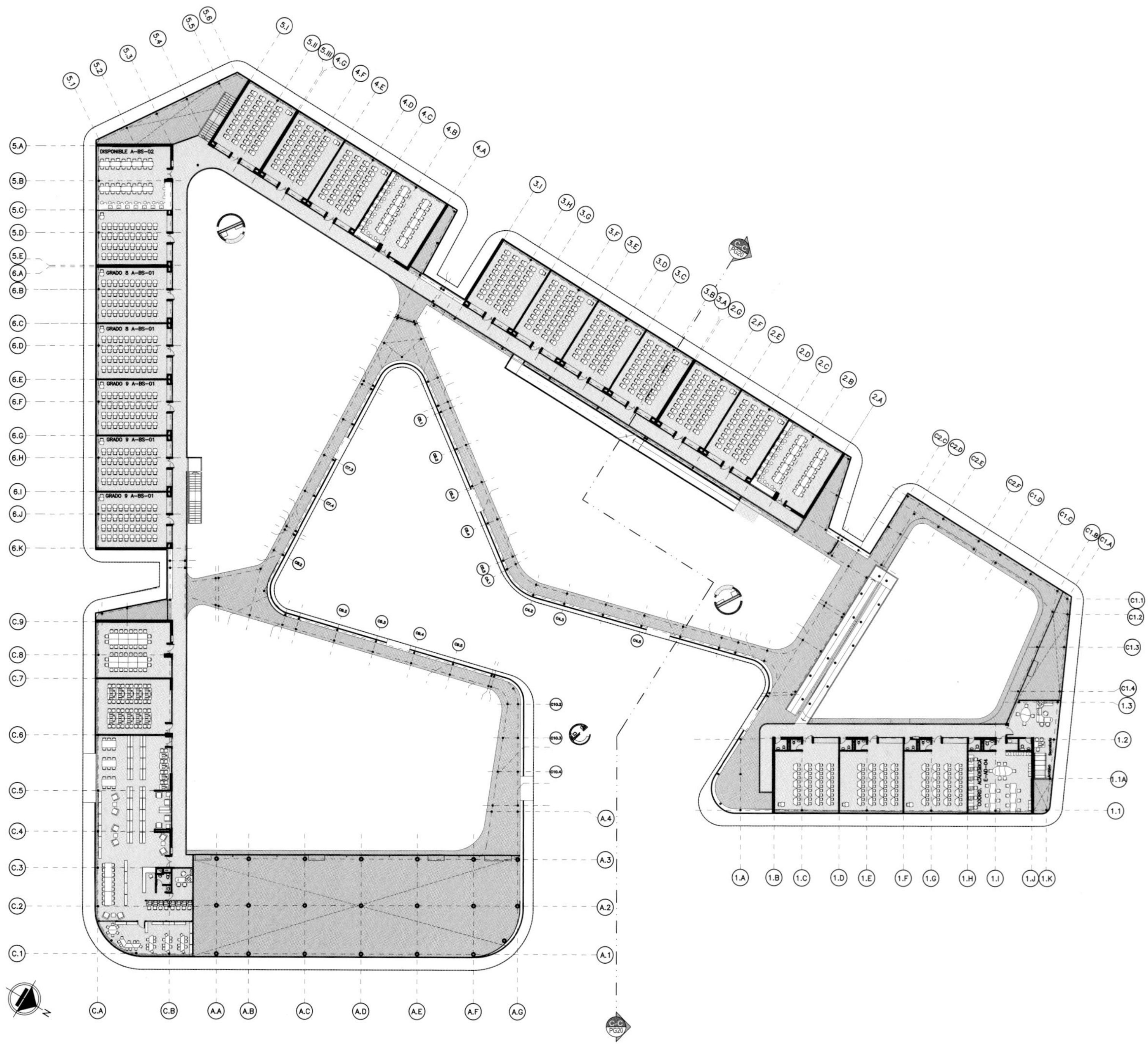

0 5 10

PLANTA SEGUNDO PISO
ESC 1:500

NORVEG COAST CULTURAL CENTER

Norveg is situated in the Community Rorvik which has long tradition for fishery, and represents the utmost of the Norwegian coastal culture through ages. Today there is a boat-building industry carrying on the tradition, but in a modern way. Being situated by the coast, represents in one way a challenge bringing visitors to the place, ensuring economic stability in the organization of the center. Therefore the architect stated that a building of significance was needed to ensure attention to this community.

The architect "visited" the ancient times of fishery and used the culture for inspiration in creating the idea. Thus the idea is based on the image of 3 sails which lean against a modern vessel, such uniting the sailing-boat tradition and the modern ships. The building becomes an evolution of a coast-cultural history visualized in architecture. The building even consists of an after-deck or a hind part to complete the interpretation of the ship inheritage.The building is 1,730 m². The organization follows the architectural elements. The main central vessel or hull as the spine of the building housing the administration,kitchen and technical plants. The sails covering the foyer,restaurant and temporary exhibition. The big rock on the other side symbolizing the shore that the ship is docking to, containing the multimedia and concert/auditorium space. At last the after-deck containing the coast cultural exhibition also designed by the same architect.

Climate by the sea demands carefulness in the choice of materials. Therefore the use of Alucobond in the Sails was necessary because of its endurance. The main ship consists of concrete, cast by horizontal formwork boards to illude the ship, and the afterdeck-walls are covered with wooden boards specially impregnated to interpret the old wooden boats.

The building has already managed to arouse a great interest outside Rorvik and the northern part of Norway, but the most important part is that it already has achieved to arouse optimism in the Community, creating other investments, and leading to other buildings and enthusiasm in the society. In such way it has in its small scale established a kind of a Bilbao-effect for a community of 10.000 inhabitants and is still carrying on its mission as an architectural symbol of history in evolution.

COMPANY	Gudmundur Jonsson Arkitektkontor
CREATIVE DIRECTOR	Gudmundur Jonsson
DESIGNER	Gudmundur Jonsson
PHOTOGRAPHER	Thomas Mayer
CLIENT	Vikna Kommune
COUNTRY (DISTRICT)	Norway

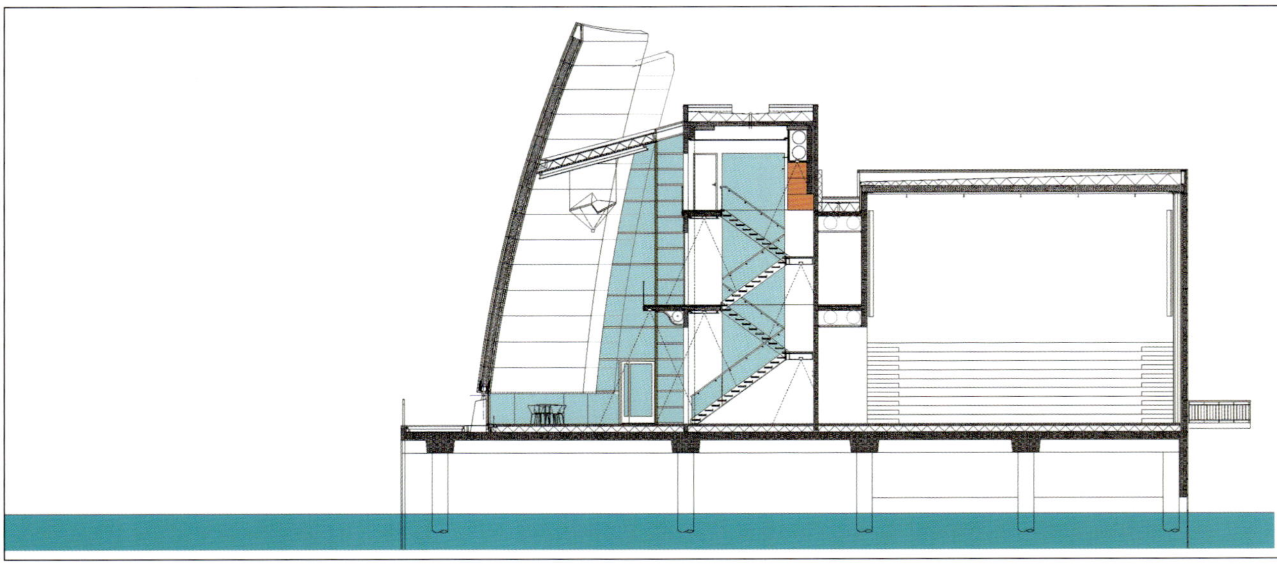

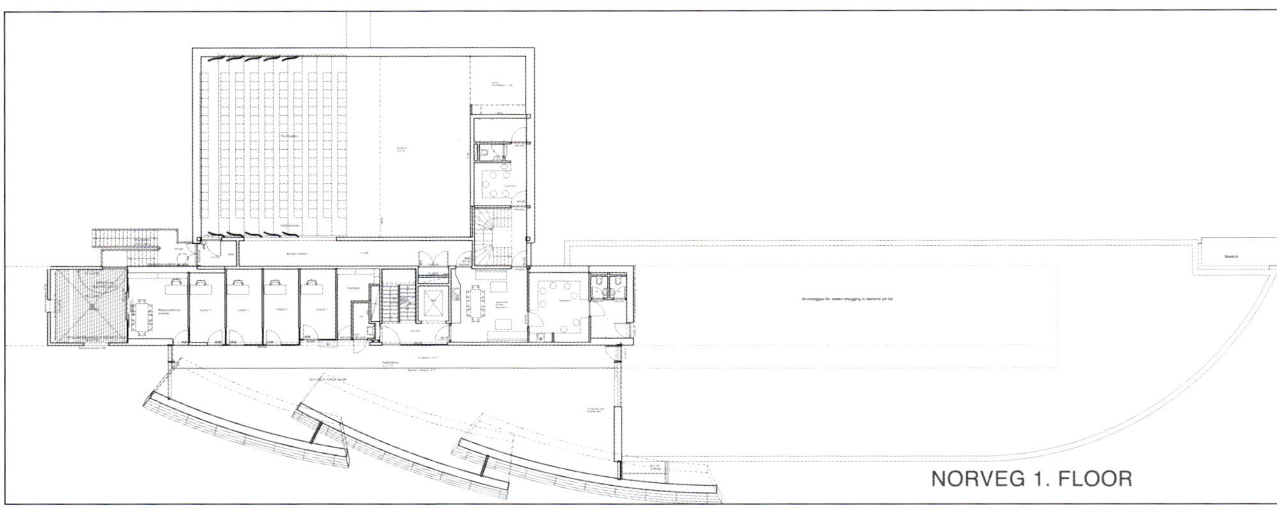
NORVEG 1. FLOOR

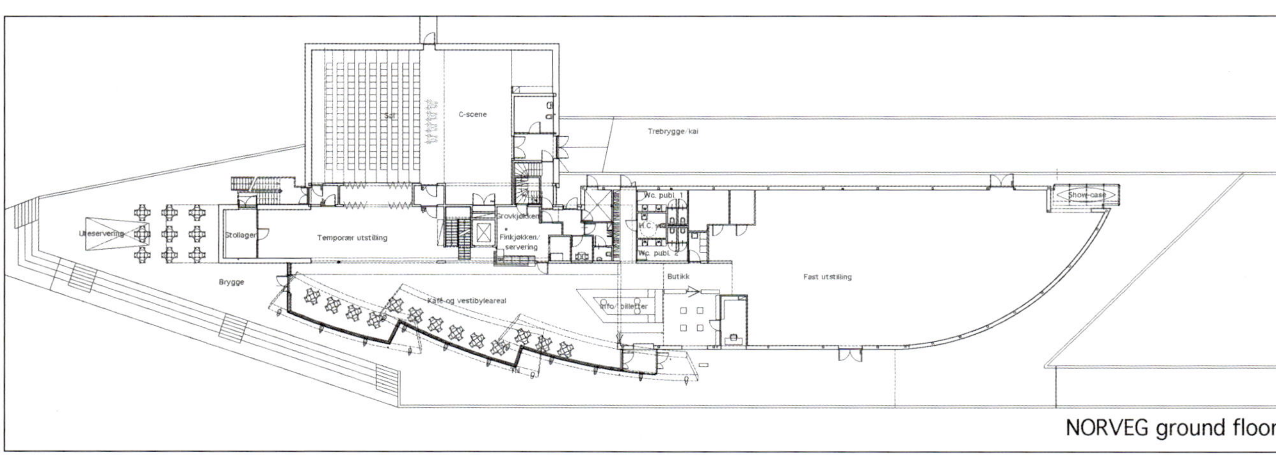
NORVEG ground floor

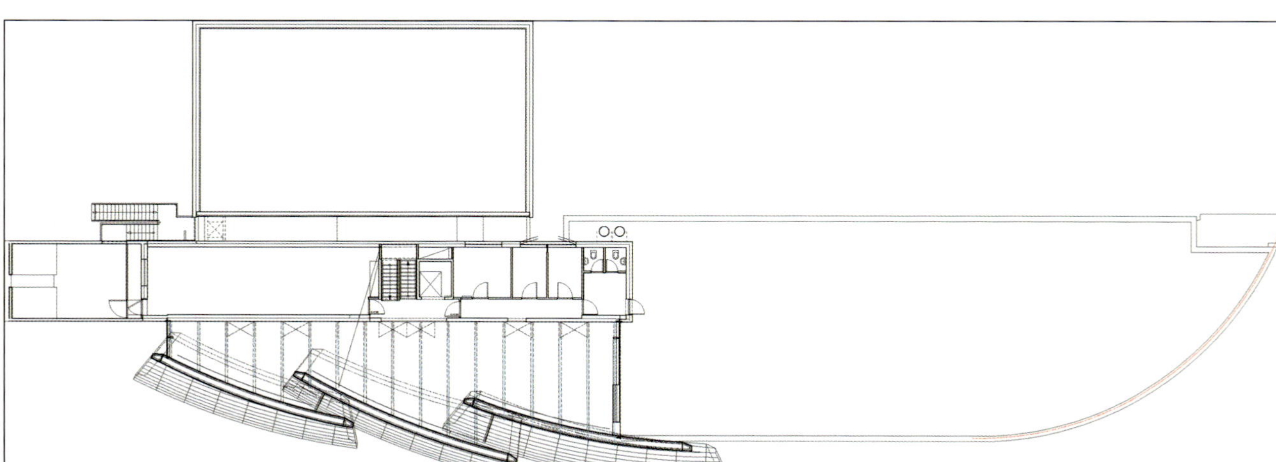

NORVEG

SVALBARD SCIENCE CENTRE 78°NORTH

The project was commissioned through an invited competition. The new structure is an addition to an existing university and research building, which is extended to about 4 times its original size. The project also provides new facilities for the Svalbard Museum.
The project is the very largest building in Longyearbyen and Spitzbergen. The insulated copper-clad skin is wrapped around the program demanded, creating an outer shell adjusted to the flows of wind and snow passing through the site. Climatic 3D simulations has been undertaken to assure that the accumulation of snow would not create undesired conditions in front of doors and windows. In the process, the skin has been flexible to adjustments, both geometrical changes answering to the climatic studies and alterations of program. The building is elevated on poles to prevent the melting of the permanent frost - the only thing fixating the construction.
The main structure is in timber, to facilitate on-site adjustments and avoid cold bridges. The outer copper cladding retains its workability even at low temperatures, thereby extending the construction period further into the cold season.
An important consideration has been to create vital public spaces and passages in the building, an "interior campus" area providing warm and lighted meeting places during the dark and cold winter. The pine-clad spaces have complex geometry relating to the outer skin of the building- the effectiveness of the circulation is maximized but at the same time it offers varied vistas and experiences. The technical infrastructure is hidden in the tilted walls of the interior.
The use of color has been a necessity in a natural condition where colors are scarce. Both physical and virtual models have been important tools in the design process, while an accurate 1:50 construction model has facilitated work on site. The Danish / Icelandic artist Olafur Eliasson will provide an extensive glass installation on the main lobby window.

COMPANY	Jarmund / Vigsnæs AS Architects MNAL
DESIGNER	Jarmund / Vigsnæs AS Architects MNAL
PHOTOGRAPHER	Nils Petter Dale
CLIENT	Statsbygg / Norwegian Directorate of Public Construction and Property
COUNTRY (DISTRICT)	Norway

NABITO SENSATIONAL PARK

The goal of the project is to invite users to a path in which scenes are always changing. You will have the sensation to discover always different spaces but with the same kind of characteristics. The five human senses are the main theme of the space; the material and the vegetation will be related to them .The user will not have an entire look over the park, but he will do a series of different experiences. The variation of high and inclination, dimensional games are some of the ludic peculiarity of the Park.

We use the senses as a big metaphor. We use senses to relate ourselves with surroundings and other people. We would like to give a gift to the city: a relational space.

COMPANY	Nabito Architects
PHOTOGRAPHER	Bebo Ferlito
CLIENT	Frosinone's Municipality
COUNTRY (DISTRICT)	Spain

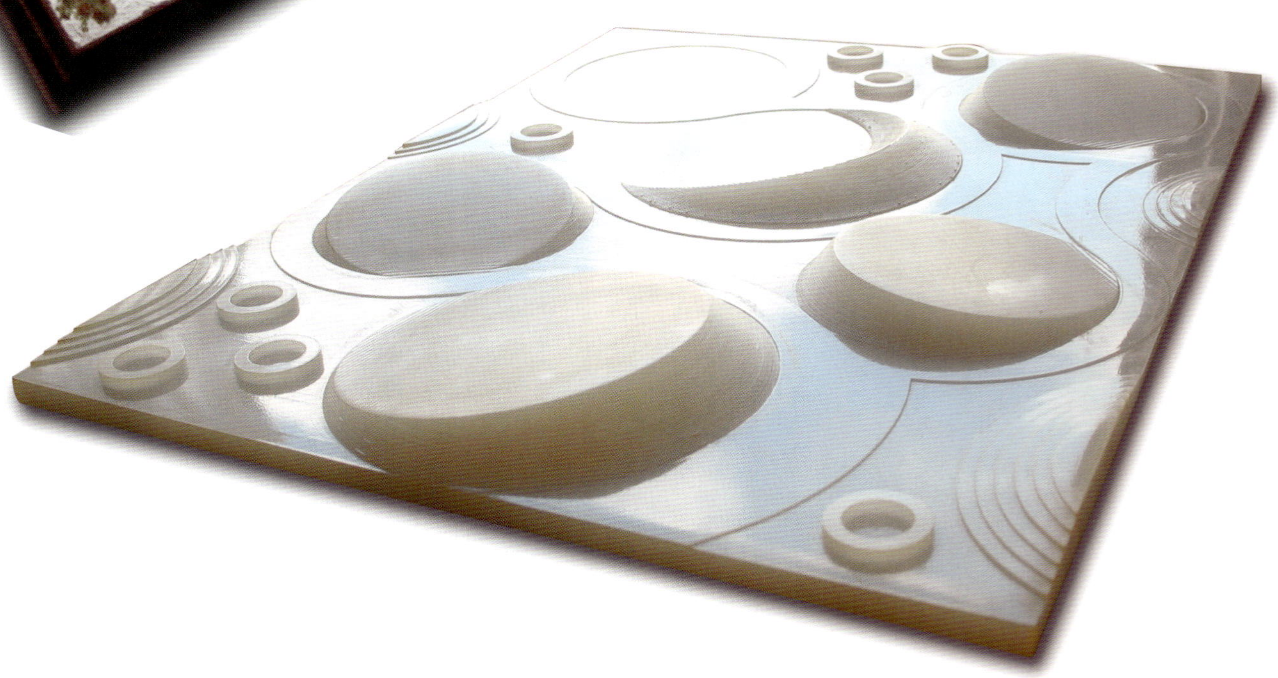

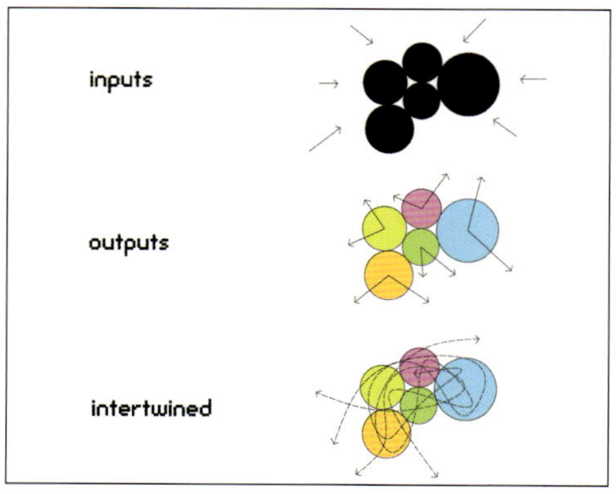
inputs
outputs
intertwined

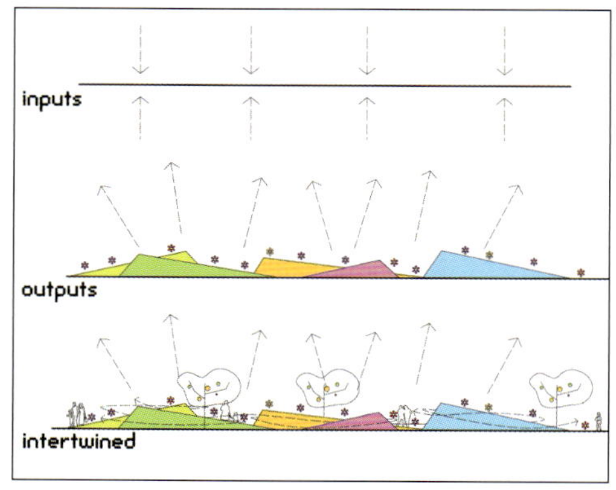
inputs
outputs
intertwined

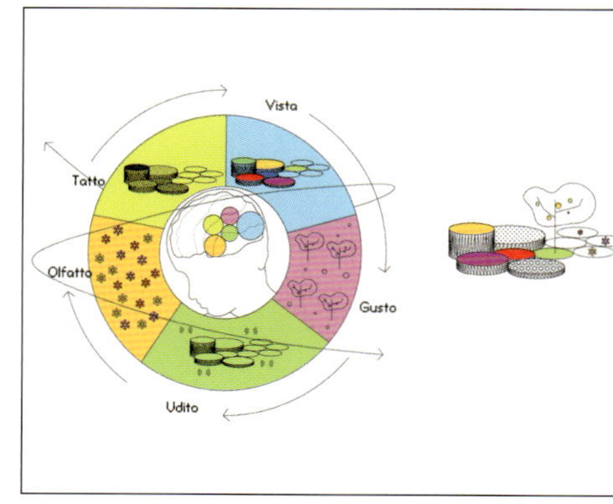
Vista
Tatto
Olfatto
Gusto
Udito

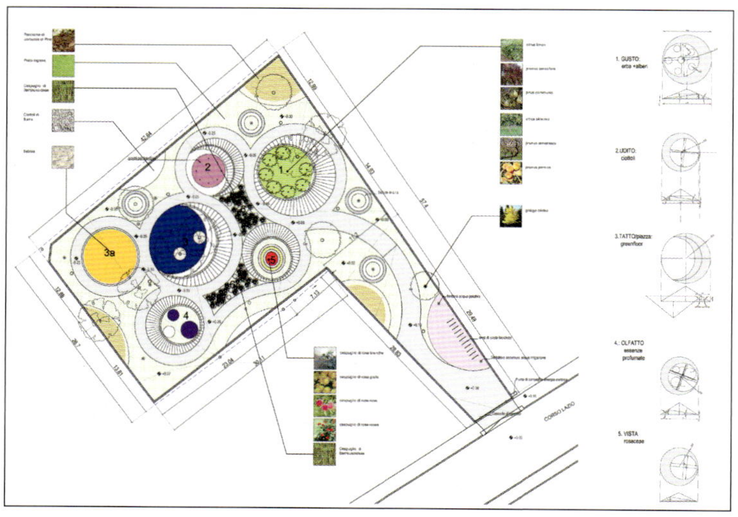

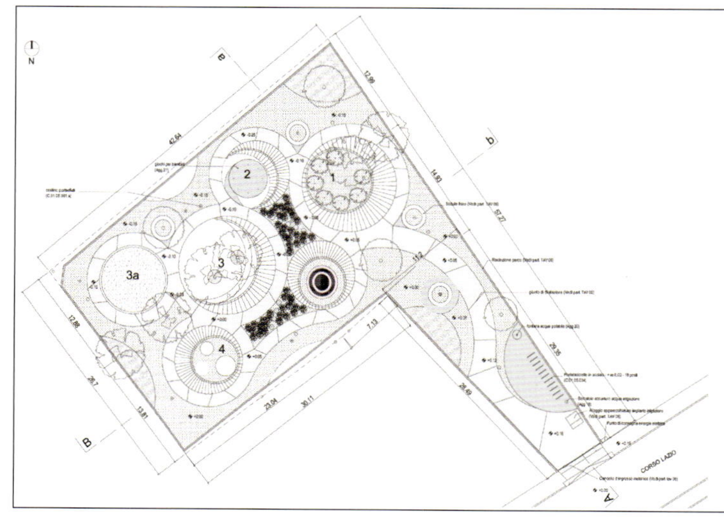
CORSO LAZIO

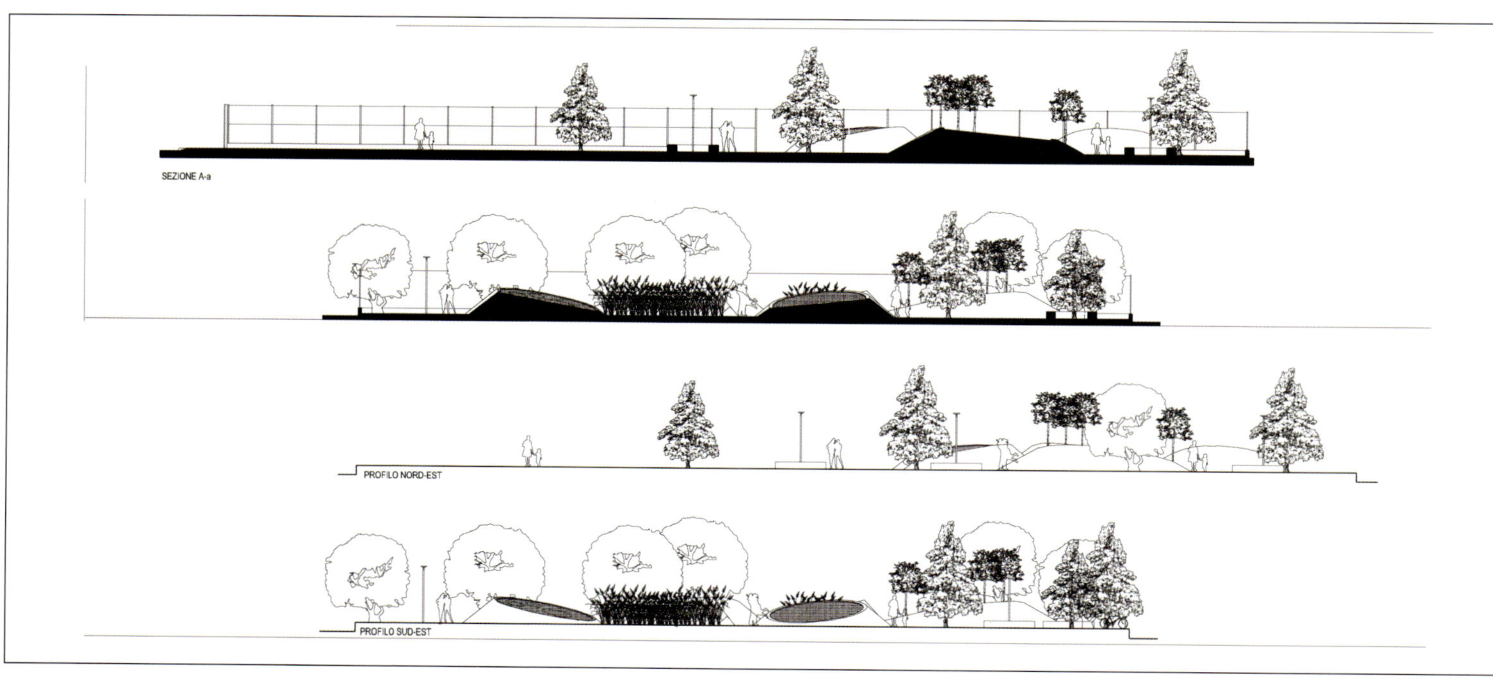
SEZIONE A-a
PROFILO NORD-EST
PROFILO SUD-EST

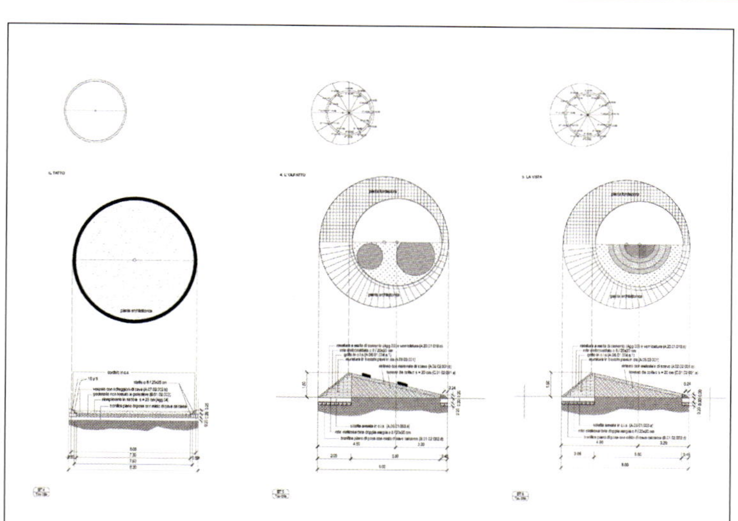

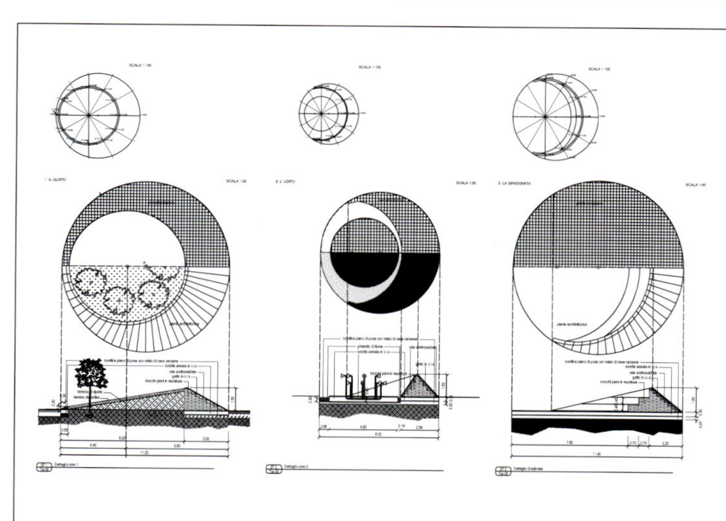

TRAM STOP

Alicante is a 400,000 inhabitants city of the southeast Mediterranean Spanish coast. Over the last years, there has been building a new tram infrastructure, using the old rails of the local train. This line connects all the towns of the coast, ending in Denia, a northern city of the province, where ships departure to Ibiza. This stop, is the central stage of a new line of the tram, that links the centre of the city to the residential areas of San Juan beach.
The construction of the Tram Stop was the opportunity to bring back a stolen space to the city: to turn a traffic circle into a public space. Through a fractal access system deformed in each side to avoid the existing trees, the travelers can arrive in a frontal way to the platform in 32 different possibilities.
Over the platforms, 2 empty boxes (36 m long, 3 m wide, 2.5 m high) create a floating void slightly over the travelers' heads. It matches the size of the train, creating an intermediate scale between buildings and urban elements.
There is no difference between structure and envelope, neither between roof and walls. It is an isotropic material in both conception and construction.
The holes reduce the weight as increase the resistance to normal tensions, and equally decrease wind pressures among the surfaces. Light and air pass through, smoothing the shadow and generating a soft breeze in summer months. At night the boxes are transformed into two giant lamps.
Benches are spread over the garden close to the vegetation and the paths, creating a public place overlaying the quiet of the seated people and the movement of the people walking.

COMPANY	Subarquitectura
DESIGNER	Subarquitectura
COUNTRY (DISTRICT)	Spain

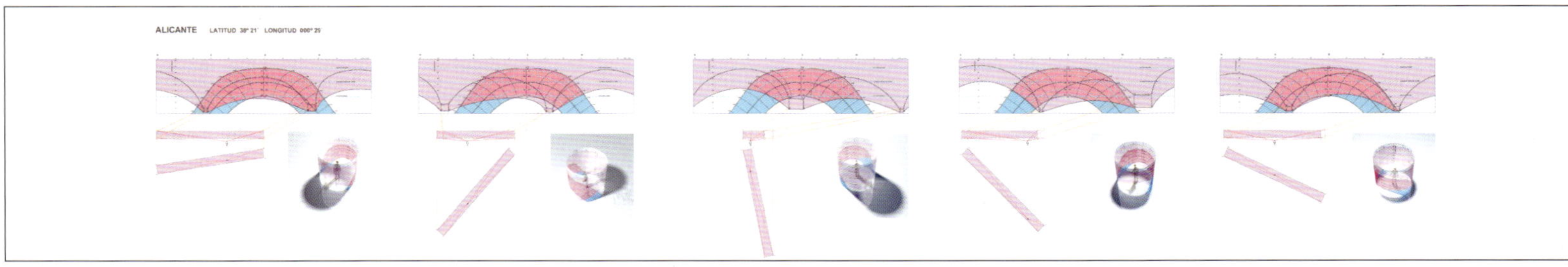
ALICANTE
LATITUD 38° 21'
LONGITUD

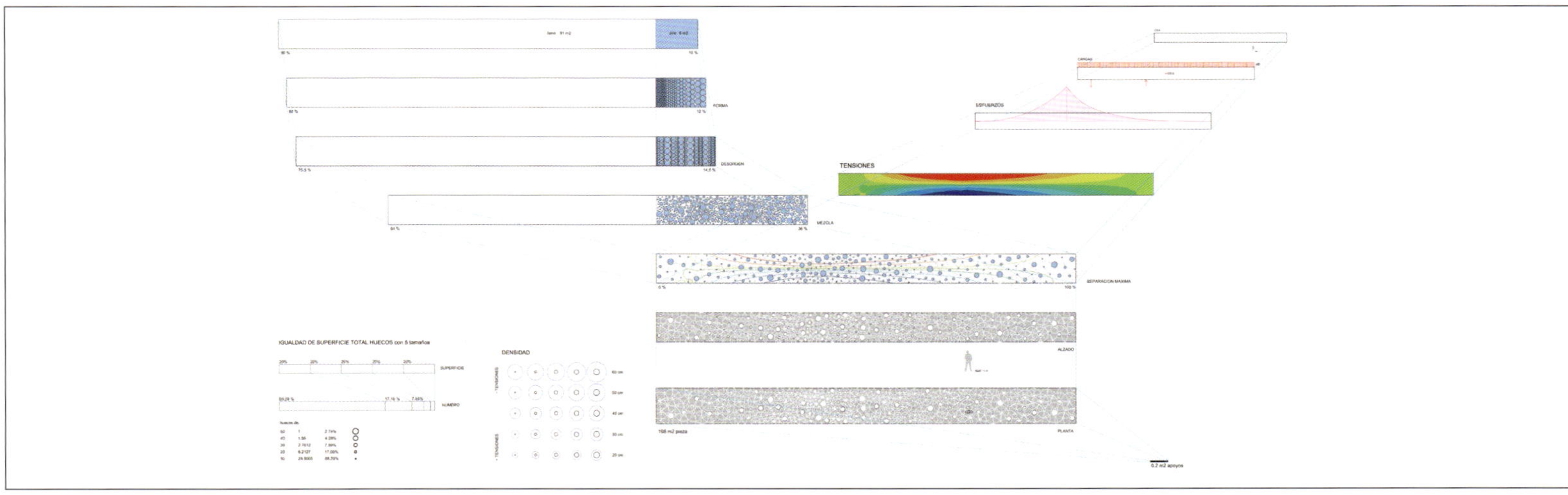
TENSIONES

RE-SKIN / MORE WITH LESS

What initially began as a speculative proposal to reshape the UTS tower on Broadway has evolved into a broader architectural idea for re-purposing inefficient or outdated buildings as an alternative to demolishing and rebuilding (which comes with a huge financial and environmental expense). LAVA has developed a simple, cost effective and easily constructed building skin that can potentially transform the identity, sustainability and interior comfort of an existing structure such as the UTS tower.

The 'skin' is a translucent cocoon that can create its own 'micro climate'. It can generate its own energy with photo-voltaic cells, could collect rain water, improve the distribution of natural daylight and it can use available convective energy to power the building's ventilation requirements.

A pre-existing building is wrapped with three dimensional lightweight, high performance composite mesh textile. Surface tension allows the membrane to freely stretch over a light steel frame around walls and roof elements achieving maximum visual impact with minimal material effort.

The skin with embedded LED strips could act as an intelligent media surface and be used for dynamic animation and to communicate information into the public realm – effectively integrating principles of architecture, fashion, media and communication design into a new hybrid typology.

"A re-skinned UTS Tower could be an example of sustainability, innovation, cutting edge design and creative education, without demolishing and rebuilding the 1960s icon." says Chris Bosse, Director of LAVA.

"When it was built the Broadway tower was cutting edge, with latest building technologies and principles that have partially become obsolete."

The re-skinning technology could be easily applied to other buildings in need of a facelift such as the Goulburn street carpark, Sydney. One quickly and cost efficiently enhance their performance and aesthetics through this minimal intervention.

The re-skin concept continues LAVA's research into sustainable public architecture by combining lightweight contemporary materials with the latest digital fabrication technologies with the aim of achieving more (architecture) with less (material/energy/time).

COMPANY	LAVA
COUNTRY (DISTRICT)	Australia

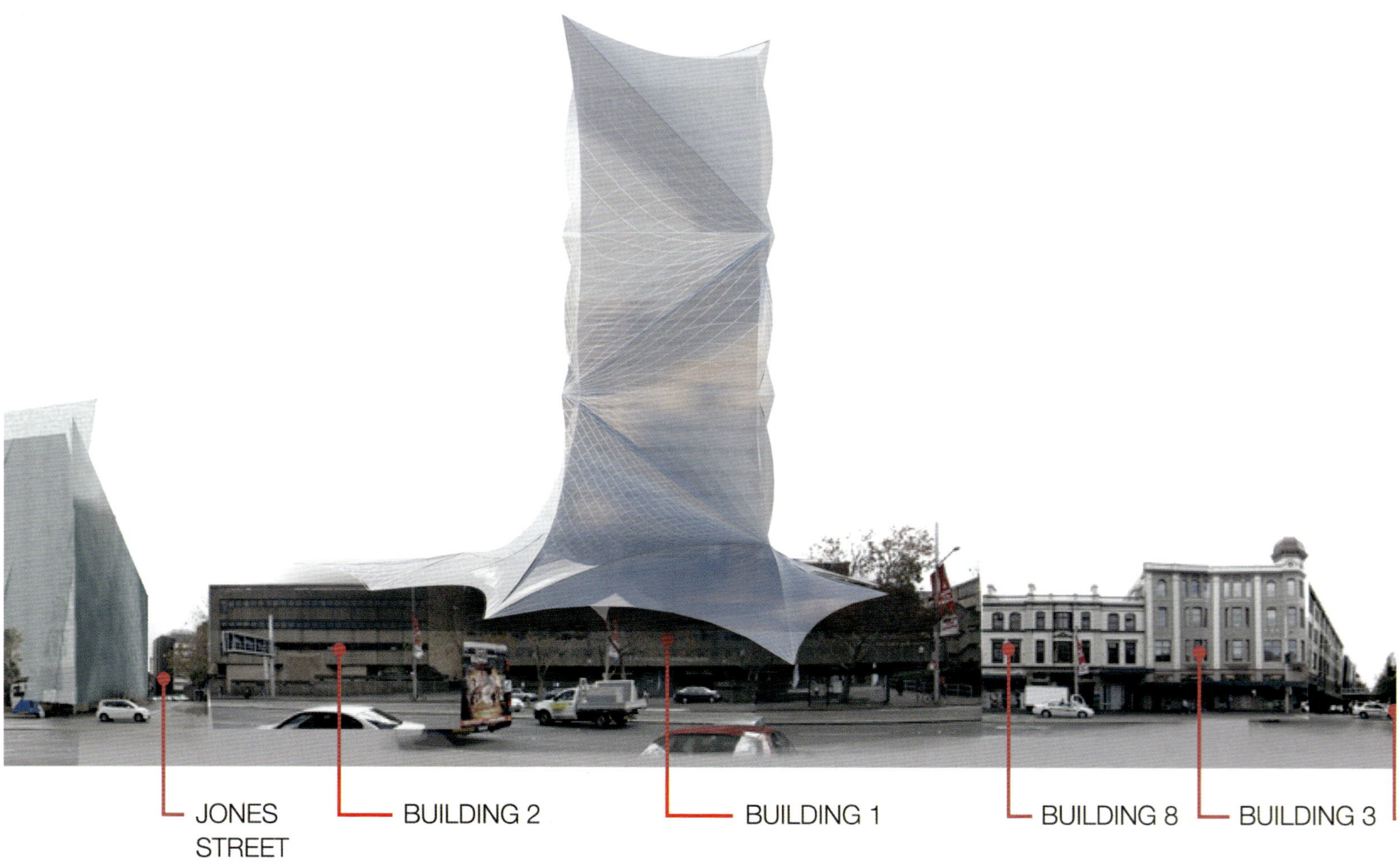

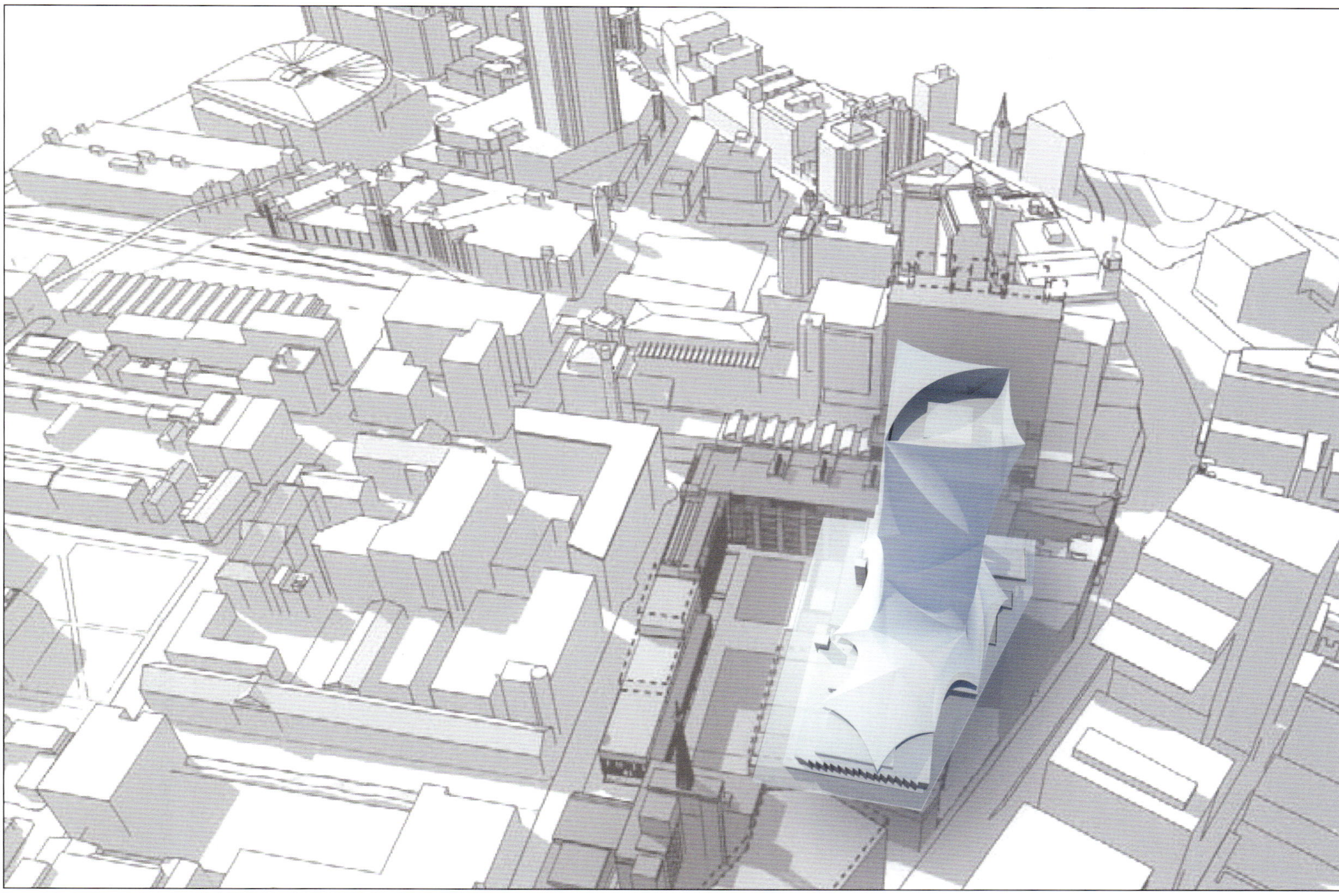

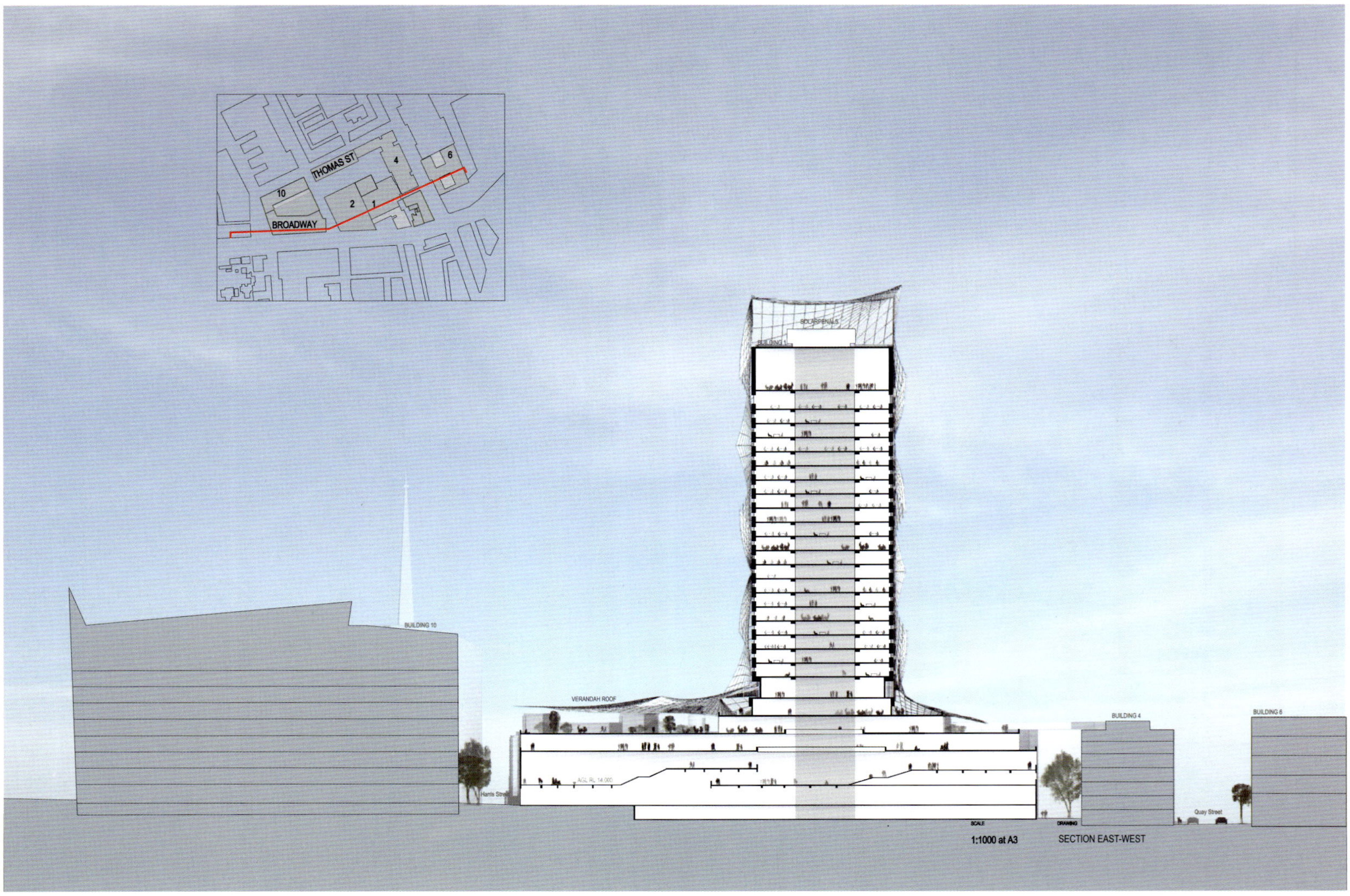

Skin

Structure

element	number of elements	position	bend radius m	diameter profile mm
	1	horizontal	18	400
	2	horizontal	28	400
	1	horizontal	60	400
	2	diagonal	80	600
	2	horizontal	132	400
	1	diagonal	99	600
	4	vertical	72	200
	4	horizontal	67	400

element	number of elements	position	bend radius m	diameter profile mm
	3	vertical	131	200
	4	diagonal	92	600
	4	diagonal	96	600
	4	horizontal	99	400
	1	horizontal	132	400
	1	diagonal	99	600
	2	diagonal	45	600
	4	diagonal	40	400

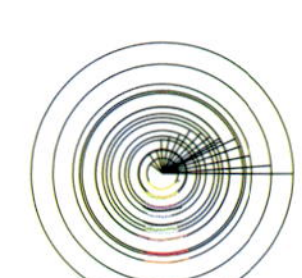

bend radia

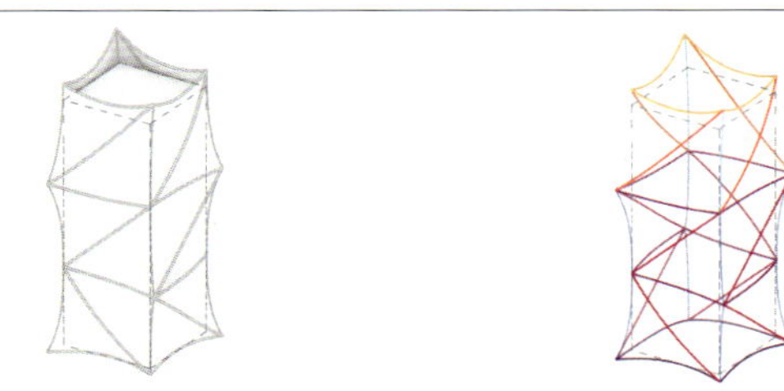

Skin

Structure

element	number of elements	position	bend radius m	diameter profile mm
	2	vertical	75	200
	2	vertical	92	200
	8	vertical	60	200
	4	horizontal	65	400
	8	horizontal	132	400
	8	diagonal	99	600
	4	diagonal	469	600
	4	horizontal	46	400

profile versions

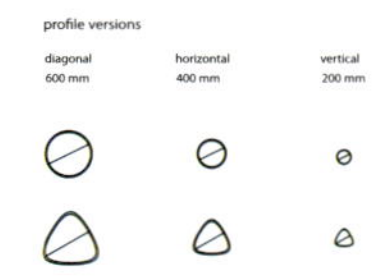

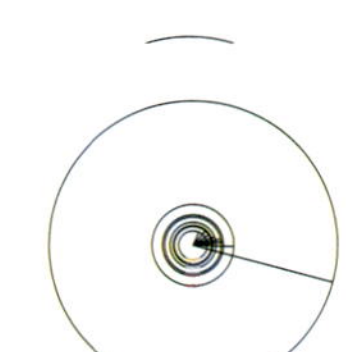

bend radia

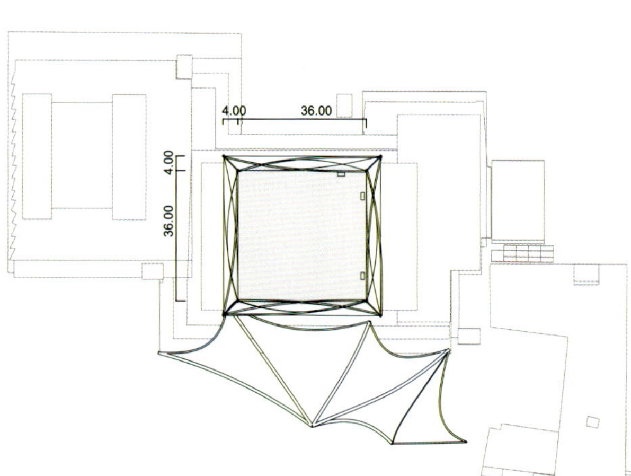

top view 1:1000

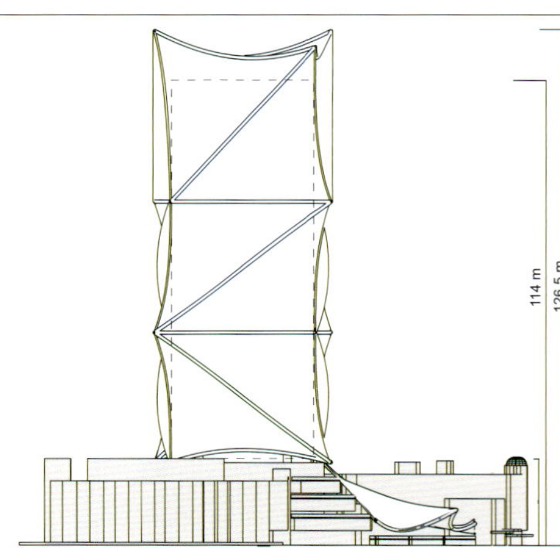

elevation 1:1000

UBUNTU CENTRE

The Ubuntu Centre provides pediatric HIV testing and treatment, counseling, education, and community empowerment. The design is focused on de-stigmatization and normalization of HIV testing and treatment. It provides access to a state-of-the-art facility in a beleaguered post-apartheid community. The design is a model for sustainable development that begins with environment and extends to the preservation of life.

The folded concrete forms read as independent volumes which lean on one another for support, sending the message of Ubuntu, which literally means: "I am because you are." The distributed mass of the building allows pedestrian walkways to continue through the building uninterrupted; rather than entrances being punctured in the facades, the voids are a continuation of the township pathways. This creates a critical sense of community ownership which allows this building to survive in the township context. The clinic is placed an route to other life services to enable anonymous visitors. While fulfilling the centre's service based mission, the architecture attempts to minimize the potential social stigmatization of users. The design sends the message that every child, regardless of race or background, deserves access to world-class health and education.

Concrete, the age-old material of infrastructure creates a sense of permanence and safety. The large, smooth surfaces fold to double as roof and walls which envelope the spaces along the length of the site. The resulting shapes are open on either side, extending a welcome to the community, rather than forming a barrier. The large openings are massive window walls, which allow natural light to penetrate deep inside the spaces of the building. The translucent glass window walls are draped with a curtain made of local gum pole members, called, "Izibonda" which provide both shading and security. The folded concrete surfaces assert the building as a permanent part of the modern world, while the gum pole curtains are inspired by the centuries-old woven thatch craft. The combination of the two initiates a material dialogue between the modern and ancient, the formed and the crafted, and is continued throughout the building in every detail.

COMPANY	Field Architecture
DESIGNER	Stan Field and Jess Field
PHOTOGRAPHER	Jon Riordan, Richard Mills, Jess Field
CLIENT	Ubuntu Education Fund
COUNTRY (DISTRICT)	USA

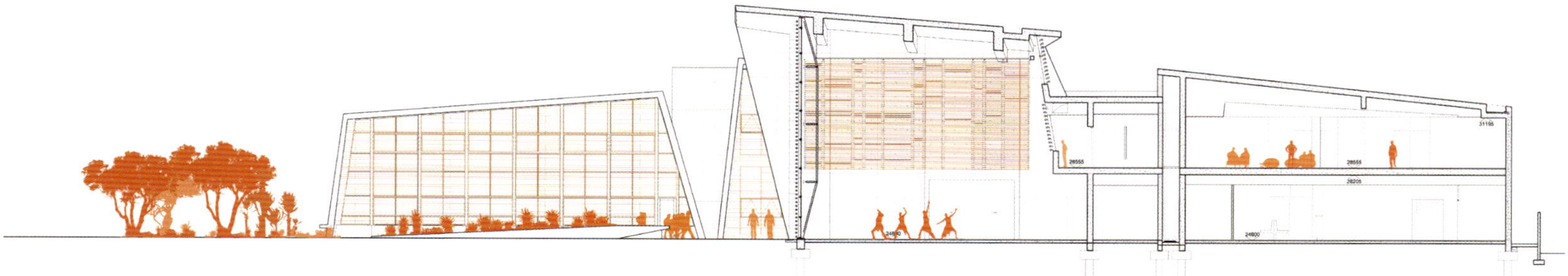

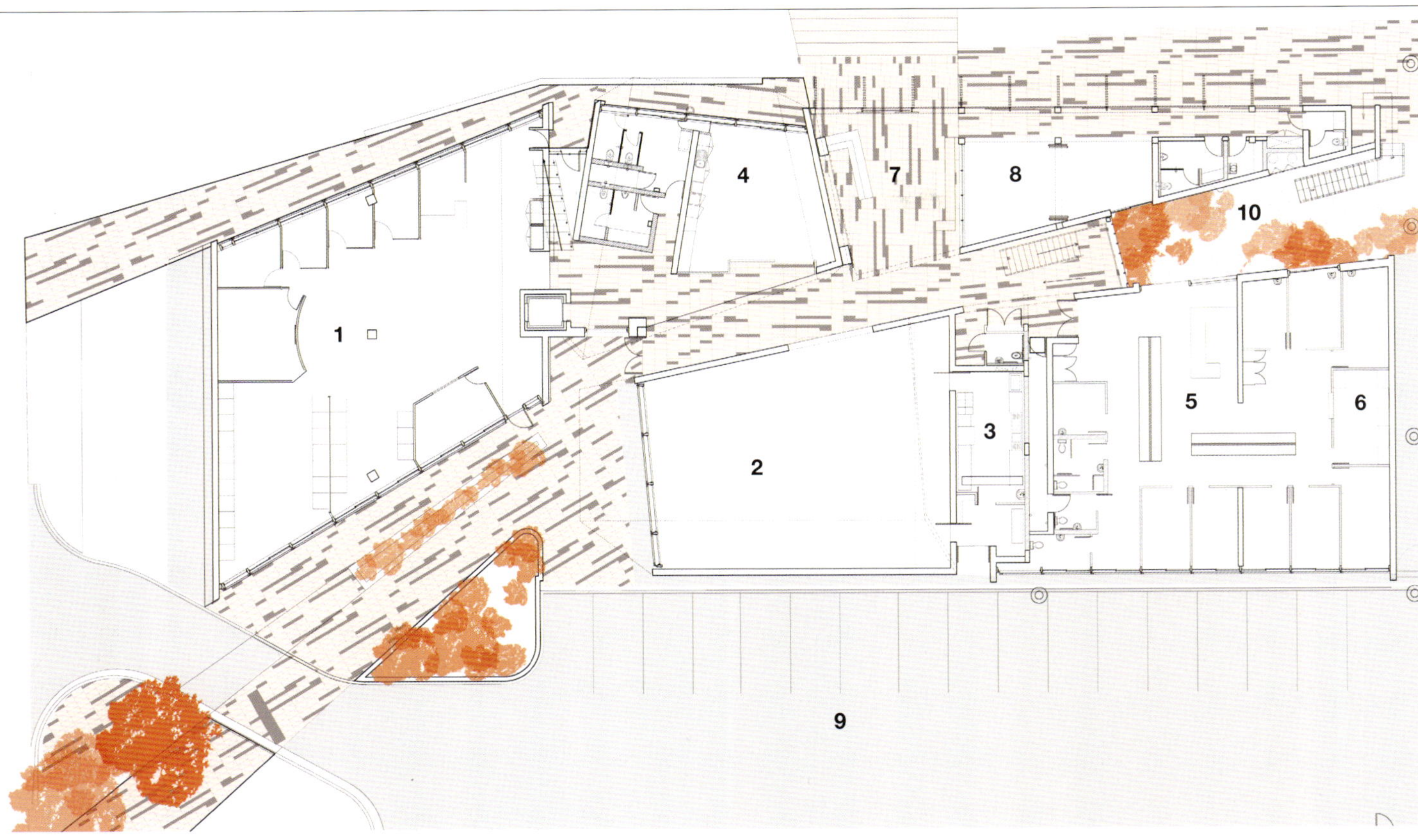

1 Resource/ Computer Learning Centre
2 Multi-Purpose Hall
3 Community Kitchen
4 Staff Lounge
5 Pediatric HIV/TB Clinic
6 Pharmacy
7 Reception/ Entrance Hall
8 Flexible/ Expandable Meeting Rooms
9 Parking
10 Garden Court/ to Rooftop Vegetable Garden

ABUJA NATIONAL COMPLEX

The Cultural Centre and the Millennium Tower of Nigeria, which together with the National Square, make up a single unit, are an eloquent witness to the quality of the great development of the City of Abuja, which from 1991 has been the new capital of Nigeria.
The projected complex extends over two adjoining lots in the cultural, religious and administrative heart of the city. It is set in a dominant urban site, at the intersection of the central axis of the new metropolis, designed by Kenzo Tange, and the cult axis that unites the Catholic Cathedral and the Great Mosque.
The site alongside the Great Mosque takes in the Cultural Centre and a Botanical Garden where, among other things, the Museum of Nigerian Art and the scientific discovery of Nature are blended harmoniously. It will be the venue of the cultural identity of Nigeria designed to foster meetings, studies and relaxation.
On the lot adjacent to the Great Mosque we find the Millenium Tower, a 'lighthouse tower' of 170 metres high which dominates 'National Square' rising above an underground parking lot with places for 1100 cars. The Millenium Tower grows from the ground, like a flower surrounded by transparent wings on which is stamped the luminous symbol of the Nation that is visible also by day and is crowned with white and green laser rays.

COMPANY	Studio Nicoletti Associati
CREATIVE DIRECTOR	Manfredi Nicoletti
DESIGNER	Manfredi Nicoletti
PHOTOGRAPHER	Studio Nicoletti Associati
CLIENT	Federal Republic of Nigeria, Ministry of Culture and Tourism
COUNTRY (DISTRICT)	Italy

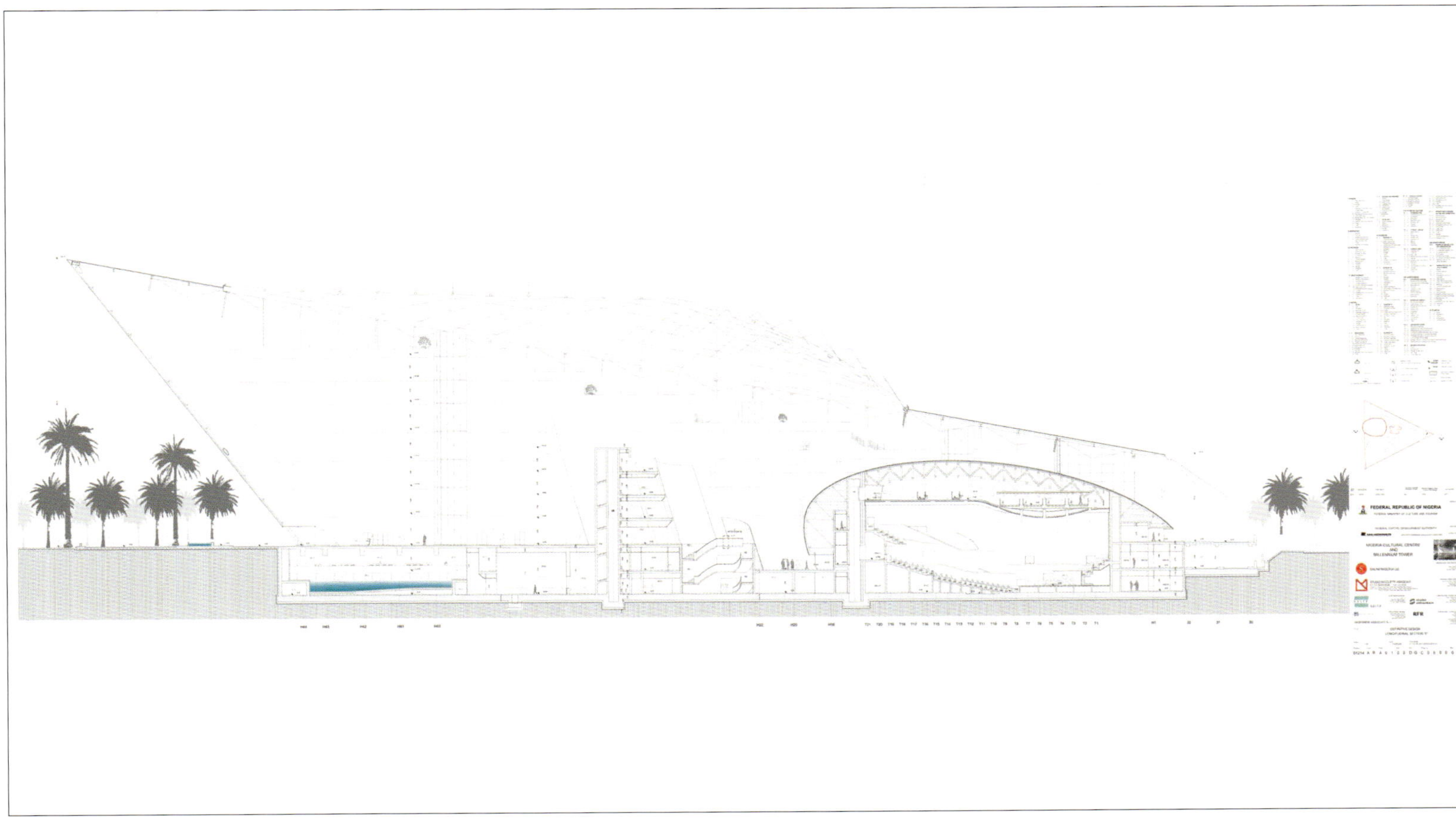

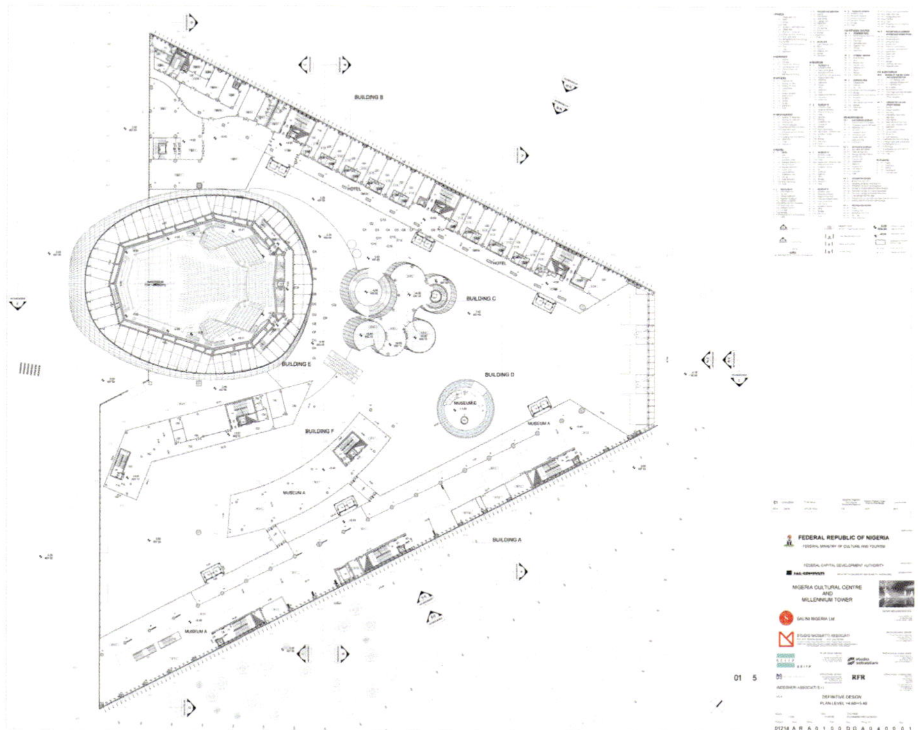

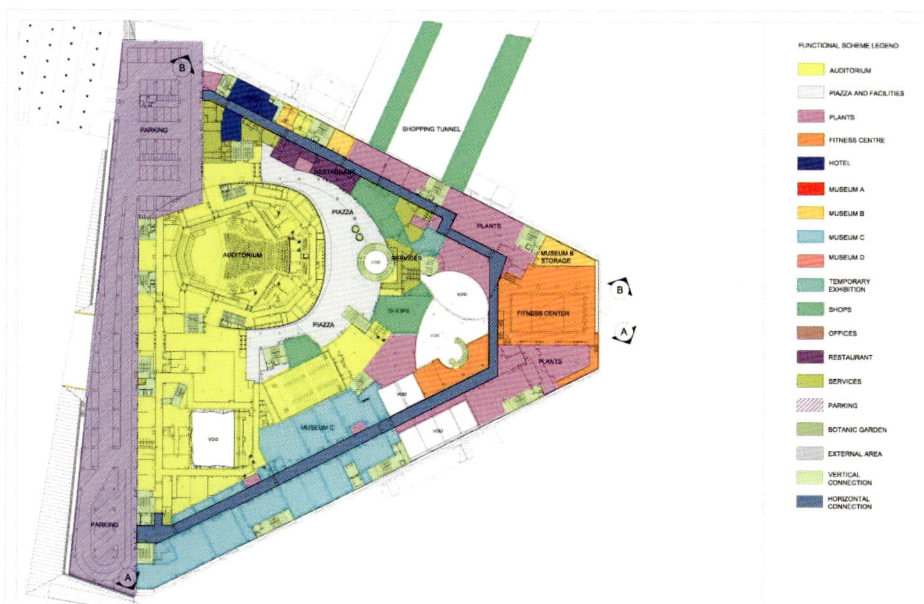

NIGERIA CULTURAL CENTER FUNCTIONAL SCHEME

LEVEL -4.45

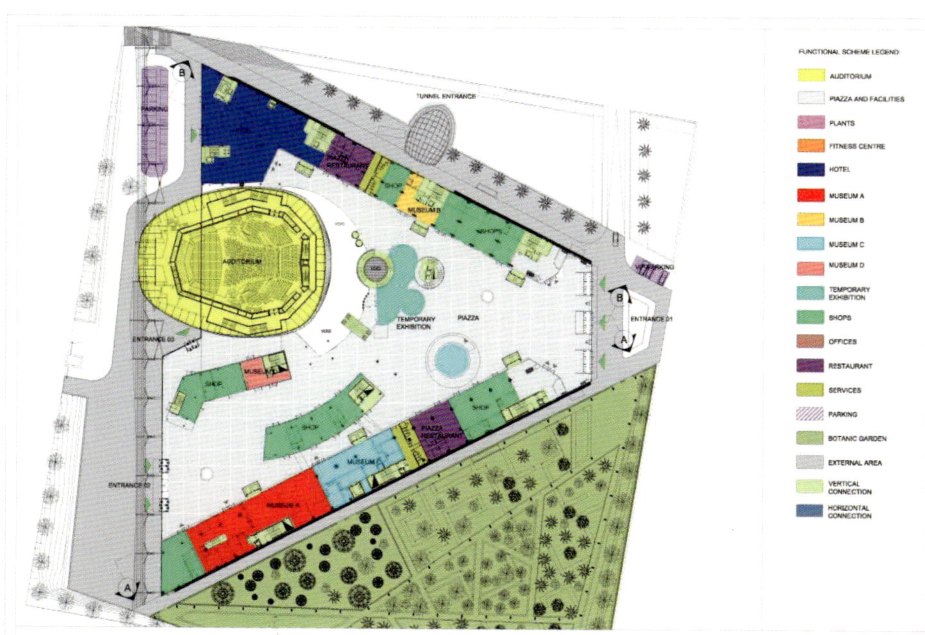

NIGERIA CULTURAL CENTER FUNCTIONAL SCHEME

LEVEL +0.05

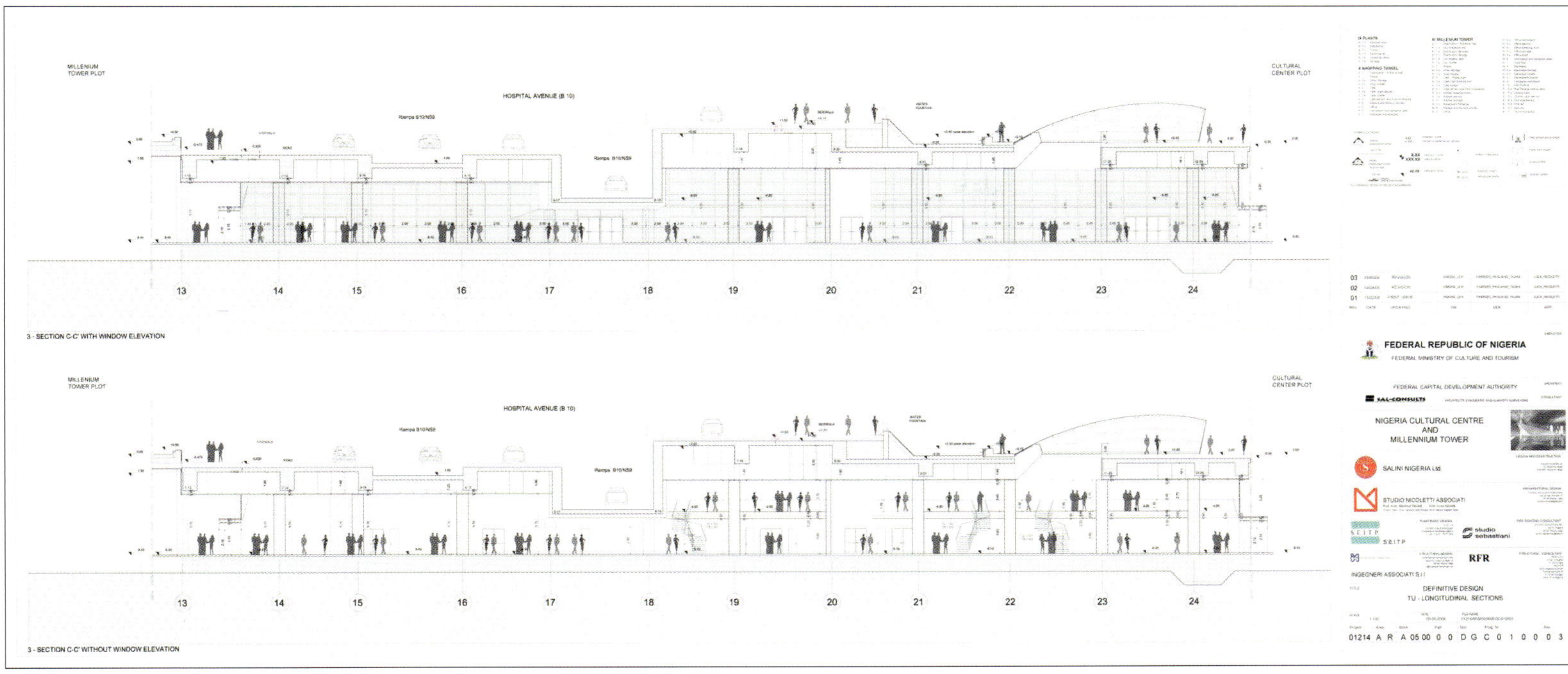
MILLENIUM TOWER PLOT
HOSPITAL AVENUE (B 10)
CULTURAL CENTER PLOT
3 - SECTION C-C' WITH WINDOW ELEVATION
3 - SECTION C-C' WITHOUT WINDOW ELEVATION
FEDERAL REPUBLIC OF NIGERIA
NIGERIA CULTURAL CENTRE AND MILLENNIUM TOWER
SALINI NIGERIA Ltd
STUDIO NICOLETTI ASSOCIATI
DEFINITIVE DESIGN
TU - LONGITUDINAL SECTIONS

M4 FŐVÁM TÉR UNDERGROUND STATION

Having the new underground station, "FŐVÁM TÉR" will become a new gateway of the historic downtown of Pest. Only a complex structural system could fulfill the requirements emerging from the proximity of the Danube and the given construction site. The "FŐVÁM TÉR" station is composed of a cut-and-cover box and tunnels.

The station box is supported by three levels of reinforced concrete beams. The structure is similar to a net, which keeps the walls of the box like a bone structure. The design of the box is determined by this sight of concrete net structure.

More information: http://www.sporaarchitects.hu

COMPANY	Sporaarchitects
DESIGNER	Sporaarchitects, Palatium Stúdió
PHOTOGRAPHER	Tamás Bujnovszky
CLIENT	DBR Metró Projekt Igazgatóság
COUNTRY (DISTRICT)	Hungary

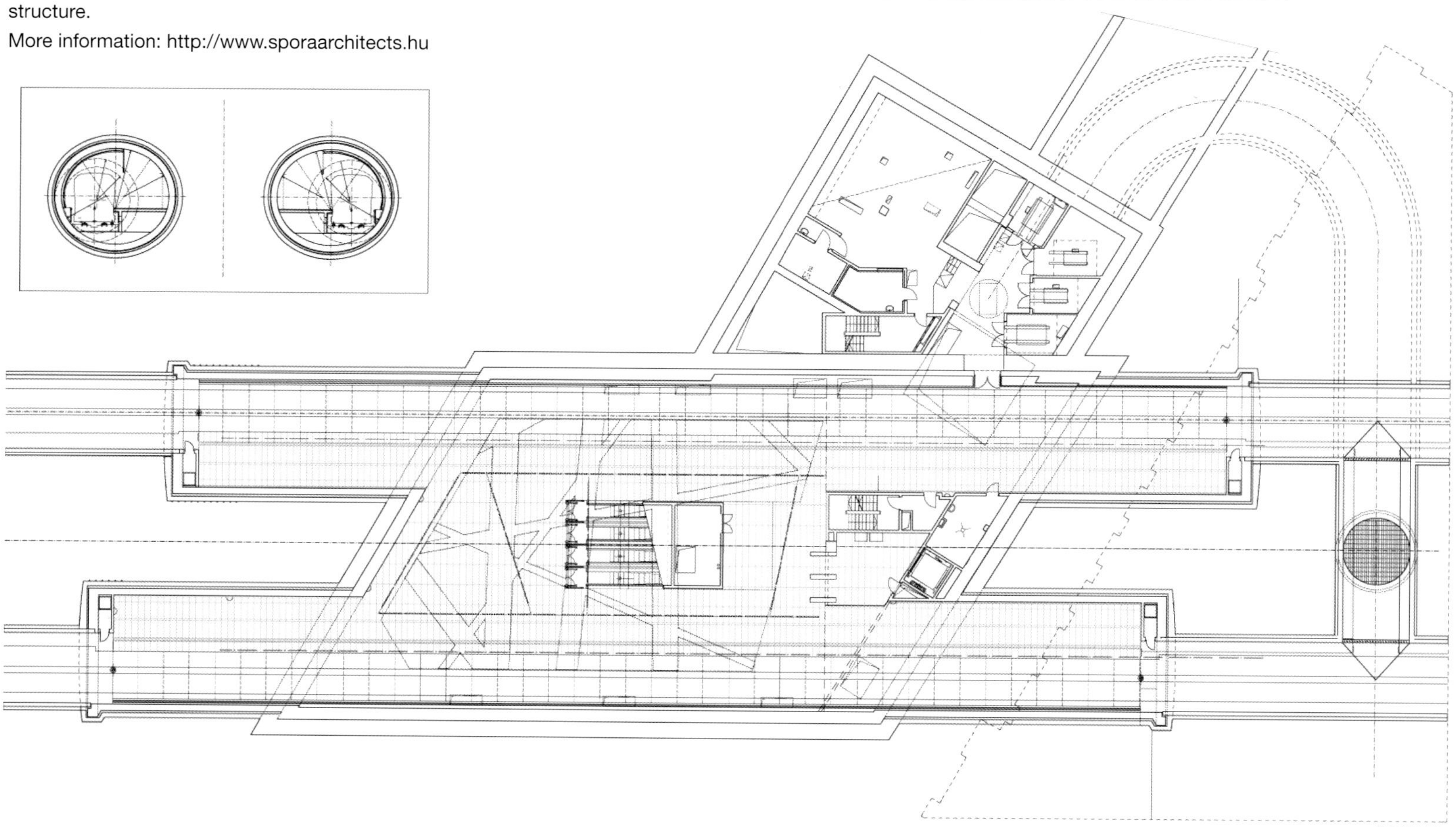

PLATFORM LEVEL

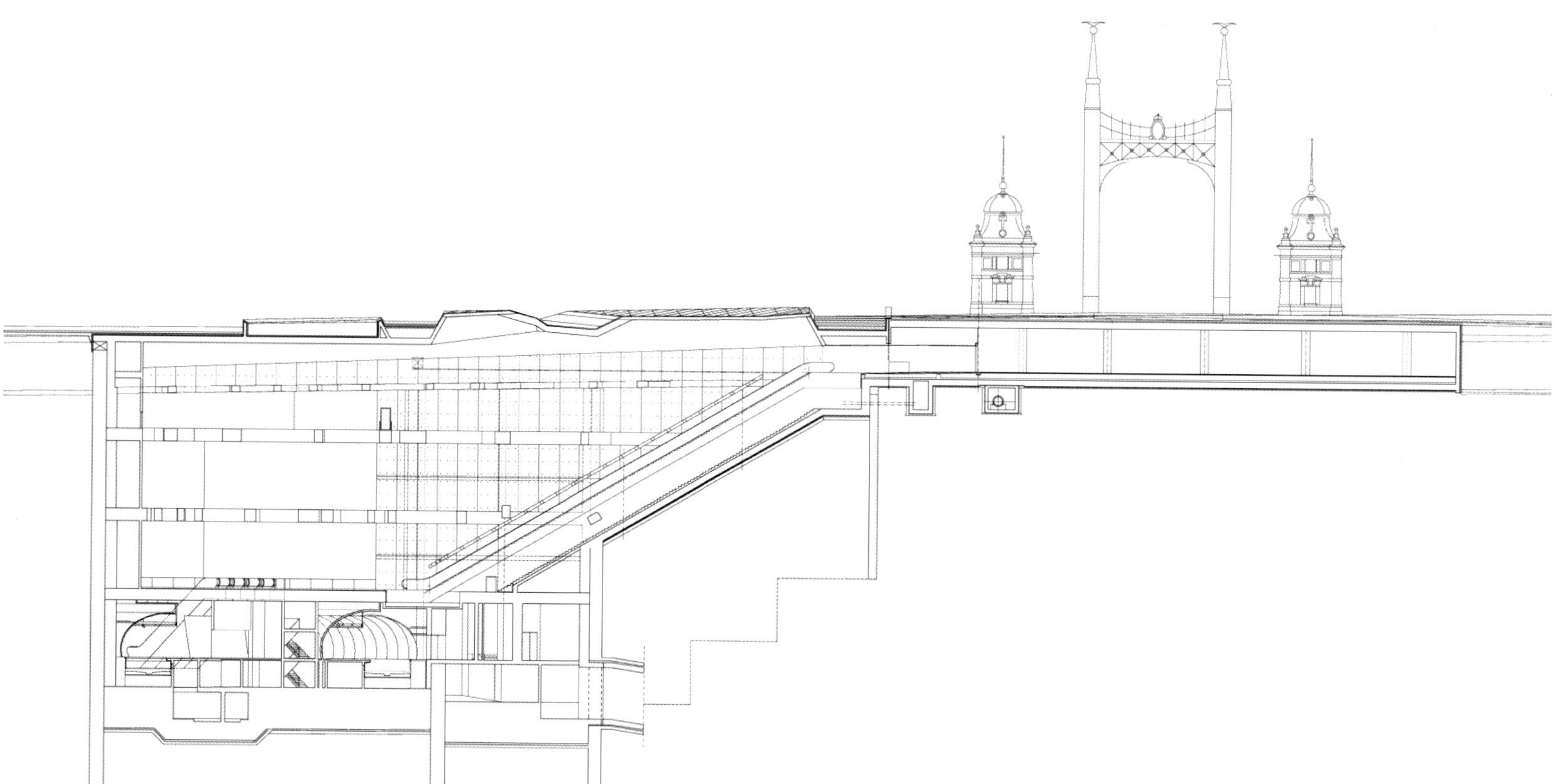

LIGTHSAILS

Lightsails as guiding symbols for the exhibition around the Millstaetter lake, Austria. The lighthouse is used as a metaphor to guide the visitors around the different exhibitions. Nowadays the lighthouse is used as a symbol of holidays, sea, adventure and water.

The objects are abstract sails, as a "light-space installation".The objects are orientated to the lake.

The lake Millstättersee is getting a tribune out of water, because the energy of the lake is trapped, converted and reflected as light. So the sails are working as a transmitter and receiver at the same time.

The illumination is reacting to the surrounding – the more people approaching the sails the more vibrate light. The illumination is also reacting to the temperature – they are constantly changing the color. The colder the temperature the warmer the color if light is getting.

COMPANY	Söhne & Partner Architekten
DESIGNER	Söhne & Partner Architekten
PHOTOGRAPHER	Gisela Erlacher
CLIENT	MTG
COUNTRY (DISTRICT)	Austria

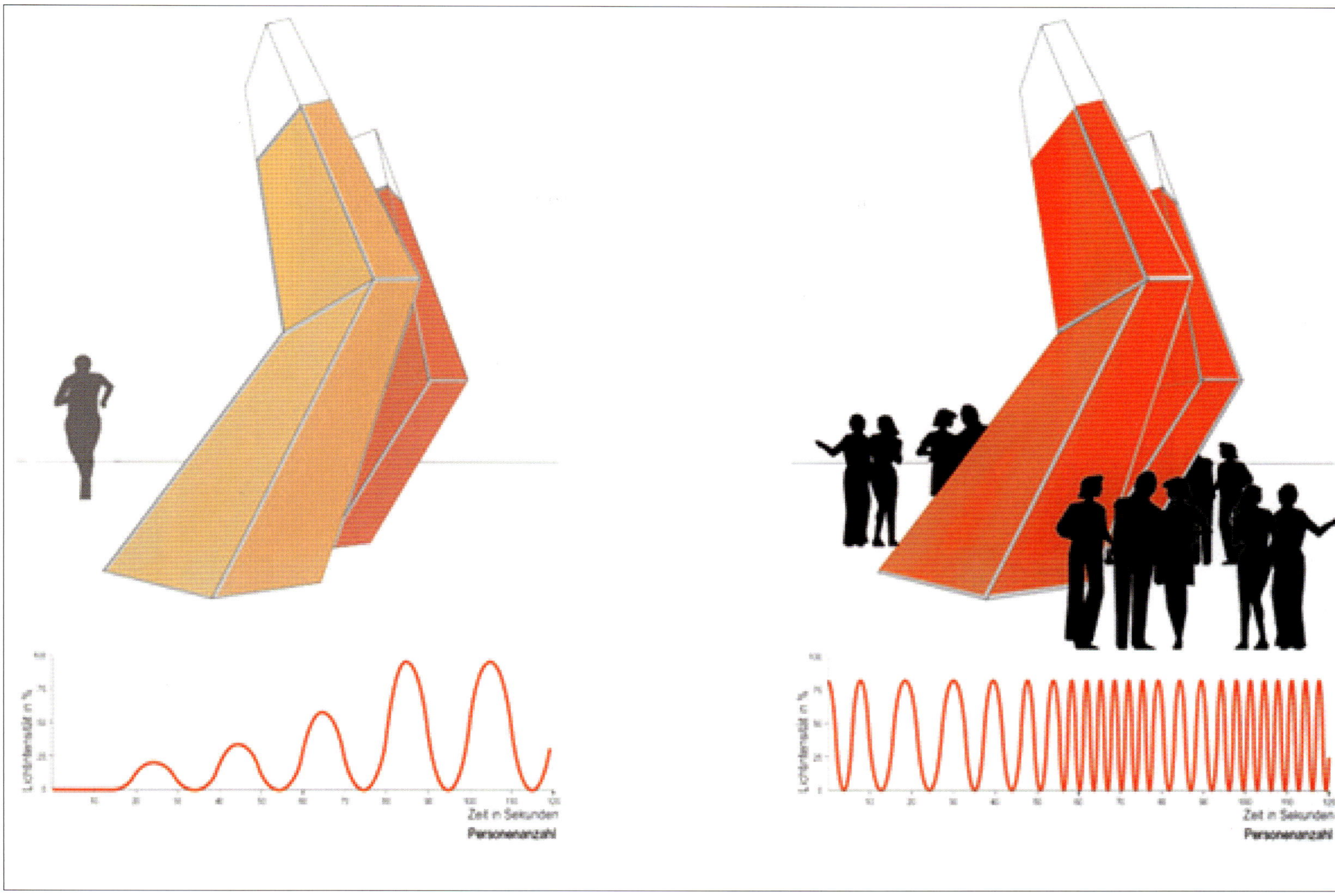
Zeit in Sekunden
Personenanzahl
Zeit in Sekunden
Personenanzahl

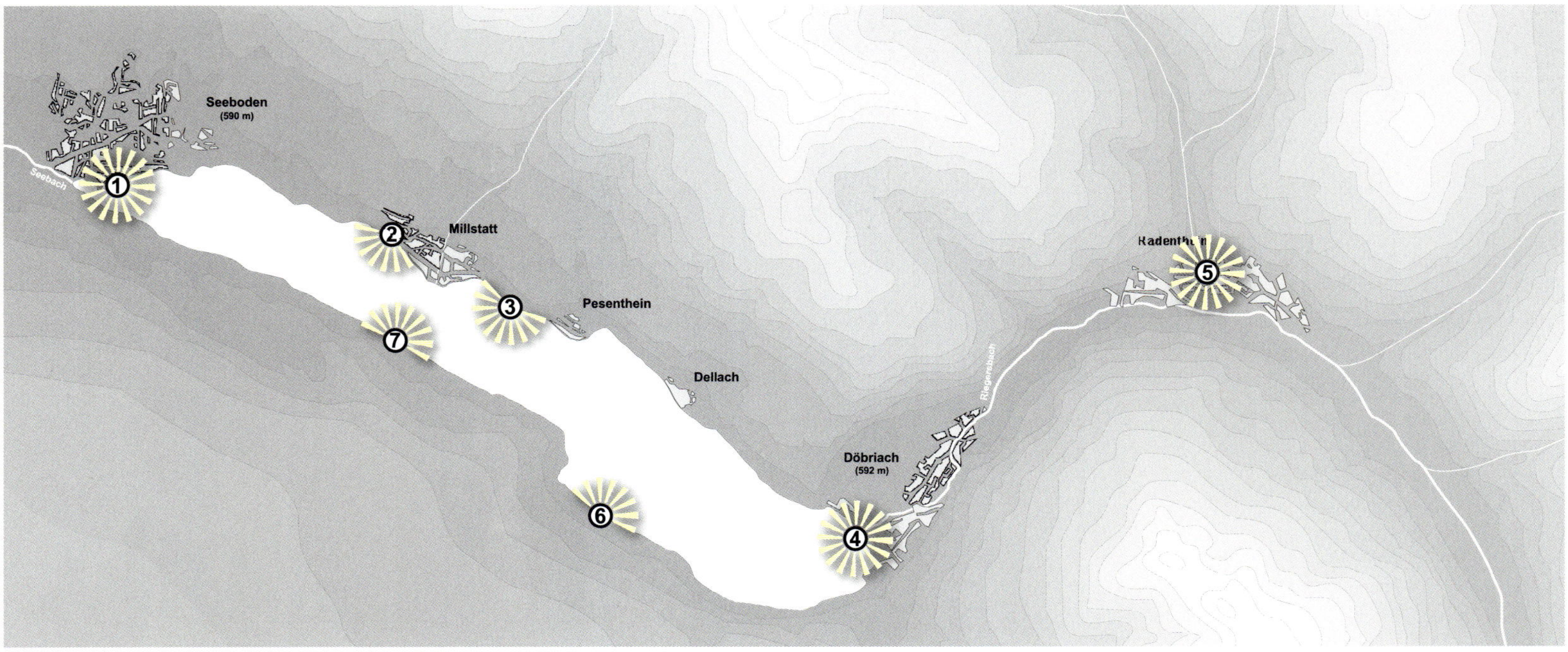
Seeboden
(590 m)
Seebach
Millstatt
Pesenthein
Dellach
Döbriach
(592 m)
Radenthein

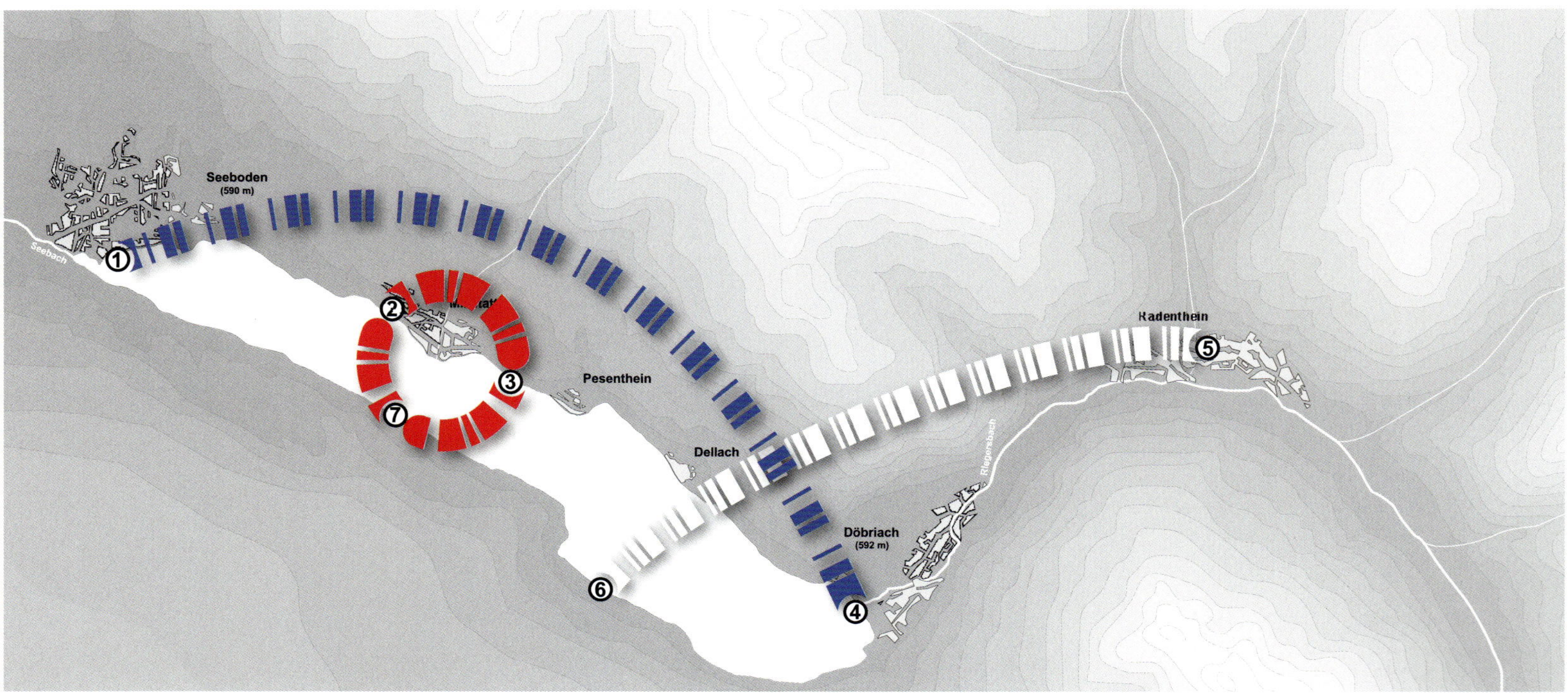
Seeboden
(590 m)
Seebach
Pesenthein
Dellach
Döbriach
(592 m)
Radenthein

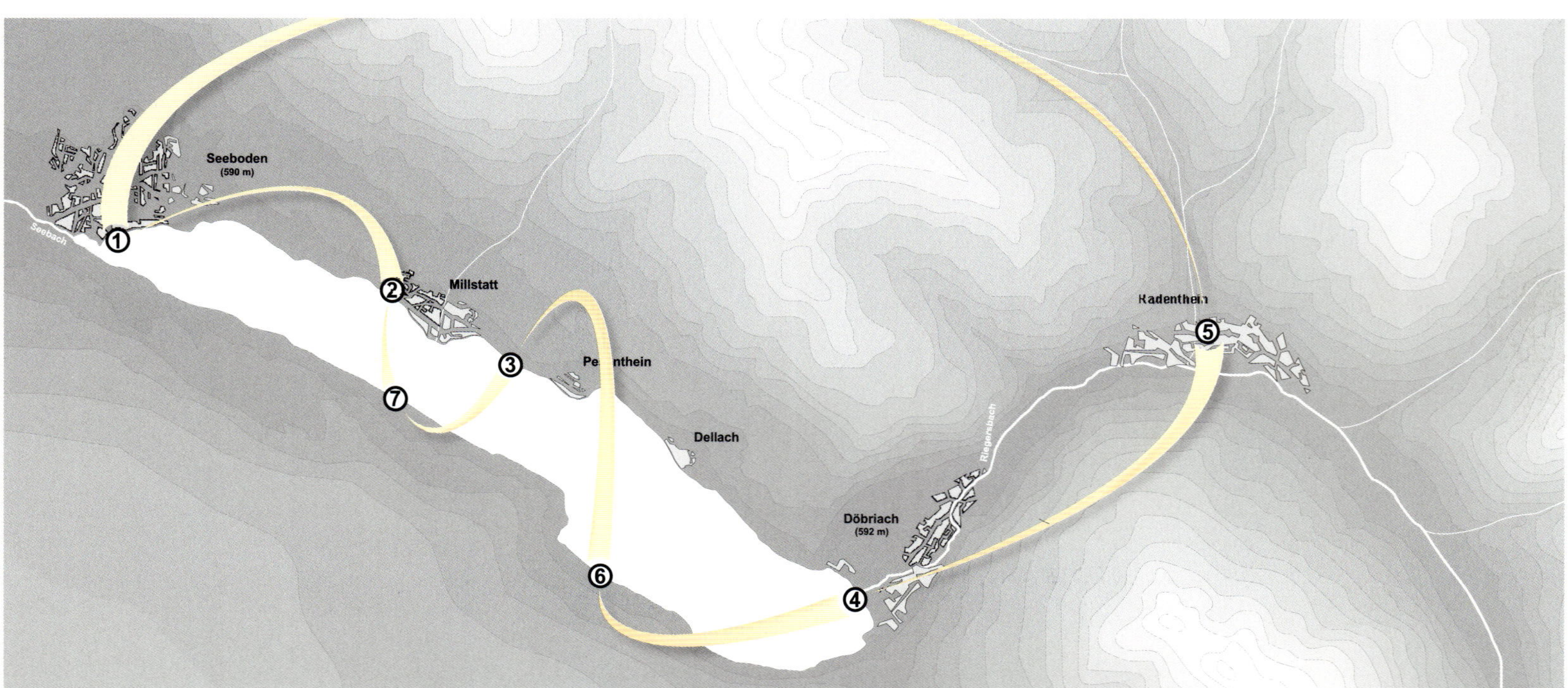
Seeboden
(590 m)
Seebach
Millstatt
Dellach
Döbriach
(592 m)
Radenthein

PERES PEACE HOUSE

A home port for all sailors and a haven for the shipwrecked. To imagine a place that is not virtual, but real. To be dedicated to Peace, is an immensely taxing undertaking of profound ethical significance. Peace is a spiritual condition, an aspiration: tension and utopia. The projection of will into the future is also an expression of hope that our children and future generation will live in a better world. Peace cannot be enclosed in wrapping: it's rather a sensation of fullness and serenity that can be communicated through a place, or through architecture. I have thought of a series of layers, a building that represents time and patience in strata of alternating materials representing places that have suffered heavily. Concrete is composed of alternating and superimposed types of sand and aggregate. A stone basement to raise the building, a meeting place from which two long staircase lead to a place of "rest", whose size and height, full of light from above, helps us to forget the troubles of the world, and fill us with the positive attitude that is needed for our meeting with other men and other women. The outside of the building has alternate layers of concrete and translucent glass. The transparency of the glass will filter the light through to the inside during the day, and by night will send it back outside, entrusting this magical image with the spiritual and concrete message the site will inspire.

Architecture today must set itself as an aid, a hand to help us cope with the difficulties of understanding. This project represents the venue of an encounter, a debate, reasoning and solutions. The Peres Centre for Peace is a parallelepiped. Obtained by irregularly shaped glass and concrete layers standing on a monolithic base: at one end of the building is the entrance to the car park, at the other is the pedestrians entrance. At this point the basement becomes a large plaza, an empty space dissected lengthwise by two symmetrical ramps leading inside. This dark and low-ceilinged area leads to the inside of the well of light that is open for the whole height of the building, where the reception area is situated. From here the alternating light and dark layers are visible; the former, in glass, lit from the outside and the latter, in concrete mixed with other materials and local earth.

The rest of this floor (which totals 550 m^2) is designed to house the reception area and exhibition hall. The remaining six floors, each covering a space of 600 m^2 and a height of 3-4 m. house on the first one, office facilities, a library and cafeteria; on the second floor there is an auditorium to seat 200 people (with a height of 7 m.), the press room and the press conference hall; the members and guest cafeteria is on the third floor with the library and the Mediatheque, the fourth and fifth floors offices and meeting rooms and the sixth contains ten apartments.

COMPANY	Massimiliano Fuksas Architetto
DESIGNER	Massimiliano Fuksas Architetto
CLIENT	Peres Center for Peace
COUNTRY (DISTRICT)	Italy

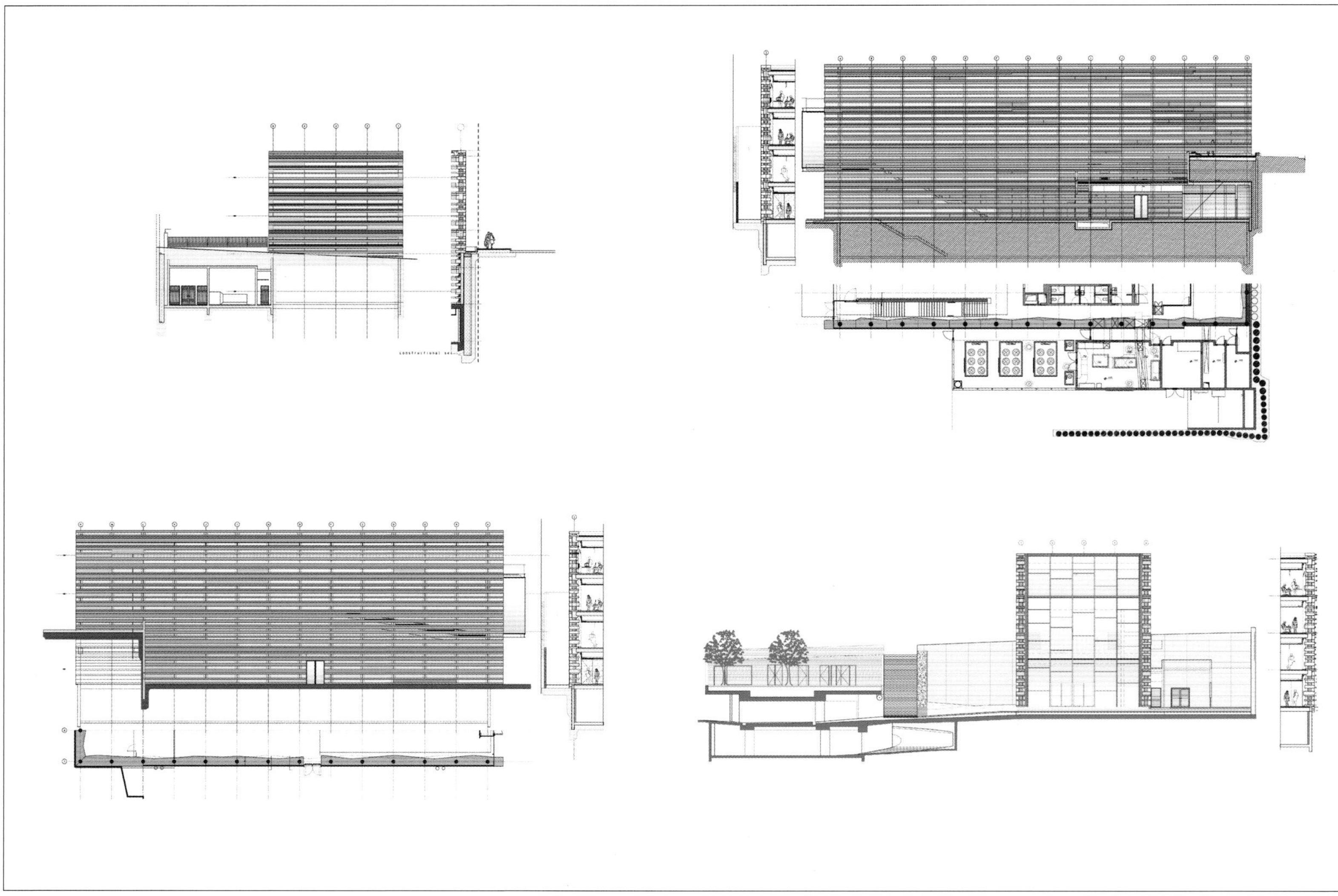

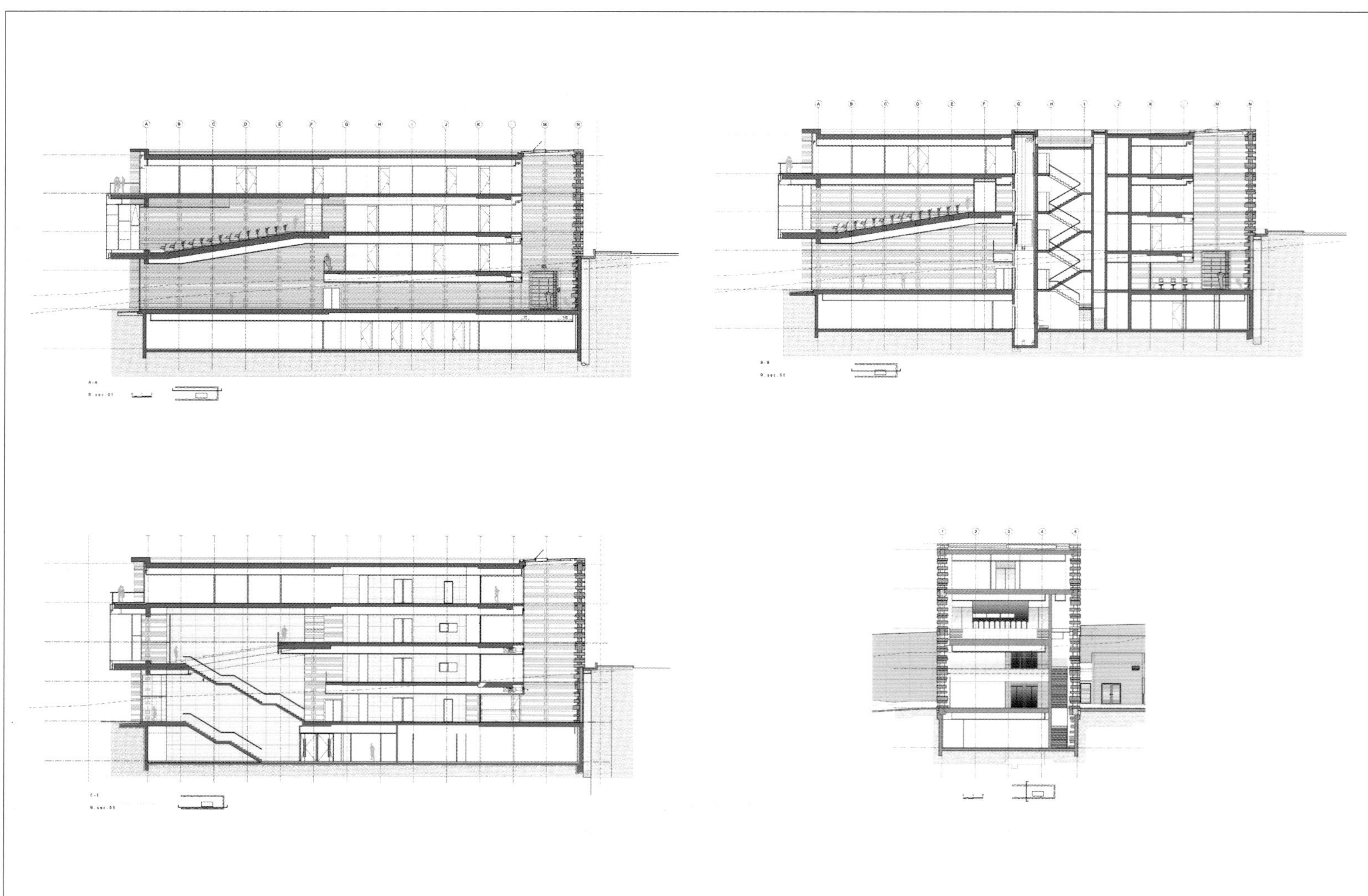

SAN PAULO PARISH COMPLEX

This project won the national competition organized by the Italian Episcopal Conference to design new parish centres: "to provide an innovative and decisive landmark in accordance with the latest international research and symbolising the rebirth of the city after the earthquake".
The new parish complex is composed of two main elements, which also serve the purpose of providing a religious centre. The first feature, the church, is a monolith designed in a pure geometric form, a box within a box measuring 30x22.5m by 25 m in height.
The second feature, an elongated low parallelepiped, holds the Vestry, Pastoral Ministry rooms and Canonical House. A third translucent structure, the Weekday Chapel, both joins together and distinguishes the two main structures. A thrust towards spirituality and quiet prayer blend together in an interplay of beams of natural light crossing the structure both transversely and vertically, projecting towards the main features, the Altar, Ambo and Baptismal Font.
The striking structure is raised one and a half meters above grade level. It can be reached by crossing a parvis, along walkway leading to the entrance, a clean horizontal cut into the absolute compactness marking the entire front elevation. A beam of light which interacts with the outside.
All the furniture have been designed by local craftsmen. They even help alter how we perceive the works of certain artists.The artist Enzo Cucchi designed the monumental "Pole-Cross" sculpture outside the church, which is 13.50m tall and made of concrete and white Carrara marble,actually turning into an architectural feature itself.The artist Mimmo Paladino created the 14 stations along the Via Crucis.

COMPANY	Massimiliano Fuksas Architetto
DESIGNER	Massimiliano Fuksas Architetto
CLIENT	Conferenza Episcopale Italiana – Diocesi di Foligno
COUNTRY (DISTRICT)	Italy

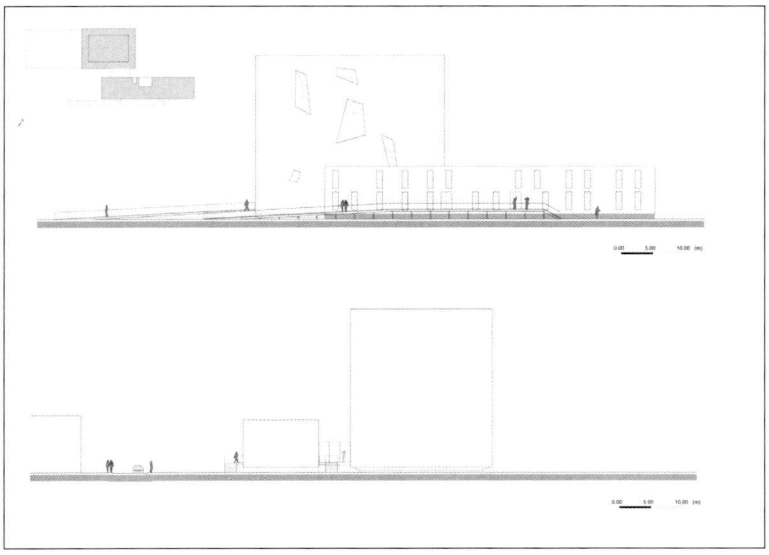

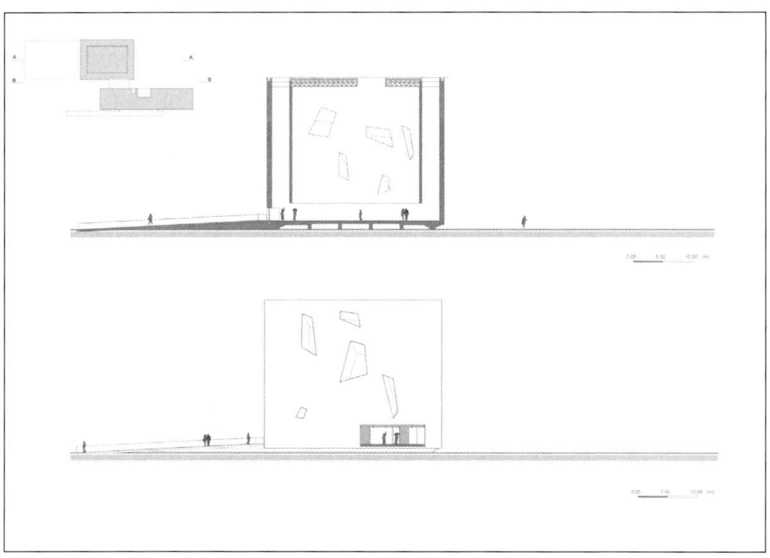

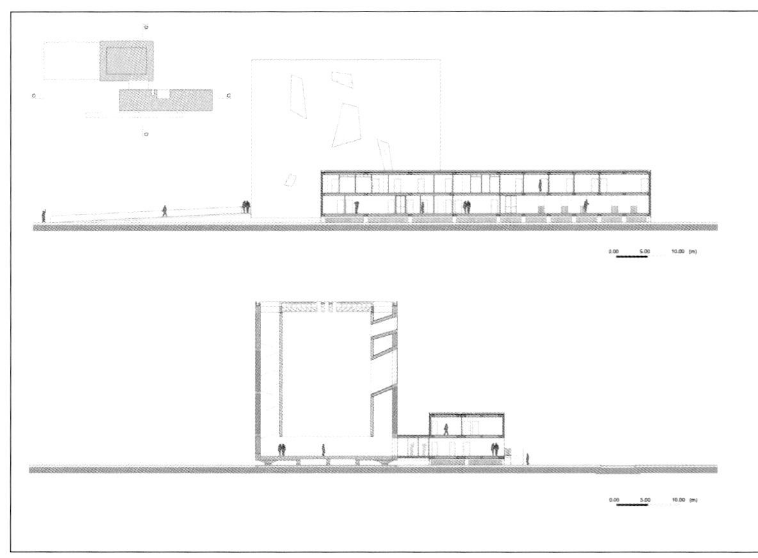

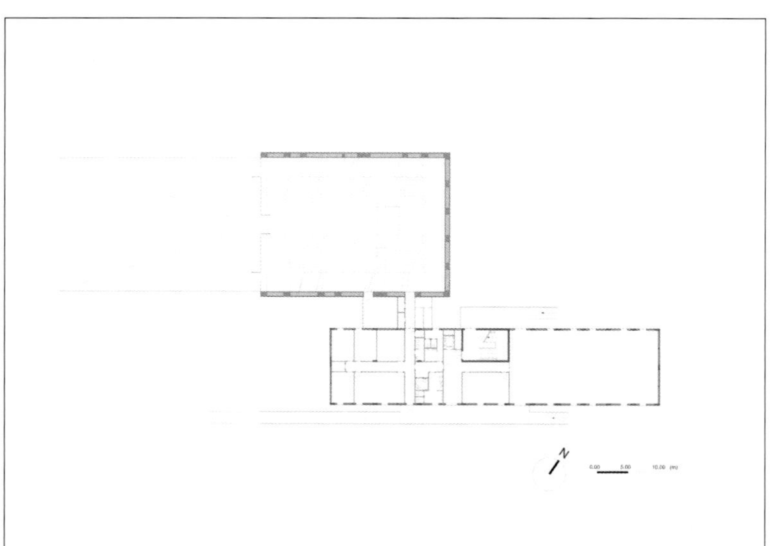

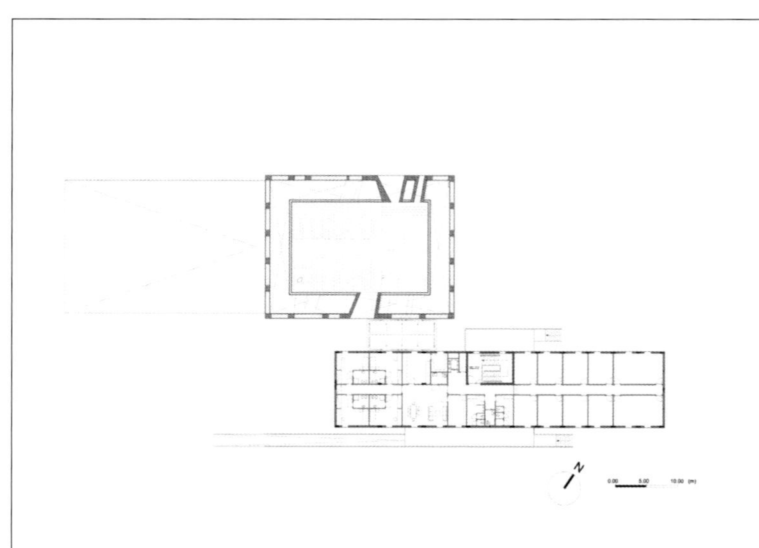

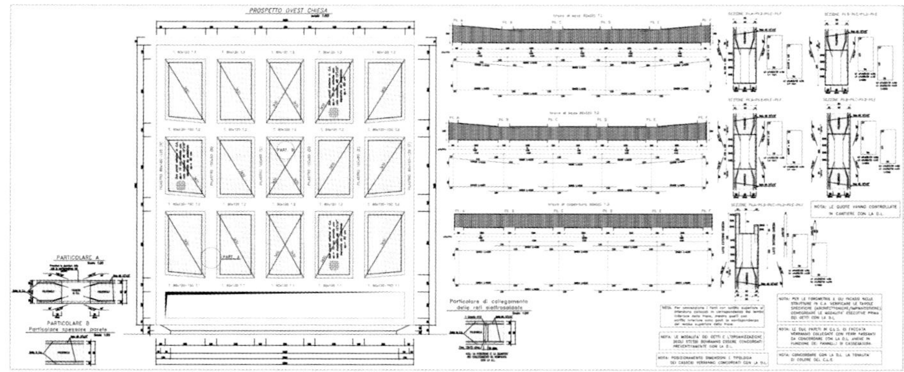
PROSPETTO OVEST CHIESA
PARTICOLARE A
PARTICOLARE B
Particolare spessore parete
Particolare di collegamento delle reti elettrosaldate
NOTA: LE QUOTE VANNO CONTROLLATE IN CANTIERE CON LA D.L.

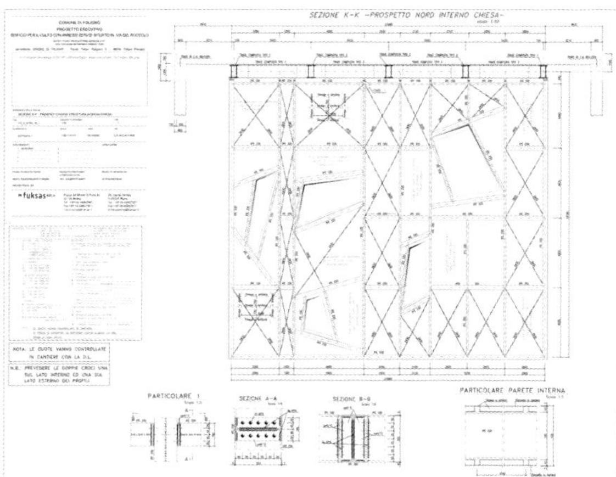
SEZIONE K-K -PROSPETTO NORD INTERNO CHIESA-
PARTICOLARE 1
SEZIONE A-A
SEZIONE B-B
PARTICOLARE PARETE INTERNA

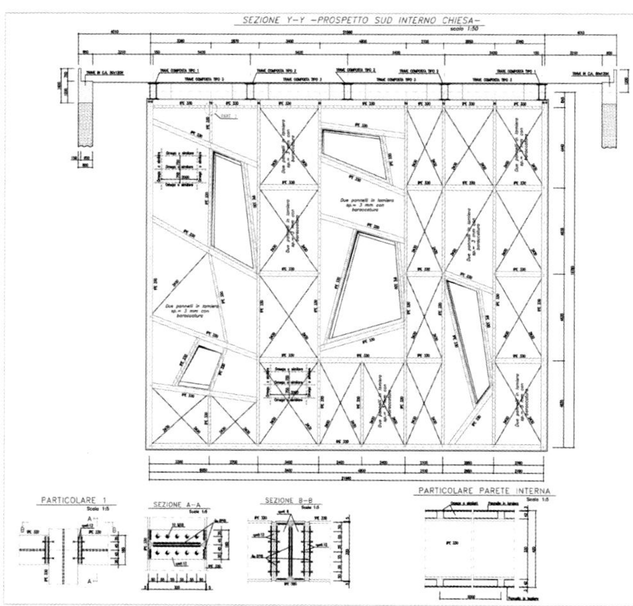
SEZIONE Y-Y -PROSPETTO SUD INTERNO CHIESA-
PARTICOLARE 1
SEZIONE A-A
SEZIONE B-B
PARTICOLARE PARETE INTERNA

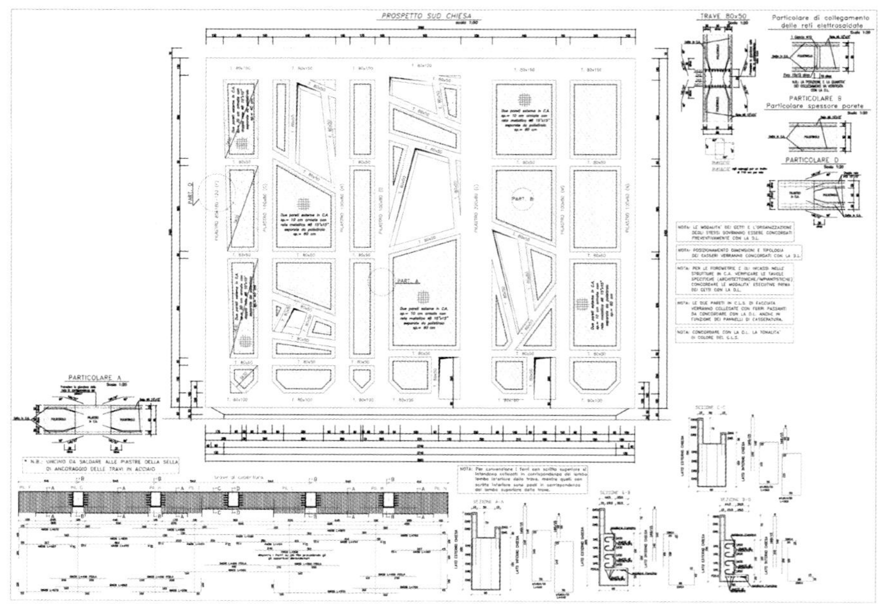
PROSPETTO SUD CHIESA
TRAVE 80x50
Particolare di collegamento delle reti elettrosaldate
PARTICOLARE B
Particolare spessore parete
PARTICOLARE D
PARTICOLARE A

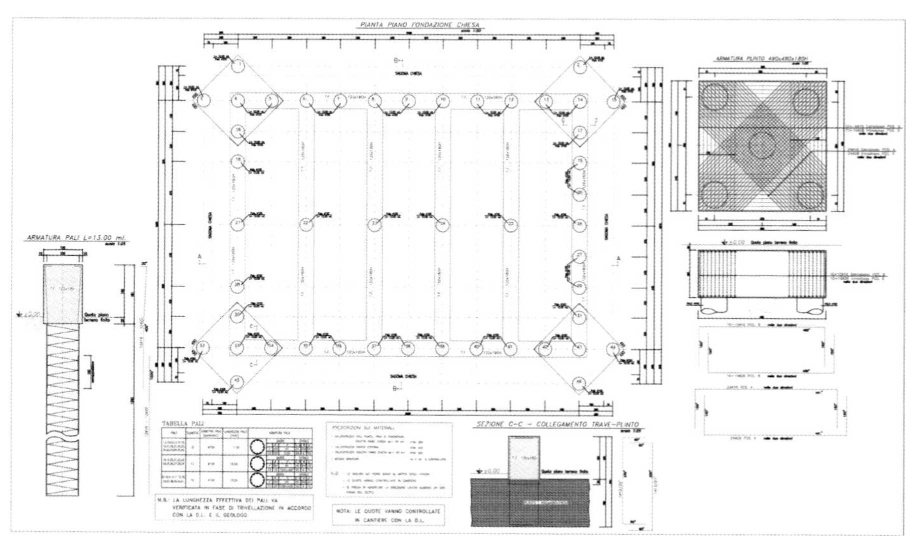
PIANTA PIANO FONDAZIONE CHIESA
ARMATURA PLINTO
ARMATURA PALI L=13.00 ml
TABELLA PALI
SEZIONE C-C - COLLEGAMENTO TRAVE-PLINTO
N.B. LA LUNGHEZZA EFFETTIVA DEI PALI VA VERIFICATA IN FASE DI TRIVELLAZIONE IN ACCORDO CON LA D.L. E IL GEOLOGO
NOTA: LE QUOTE VANNO CONTROLLATE IN CANTIERE CON LA D.L.

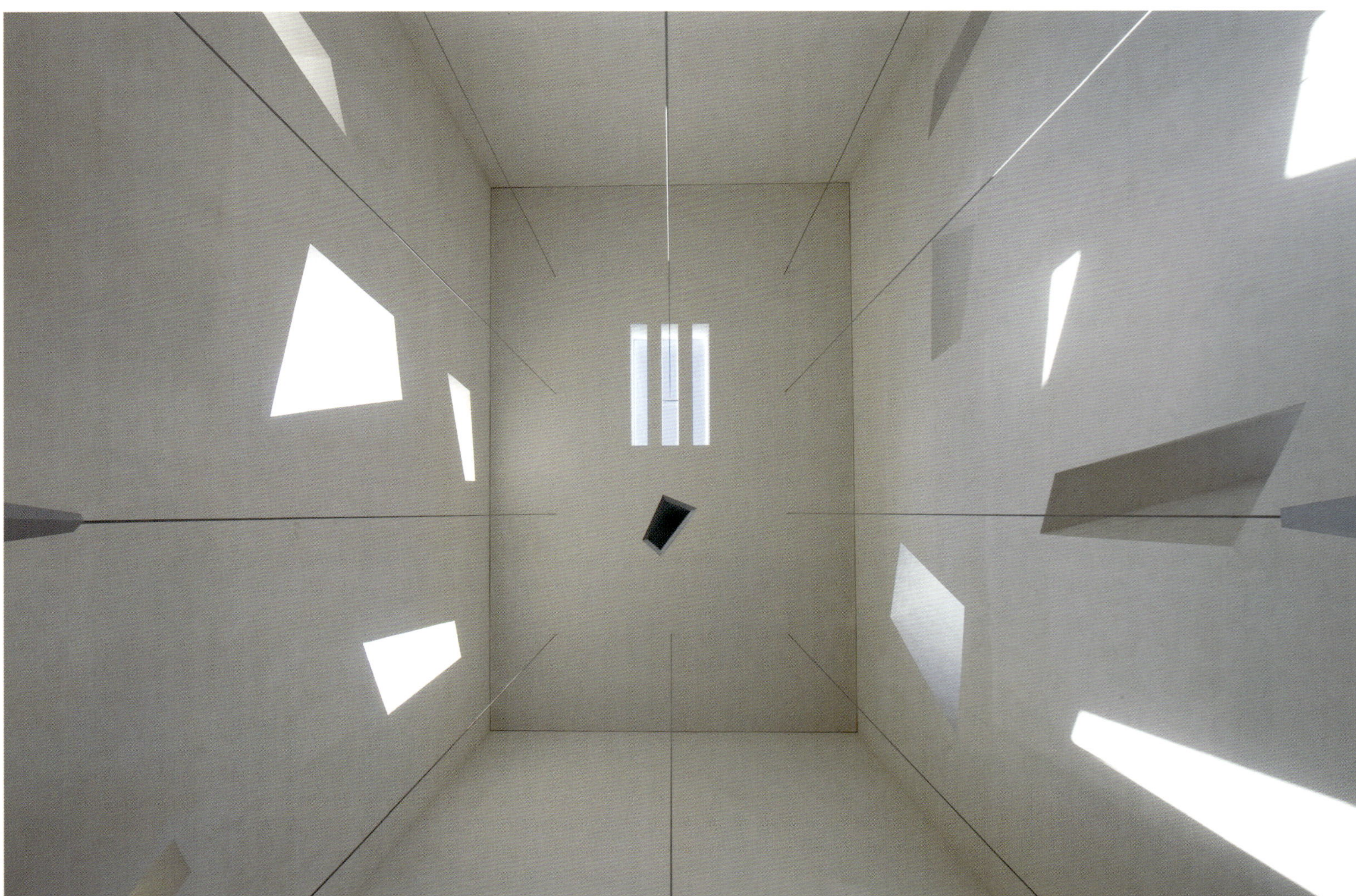

KAROO WILDERNESS CENTER

The landscape of the Karoo is elemental, in excess of nothing. From its inception, life in the Karoo has been defined by struggle. The minimal amount of rainfall has resulted in a parched condition in which each species of plant and animal has had to adapt, utilizing an economy of means in order to exist. Human inhabitation, a relatively recent phenomenon in the palpably long history of life here, has demanded more of the landscape than it can sustain, bringing it to the brink of irreversible depletion.

The Karoo Wilderness Center represents a significant shift in perspective and practice, sponsoring and provoking the learning, dialogue, and action necessary to redefine the consequence of human inhabitation on the land. The Center aims to re-establish the connection between the built and natural world as one that is mutually beneficial. Forming an exemplary model of sustainability, the Center generates its own energy, harvests its own water, processes its own waste, and provides thermal comfort using no municipal water or power. Learning from the continuum of life in the Karoo, the architecture of the Center provides a lasting connection to the landscape, and fosters an understanding of the interdependence of ecosystem health, and human well-being.

Water, its absence as much as its presence, is a critical aspect of the formation and cognitive experience of the Karoo landscape. It is the relative scarcity of water that has determined the physical constitution and adaptations of the flora and fauna to the environment of the Karoo. Exemplified by the Aloe ferox - the predominant succulent found on the site and region - the structure and form of plant species is characterized primarily by strategies to collect and retain water and provide a shield from the sun. These qualities, which are result of opportunistic utility, make the Karoo what it is today, and are expressed through the architecture of the Center.

The reconstitution of local materials through the architecture of the Center provokes an intimate experience of the immediate site. Concrete walls provide thermal mass, as well as critical earth retention. Formed using aggregate from the site itself, the concrete walls extend the colors and hues of the earth through the buildings, recalling the raw material of the ground. Constructed using shallow horizontal pours, each layer is expressed, creating strata that reveal the wall's method of formation, echoing the geologic striations visible in the surrounding mountains. The curved undersides of the roofs are clad with thin wooden strands that bend to define the cupped form of the roof. Small gaps between each slat allow the imperfections and character of each piece to be celebrated, giving the effect of a hand crafted tapestry.

COMPANY	Field Architecture
DESIGNER	Stan Field and Jess Field
PHOTOGRAPHER	Field Architecture
COUNTRY (DISTRICT)	USA

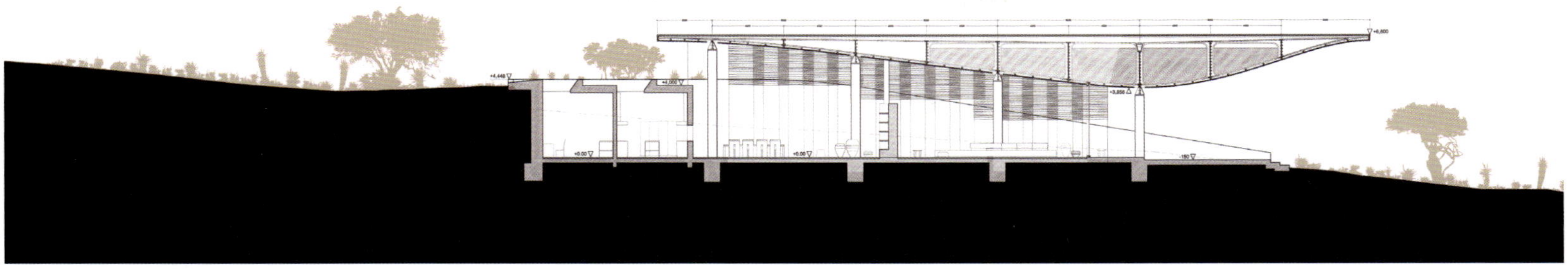

Section aa
Scale 1:200

Section bb
Scale 1:200

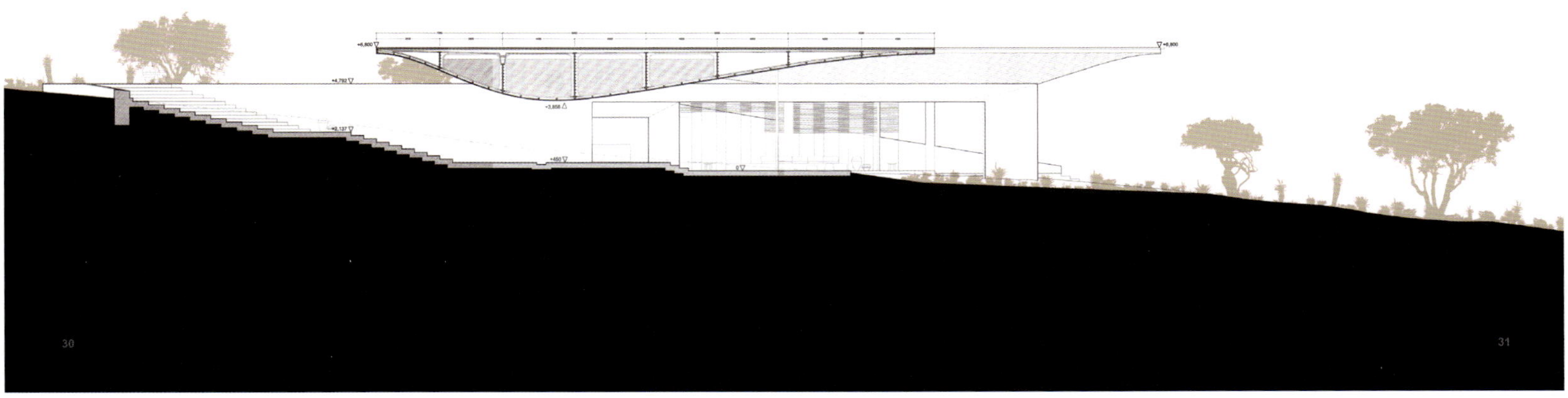

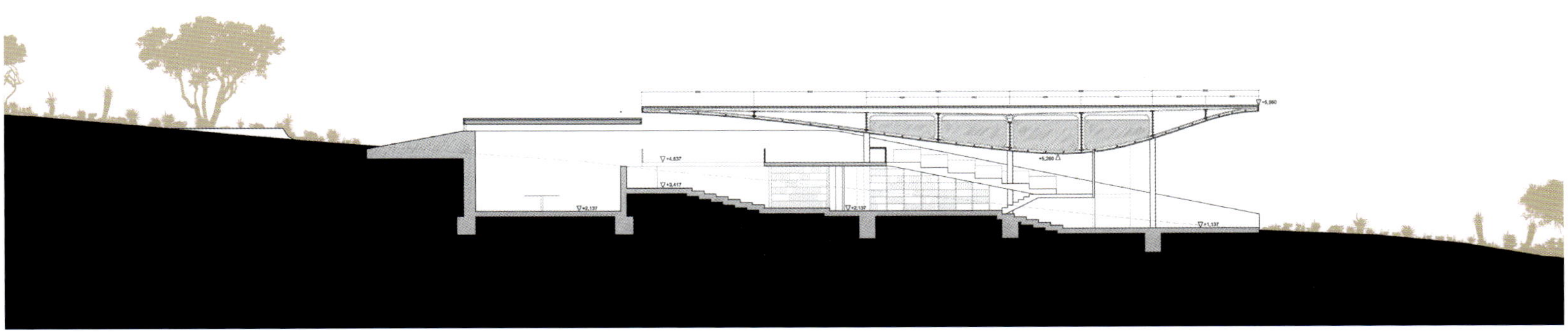

Section cc
Scale 1:200

Section dd
Scale 1:200

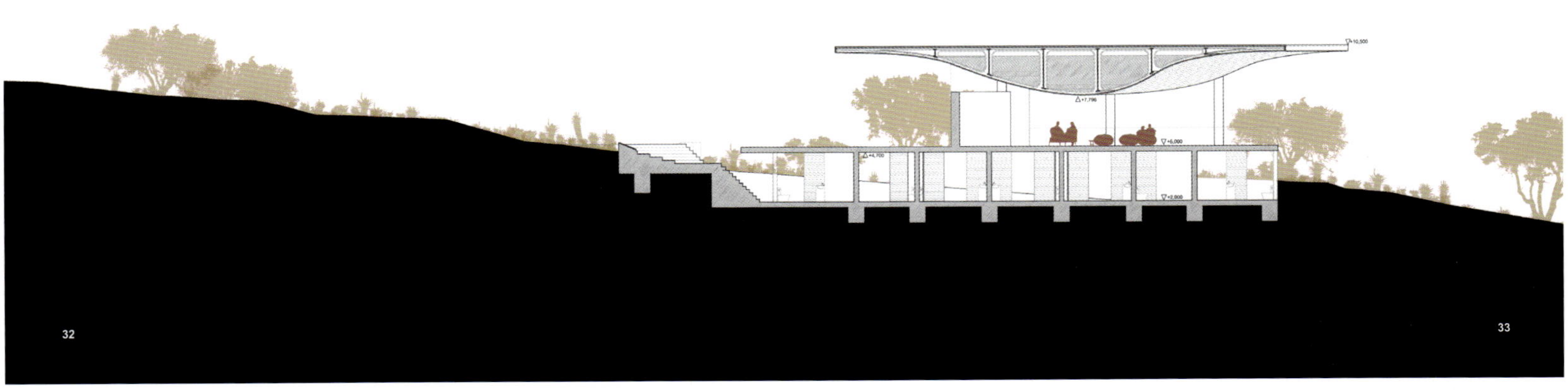

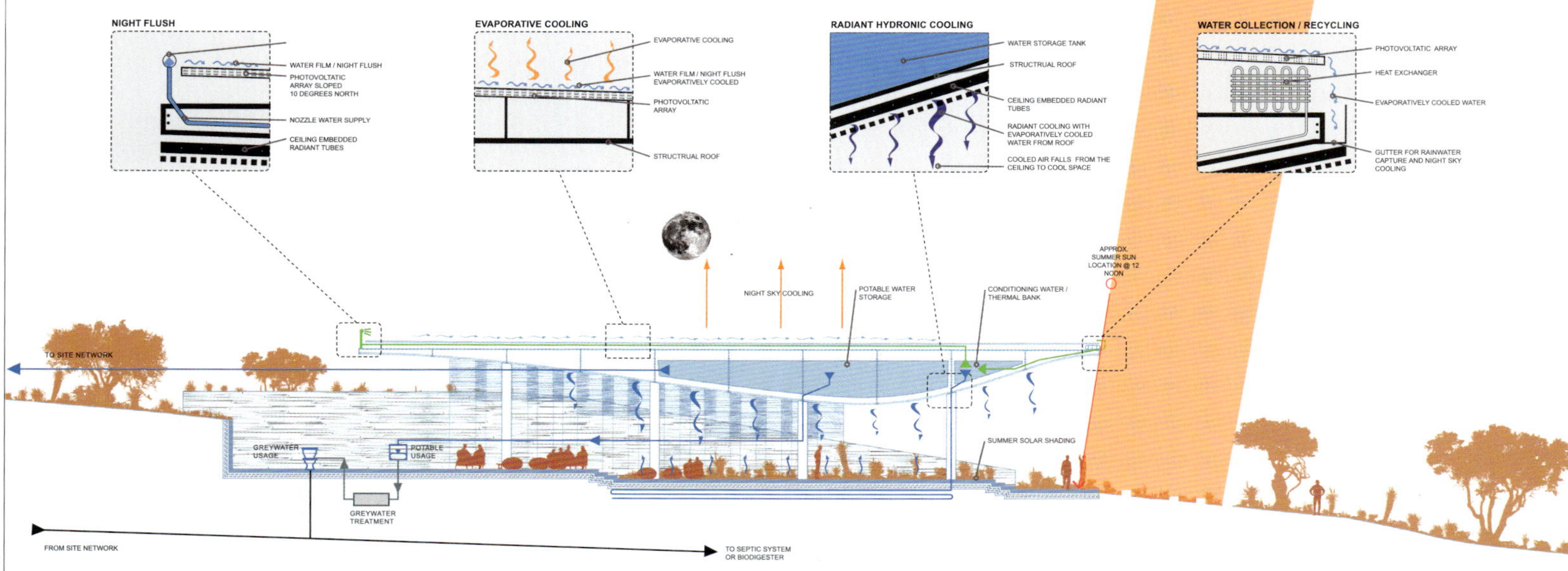

Proposed Summer Strategy

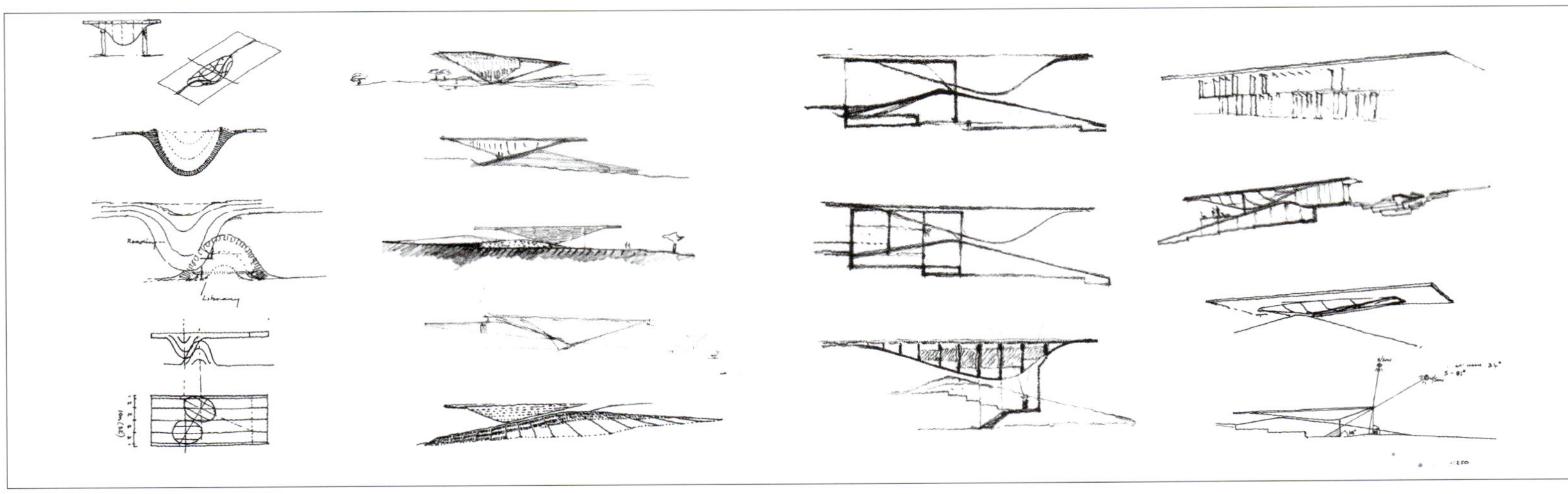

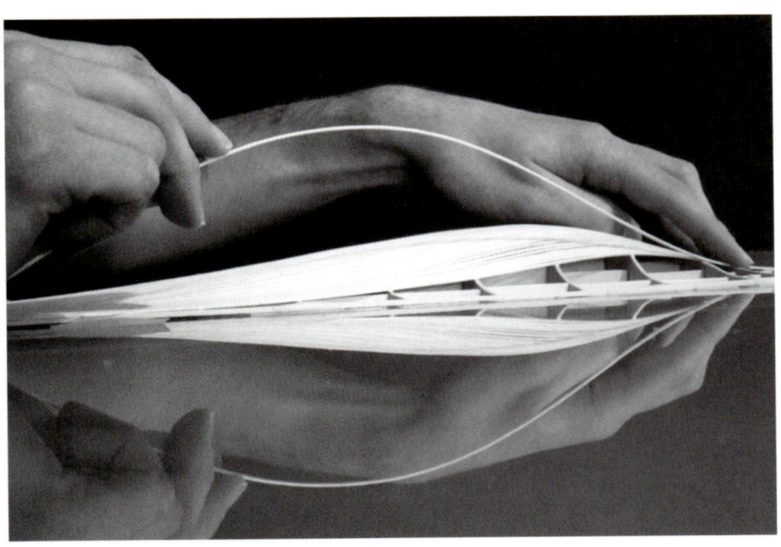

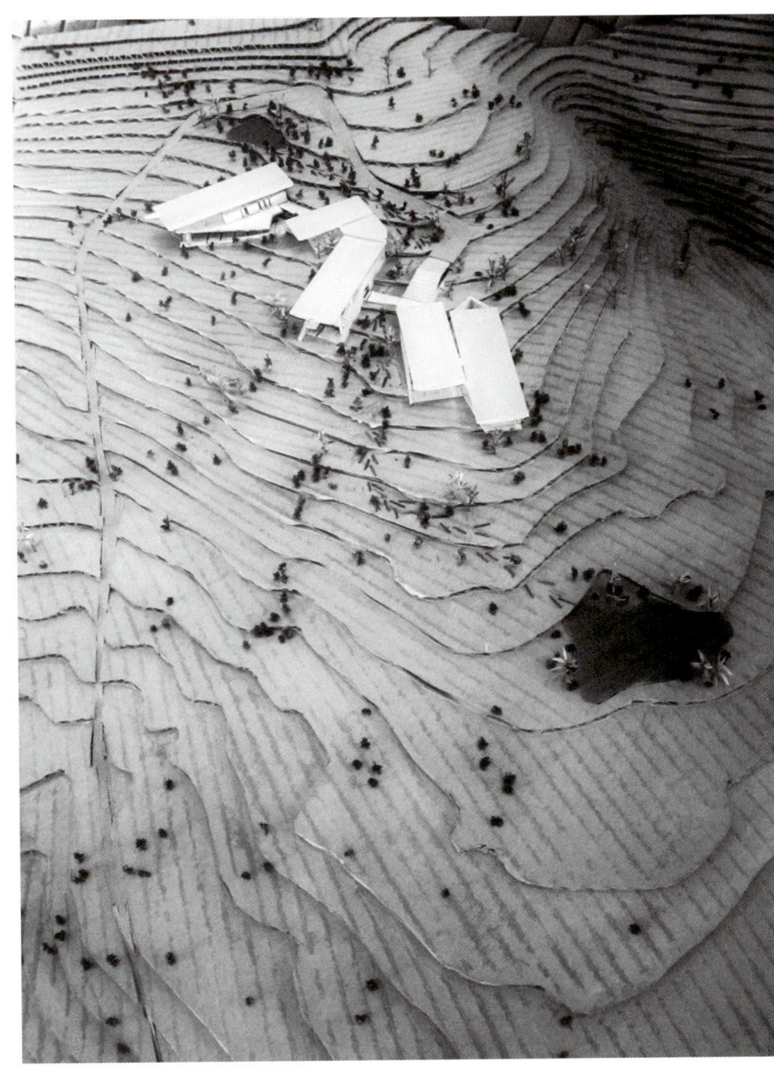

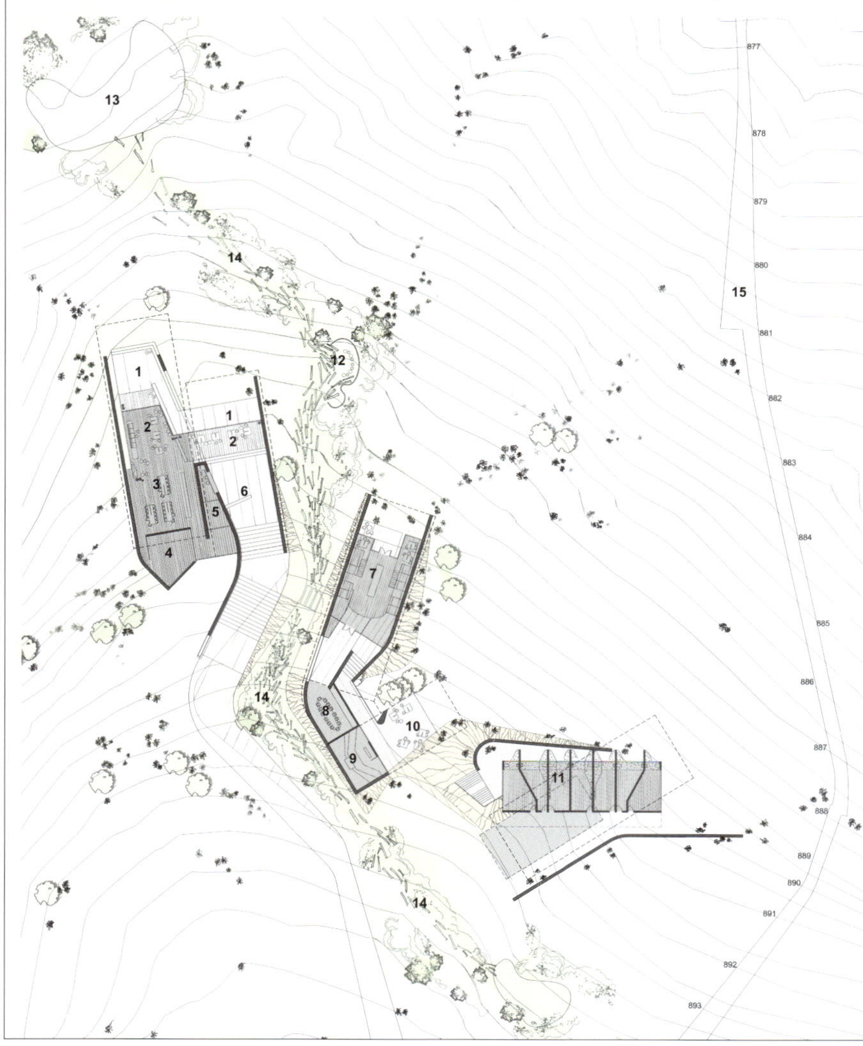

Site Plan

Scale 1:750

1. Stoep (terrace)
2. Lounge
3. Dining
4. Kitchen
5. Reception and office
6. Arrival Lobby
7. Library
8. Conference Room
9. Theater
10. Outdoor Classroom
11. Residences
12. Boma (traditional outdoor dining enclave)
13. Water Hole
14. Living Corridor
15. Road

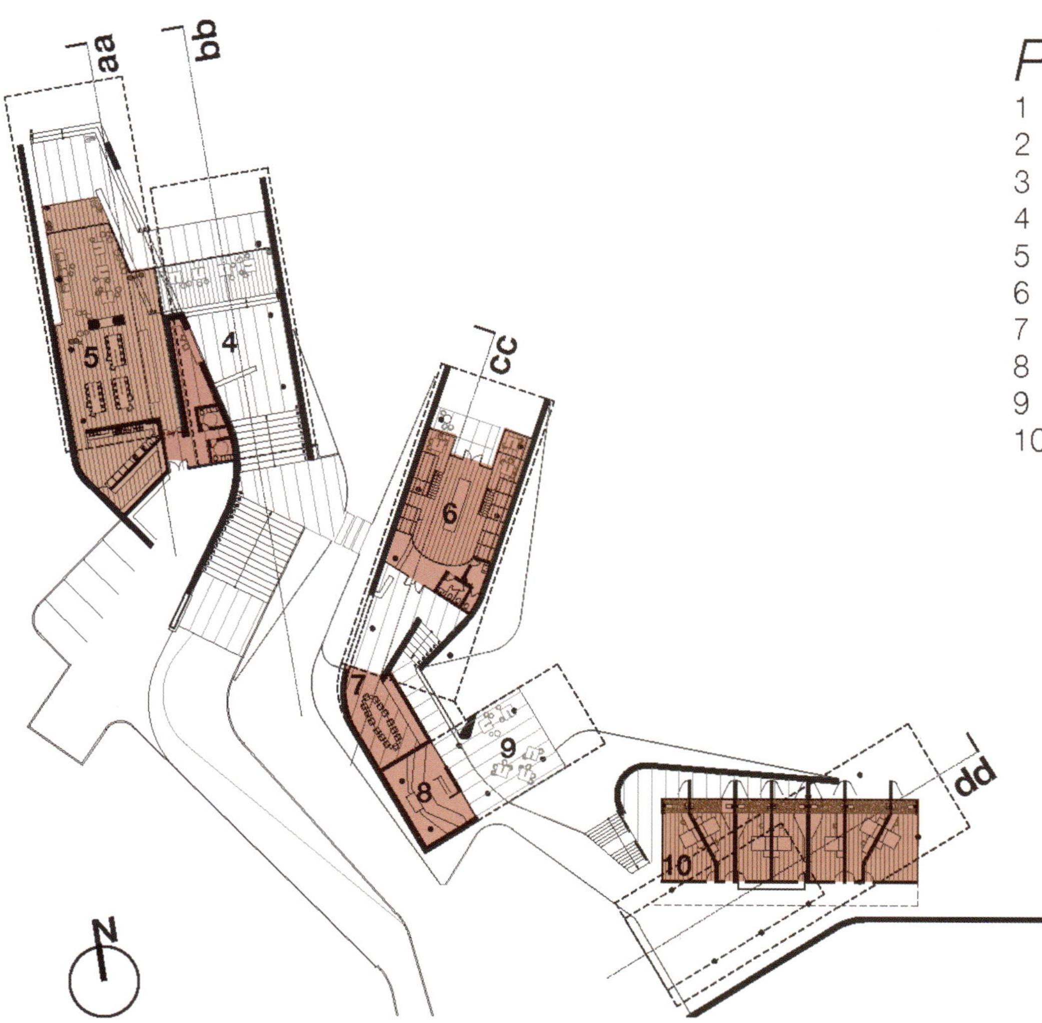

Plan

1 Access Road
2 Living Corridor
3 Water Hole
4 Reception and Office
5 Lodge: Kitchen/Dining/Lounge
6 Special Collections Library
7 Conference Room
8 Theater/ Lecture Hall
9 Expandable Outdoor Classroom
10 Laureate Residences

BUENOS AIRES FOOTBALL (BAF)

The complex is located on a lot of 5 hectares in a suburban zone full of clubs and closed neighborhoods.

Considering the natural character of the site and its potential atmosphere, the idea was to suggest an architecture that was anchored in the terrain. While related in part to the green banks, it simultaneously would be clearly distinct in the abstraction and artificiality of its geometry and materials. We wanted the building-terrain relationship to be in harmony and the natural-artificial combination to be magnified by their contrast.

Another important decision regarding the implantation was to separate the program into two structures with horizontal proportions to control the impact of the construction and create spaces and joints where the entrances, the connections, the fields, and finally the lagoon and landscape begin to appear.

Regarding the program, the project is composed of Building 01 of 1,020m², Building 02 of 1,437m², a point of control at the entrance, 50 parking spaces, 2 football fields for 11 players, and 4 football fields for 8 players. The reflecting pool in the artificial lagoon of 220m² completes the program, which anchored the whole idea. As a result of economics and aesthetics, we had to transplant a great volume of earth to the natural terrain to be able to satisfy the minimum inundation codes for the city.

All of the living spaces and team sports are located in Building 01 which includes a reception hall, 18 apartments, and mixed-used spaces. On the ground floor, Building 02 contains the service quarters, and sport-specific spaces including lockers, work-out rooms, personal and public changing rooms, and a gym with independent entrances and exits directly to the fields.

The social and administrative areas are located on the first floor. This includes a restaurant/bar (also used as a salon for parties or events), terrace, kitchen, and a space for offices. On this floor there is a big opening not only to capture the best views of the landscape for whoever simply wants to enjoy having something to eat or drink, but also to offer a general panorama of the whole complex and fields for whoever wants to see the individual fields or entertainment spaces from the leisure of a covered space.

For the formal and spatial development of the project, models played a fundamental role. The results responded to three principle objectives. For one, the buildings were to be dismantled, fractured, and faceted seeking to colonize the terrain, adapting it to the project. Another objective was to generate diverse, atypical spaces that surprise you and provoke multiple sensations. And, lastly, the architecture was to be totally contemporary. We believe that we as architects build the present world, understanding how we are part of a constantly evolution and seeking to be between the past and the future.

COMPANY	Andres Remy Arquitectos
CREATIVE DIRECTOR	REMY-Speziale Linares
DESIGNER	Andre Remy, Carlos Arellano, Hernan Pardillos, Denise Presson, Lilian Kandus. Juan Etala, Diego Siddi, Coral Banegas, Javier Speziale, Guido Piaggio, Matias Quintela, Gullermo Gauna
PHOTOGRAPHER	Alejandro Peral
COUNTRY (DISTRICT)	Argentina

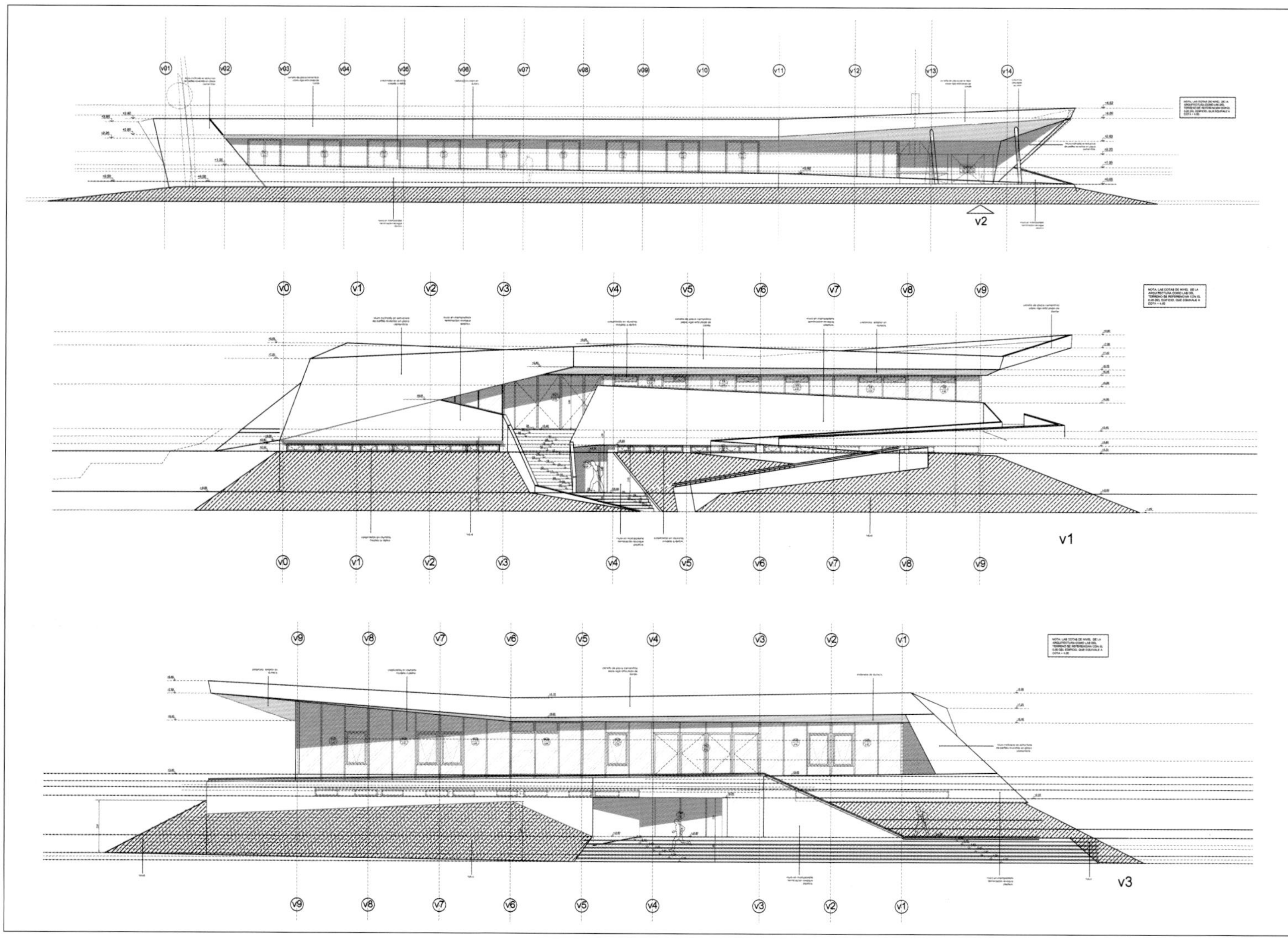
v2
v1
v3

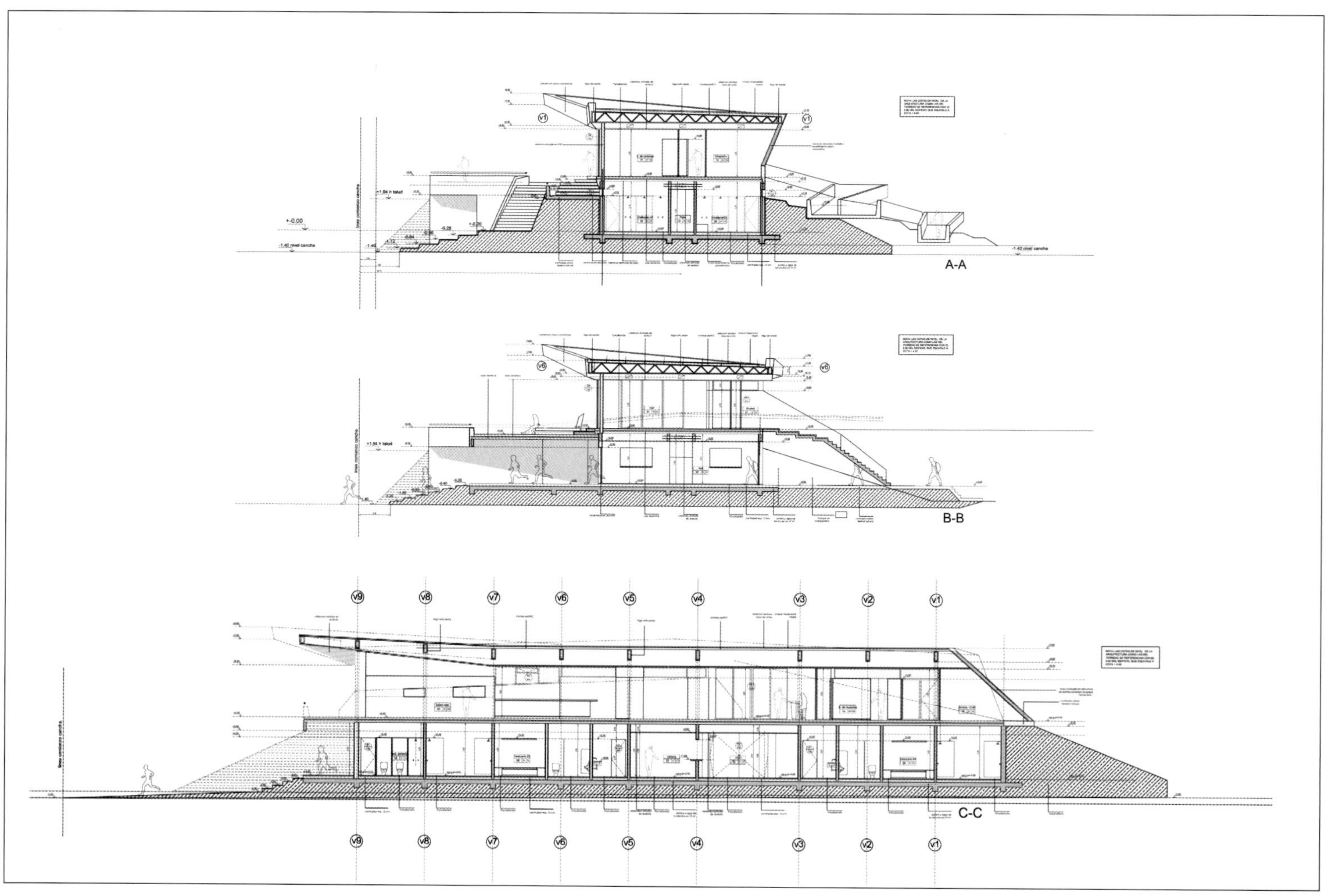
A-A
B-B
C-C

MasterCard
MasterCard
POWERADE
Buenos Aires Football

MEDITATION HOUSE

This is a project with very strong emotional implications.
We had to understand the mood of the user, who at such this moment would not care very much for an aesthetical analysis of any place, but at the same time we wanted to create a space that can create a spiritual mood, for this we referred to ancient buildings that were designed for this purpose, as the Egyptian "Mastabas" or some Mayan buildings in Palenque.
A project of this nature must encourage introspection and peaceful visual harmony through a discrete use of materials and lighting. The construction is located in a residential area and being planned as an isolated construction from the surroundings, an indoor illuminated yard was built. The building facade is completely covered by Grissal flamed granite.
The building welcomes the visitors with a 6´4 wide and 30´ high triangular shaped wooden door which leads to an access tunnel in the same shape, creating a solemn atmosphere as you enter. This darkening experience at the entrance ends when the hallway opens to a large, double height granite hall illuminated by the northern light coming from the indoor courtyard with a tall Dracaena at the center and a symbolical abstract sculpture by artist Saul Kaminer as the only artwork piece for decoration.
No furniture was used inside this place, only a floating bench surrounding the room, that is made out of the same wood used in all the building. It also serves to hide all of the air conditioning, speakers and recessed lighting which adds a dramatical touch. This way the rooms show no added ornament but the light and shades playing on the granite volumes. The ceiling is made of dark cumaru wood and floats without touching any wall and a skylight puts a highlight on this detail.

COMPANY	Pascal Arquitectos
DESIGNER	Carlos Pascal / Gerard Pascal
PHOTOGRAPHER	Víctor Benítez
CLIENT	Comunidad Monte Sinai
COUNTRY (DISTRICT)	México

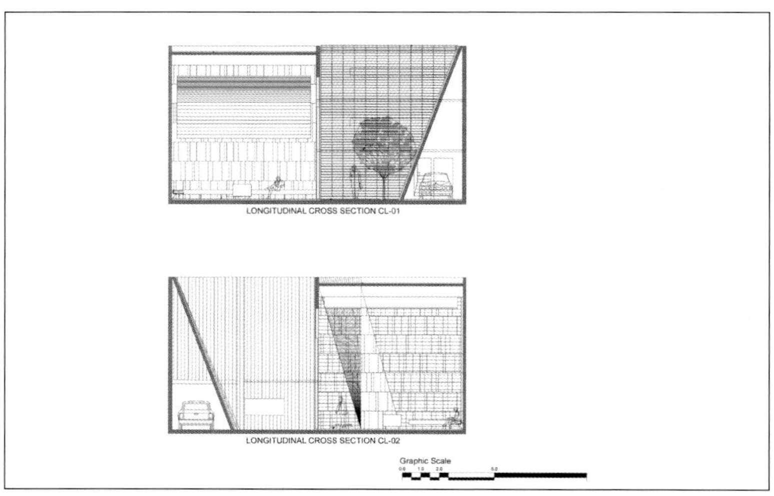

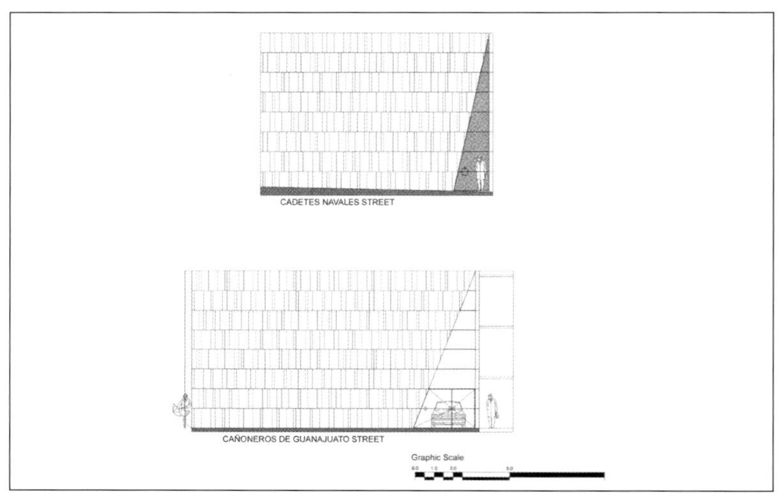

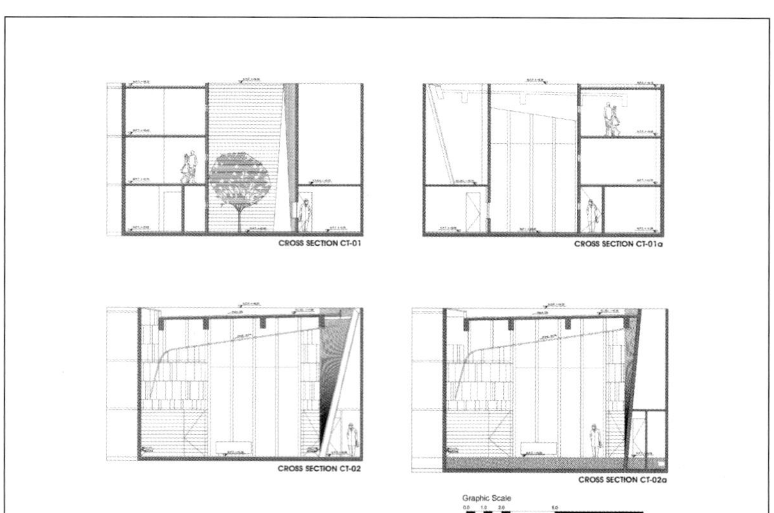

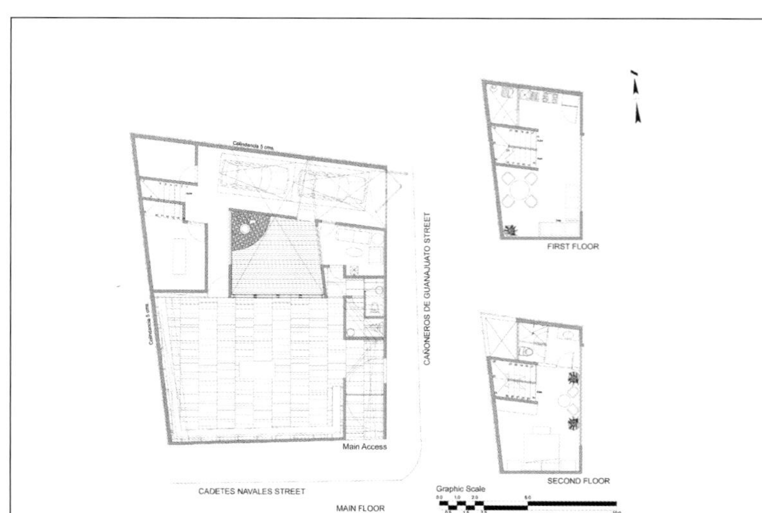

ANNEX OF THE CHAMBER OF TRADES-VAL D'OISE

The chamber of Trades of Val d'Oise (French department) decided in the mid 2000's to create a professional training center for apprentices in Villiers-le-Bel (French city). To highlight such a successful facility in such a difficult area, the administration decided to project its extension and its local branch on an adjoining site. This new building is composed of offices and professional training rooms accessible to the public.

In order to develop the educational objective of the Chamber of Trades, the site plan was thought as a micro campus. Surrounding the park, the future extension will be settled at the edge of the site; the closest edge from the neighboring school. On the north side of the park, the street Louis Perrin is rapidly expanding. On the south side, an highway linking La Francilienne (Parisian highway) to Garges-les-Gonnesse is being built. To answer those contextual appeals, the project fits into a non-oriented circle addressing itself to everyone. The building was thought as a "folly". The circle is divided into two halves along a north/south axis. The entrance faces the south, where the school and the bus stops are situated. The building can easily be located by everyone walking down the street. The north side of the building welcomes the six offices. Those workspaces have a view on the whole park and enjoy natural light all year long.

Moreover the circular shape allows optimizing surfaces (20%): workspaces at the periphery and services in the center. As surface gains the heated volume and the energy consumption were reduced. A perforated double skin is set up around the building to ensure both privacy and safety to users. The system also provides shade to interior spaces. Distant from the facade, it creates a terrace all around the building and extends the interior floor.

The solar shading system is framed with 96 "arches" strictly identical and articulated in 3 points (foot, elbow, top). Those arches are anchored in the ground along an ellipse whereas they are attached to the roof along a circle. Perforated aluminum steel sheets are fixed on this frame thanks to rivet. Perforations vary according to the different aspects of the building.

COMPANY	Colboc Franzen & Associates
CREATIVE DIRECTOR	Benjamin Colboc, Manuela Franzen, Arnaud Sachet
PROJECT MANAGER	Yann Follain
PROJECT TEAM	Jerome Garnier, Kerstin Heller, Gerald Barras-Pin, Arnaud bag, Pauline Taboury
PHOTOGRAPHER	Cécile Septet
CLIENT	Chamber of trades of the "Val d'Oise" (France)
COUNTRY (DISTRICT)	France

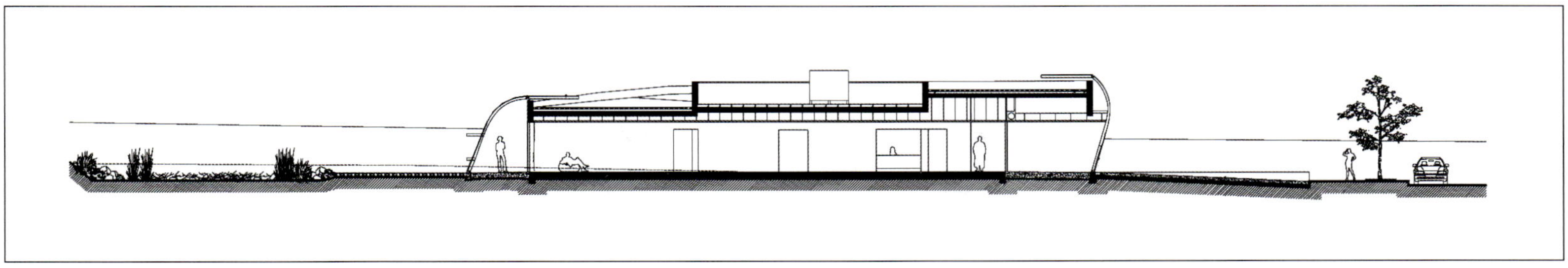

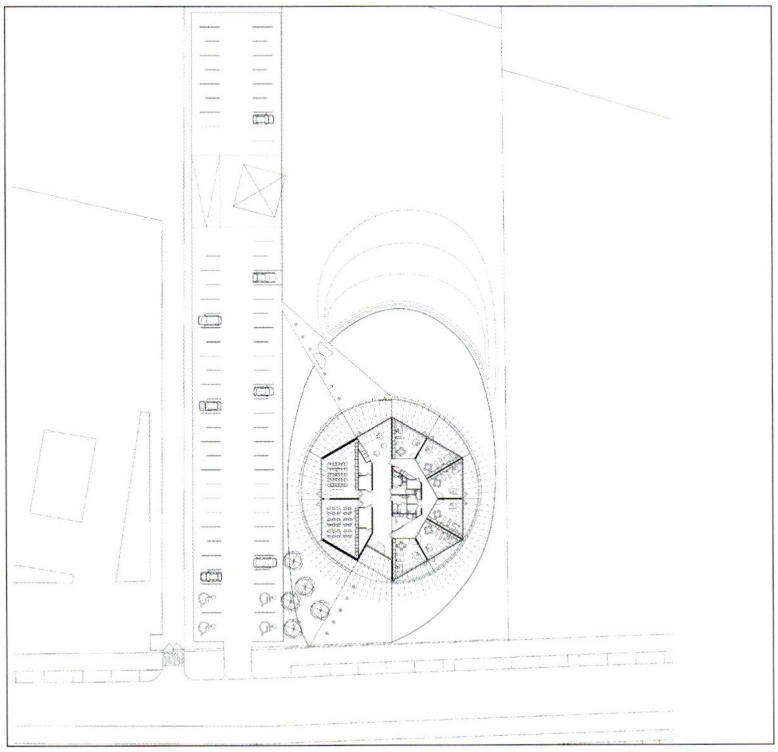

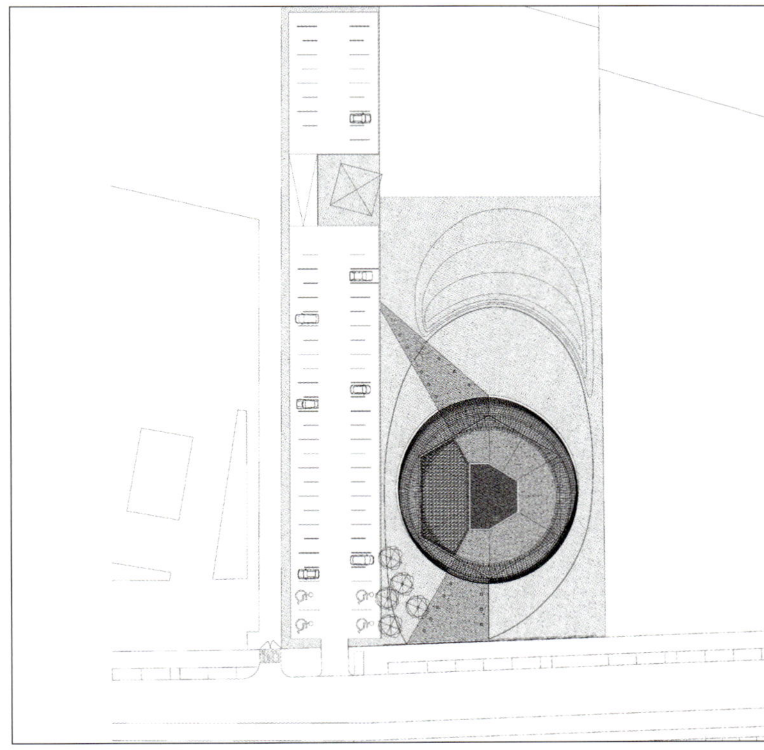

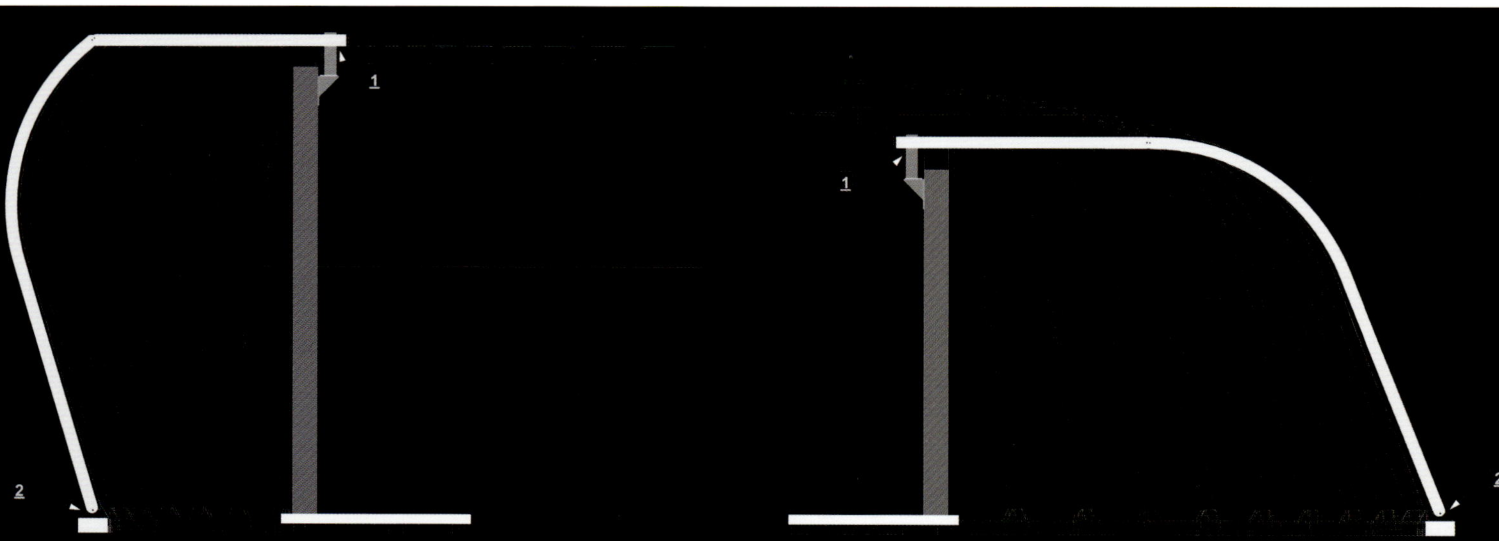

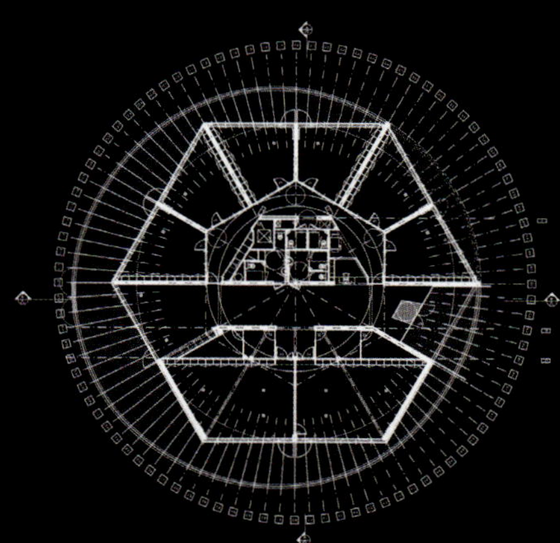
PLAN RDC

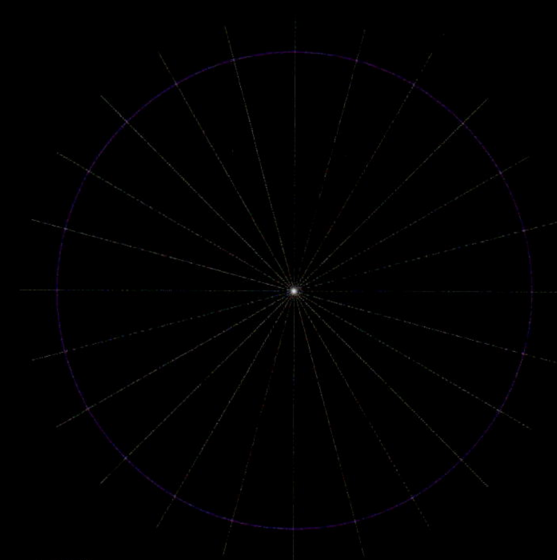
AXES

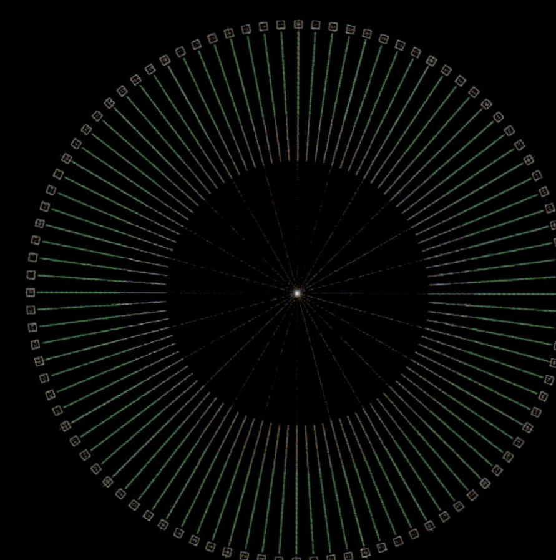
FILES

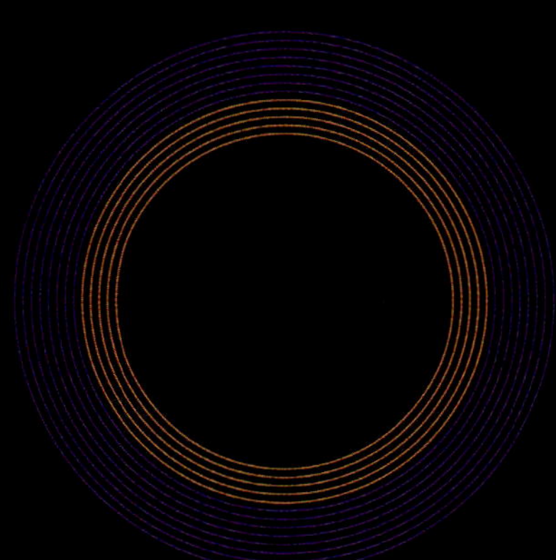
BANDES HORIZONTALES

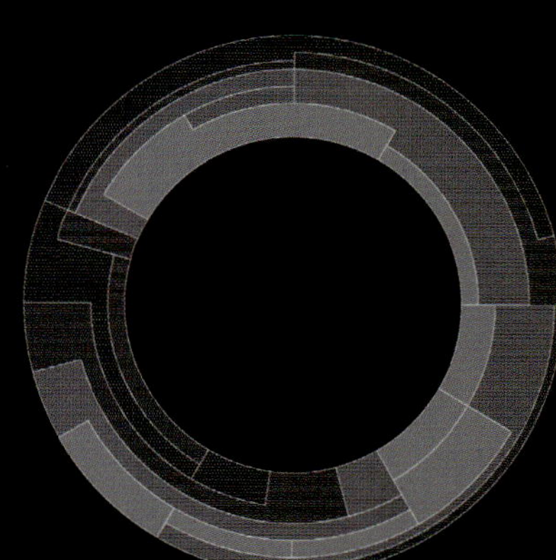
REPARTITION PERFORATION

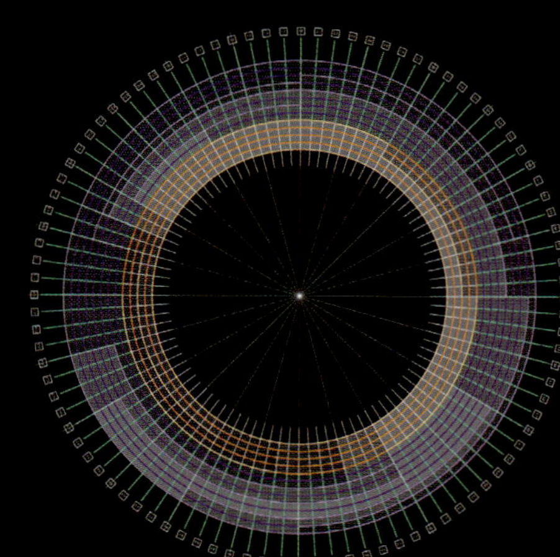
SYNTHESE

SERVICE ECONOMIE ET FORMATION

FAREWELL CHAPEL

A farewell chapel is located in a village close to Ljubljana.
The site plot is next to the existing graveyard. The chapel is cut into the rising landscape and it is following the landscape trajectories around the graveyard. Three curved walls are embracing and dividing the programs. External curve is dividing the surrounding hill from chapel plateau and also reinstates main supporting wall.
Services such as storages, wardrobe restrooms and kitchenette are on the inner side along the wall. Internal curve is embracing main farewell space. It is partly glazed and it is opening towards outside plateau for summer gatherings. Roof is following its own curvature and forming external porch.
The cross as catholic sign is featured as laying feature positioned on the rooftop above the main farewell space. It also functions as luminous dynamic element across the space during the daytime and lighting spark at a night time.
Materials are polished concrete, larch wood, glass.

COMPANY	OFIS arhitekti
DESIGNER	OFIS arhitekti
PHOTOGRAPHER	Tomaz Gregoric
CLIENT	Community of Krasnja
COUNTRY (DISTRICT)	Slovenia

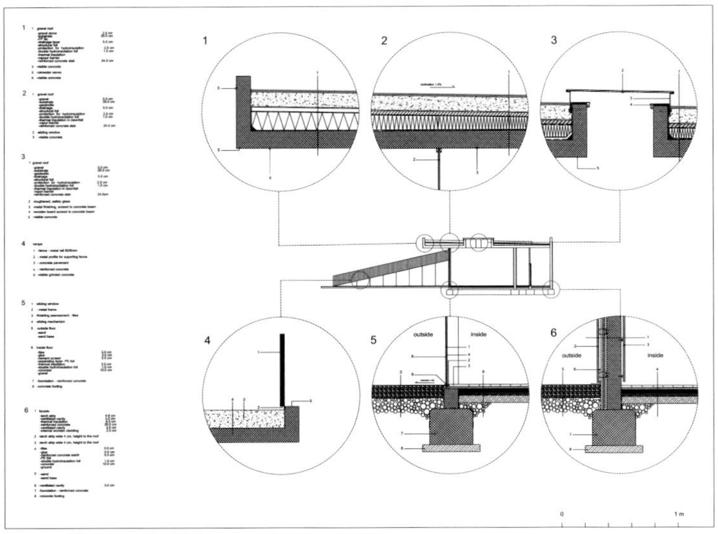
1
2
3
4
5
6
outside
inside
0
1 m

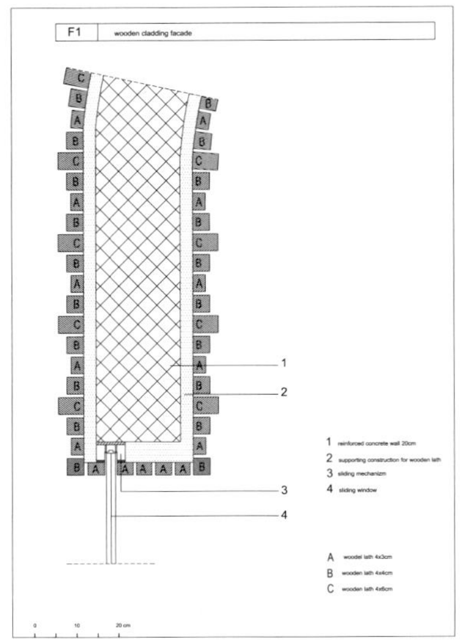
F1
wooden cladding facade
1 reinforced concrete wall 20cm
2 supporting construction for wooden lath
3 sliding mechanizm
4 sliding window
A woodel lath 4x3cm
B wooden lath 4x4cm
C wooden lath 4x6cm

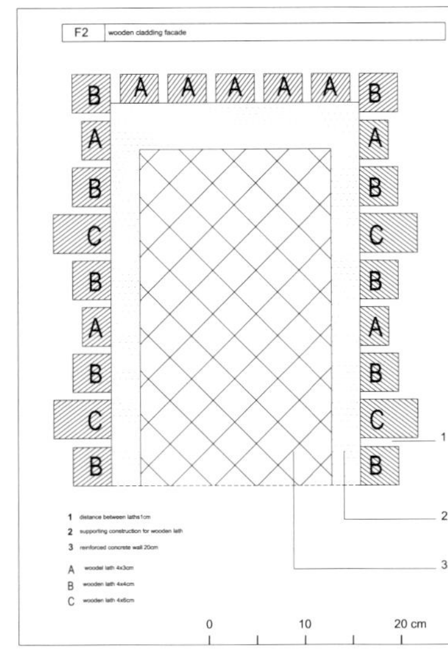
F2
wooden cladding facade
1 distance between laths1cm
2 supporting construction for wooden lath
3 reinforced concrete wall 20cm
A woodel lath 4x3cm
B wooden lath 4x4cm
C wooden lath 4x6cm
0
10
20 cm

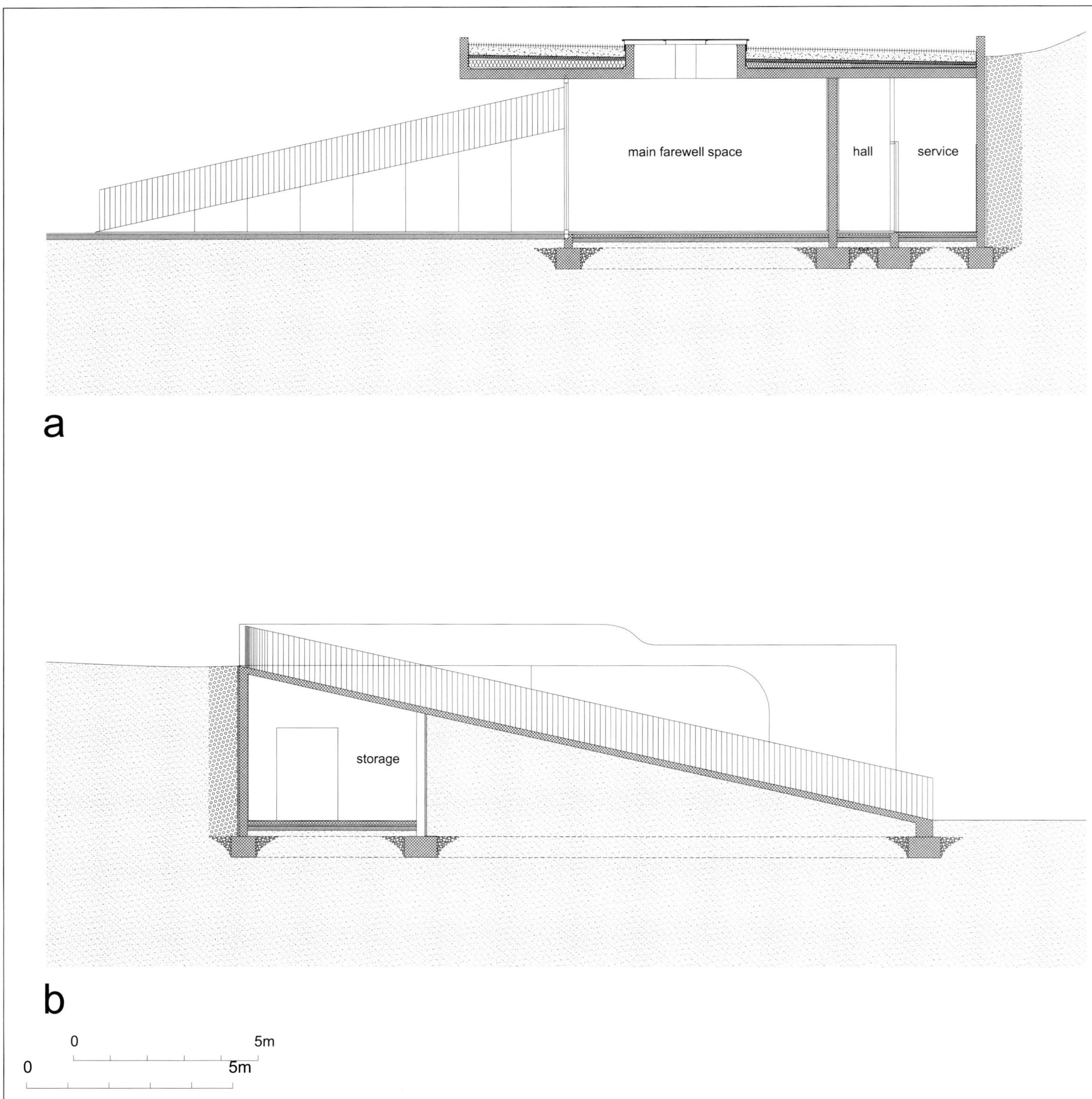
main farewell space
hall
service
a
storage
b
0
5m
0
5m

RESIDENCE

TREEHOUSE IN SEATTLE

Treehouse is a single family residence located at a park in Seattle, WA. Built on an inaccessible, steep slope lot, the project overcame significant design and construction challenges to create a unique home elevated in the trees. The project had three primary design objectives: 1) minimize long term site impacts; 2) design a cost effective and resource efficient building; 3) use view, light and enclosure to accentuate the experience of living in the tree canopy. In 1999, the owners discovered an "un-buildable" lot while searching the internet for cheap vacant lots in Seattle. At first attracted by the price, the owners soon realized that the lot was adjacent to the park where their community garden plot was located. Despite the challenges posed by the lot itself, the vacant lot seemed too good to pass up for the sale price of $15,000. Ten years of planning/design, construction and sweat equity later, their project has been realized.

COMPANY	SHED Architecture & Design
DESIGNER	SHED Architecture & Design
PHOTOGRAPHER	SHED Architecture & Design
COUNTRY (DISTRICT)	USA

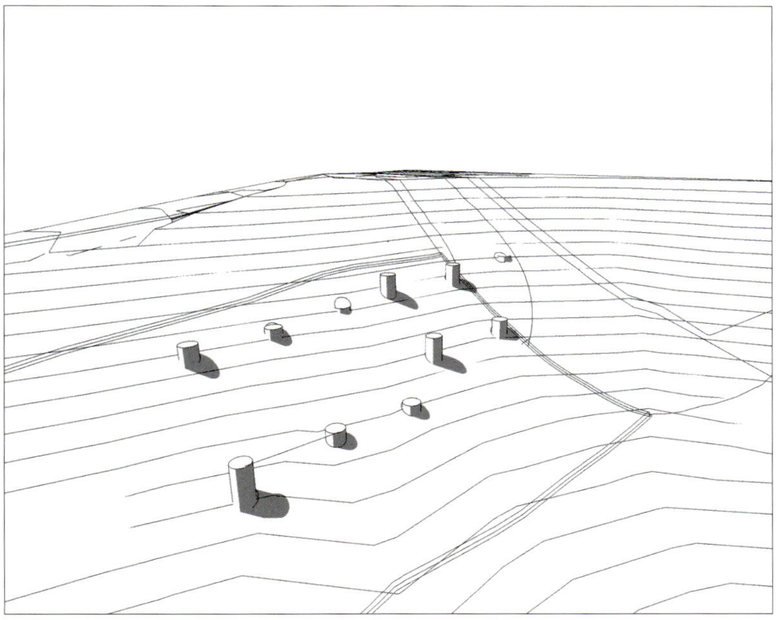

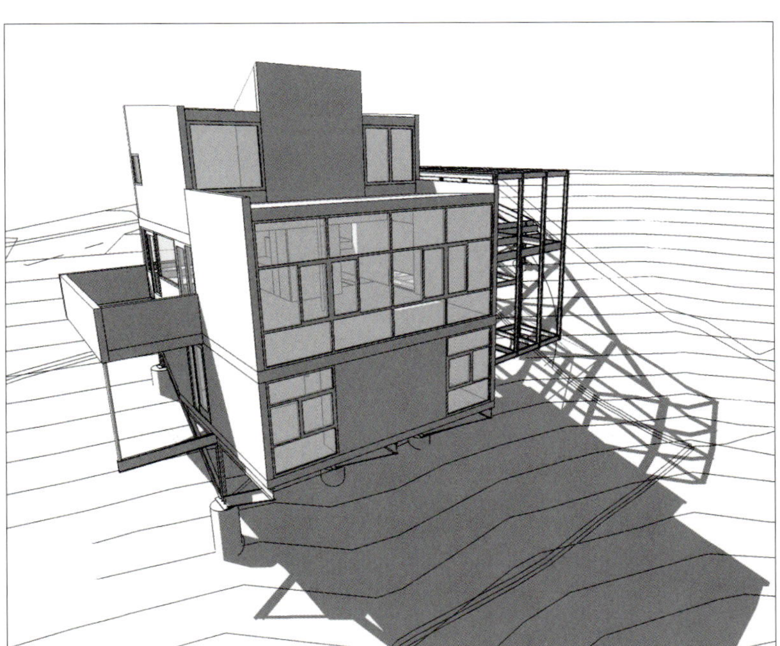

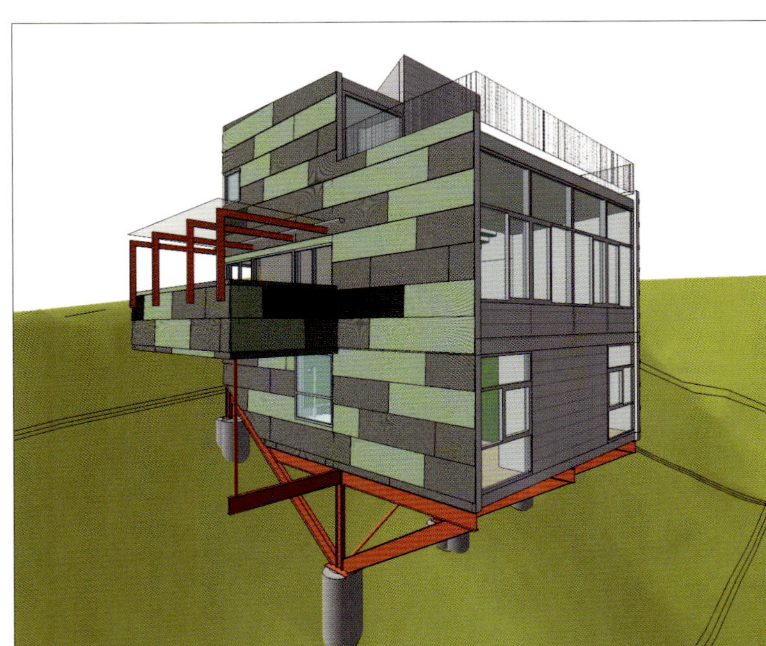

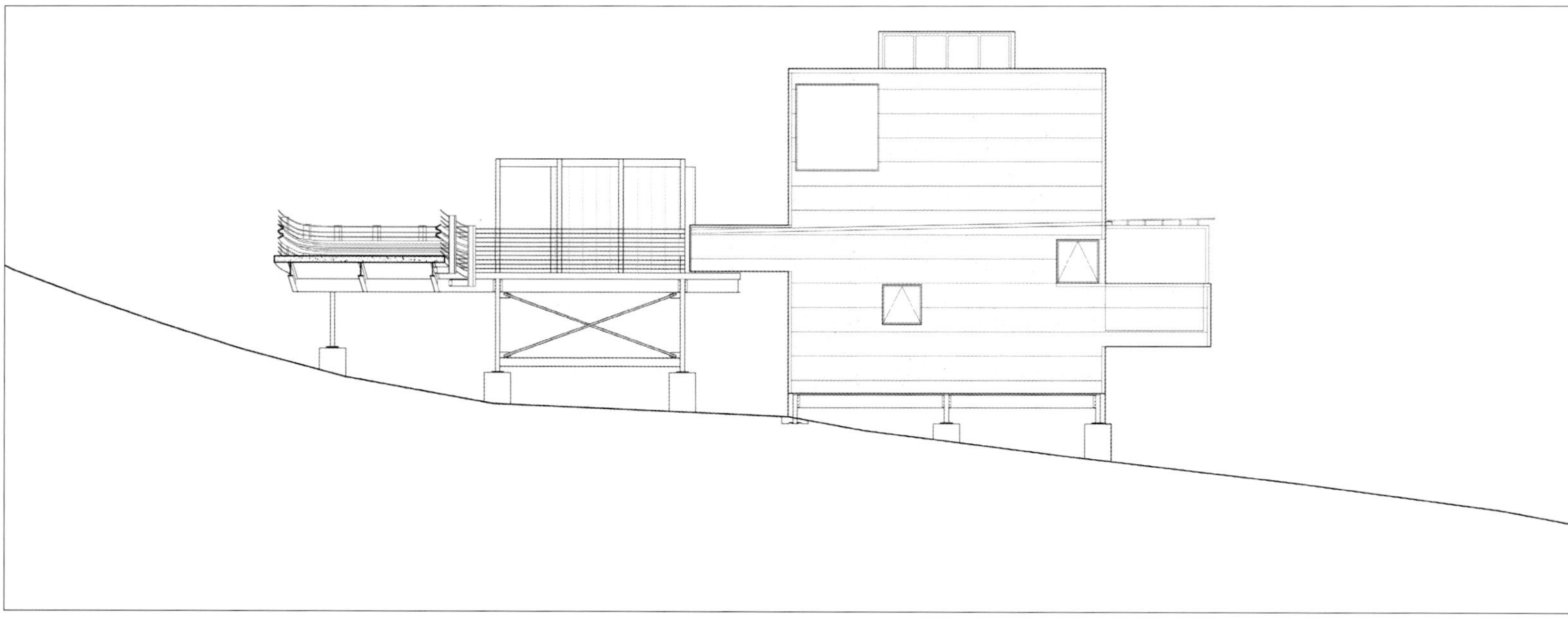

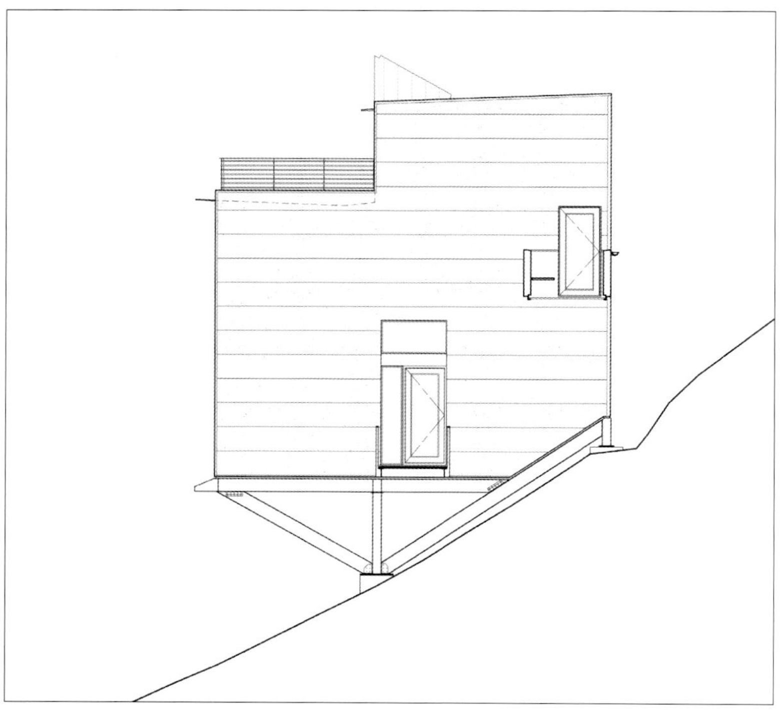

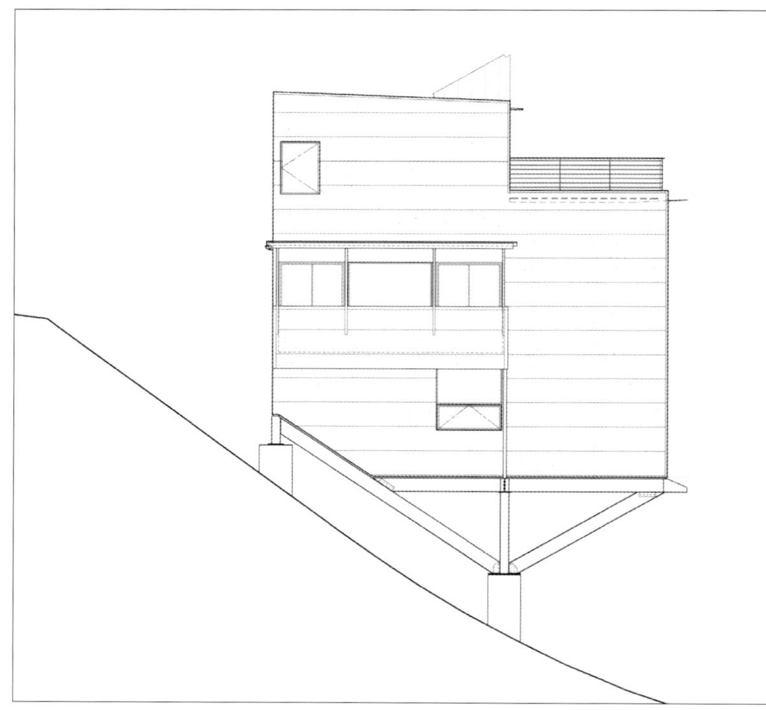

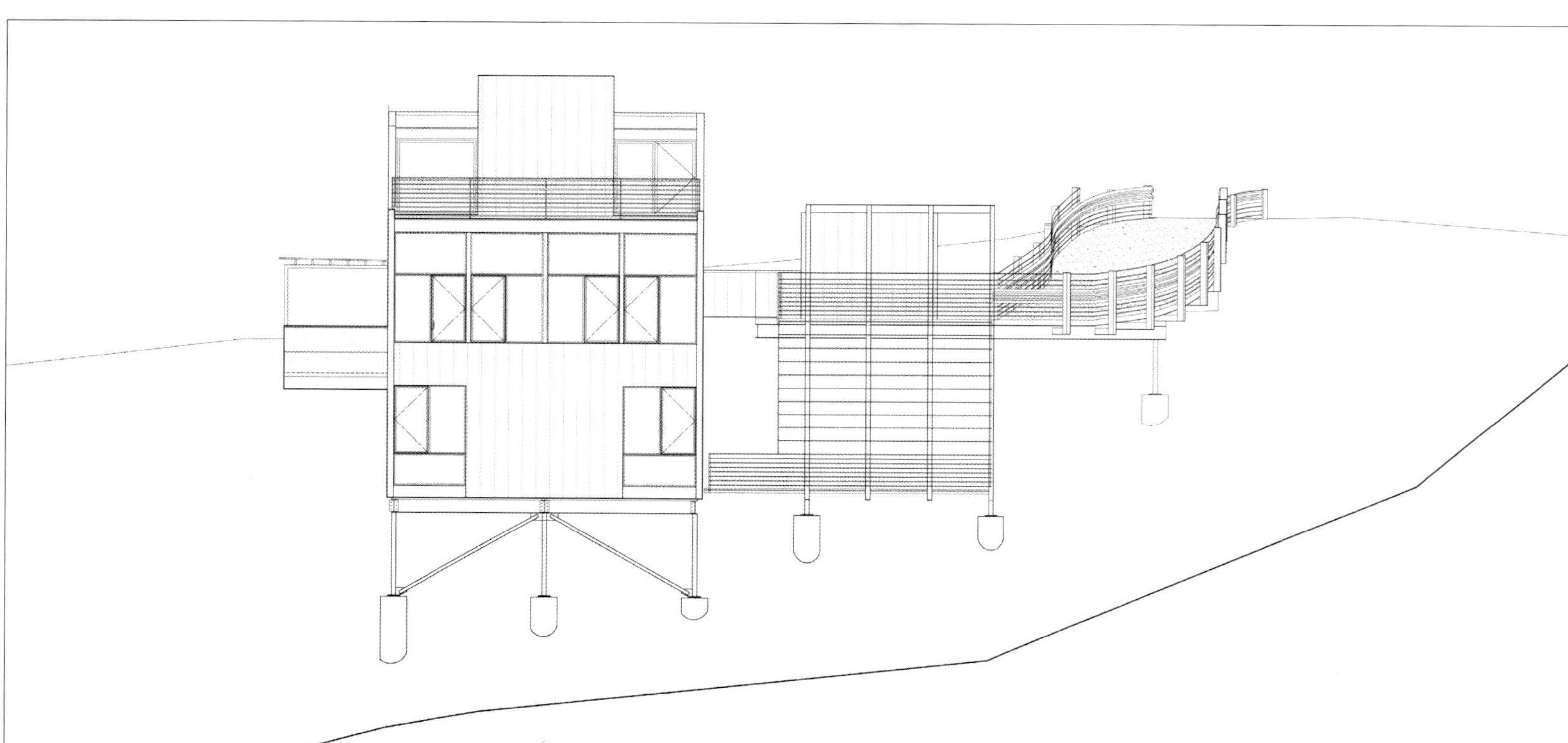

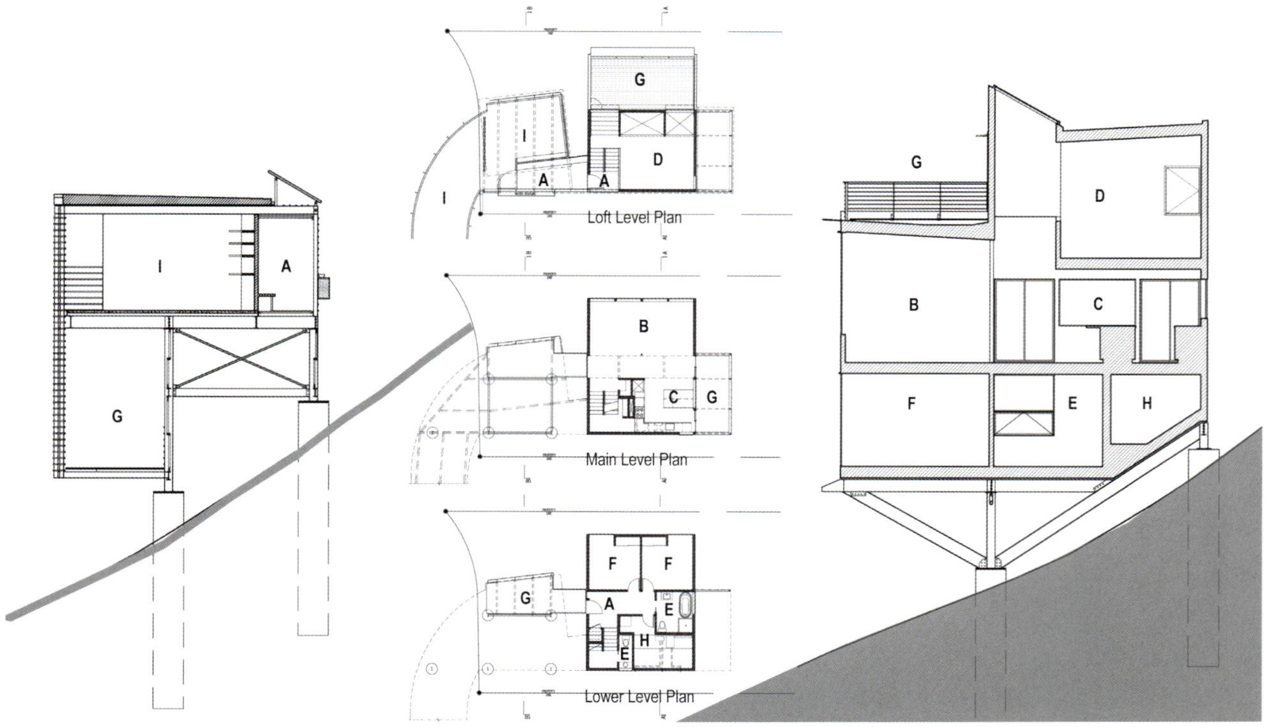

Carport
Section B-B

Floor Plan Key

A Entry
B Living / Dining
C Kitchen
D Loft / Office
E Bathroom
F Bedroom
G Deck
H Laundry / Storage
I Carport / Driveway

House
Section A-A

MAGAZINE CAMERA
TYPE A-5A

HOUSE A

The location is Abeno-ward Osaka, JAPAN. Though it is a superb location just 10 minutes from Tennoji Station, it is in the downtown streets filled with traditional emotion. There are traditional tenement houses, old houses and shops, just 1 block from the main street. I planned the house in the narrow vacant land for 56-square-meter in this area. The house is light and open, and the residents can enjoy their hobbies.

Its owner, the K family, which consist of a couple and one daughter, like music. Especially, their daughter, who is 27 years old, is a musician and received the fifth winner in a recital. This family requested "Hobby Room, Live Studio" in their house that they can enjoy music. Sometimes, they will open mini concert with other band members and usually, they will use the room as an art gallery. And sometimes, they want to have a party with close friends by drinking. To maximize the locality with good access, which can create linkages between people through hobbies, such space was required.

Use as a distribution, I planned the first floor for "Hobby Room (studio and gallery and bar, live) " and a few floors as a living space. For Live Studio, because high sound insulation is required, I used the RC structure for the first floor, and I considered soundproof for doors, sashs, ventilators, and among others. On the other hand, I tried to make cost down in total for the second and the third floor, by using simple space of Japanese traditional wooden structure.

COMPANY	Hamada Design Co.,Ltd
DESIGNER	Takeshi Hamada
PHOTOGRAPHER	Yohei Sasakura
CLIENT	K families
COUNTRY (DISTRICT)	Japan

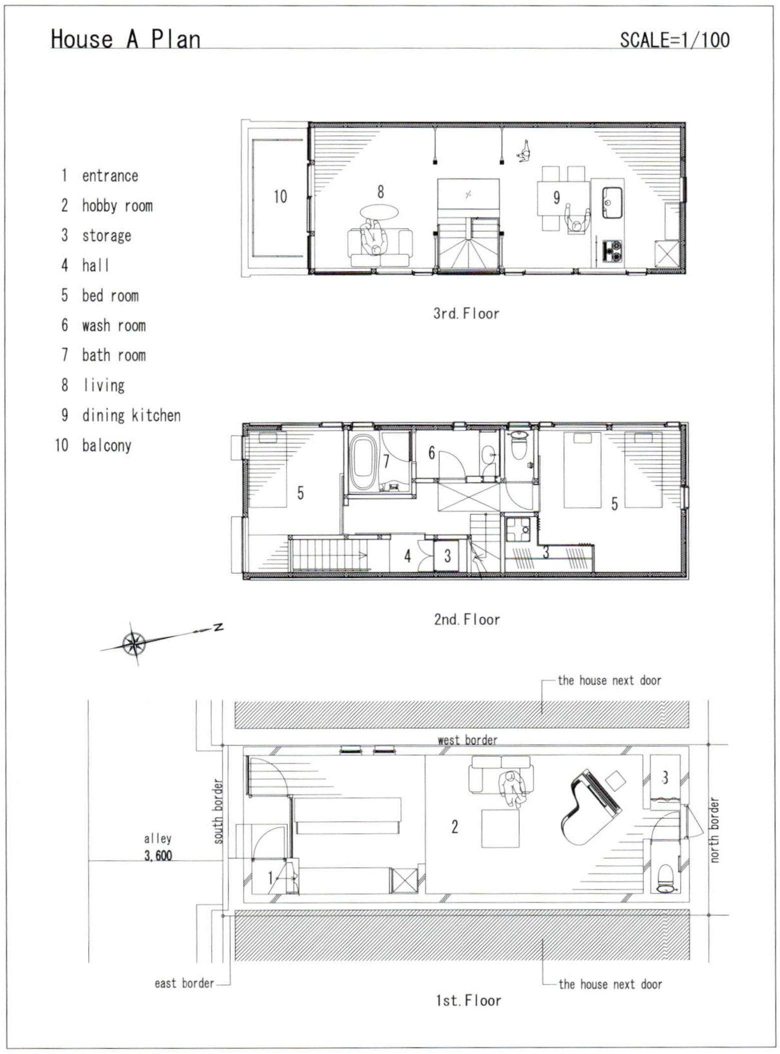
House A Plan
SCALE=1/100
1 entrance
2 hobby room
3 storage
4 hall
5 bed room
6 wash room
7 bath room
8 living
9 dining kitchen
10 balcony
3rd. Floor
2nd. Floor
the house next door
west border
south border
north border
alley
3,600
east border
the house next door
1st. Floor

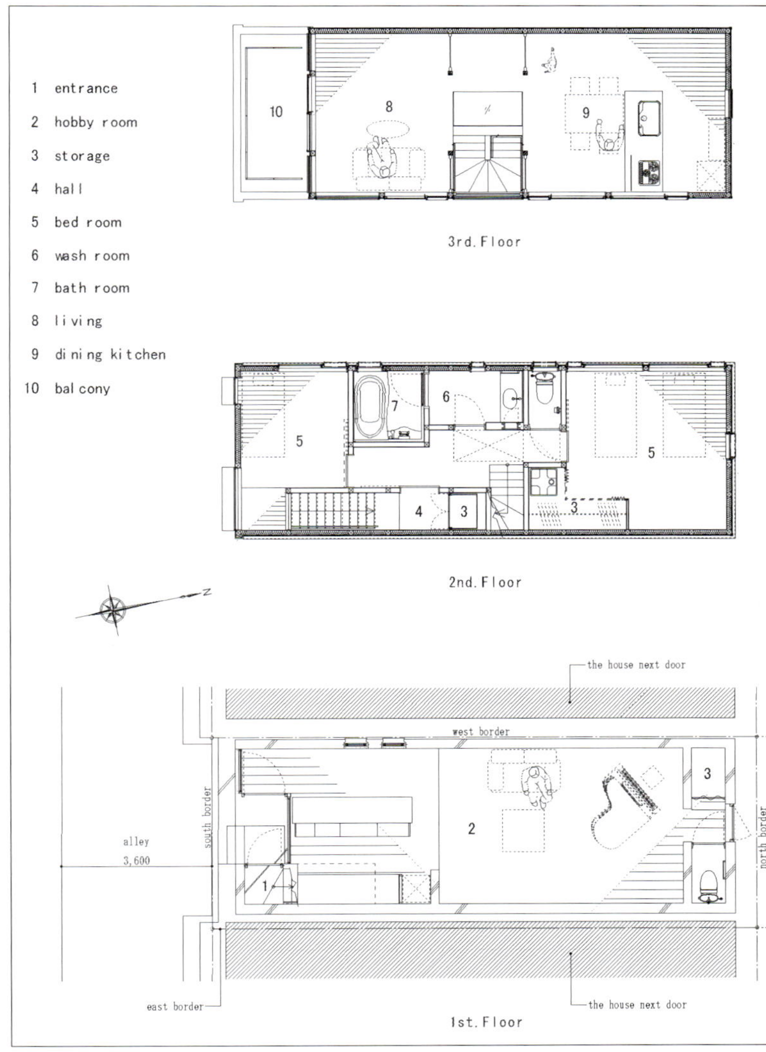
1 entrance
2 hobby room
3 storage
4 hall
5 bed room
6 wash room
7 bath room
8 living
9 dining kitchen
10 balcony
3rd. Floor
2nd. Floor
the house next door
west border
south border
north border
alley
3,600
east border
the house next door
1st. Floor

FOUR-CORNERED VILLA

The site is situated on a horse shoe shaped island and faces north and east. The cross like shape of this simple villa reaches towards four very different views. The space is open and defined at the same time. The exterior is treated all black and to contrast the interior is very light. Dark color makes the building disappear totally when seen from the lake. The roof is flat – there is some warm irony to the clichés of modern architecture. The building is insulated well and heated by wood only resulting in a carbon neutral building. There is no running water and the electricity is provided by the sun. Vegetables and herbs are cultivated on site and the Vaskivesi Lake is known as a good place to catch pike-perch. The simple and ascetic life at the countryside differs dramatically from the hectic city life and provides a possibility to live a life with a minimum impact on the nature.

COMPANY	Avanto Architects Ltd
DESIGNER	Avanto Architects
PHOTOGRAPHER	Kuvio
COUNTRY (DISTRICT)	Finland

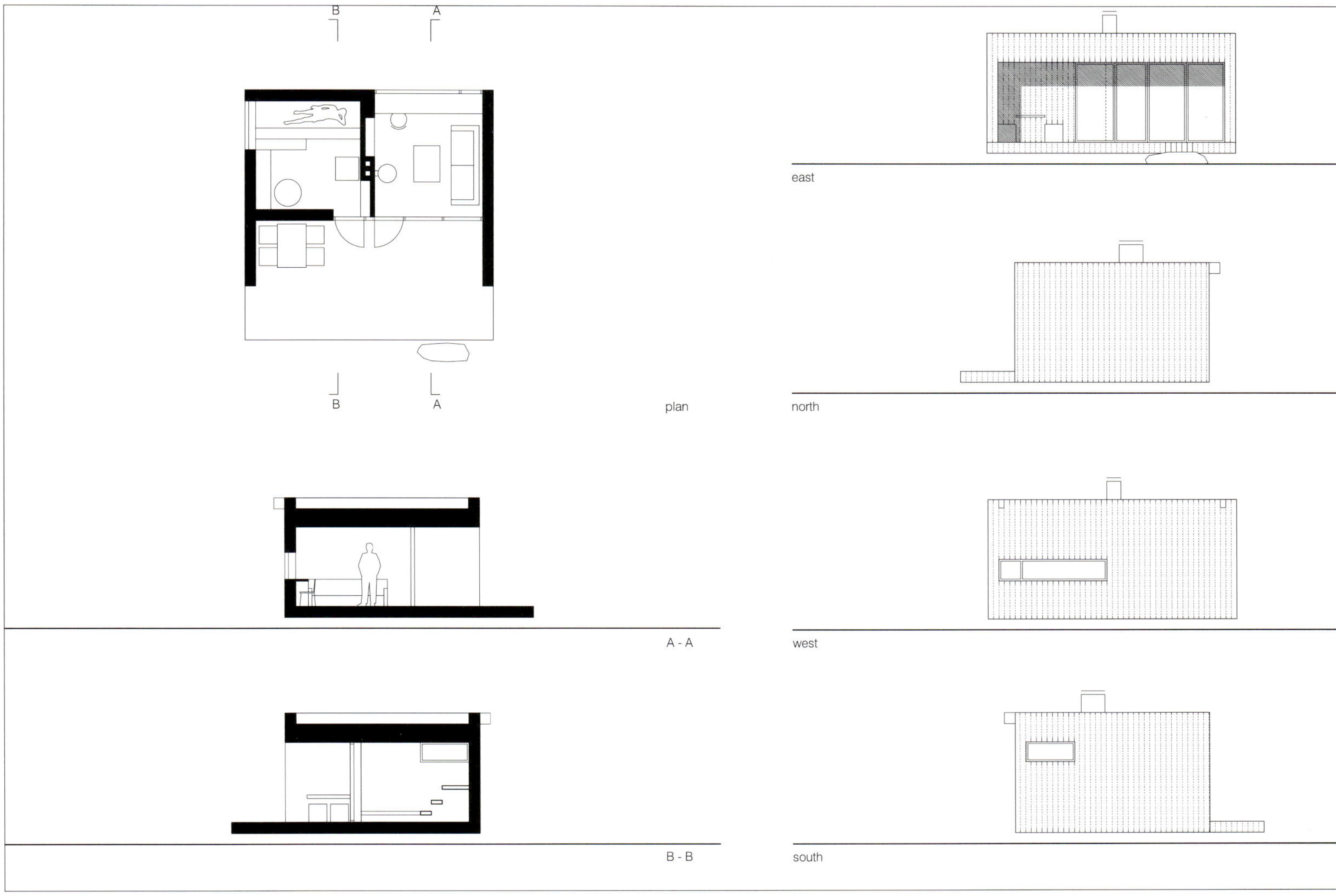
B
A
B
A
plan
east
north
west
south
A - A
B - B

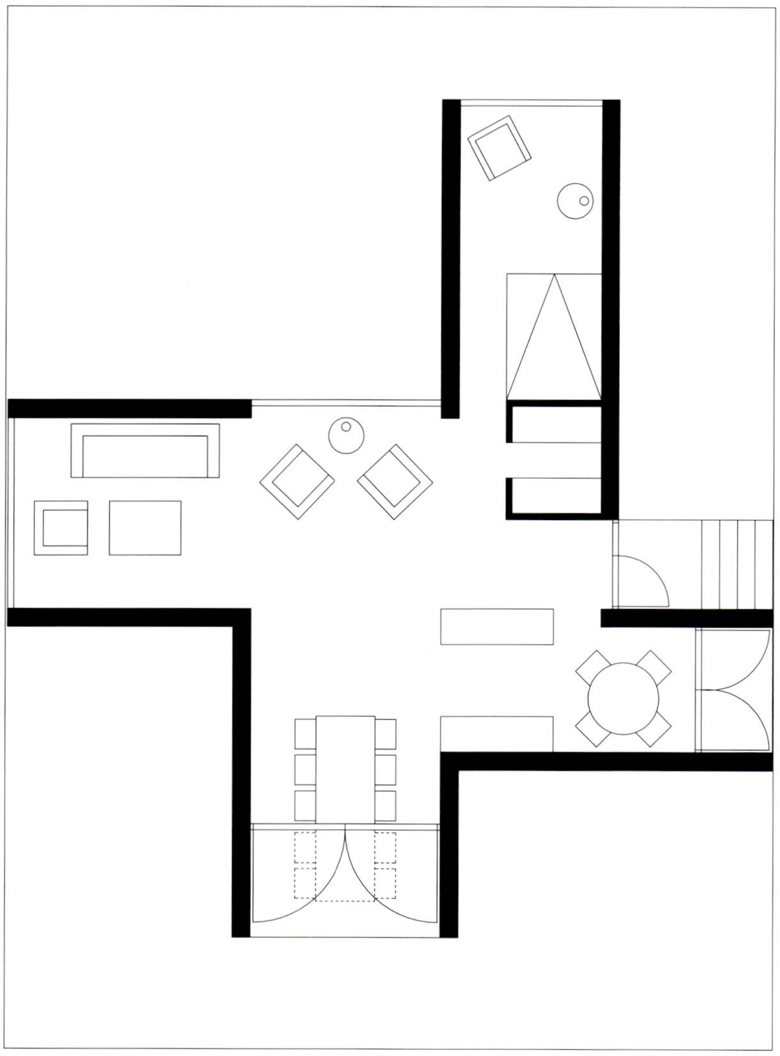

REFUGE IN LA VALL DE LAGUAR

This house, situated in a village perched on a mountain overlooking the Mediterranean sea, is located on site with a not very easy accessibility, full of cherries fields and open views.
The planning regulations only allowed to build a small volume to store agricultural tools not exceeding 25m², and a buried cistern underneath to water of 50m² . The main space of this construction becomes in this case a living room and kitchen, and upon it, taking advantage of the height permitted, one bedroom. Inside the cistern, a studio, one bedroom and a bathroom occupy the space of the water. To allow the lighting of these underground space, two large skylights allow incoming daylight, while on the surface these two skylights become in seats.
To simplify the distribution of such small space, one of the side walls gets thicker to make room for storage space, cupboards and fireplace, leaving the rest of the space released.
The exterior of the house tries to blend with the environment. It uses local stone laid dry, following the construction system of the stone of the retaining walls of the terraces in the area.

COMPANY	Enproyecto Arquitectura
DESIGNER	Sergio García-Gasco Lominchar, Jorge Cortes, Borja García
PHOTOGRAPHER	Enproyecto Arquitectura
COUNTRY (DISTRICT)	Spain

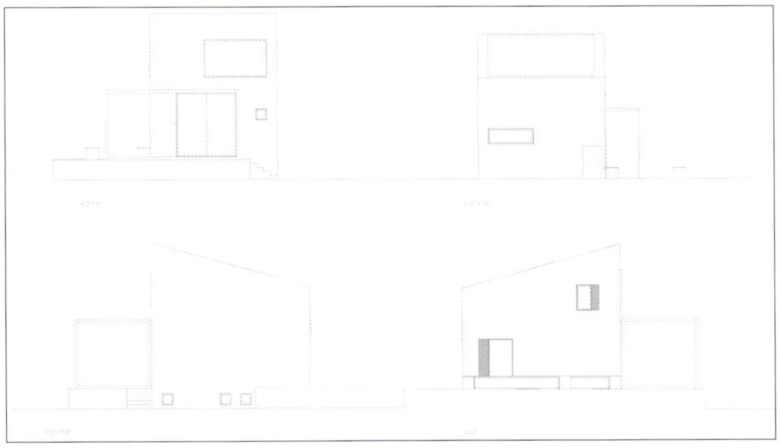

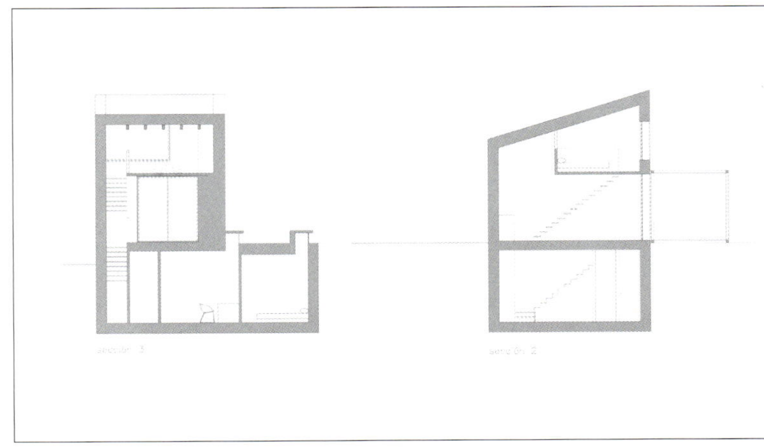

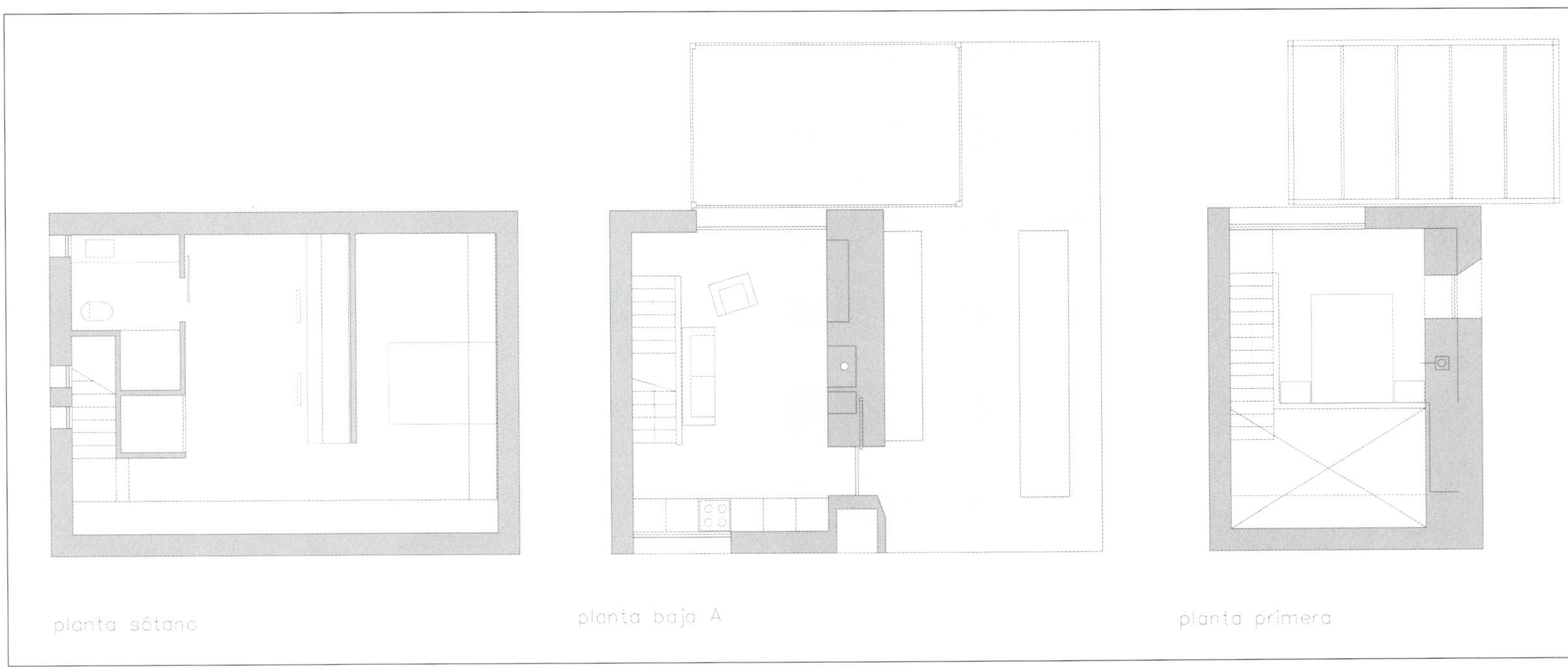
planta sótano
planta baja A
planta primera

HOUSE D

The housing is located in the place one block from the main street in Osaka's suburb, but I cannot say it's quiet. There are a lot of different buildings such as an iron factory, an elementary school, and a parking space near the house.

In this planning, I call the garage in the building site "Light Well" and I deploy the building in L type around the garage. There is only road in the north side and I intentionally didn't make a window on this side and planned that all rooms can take lights and air from this "Light Well". I put Gal-Barium Steel Plate on the road side of the housing and it configures the feature of this housing with wooden doors.

I planned simple space structure that all rooms enclose "Light Well". Second floor has living room, dining room, kitchen. The floor is lime stone, and we could feel at home of our families by open design of stairs. The other part of second floor is bathroom and toilet. The floor is lime stone as same as LDK, and it's open space faced with "Light Well".

I planned children room in the third floor, and it's next to free space and separated by wooden sliding door. There is no wall on this floor so that we would arrange the space depending on the change of family structure in the future and daily intended use.

COMPANY	Hamada Design Co.,Ltd
DESIGNER	Takeshi Hamada
PHOTOGRAPHER	Takeshi Hamada
COUNTRY (DISTRICT)	Japan

1 garage
2 entrance
3 hall
4 LDK
5 bed room
6 free room
7 wash room
8 bath room
9 lightwell
10 void
11 balcony

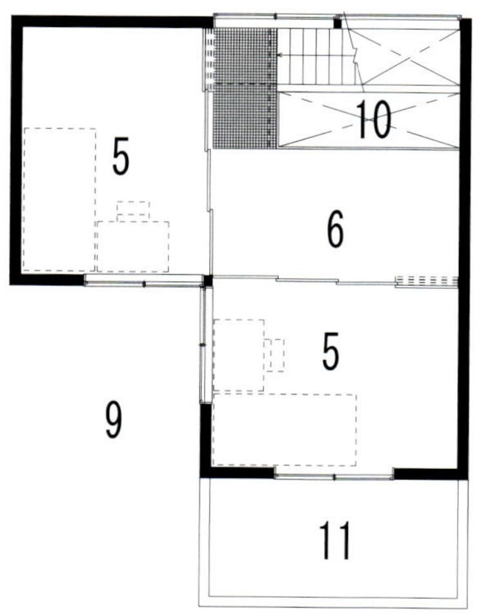

3rd. Floor

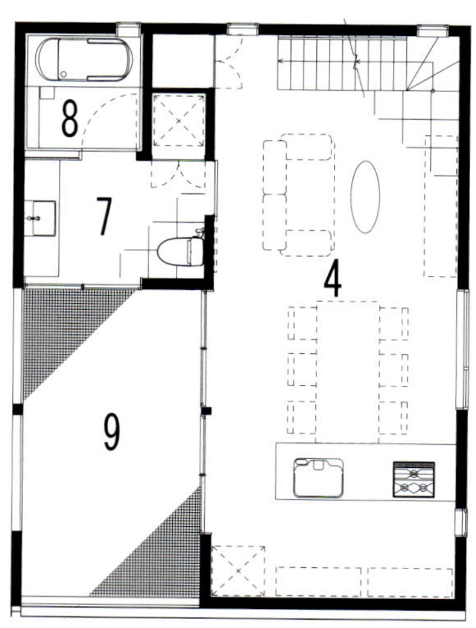

2nd. Floor

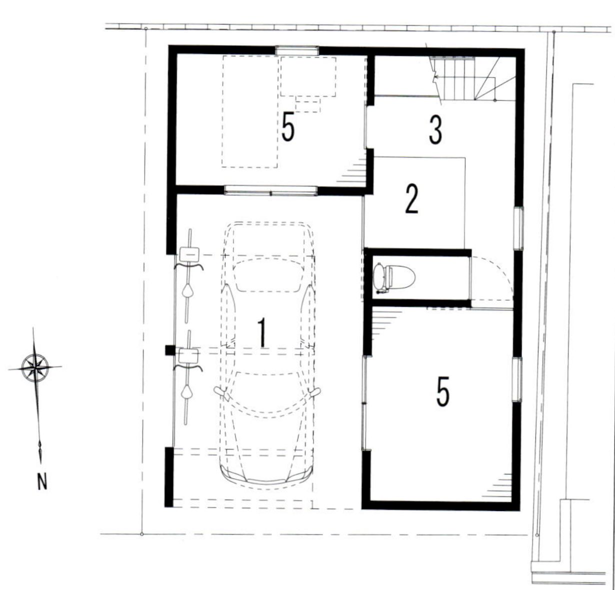

1st. Floor

INSIDE OUT

This is a project of a house for a married couple and two cats, located in Tokyo. The project had started based on the idea that human and cats live in a same house, rather than cats living in a house designed for human — and finally this idea brought out a concept: "a house inside which you feel being outside."
The shape of the building was decided as an irregular quadrangle in accordance with the irregularly-shaped quadrangular site. The roof and wall sides of the volume have carefully designed openings, through which light, wind or rain could enter into the building. Plants are planted on the ground under the roof opening which allows rain to enter. The boxes for bedroom and for bathroom are put in the outer volume, and a living room is located above the bedroom box and a deck above the bathroom box.
Inside the volume, there is a space in which you would feel yourself being outside: light, wind or rain could enter, so that your way of living depends on the weather. However, in this house, you would always positively seek to find another images of life. Areas on the floor on which rain falls vary according to the wind direction, so you would seek to find the area where you don't get wet. As you live longer, you would find out, from your experiences, various things about the relation between the extent to which rain enters on the one hand, and the location of objects, furniture and yourself on the other. And, there is no air-conditioner in this house. During intermediate seasons or summer, both human and cats live in natural draft, or, in another words, they live in the air environment which is almost the same as the outside. On windy or chilly days, you could stay in the indoor boxes or the living room with glass sliding doors closed. Figures and other many items which had been collected are located not only indoors, but many of which are also put on the outdoor shelves to the extent that it is possible. Cats walk on the thin line on which rain doesn't fall and find places in the sun to take a nap. The couple stay in the living room upstairs with glass doors open, sometimes even on rainy days. They often live a life in which they feel themselves being outside even while being inside.
People living in the modern era attempt in the modern way to reduce energy consumption and to coexist with nature — this is also a positive attempt to find what ways of life are possible beyond energy problems and this, in turn, beyond way of life, leading to the important themes about human mental activities. The couple and cats who had lived in an apartment are now pioneering the new images of life every day in the weather-dependent house inside which they feel being outside.

COMPANY	Takeshi Hosaka Architects
DESIGNER	Takeshi Hosaka
PHOTOGRAPHER	KOJI FUJII / Nacasa&Pertners Inc.
CLIENT	Masayoshi & Yoko Matumoto
COUNTRY (DISTRICT)	Japan

North elevation S=1/100

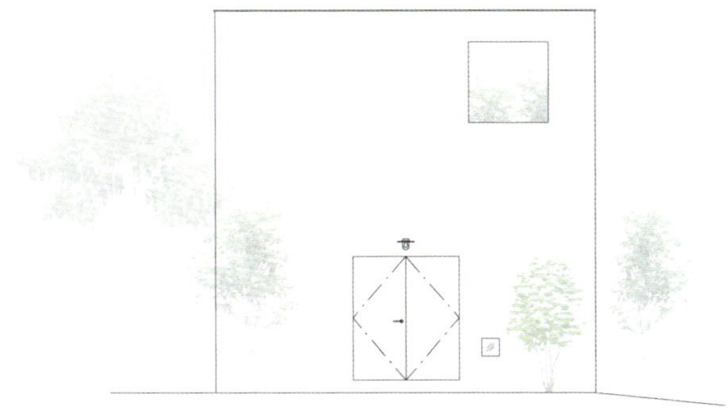

South elevation S=1/100

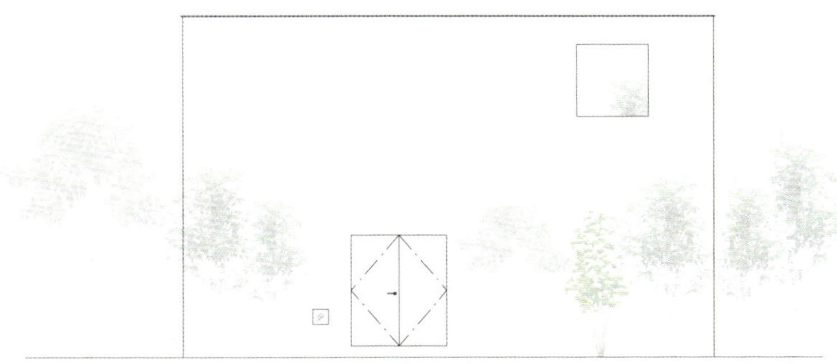

East elevation S=1/100

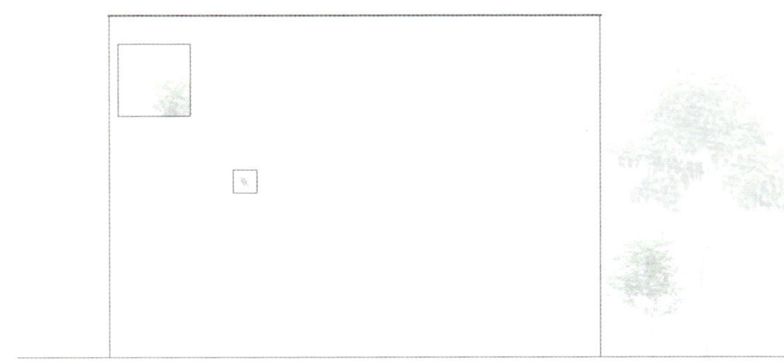

West elevation S=1/100

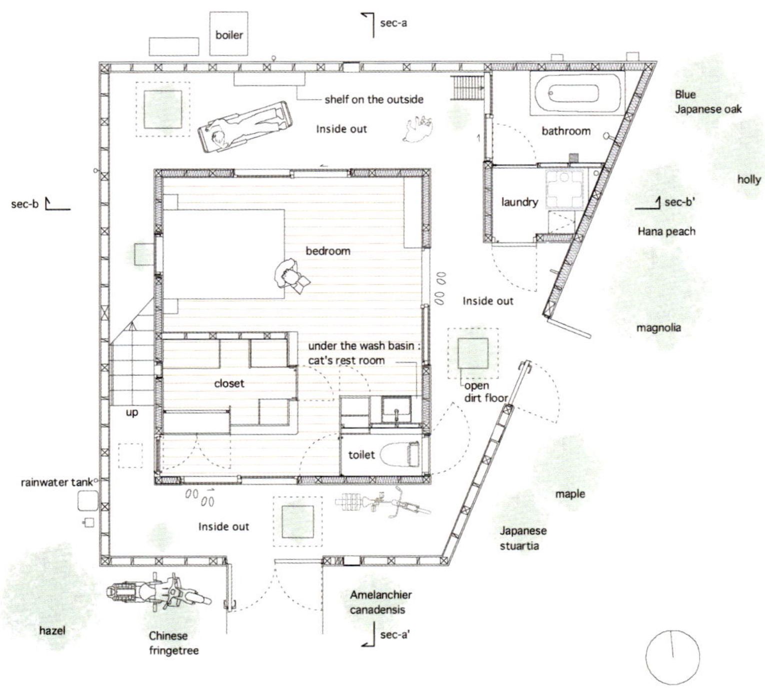

1F plan S=1/100

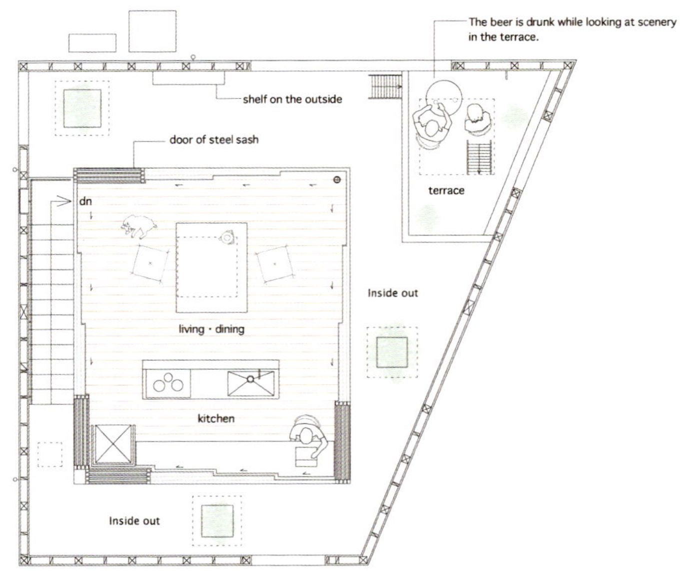

2F plan S=1/100

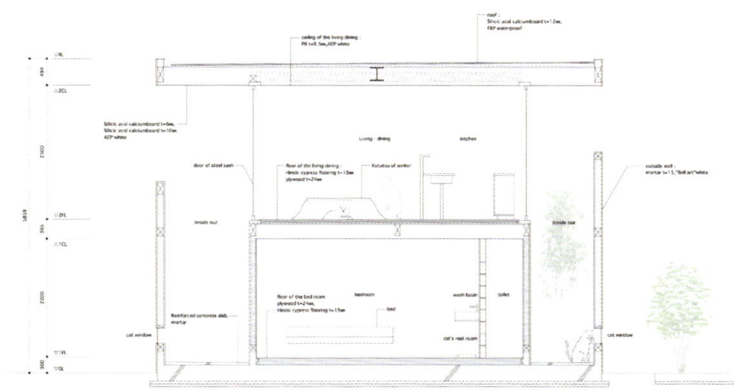

a-a'section S=1/50

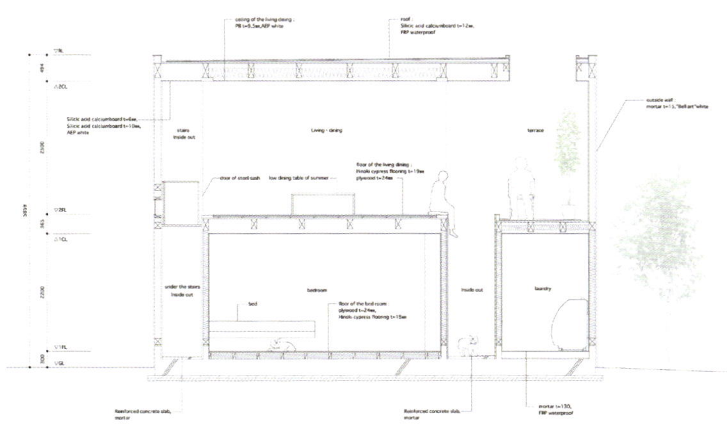

b-b' section S=1/50

VILLA IN DARVISHABAD

This project is a spatial dialog between traditional Persian Architecture and aspects of modern architecture. It creates an architectural space through the incorporation of modern architecture tenets with traditional Persian architecture. The diagram shows how this combination can happen in a coherent way, to make a new space which has got a new and different quality from what it has made from.

The Idea:

I have always thought there is something strange about people in countries such as Iran! There was a history of 4000 years in culture and architecture and in a short period after modernism everything changes. There are people who lost their culture and didn't understand modernism either! They just modernized. What I try to do is to create a new architecture with new spatial qualities which is neither Persian nor Modern but at the same time contains both qualities! To explain, in this house we have free space on the ground floor as the free space exists in modern architecture (I mean roots of modern architecture). On the other hand we have a kind of space surrounded by walls on top (the second floor)! This space opens toward the center, opens in a vertical direction toward the sky and the ground, a quality that you can find almost in all types of Persian architecture. But the interesting part is the space in the middle (first floor), in fact as this modern space on the ground floor and this Persian space in the second floor start a dialog, a new space born in the middle! This space has got both qualities at the same time but is completely different and has got its own personality,we can call it Modersian space.

COMPANY	Rai Studio
DESIGNER	Pouya Khazaeli Parsa
PHOTOGRAPHER	Mohsen Jazayeri Mehrdad Emrani
CLIENT	Nastaran Shahbazi
COUNTRY (DISTRICT)	Iran

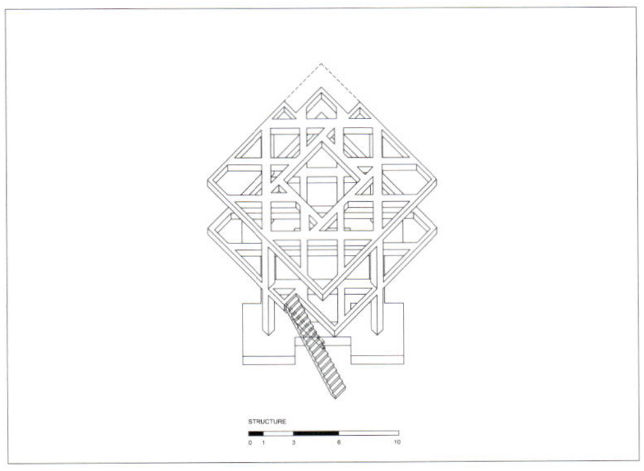
STRUCTURE
0 1 3 6 10

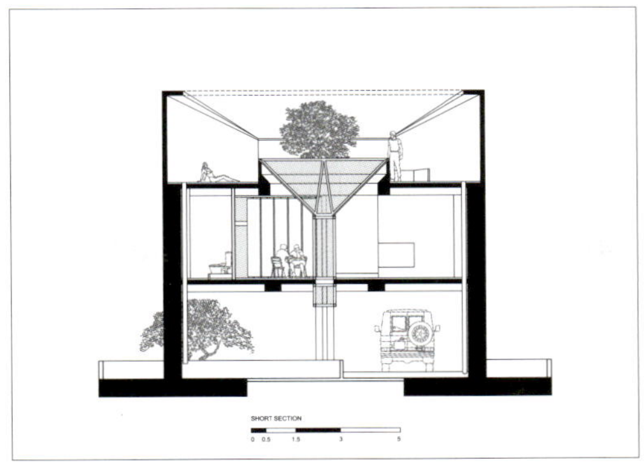
SHORT SECTION
0 0.5 1.5 3 5

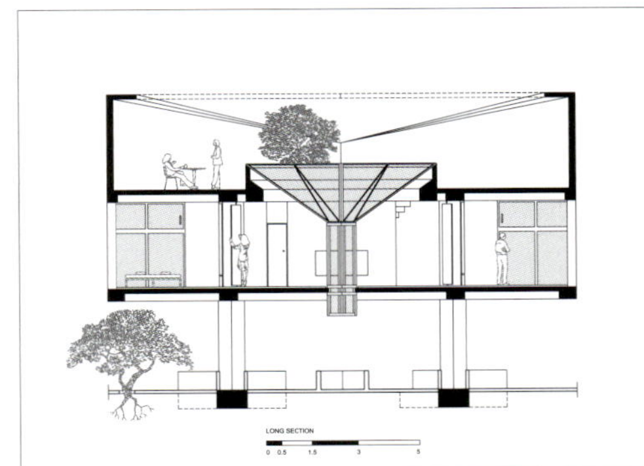
LONG SECTION
0 0.5 1.5 3 5

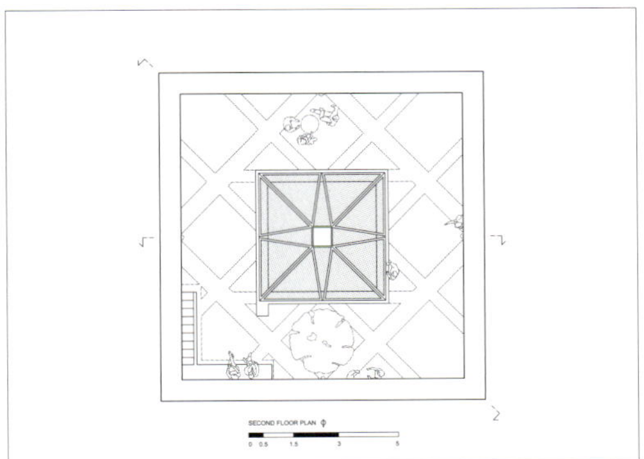
SECOND FLOOR PLAN
0 0.5 1.5 3 5

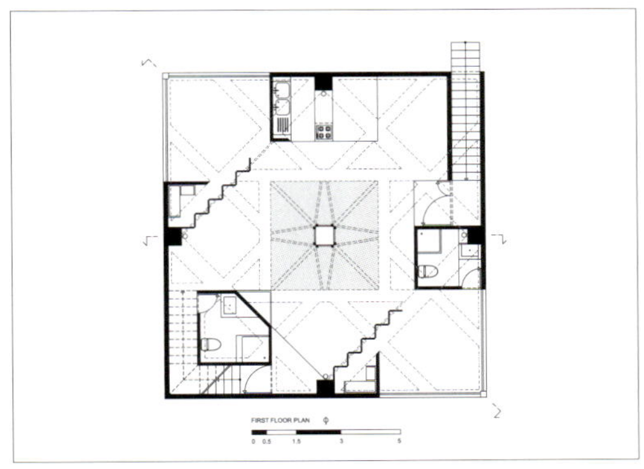
FIRST FLOOR PLAN
0 0.5 1.5 3 5

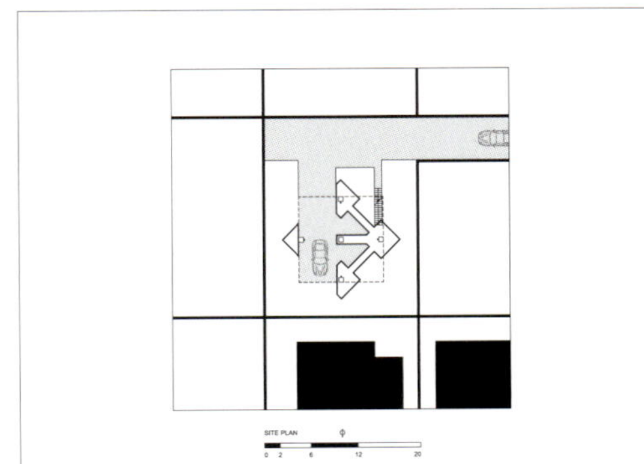
SITE PLAN
0 2 6 12 20

HOUSE TRANSFORMATION

Situated away from the village, this house included an adjacent barn and had a too vast volume to be renewed in its totality. Only elements which can easily be reused were preserved, cellars and floors of the pre-existent house. The rest was demolished.
Volumes of visible tinted concrete replaced the double-sided roof and the transformed area. The big openings so created allow the light to penetrate more generously.
The geometry of the superstructures results. Both from a formal desire and from a will to remove the wall thickness, the various-slope faces enhance the highly varied game of the shadows throughout the day. There is no corridors. Circulation is made along the external wall, from room to room. The overall view continues beyond the windows, opening onto the surrounding landscape.

COMPANY	Clavienrossier Architectes
CREATIVE DIRECTOR	Valéry Clavien & Nicolas Rossier
DESIGNER	Valéry Clavien & Nicolas Rossier
PHOTOGRAPHER	Roger Frei – Zürich
CLIENT	Yann & Daniéla Roduit, Charrat (vs) Switzerlan
COUNTRY (DISTRICT)	Switzerland

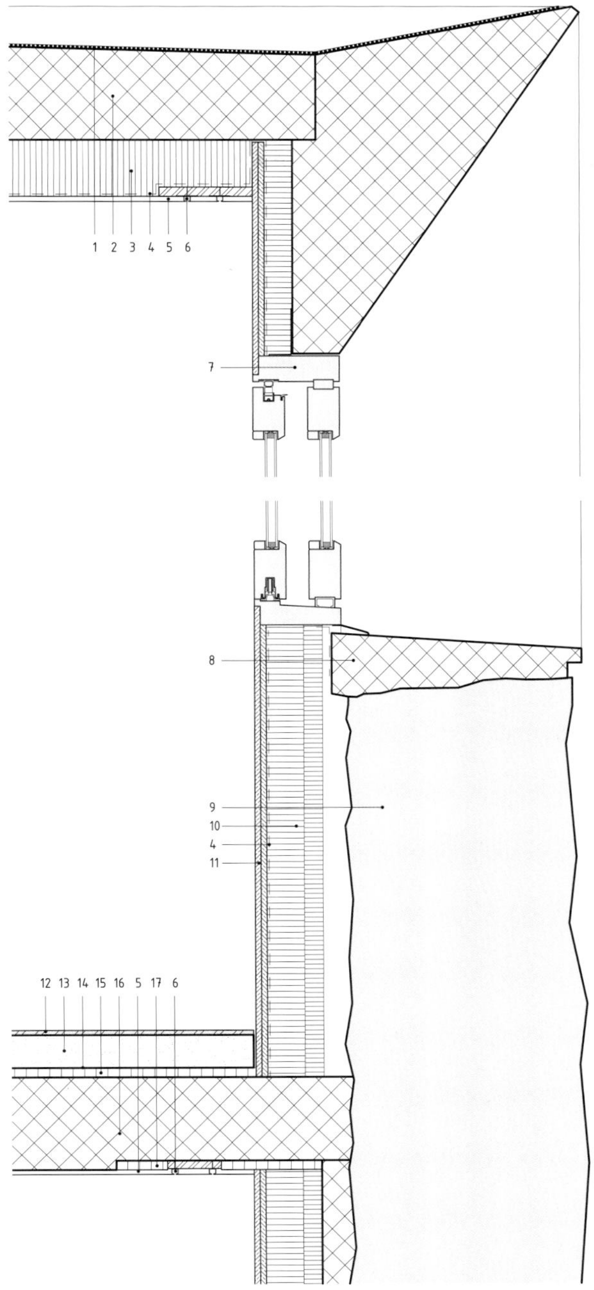

1	bitumen roofing felt, 2 layers	7mm
2	reinforced concrete slab	22-30cm
3	thermal insulation	12cm
4	vapour barrier	-
5	plaster	1cm
6	curtain rail	-
7	larch sliding window	-
8	fair-face reinforced concrete, couloured	
9	existing stone wall	60cm
10	thermal insulation, 1x4cm, 1x8cm	12cm
11	reinforced plasterboard	2.5cm
12	oak parquet flooring	1cm
13	screed with underfloor heating	7cm
14	separating layer	-
15	impact sound insulation	2cm
16	concrete slab	20cm
17	thermal insulation, expanded polystyrene 2cm	

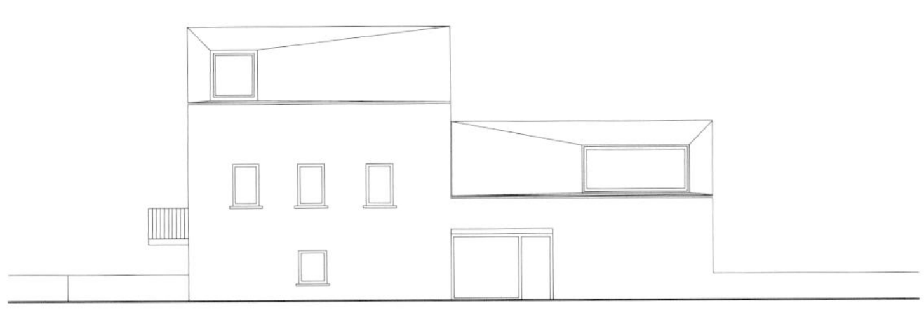

elevation north

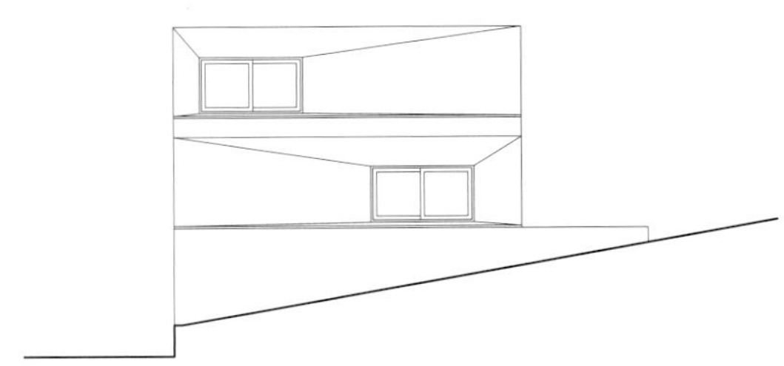

elevation west

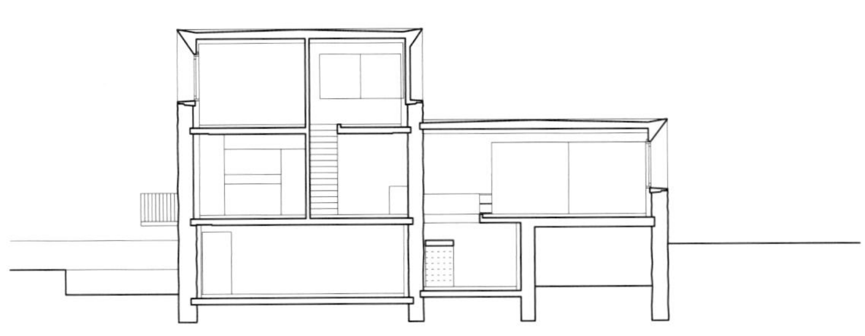

section

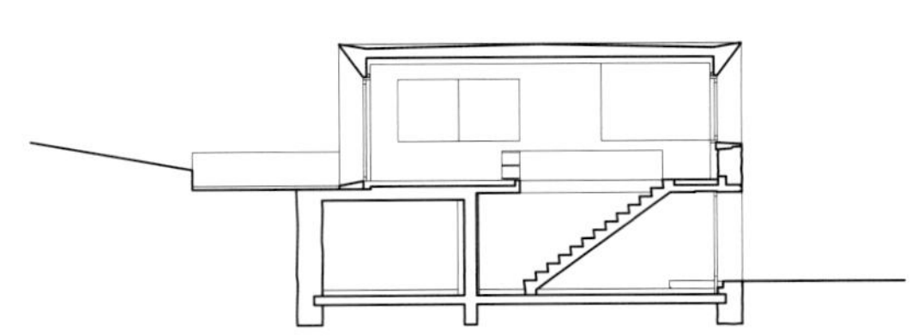

section

DEVOTO HOUSE

This project was a great challenge to the studio, considering that it was going to take part of the urban structure. The lot of 18 x 24 meters is located in Devoto. It is between two existing buildings that threatens the project when the problem of isolation and view. For this reason this project is leaning towards its neighbor, creating an introspective posture that creates the views from the inside rather than from the outside.

An architecture that generated its own views. In this manner the project was able to solve the basis of isolation and views from the garden. This had been a constant worry from the clients since the beginning of the project.

The house of 500m² was done for a young couple with kids. It was larger than the dimensions of given lot, threatening the space of the garden. For that reason, the first floor was given less program, leaving open the exterior spaces.

The living, kitchen and dining rooms expose the garden that penetrates all the volumes in the house. The space distort the conventional plans of an urban house. The stone wall guides the inhabitant within the house, therefore, the rough texture of the streets are softened by the water that flows down the stone wall, a walk that is colored by the different qualities the water gives the space.

The green area between the living room and the neighbor guides the way to the entrance of the house. It is surrounded by the natural setting and different tones that the light of the sun gives to the space. In this project, the impact of the sun path was carefully studied, especially to place the swimming pool. One more time, water takes a big role in the creation of this house. This time the swimming pool is elevated from the ground creating a glass wall that allows views from within and the outside, creating views from different points in the house and focal point outside the house.

The house is formed vertically having a shifting effect. The bedrooms are located in the east overlooking the heart of the house, the garden. The last floor place includes a spa; having a jacuzzi, sauna and a gym with an exterior space. Privately set for the couple.

This project goes beyond the rigid setting. It translates the urban setting into a natural setting subtlety. It pushes the boundaries of the conventional urban home to a spacious living where one has the best of both, the natural and the urban setting.

COMPANY	Andres Remy Arquitectos
DESIGNER	Remy
PHOTOGRAPHER	Alejandro Peral
COUNTRY (DISTRICT)	Argentina

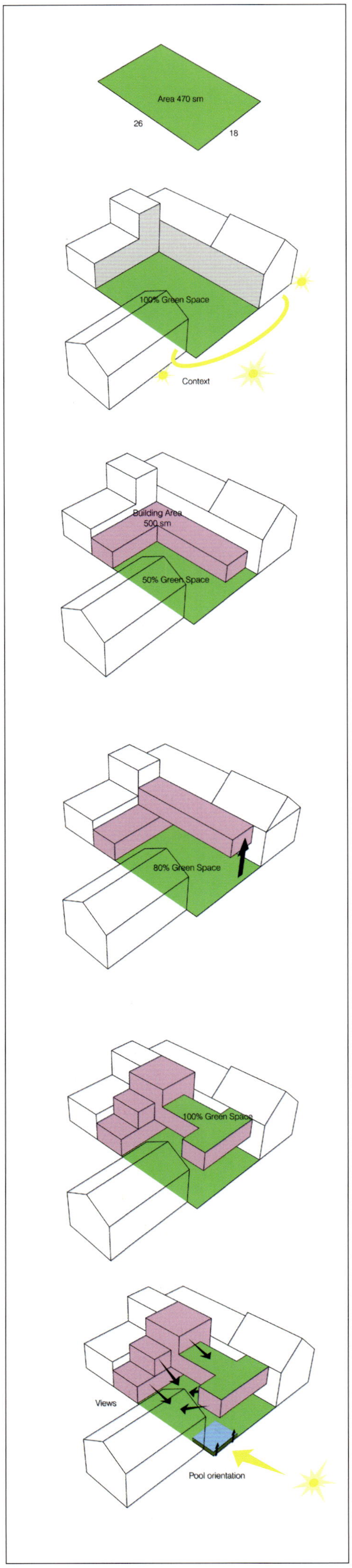
Area 470 sm
26
18
100% Green Space
Context
Building Area
500 sm
50% Green Space
80% Green Space
100% Green Space
Views
Pool orientation

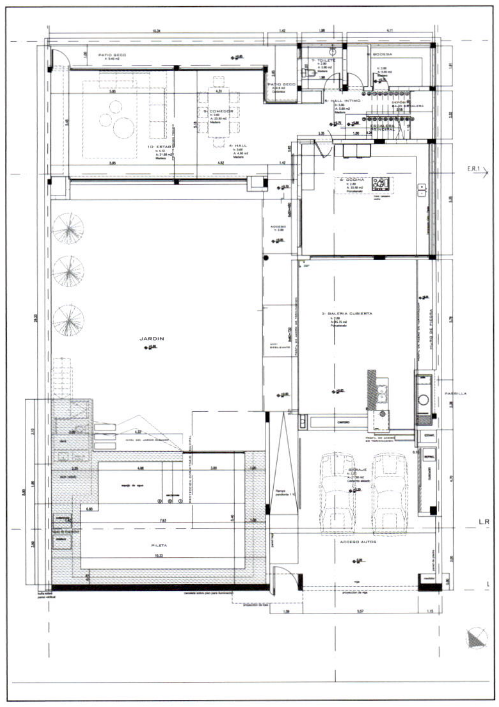

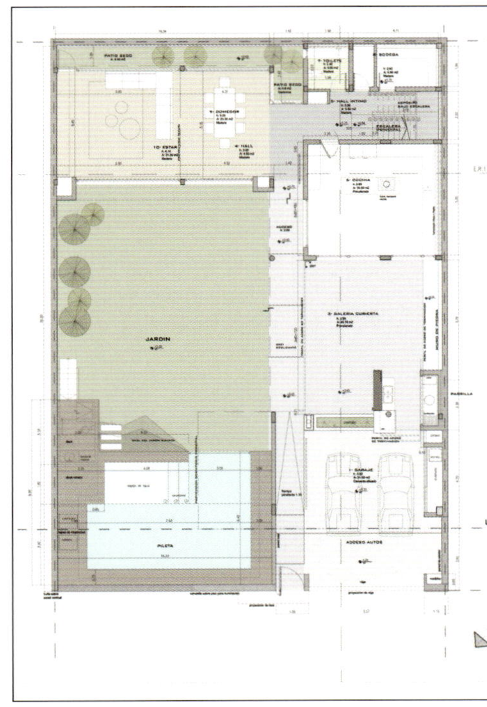

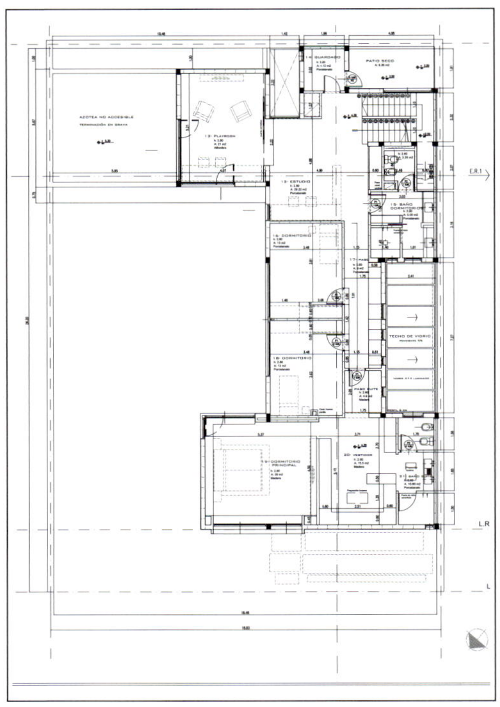

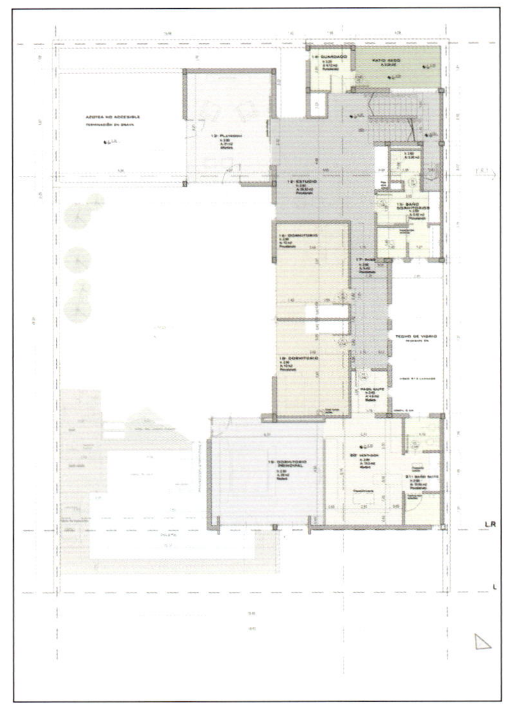

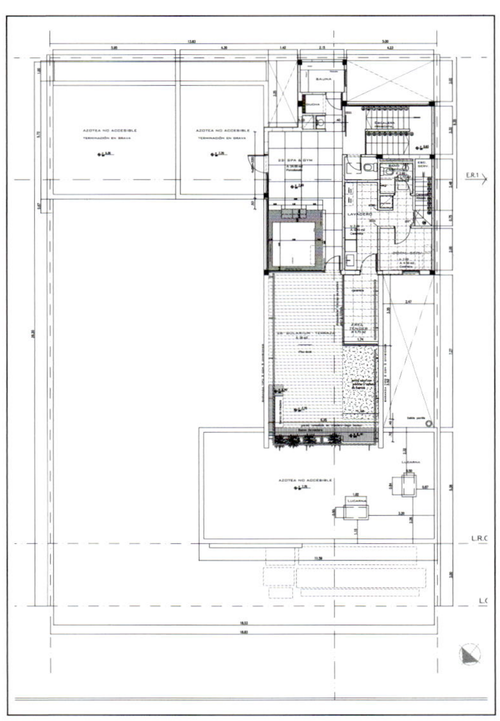

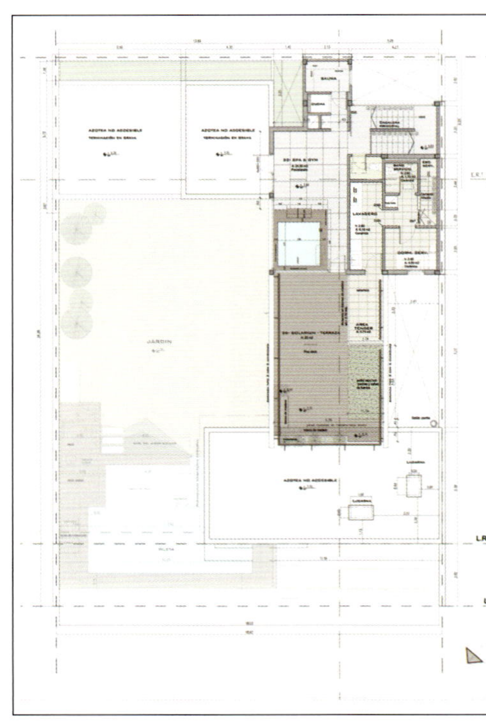

THE R HOUSE

Sevres is located in the Parisian suburb. A couple and their three kids acquired a plot of land, which was, at the time, occupied by an orchard and its gardener's shed.
The small construction along with the healthy trees were preserved in memory of the past. The program was discussed and analyzed. It's composed of three distinct sets: - The amenities: hall, office, laundry room, basement, garage. - The common areas: living room, dining room, the kitchen and the parental suite - The children's bedrooms organized around a multipurpose space. The methods and time of occupation are distinct and expectations are different: practicality for the first feature, collective life and reception area for the second and coziness for the third.
Furthermore, this fragmentation comes into resonance with the context: it is not just a house anymore but three volumes that come across the scale of heterogeneous nearby constructions. Due to the small size of the site volumes are superimposed.
The first volume is built backing on to the neighboring construction and runs parallel to the street. It's half buried in the slope and therefore levels the ground. Made out of masonry, quenched with a single layer of bitumen and recovered with Corten steel sheets, this first floor contains all the amenities. Walls, ceiling and floor are white and contrast with the exterior. Those elements converge on the staircase and accelerate the perspective so the visitor is quickly projected into the house. The hall leads to the office and the laundry. The cloakroom and the restrooms are hidden in the thickness of the walls.
Thanks to the first volume which levels the ground, the second floor is in direct relation with the garden. As far as the cantilever is concerned, it constitutes a canopy for the main entrance of the house. This floor is dedicated to the collective life. It's a really open and fluid space.
The second floor is divided by two "pieces of furniture". The first piece incorporates the stairs, the kitchen, the restrooms and the chimney whereas the second one is composed of the dressing and the bathroom. Those two blocks delineate the living room, the dining room and the parental suite. It's a very minimalist place.
The third and last floor is, once again, leaning on the neighboring building. The volume is wrapped with pine lath so the house can be in the line of the predominant color shades of the district. Since the volume is on the top of the construction and dedicated to the children, the wooden cladding was also a wink to tree houses. On the third floor three bedrooms and their bathrooms are organized around a multipurpose space. This double-oriented space is protected by a screen wall on the street side, and leads to a large terrace (rooftop of the second floor) on the south side. Bedrooms are also double-oriented to optimize views and natural lightening and provide natural and efficient ventilation.
All the terraces offer various points of view and different aspects depending on the season. Sustainability was a main objective of the project: exterior isolation, recyclable materials with low environmental impact, high-performance glazing.

COMPANY	Colboc Franzen & Associates
CREATIVE DIRECTOR	Benjamin Colboc, Manuela Franzen, Arnaud Sachet
PROJECT MANAGER	Arnaud Sachet
PROJECT TEAM	Florianne Bataillard, Nadège Lachassagne, Anne MERLIO
COUNTRY (DISTRICT)	France

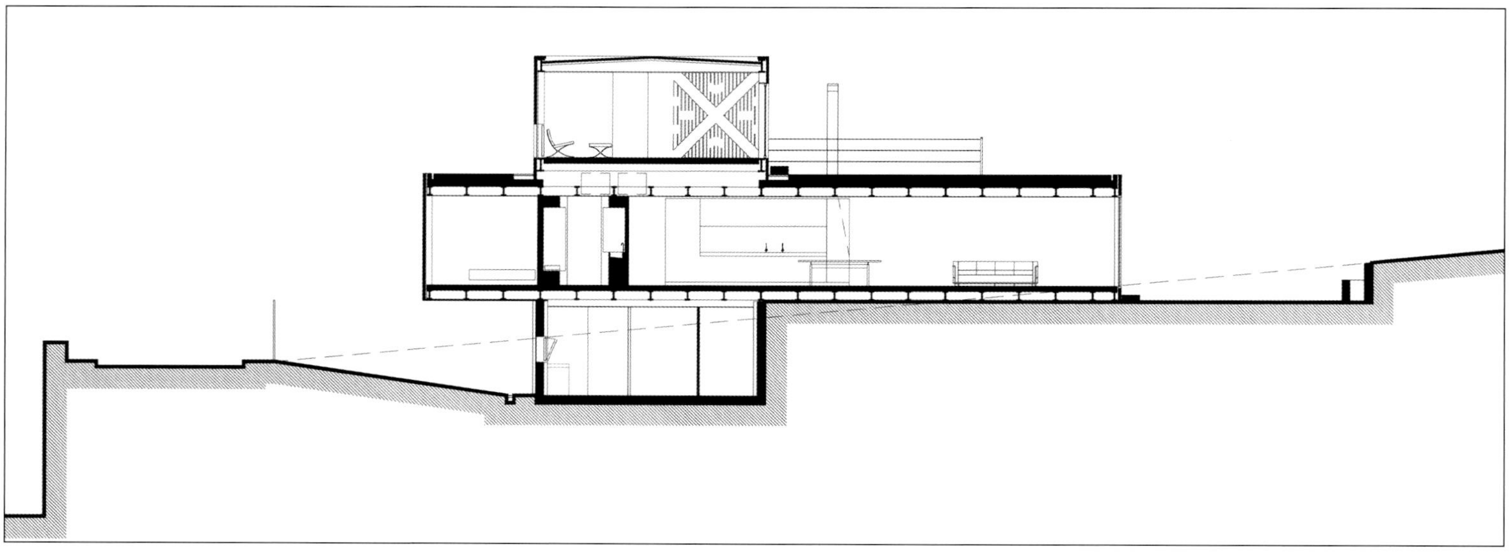

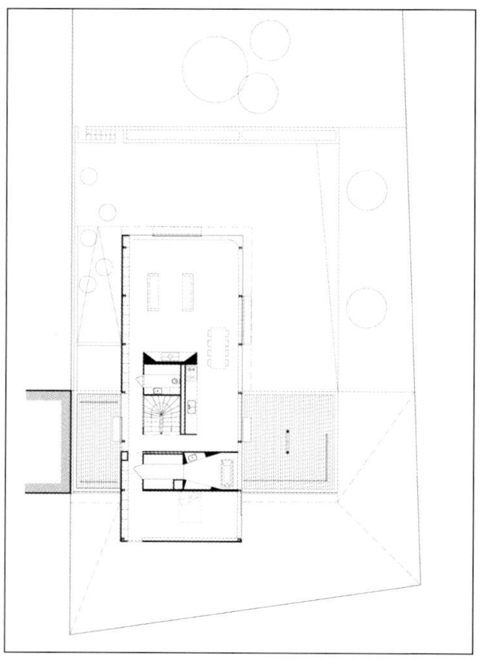

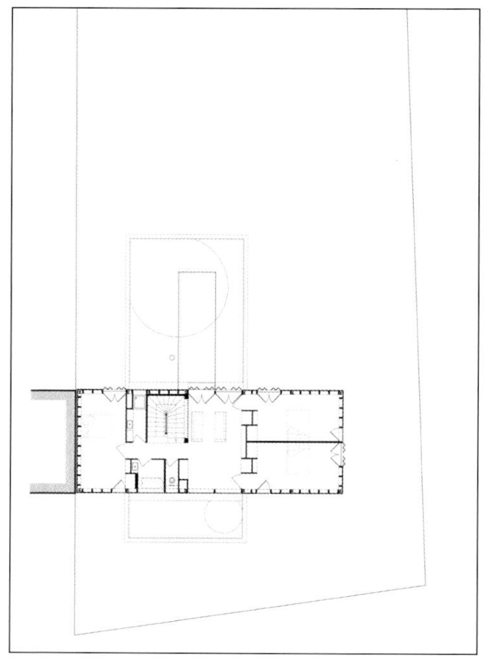

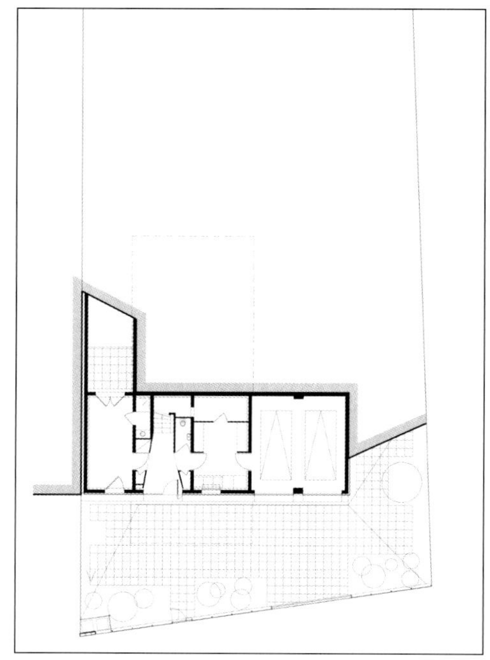

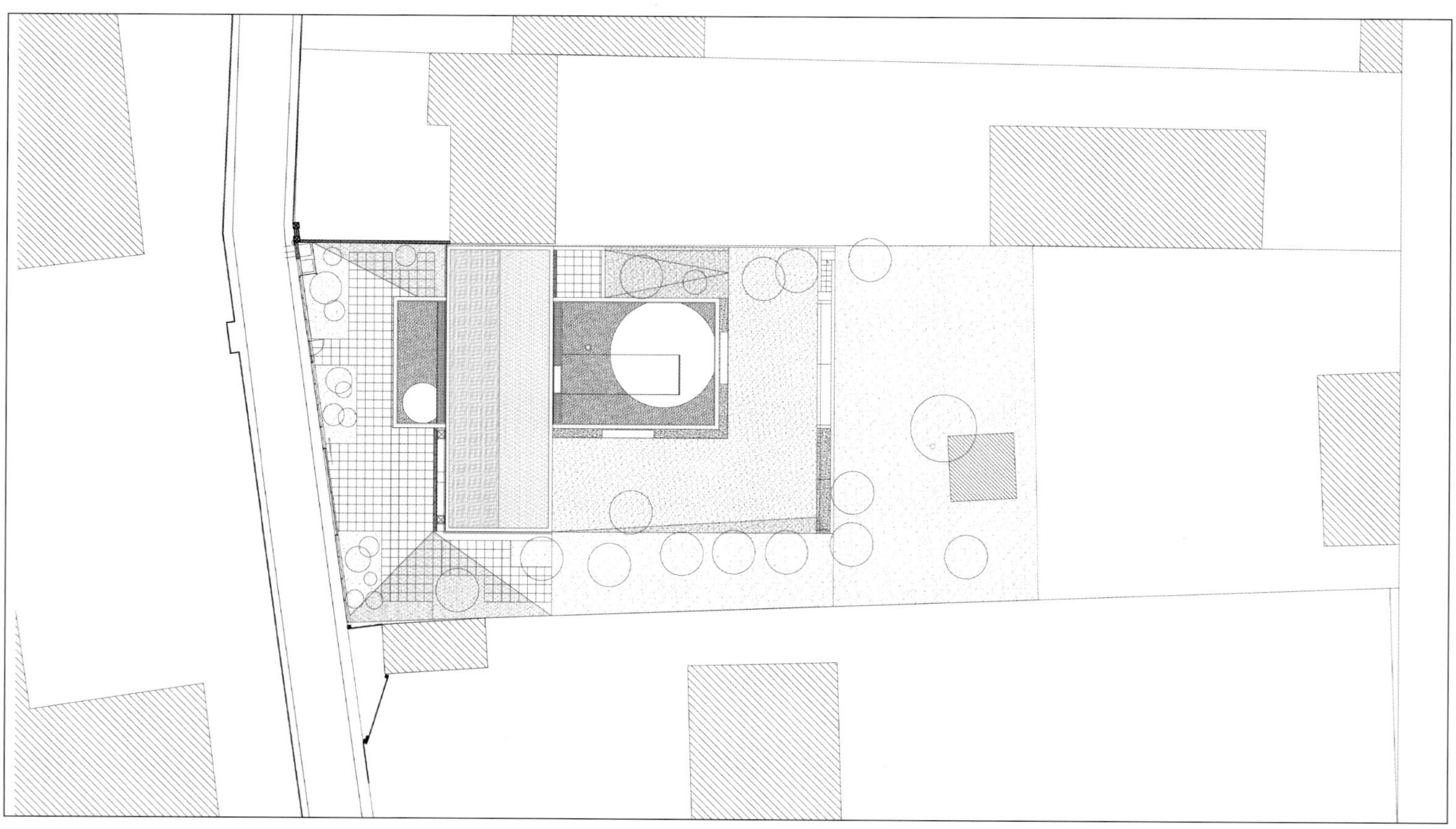

HOUSE IN MECO

Located on an woody site at Meco beach, nearby Sesimbra in the outskirts of Lisbon, this house aims to a close relation with surrounding space, a beautiful natural landscape.
A set of restrictive regulations, defined in the city council masterplan project, namely distances to borders, access, total amount of construction area and volume were a condition to be addressed and surpassed.
The resultant form proposes an almost accidental arrangement of different and overlapped solids, dealing with mass and voids. Windows are opened in a free way trying to catch the most interesting spots in the surrounding landscape or the attached external spaces and volumes.
Using different materials, the house proposes an arrangement of solids, gives opportunity to light emphasizing forms and suggest a concern in controlling the relationships between external and internal areas. Some circulations, as the staircases and bridge between upper rooms, are in white painted metal and glass, drawn as light as possible.

COMPANY	Jorge Mealha
DESIGNER	Jorge Mealha
PHOTOGRAPHER	Jorge Mealha
CLIENT	Paula Ribeiro
COUNTRY (DISTRICT)	Portugal

GROUND FLOOR PLAN

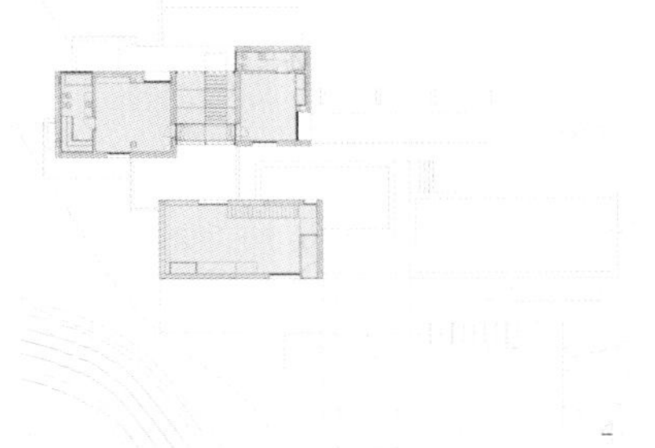
FIRST FLOOR PLAN

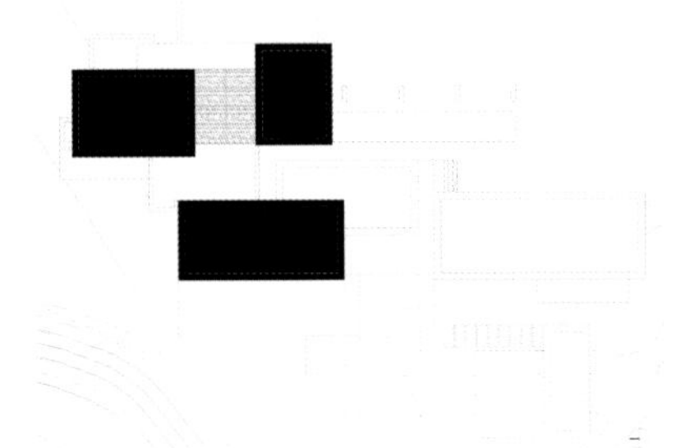
ROOF PLAN

WEST ELEVATION

EAST ELEVATION

SOUTH ELEVATION

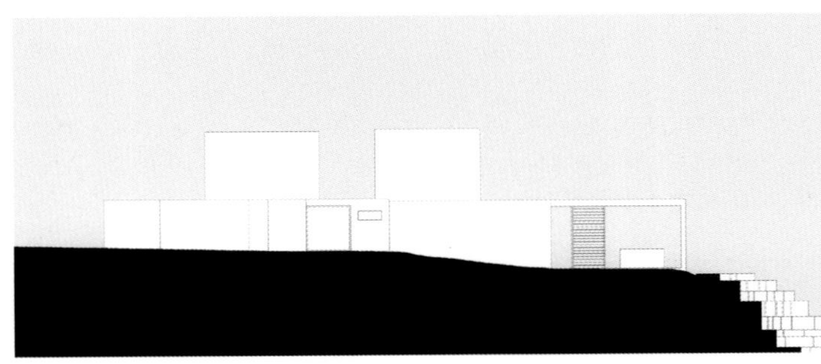
NORTH ELEVATION

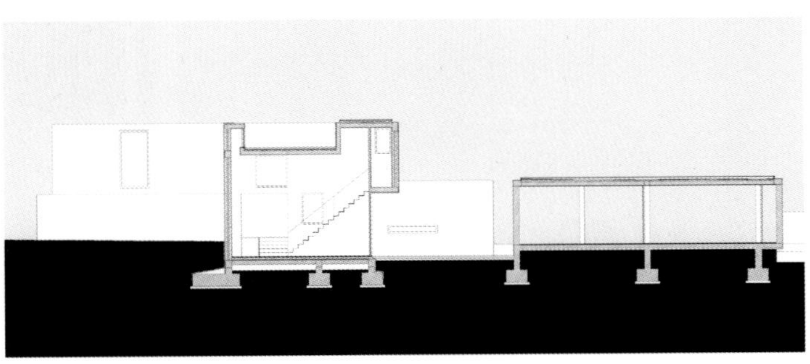
SECTION 01

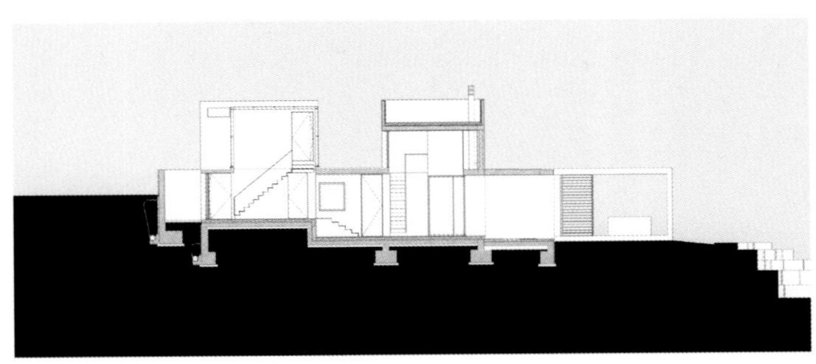
SECTION 02

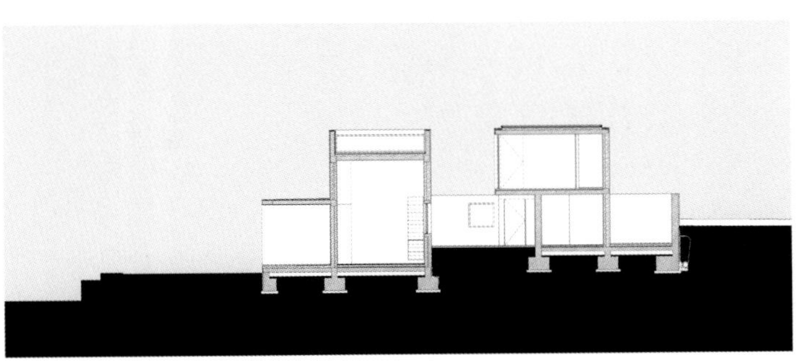
SECTION 03

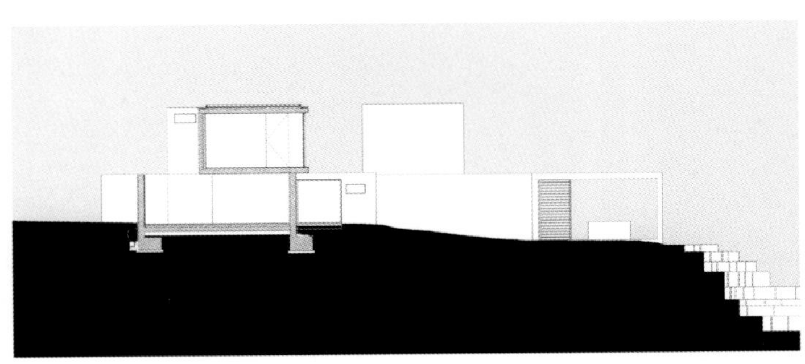
SECTION 04

HOUSE IN PAÇO DE ARCOS

Located at Alto do Lagoal in Paco de Arcos, a neighborhood of Lisbon facing the sea, this house has been built on a sloping site and proposes as main strategy an arrangement of several solids in order to attenuate the overall mass due to the functional program requested by the client.

This arrangement of different solids and voids, uses large plain surfaces and some in-between tensioned spaces to let light draw or reflect on the objects, emphasizing geometry and proposing a changeable reading of form and space during the day.

Some surfaces, covered by metal screening/shading devices, create large smooth textured plans on two facades of the house hiding windows and enhancing form, acting also as a kind of diaphragm device to filter the views between interior and exterior. Also act as a passive sunshade control between internal and external spaces.

Some circulations, as the staircase and main corridor are built in white painted 10mm metal sheet slightly detached from the walls, leaving opportunity for light, caught by the long skylight to pass in between and spread to the lower floors.

The external envelope, a"in situ" concrete structure, integrates a double row masonry of perforated ceramic blocs as external walls, including inner rigid thermal insulation panels. External walls finishes are in cement plaster painted. Windows are in standard natural aluminum color profiles integrating double thermal glass.

In the interior, the walls main finish is plaster painted in white except in the bathrooms where the walls are covered in white/grey natural striped marble.

The circulation areas floors, corridors and staircases are in plain or folded 10mm thickness metal plates, painted with white mate epoxy enamel. The bedrooms floors are finished in industrial wood parquet whit colorless wax varnish finish. Social areas are covered with polished white stone and kitchen in brilliant black ceramic sandstone.

COMPANY	Jorge Mealha
CREATIVE DIRECTOR	Jorge Mealha
DESIGNER	Arch. João Sítima, Arch. Luís Banazol, Arch. Pedro Pereira, Arch. Marcelo Dantas
PHOTOGRAPHER	Jorge Mealha
CLIENT	Margarida e António Lemos
COUNTRY (DISTRICT)	Portugal

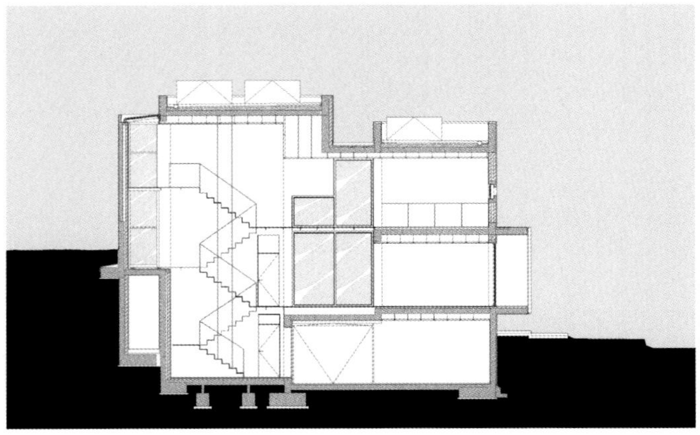

SECTION T01

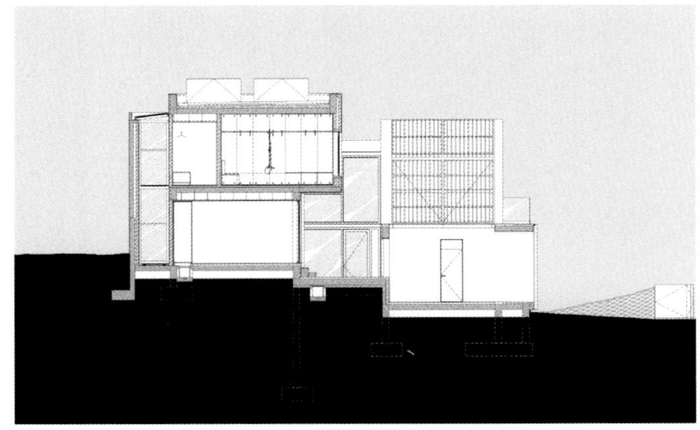

SECTION T02

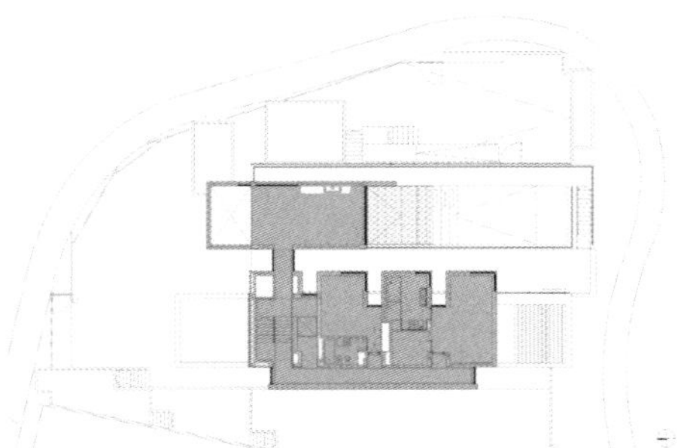

FIRST FLOOR PLAN

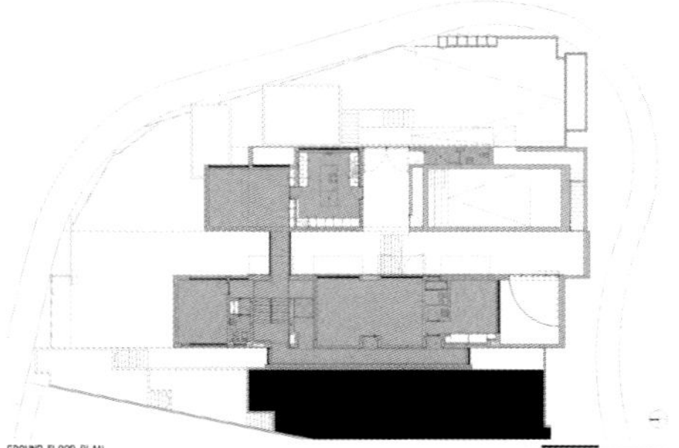

GROUND FLOOR PLAN

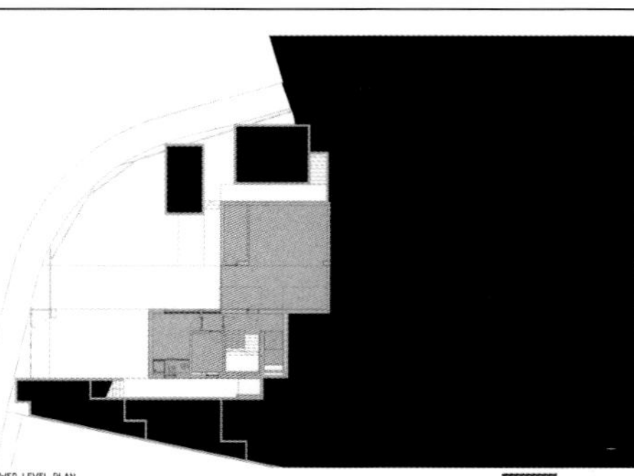

LOWER LEVEL PLAN

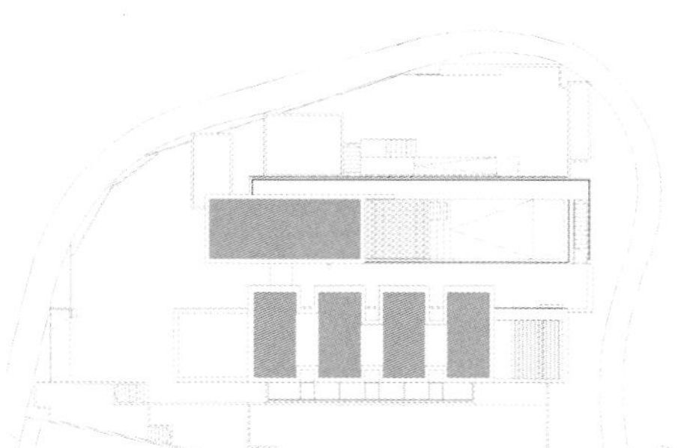

ROOF PLAN

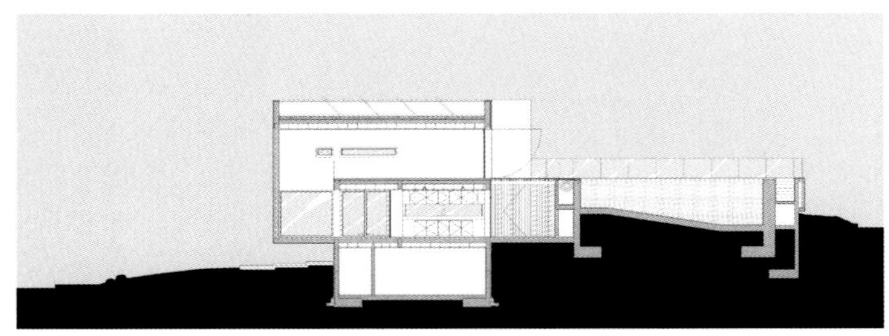

SECTION L01

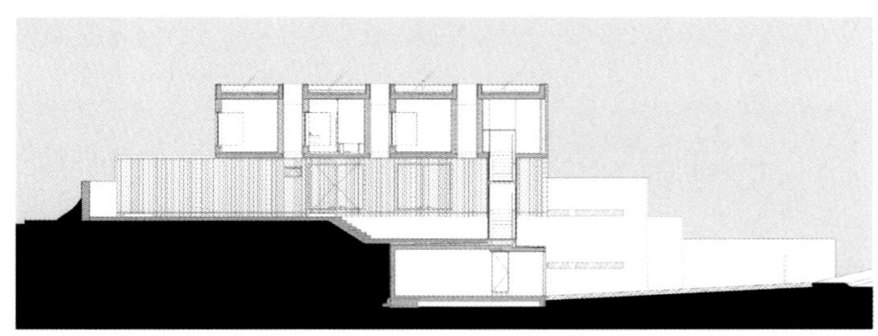

SECTION L02

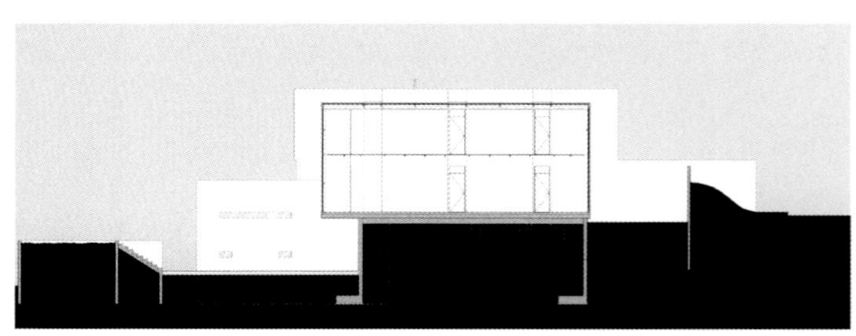

SECTION L03

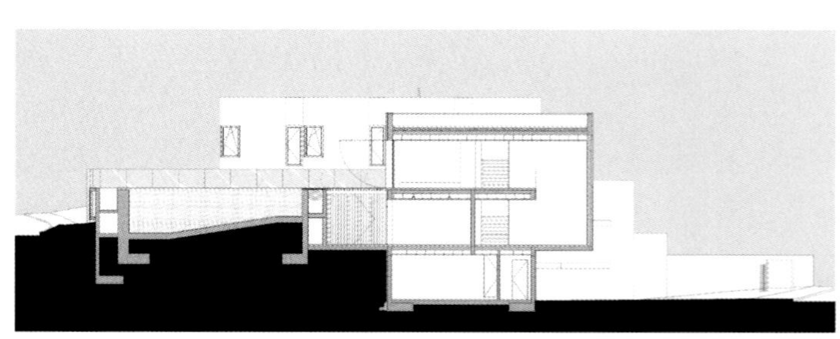

SECTION L04

FUGLSANG NAES

The estate consists of five blocks, the design of which is based upon a wish of creating a flexible concept able to contain different accommodation units within the same idea and idiom. The buildings were made so that they can be adapted to each individual resident and to the demand and will consequently be suitable for a wide segment of residents. The flats in the five blocks are situated around a centrally placed staircase (the core of the house); on the ground floor there is a parking area (also for bicycles) for the residents, depots and rooms for garbage cans. Around this core it is possible to set up three, four or five flats, which can be arranged horizontally, vertically or as a combination – and the arrangement can be different in the other blocks.

The basic idea is to build all five blocks with three to five flats depending on requirements as to size and inner arrangement. Afterwards the intention is to imitate “a stroke with an axe” in order to give the building an aesthetic distinctive character as well as functional advantages. The strokes are placed where they will give the optimum conditions for view and daylight in the depth of the building. Apart from giving view and sunlight the strokes also create a private terrace for each flat.

The inside arrangement of the flats consists of regular rooms which are contrasted by the oblique angles made by the strokes of an axe. Due to the combination of the different arrangement of the three storeys of the blocks, the number of flats and the placement of the strokes you will see five blocks with a different exterior, yet architecturally closely related.

COMPANY	CEBRA a/s, arkitekter maa
PHOTOGRAPHER	MadsBMoeller
CLIENT	M2as
COUNTRY (DISTRICT)	Denmark

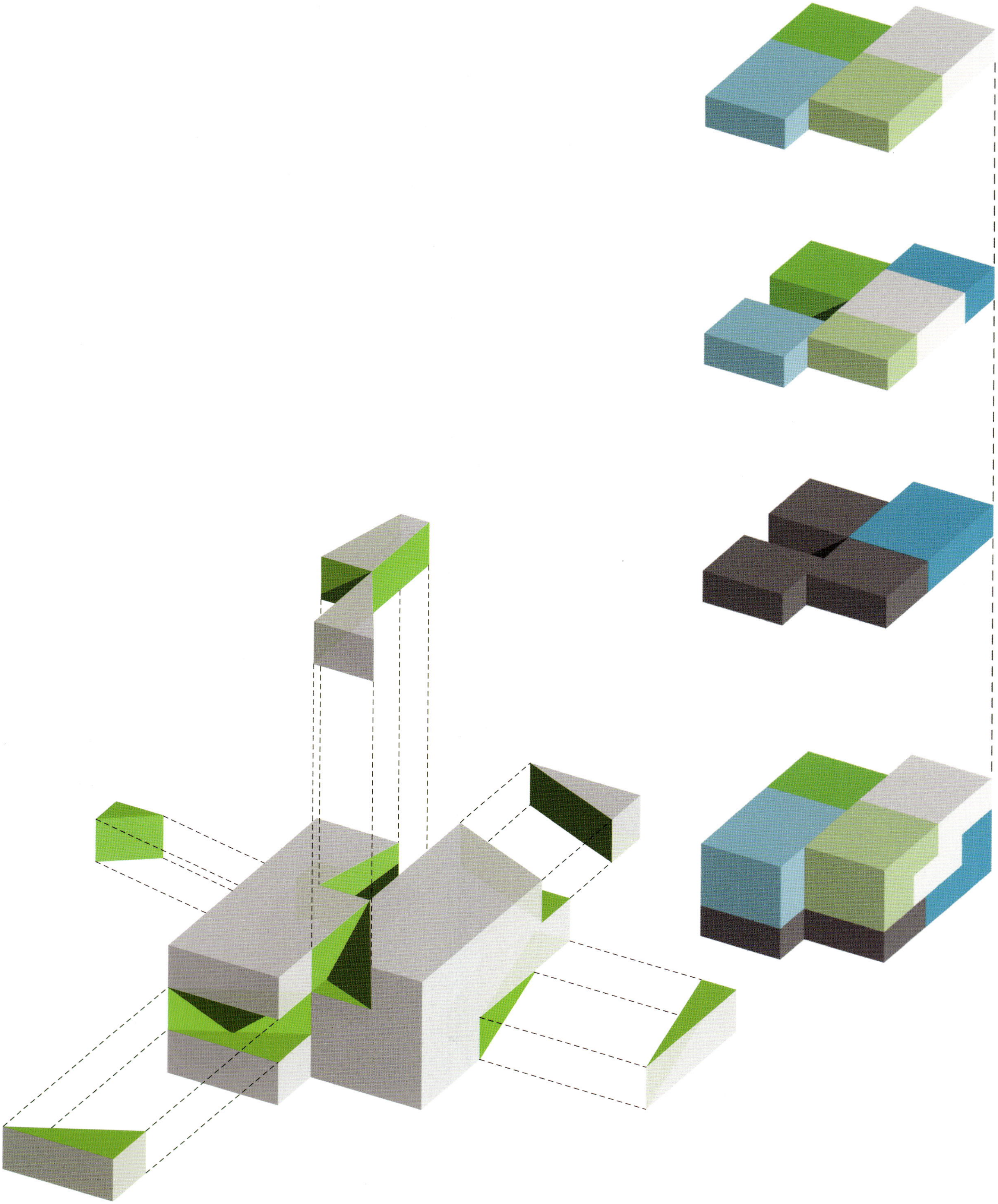

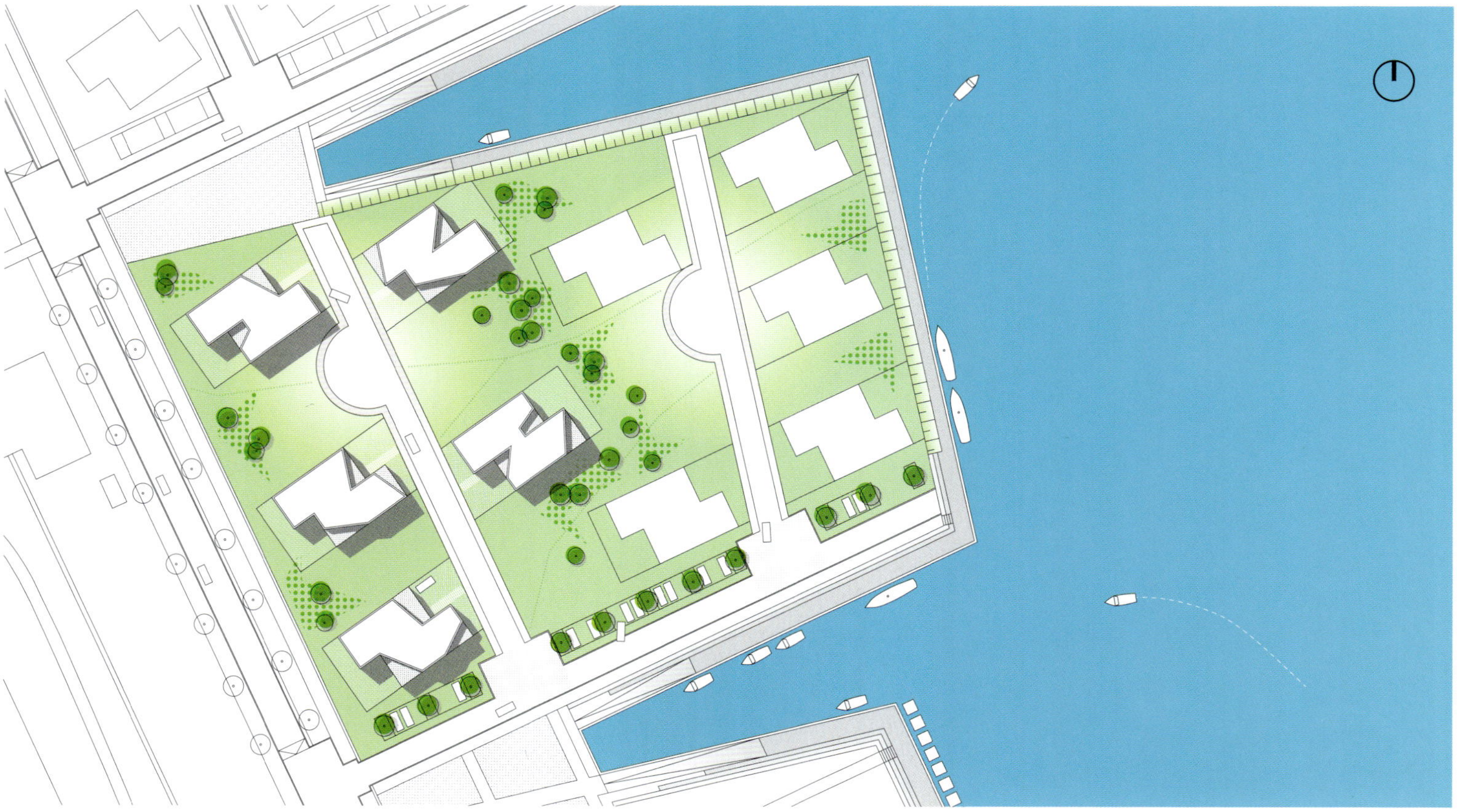

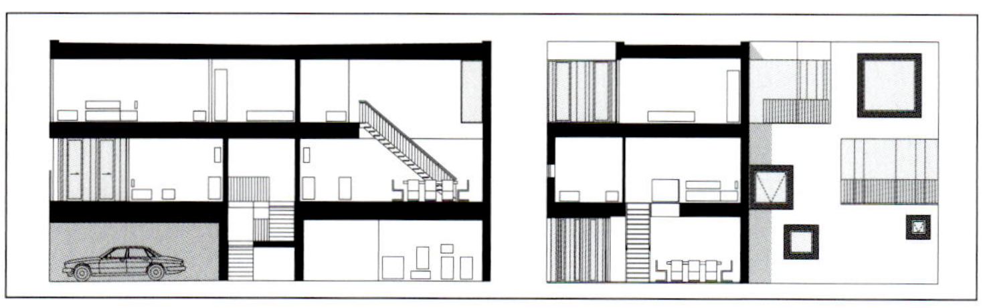

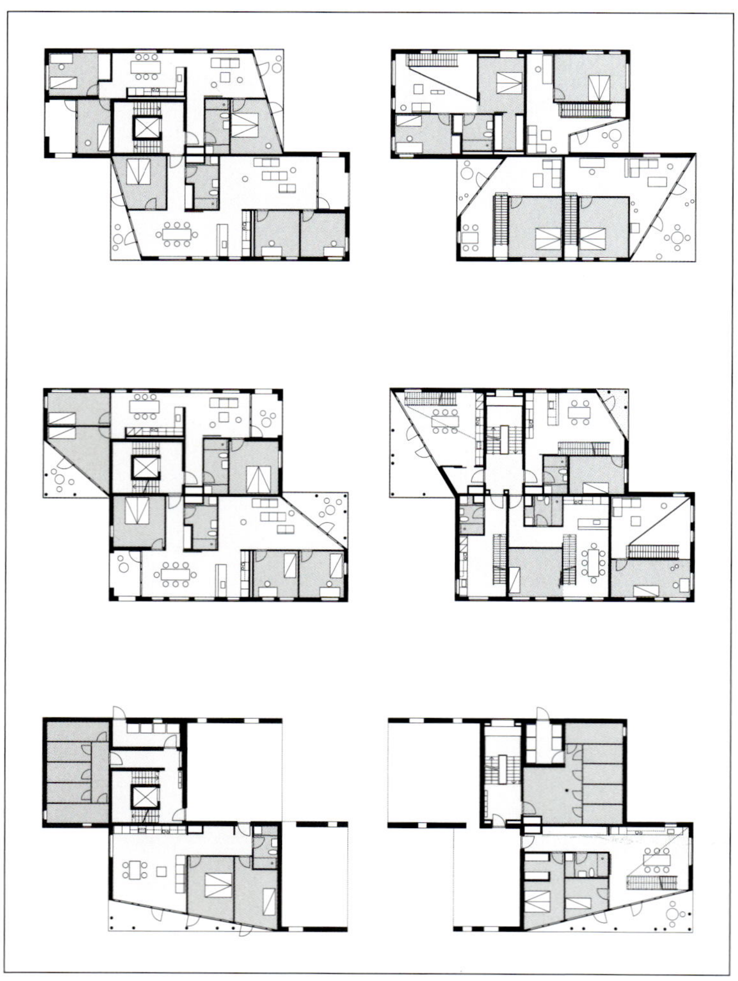

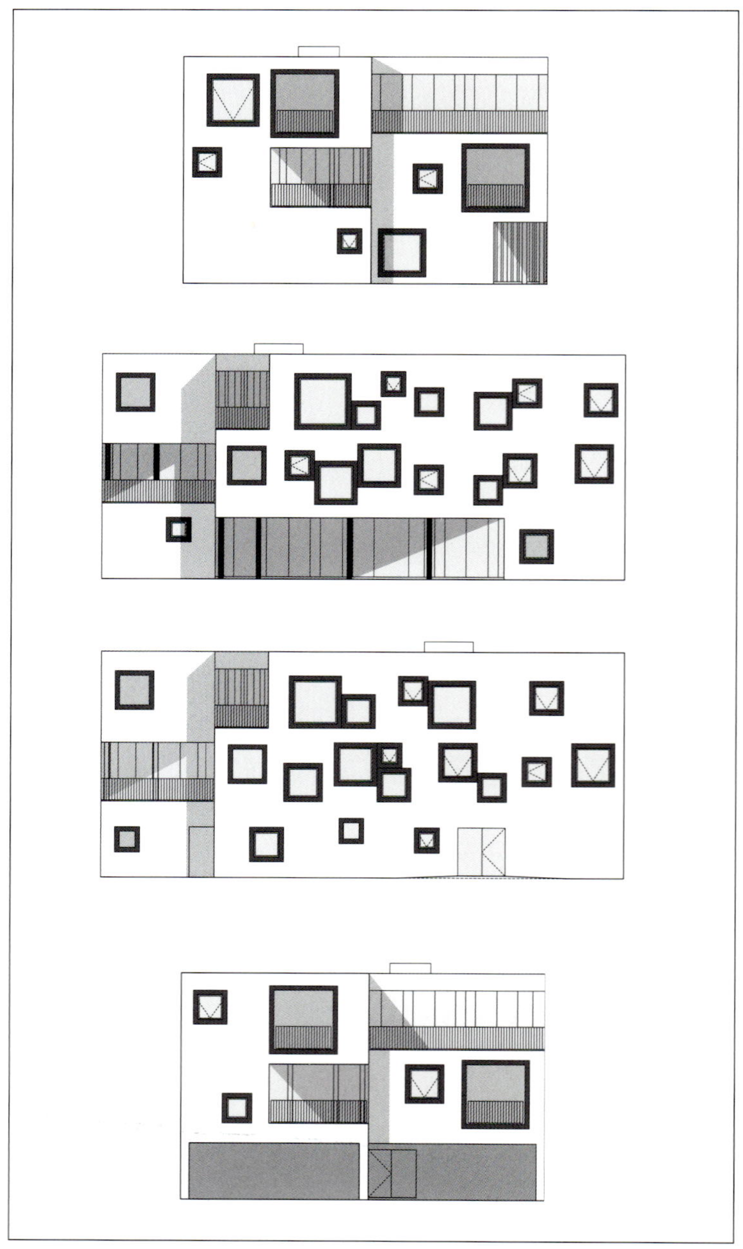

HOUSE IN NIKAIA

A family house in Nikaia. The house consists of two cubic forms, a living and a sleeping area, connected by a glass bridge. Steel constructions form the skeleton of the object wrapped by prefabricated organic blocks that act as perfect insulation during warm summers and cold winters typical for this region. Interactions of geometrical shapes, huge volumes and transparent surfaces that offer a great view in Olympus mountain.

In the main object is the living room into which one steps directly from the front entrance, the dining room and the kitchen area. In the upper level is the master bedroom, the laundry room and bathrooms. The secondary cube-shaped pavilion houses the children's bedrooms. One level for each. Through the glass corridor they have access to the main bedroom and bathrooms. Photovoltaic solar panels hidden in the roof top provide sustainable electricity for any use. Recycled and second hand materials have been used for the building. The interior and the exterior is entirely illuminated with LED modules, with low energy consumption. The floor-to-ceiling height in the main object is 7 meters, with the supporting structure that consists of a steel skeleton reinforced by diagonal elements staying visible.

With no conventional internal support walls there is opportunity for more shapely, free form space dividers, reminding of an industrial space that was never designed with rooms in mind of pollution, noise, traffic, these are only a few of the problems the young couple had to face while choosing the best location for their future home.

That is why we felt that Nikaia, a lovely and friendly green neighborhood 10 km from Larissa, was the right place.

Driving 10 km every day to work seemed like a small price for the couple to pay for a home close to nature with a 4000 m^2 yard where their children could play.

A flat and empty area was the site condition to start with. The house was placed on the north side of the rectangular shaped site. The further development of the project is to enrich the inner yard by increasing greenery and planting trees.

Our goal was to build a comfortable and functional home with enough space for each member of the family. The idea was to provide space that is separate but coherent.

The two cubes shaped form pavilions provide that kind of intimacy for the family. The construction of the building was the biggest challenge for my team, since some of the materials and the technique have never been used before in Larissa. I chose steel because of its advantages over concrete. It is light and very strong. The transportation and site handling are easier. Components are produced in factory conditions, ensuring accuracy and quality. The main advantage of steel is that it withstands unfavorable weather conditions as well as earthquakes. Fortunately, most Greek earthquakes are relatively mild but there is always the potential for more severe seismic activity.

So the construction should be built to provide safety. Steel also has positive environmental impacts. For its sustainability, refurbishment, recyclability and reusability characteristics. For those reasons it is an environmentally friendly building material.

I decided to use Ytong block because of its optimum fire resistance since fires are frequent in Greece. It is also convenient for its thermal insulation. It is ecological and durable, the CO2 emissions are very low, and, as a result, the environment is less polluted.

COMPANY	Christina Zerva Architects
DESIGNER	Christina Zerva Architects
PHOTOGRAPHER	Mihajlo savic
CLIENT	Irini and Vasilis Hristodoulias
COUNTRY (DISTRICT)	U.S.A.

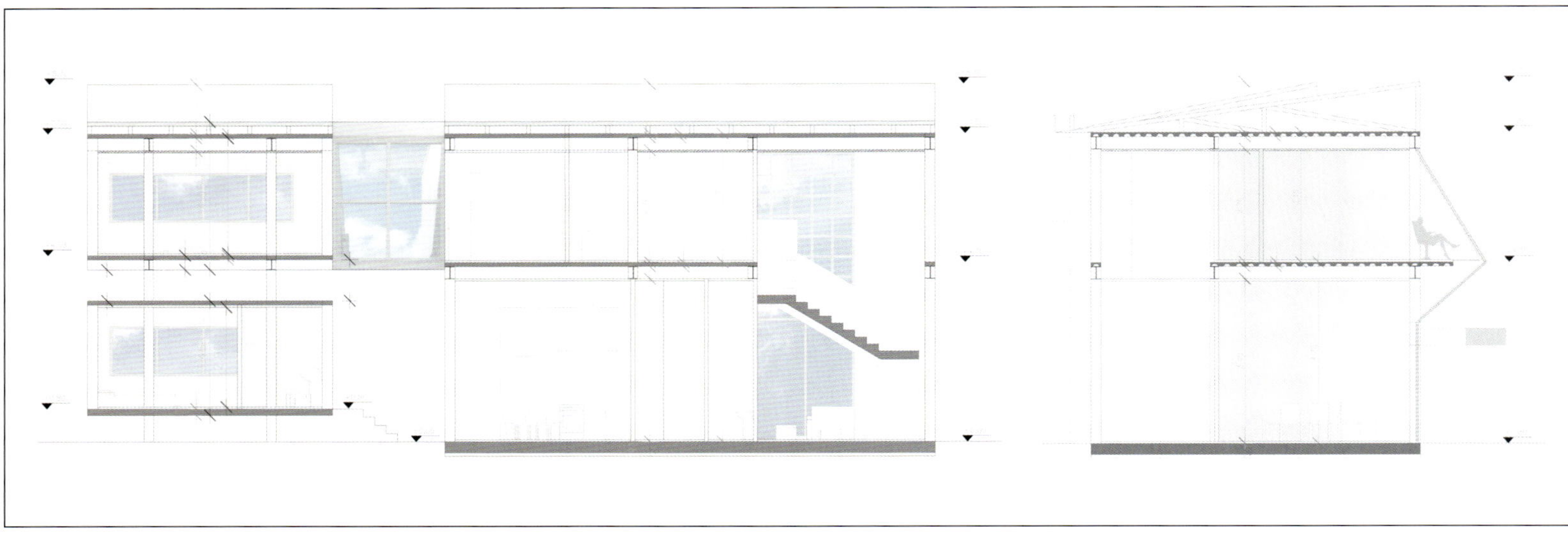

CHILDREN'S BEDROOM
MASTER BEDROOM
TV ROOM
BATHROOM
KITCHEN
CHILDREN'S BEDROOM
LIVING ROOM
DINING ROOM

ORMOND ESPLANADE

No, they said. Make it Saint Kilda. And, make it light. Make it bright. Make it tight. Add all of the green stuff too, please. And, we want it beachy. Maybe like a boat? And it better be fun. Serious fun. Hmm... How about spotted gum? Or even better, spotty gum…

Skin

A tight wrapped skin creates a shell for this vertical house. Like real skin, it's blemished and rough. Something to protect the delicate inside, at once tough and resilient, but still stretchy, smooth, supple and tactile.

Baroque

Though seemingly abstract, this house is multilayered, replete with veiled secrets, like a dreaming or wandering left for the occupant to decode – a chain of intimate revelations.

Vertical Living

A tight block turns the circulation on its head. A three level stair rises behind the circular windows providing a connection between the four distinct zones. The screen printed hoop pine balustrade links the levels through a carefully constructed narrative of image and color.

Zones for Living

A garden room lands the ground floor. A grand stair is mirrored inside and out and connects the lofty living to both the beach and the backyard. The kid's bedrooms are fun, exciting and colorful and the parent's garret is necessarily moody, sexy and private.

Lean and Green

The void also provides passive stack ventilation, grounded in a masonry level and a permeable lid.

Glazing is optimized and daylight carefully controlled. A 2.0kw solar system provides energy. Rainwater flushes and washes while grey water keeps the grass green.

This is sensory architecture that cannot be engaged in a single eyeful. A home of full of wonder and anticipation for a young family.

COMPANY	Judd Lysenko Marshall Architects
DESIGNER	Judd Lysenko Marshall Architects
PHOTOGRAPHER	Shannon McGrath
COUNTRY (DISTRICT)	Australia

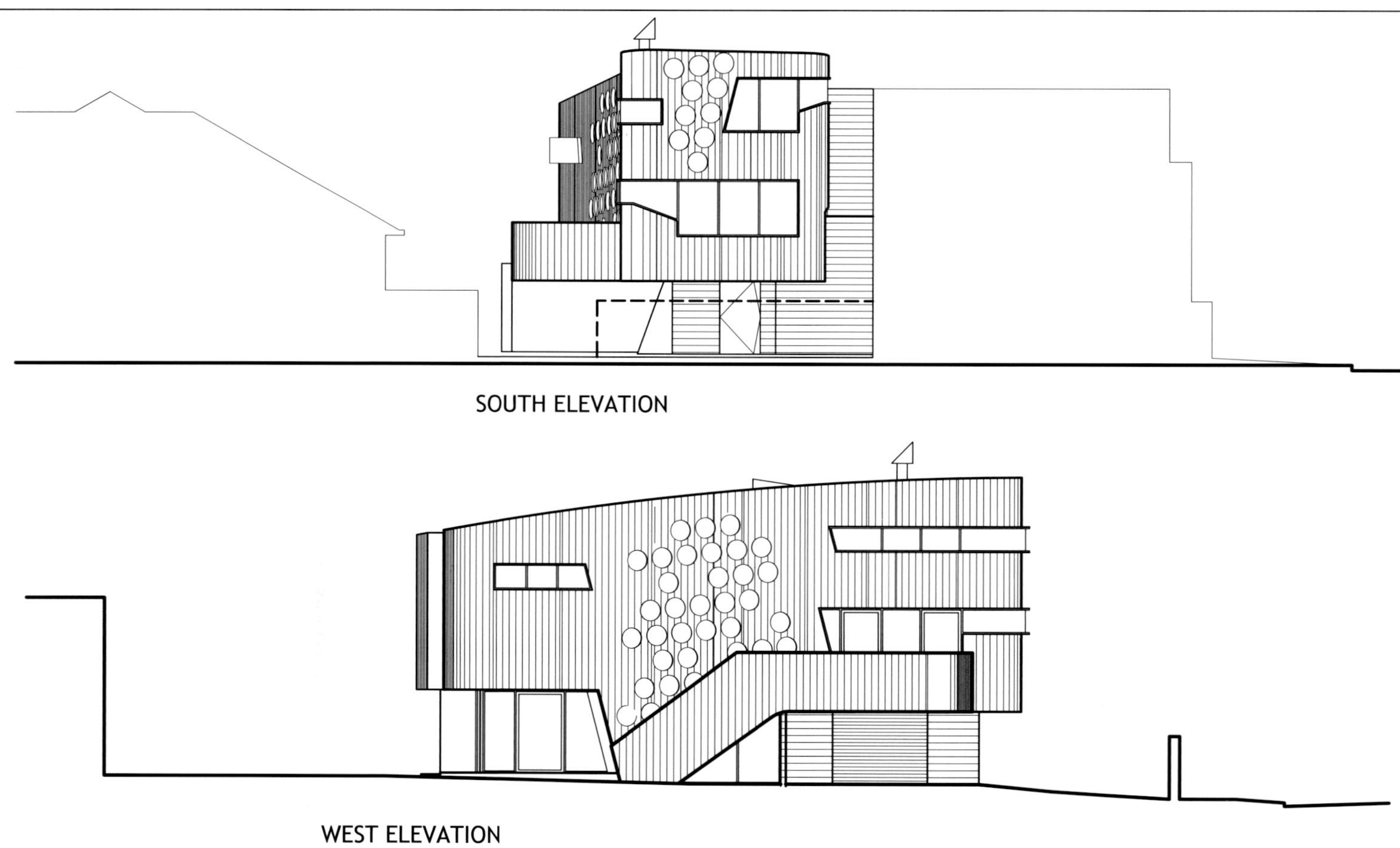

Ormond Esplanade / Elevations / Scale 1:200 @ a4

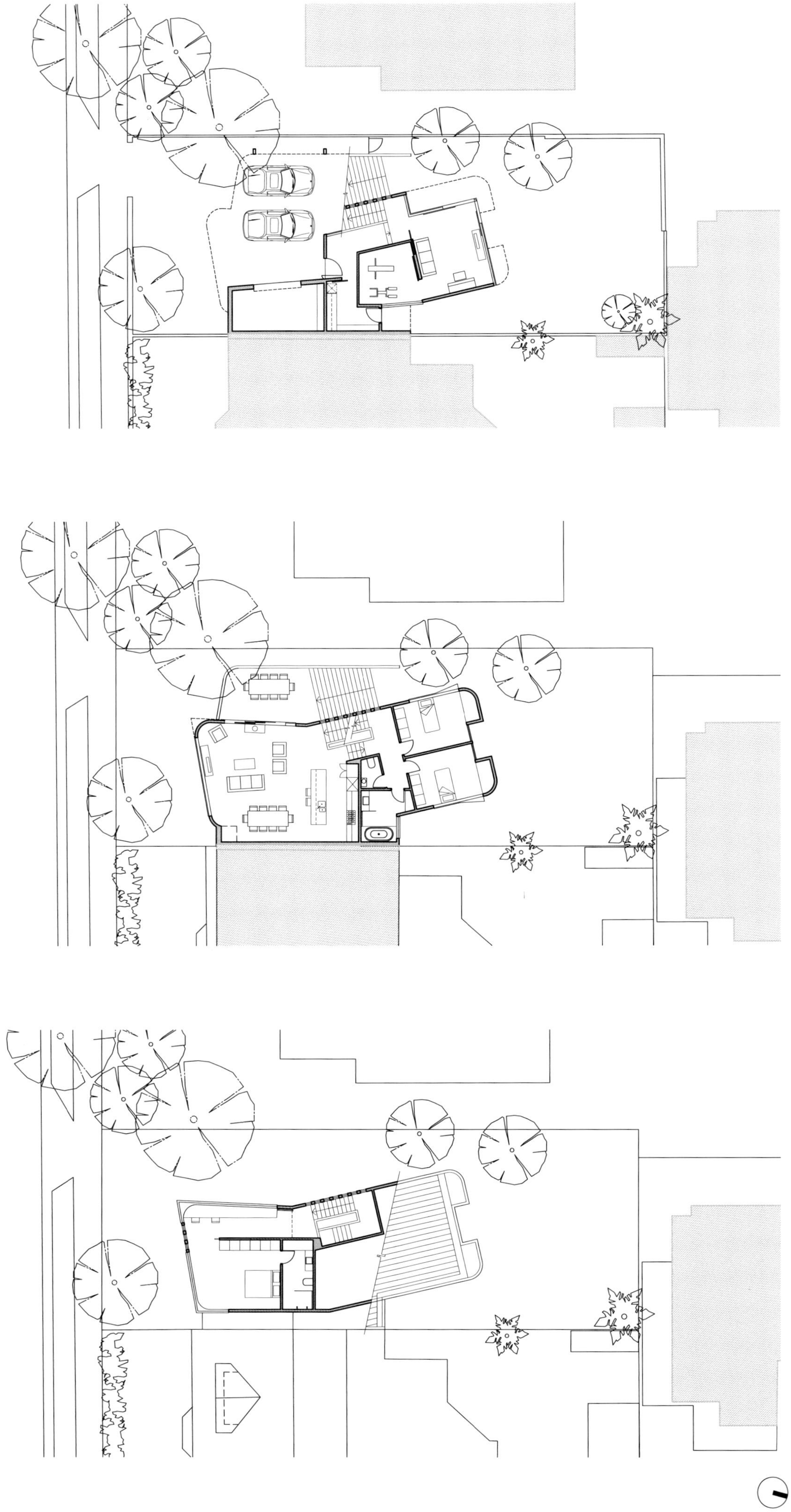

Ormond Esplanade / First Floor Plan / Scale 1:200 @ a4

97

97

RESTORATION OF AN ALPINE BARN

In the Italian Alps, barns vary from region to region in their form, materials and structure. In the Cadore which is located in the Dolomites, a UNESCO World Heritage Site, alpine barns are built from wood and stone. The ground floors in such barns were typically used as stables and the upper floors as haylofts.
We were asked to design the conversion of a barn into a holiday home in Selva di Cadore on behalf of a mountain enthusiast and his family.
The starting point was the careful removal of wooden elements and structural joints. After the building had been dismounted, many wooden beams and boards were cleaned and restored whilst others were replaced with treated wood in order to maintain the chromatic continuity of the material before being remounted.
From a volumetric perspective, some annexes that limited the original volume were removed and only essential ones were maintained and integrated in a discreet fashion.
The new exposed black steel structure respects the modular geometry of the barn and lends itself with the original wooden structure. A few steel beams are covered with wood. The building is totally energy self sufficient thanks to a photovoltaic system integrated within the roof which is made of larch. It also generates zero emissions thanks to an electric under-floor heating system.
Great attention was given to: the selection of materials (larch and fir wood, Dolomia stone, black steel, white rough plaster), their interaction and light entering from the windows. Every ambiance in the house is characterized by an accurate weaving of these five materials that creates a balanced and integrated system in each room.
Restoring a building such as this requires a coming together between architecture, landscape and interior design through the usage of materials, craftsmanship and the treatment that the wood receives. Space and materials are hence developed in mutual continuity.
The philosophy of the alpine barn is such that the wood has to age naturally through time gaining its natural protection and a new color (grey tones in the northern façades and red for the others), until it becomes completely stable.
The wood is the witness of the passing of time and of the history of the building itself.
We wanted to keep the signs of time passing such as scratches, nail marks and peculiar joints, within view and reach. The external boards show the passing of time because the wood will continue to change according to the season, natural light, and humidity.
In the interior we brought together the closed wooden boards alternating the different kinds of roughness and tones of the same wood.

COMPANY	EXiT architetti associati
DESIGNER	EXiT architetti associati (Francesco Loschi, Giuseppe Pagano, Paolo Panetto)
PHOTOGRAPHER	Teresa Cos
COUNTRY (DISTRICT)	Italy

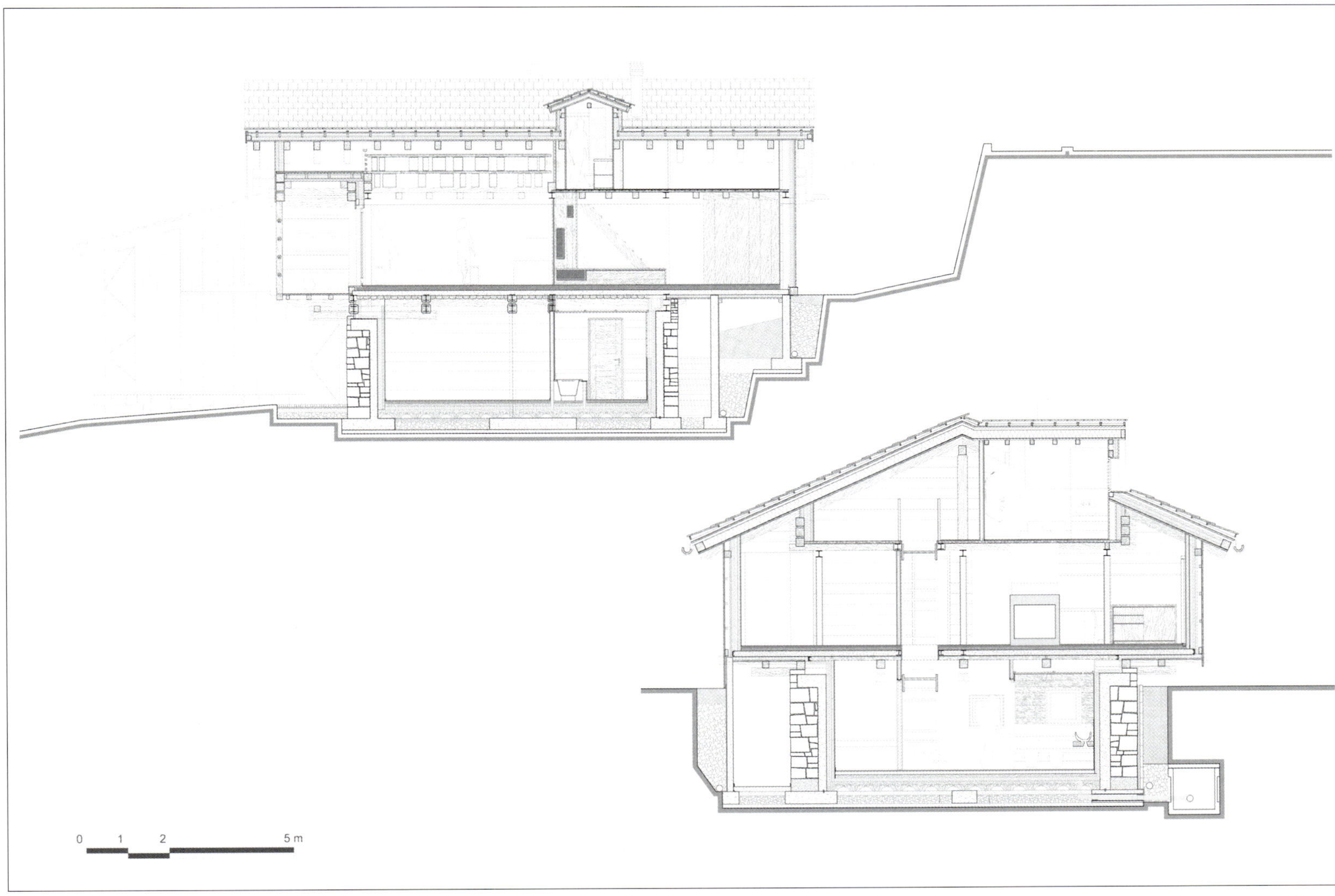
0
1
2
5 m

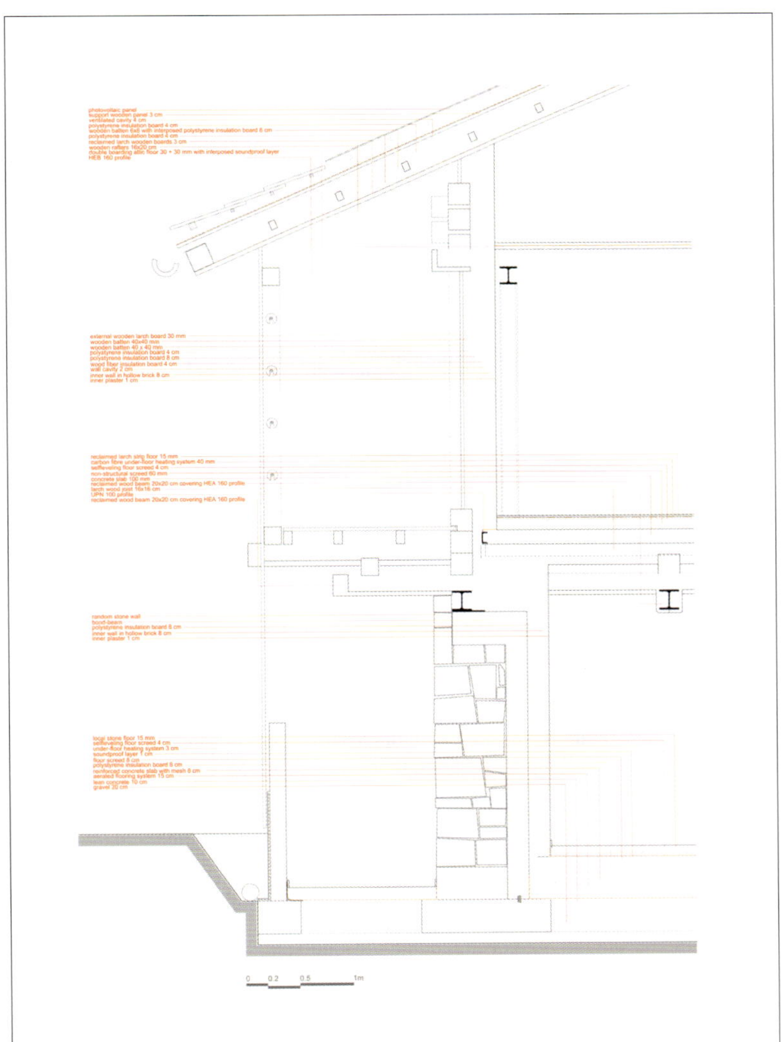

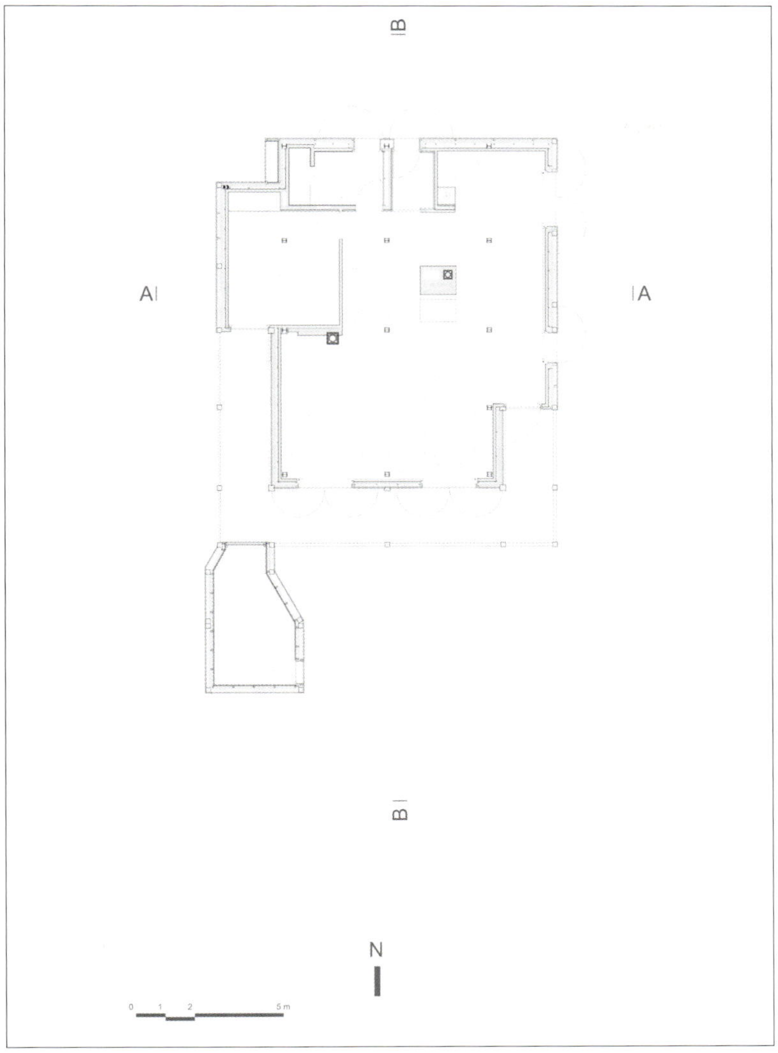
B
A
A
B
N
0
1
2
5m

TOWN RESIDENCE

Box

When a form is so familiar, we often look past it to focus on what might be in it, or on it, or perhaps we never notice it at all. Sol LeWitt's 1974 "Variations of Incomplete Open Cubes" is an exhaustive exploration of a single theme, yielding surprising and delightful results.

Similarly, this home explores simplicity of gesture, and the minutiae of geometric adjustment to uncover diverse and serendipitous forms.

Solid

The Smokey Town House investigates monumentality and permanence. Nestled on the edge of remnant scrub, the almost geological form seems at once perched and embedded in the clay stratum. The over-scaled planar elements can be read as both monumental and ephemeral, an intense mass, yet exposed and eroded.

Overlap

The scheme's twin axes overlap a single pitched roof to create a set of sheathed interiors. From the outside, these are read as a carved mass that exploits the possibilities of the tactile material – the thick folded surface defining mass and void. The resultant form is at once cavernous and expansive, lean and generous, tight and maxed out.

Twisted Axis

The interior is plainly open, but not open plan. Defined by two distinct parts severing the common from the private, the enfolding volume creates a changing spatial arrangement, through the capture and release of carefully framed views.

Deep Shade

Crafted so as to avoid intense solar exposure, the dimension of shadow and light defines the occupation of this dwelling.

This is architecture of surface and volume – a hard shell engorging a vivid and expressive belly.

COMPANY	Judd Lysenko Marshall Architects
DESIGNER	Judd Lysenko Marshall Architects
PHOTOGRAPHER	Shannon McGrath
COUNTRY (DISTRICT)	Australia

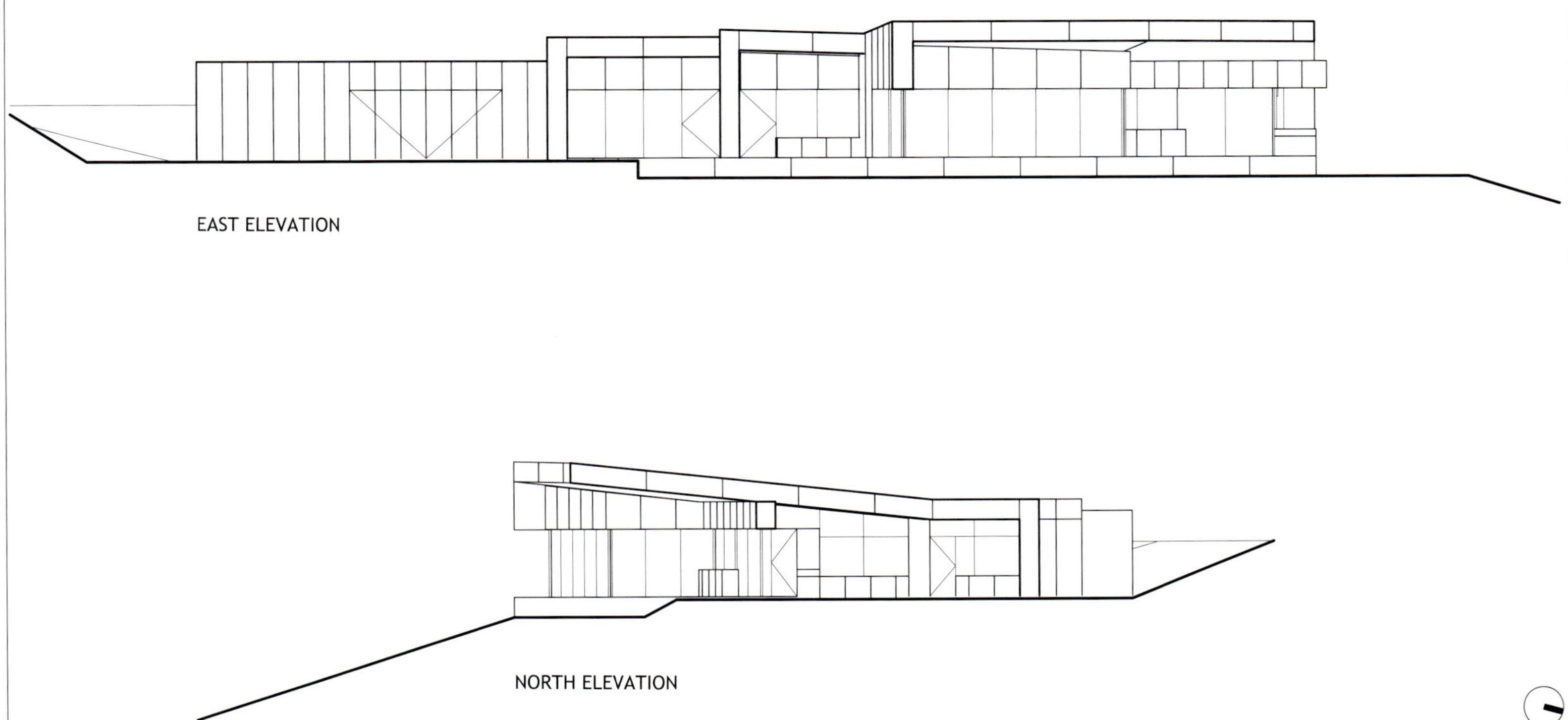

Smokey Town Residence / Ground Floor Plan / Scale 1:200 @ a4

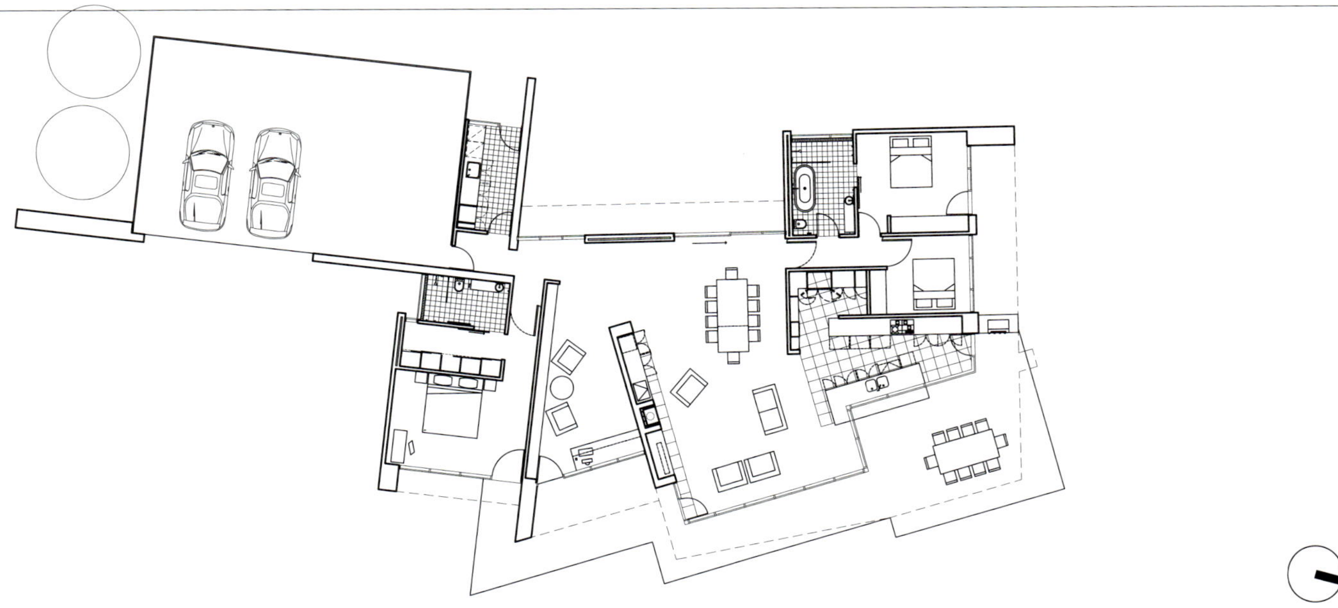

Smokey Town Residence / Ground Floor Plan / Scale 1:200 @ a4

BAMBOO FOREST HOUSE

ROEWUarchitecture has recently completed a vacation home for an extended family in eastern Taiwan. Located in a dense urban area and confined on two sides by blank party-walls the house must gain all its light and air from the street while maintaining privacy within. It was also essential to maintain security while windows are left open for natural ventilation. The narrow and elongated plot was addressed by placing a series of solid volumes along the length of the site, allowing void spaces in between to create continuity for light and air. A bamboo screen wraps around the house creating a buffer between the street and private life within.

On entering the house the experience is akin to being surrounded by an organic forest. Sun light, air and shadows filter through the bamboo poles into the spaces within. The mood and quality of the spaces changes during the course of a day and shifts with the changing seasons. In winter, a Karaoke Lounge and Spa on the second floor, form a focal point for bathing or singing.

During summer, the roof deck with its variably patterned sun-shade system and surrounding bamboo, invites cooling breezes and becomes the family's favorite spot for outdoor living.

The main source of energy consumption in Taiwanese buildings is air-conditioning during the long hot and humid summer months. By introducing several double and triple-height void spaces that penetrate through the heart of the house and open to the roof the whole house is naturally ventilated even though 2 sides of the site are party lot line walls where no openings were allowed.

COMPANY	ROEWUarchitecture
PHOTOGRAPHER	Marc Gerritsen
COUNTRY (DISTRICT)	U.K.

EDGE HOUSE

The Edge House is located at Kolbotn, a suburb south of Oslo.
The client, a young couple, had purchased a challenging site with 8 meters height difference from the access road to a plateau.
To save the plateau, the building was pushed towards the eastern perimeter of the site, suspended above the slope on slender steel columns. The entrance stair rises along the slope through the house up to the plateau.
This strategy avoids costly blasting, hiding the technical connections in the stair. It saves at the same time the existing characteristics of the site, creating a dramatic interplay between volume and site. The entrance condition and the experience from the inside attempts to underline this interplay.
The compact interior is horizontally organized around the cut for the entrance stair. Bedrooms and bathrooms are effectively organized along a corridor.
The main structure is steel, with a polished concrete floor slab. The interior is clad in Birch plywood, the exterior in naturally colored fiber cement boards.

COMPANY	Jarmund / Vigsnæs AS Architects MNAL
DESIGNER	Jarmund / Vigsnæs AS Architects MNAL
PHOTOGRAPHER	Ivan Brodey, Nils Petter Dale
CLIENT	Withheld at the owners request
COUNTRY (DISTRICT)	Norway

FYF RESIDENCE I HOUSE IN ROSARIO

FyF is located in the outskirts of Rosario the second largest city in Argentina, approximately 300 km north of Buenos Aires. The small house of approximately 200 m^2 is built in a new residential development adjacent to a traditional neighborhood. FyF can be described as a spatial and physical attempt to challenge the planar stability and flat homogeneity of the Pampas landscape in a domestic setting. The project was conceived as a monolithic solid, a monochromatic form punctuated only by subtle inflections that establish a complex physical relationship among the different spaces while maintaining a sense of identity and privacy between them.

Specifically, a supple cast-on-site reinforced concrete shell constitutes the body of the house. Determined by a structuring geometry governing the shape of the house, problematic transitions are registered into the shell through local folds and bends. Perforations in those transitions produce openings where fenestration is located, allowing for internal conditions of interstitial luminosity, cross ventilation, and oblique views.

Moreover, through shape and disposition, these openings experientially accentuate or play down the effects of the mass, while emphasizing its overall topology.

The residence is organized into a basic disposition of public and private spaces connected by a central corridor and articulated by a small light well. The internal atmosphere of the house offers a contrasting effect between calmness and fluidity. While all rooms are discretely separated, they are also connected by means of strategic openings located right at the transitions, hence adding to the main areas of the house a sense of controlled endlessness.

Because one of the clients is an agricultural engineer and a landscape designer, the project offered the opportunity to incorporate a special activity into the program: a small green house. Instead of isolating it from the rest of the house, we chose to situate the green house in a continuous spatial sequence with interior social spaces, swimming pool and solarium, thus integrating house with garden and exploiting its expressive dynamism.

Placed in close proximity to the main public areas, a pliant pool produces a cascading physical continuum with the body of the house. By torquing the volume and merging it with the ground, the pool complicates the spatial stability of the house and activates a dynamic and oblique sequence of movement and views to the landscape beyond. Tectonically, the projecting roof of the pool area is broken down into small cofferlike compartments that allow glazing facets to be flat, while indexing the complex curvature of the hyperbolic surface.

COMPANY	PATTERNS
DESIGNER	PATTERNS
PHOTOGRAPHER	Gustavo Frittegotto Courtesy of PATTERNS
CLIENT	Florencia and Fernando Garcia
COUNTRY (DISTRICT)	U.S.A.

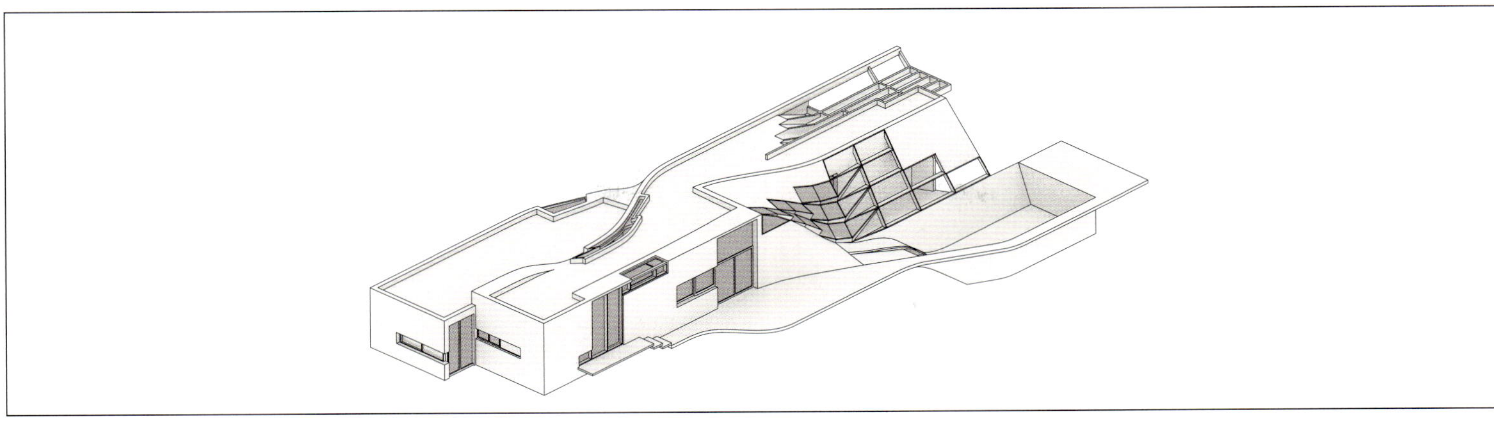

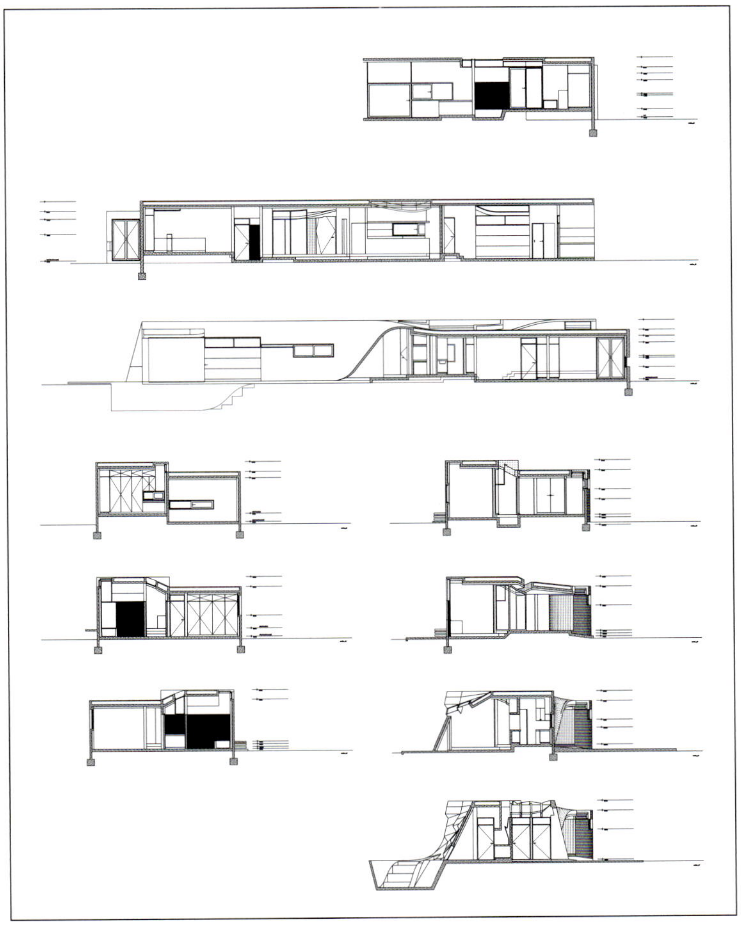

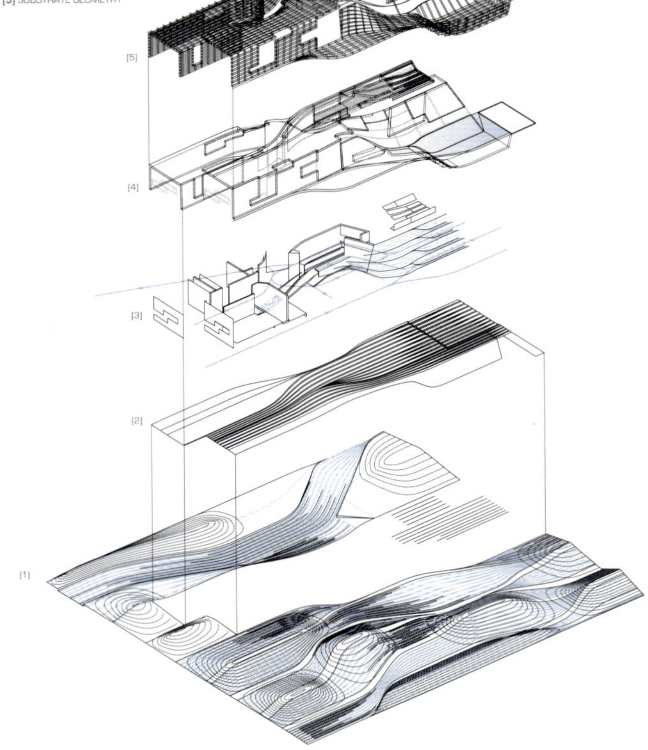

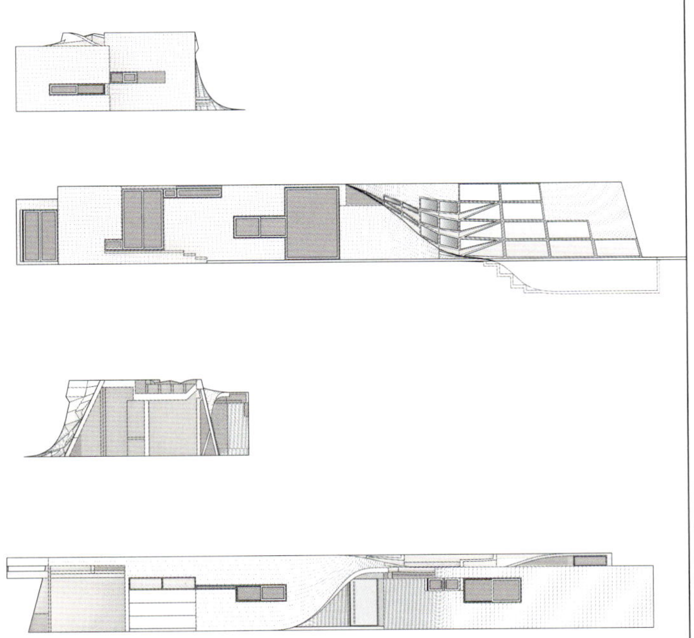

016 FyF Residence

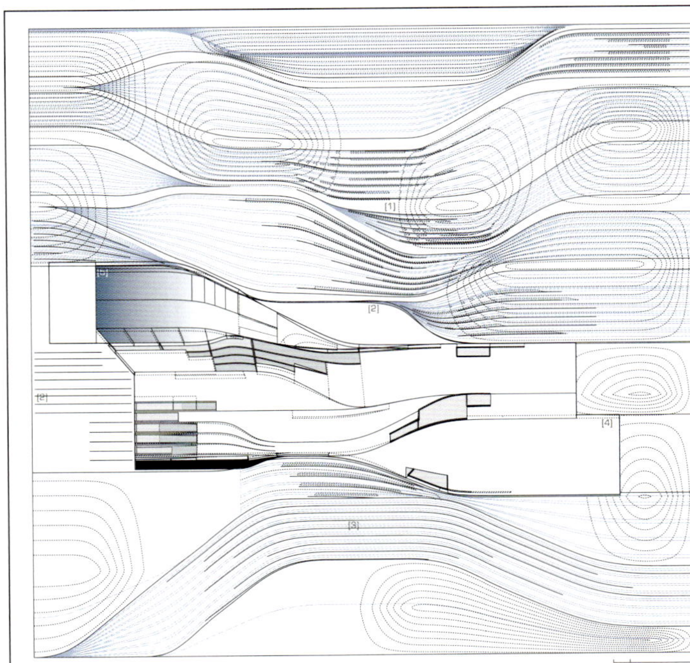

SITE PLAN
[1] TOPOGRAPHIC GARDEN
[2] TERRACE
[3] VEHICULAR DRIVEWAY
[4] CONCRETE SHELL HOUSE
[5] POOL AREA

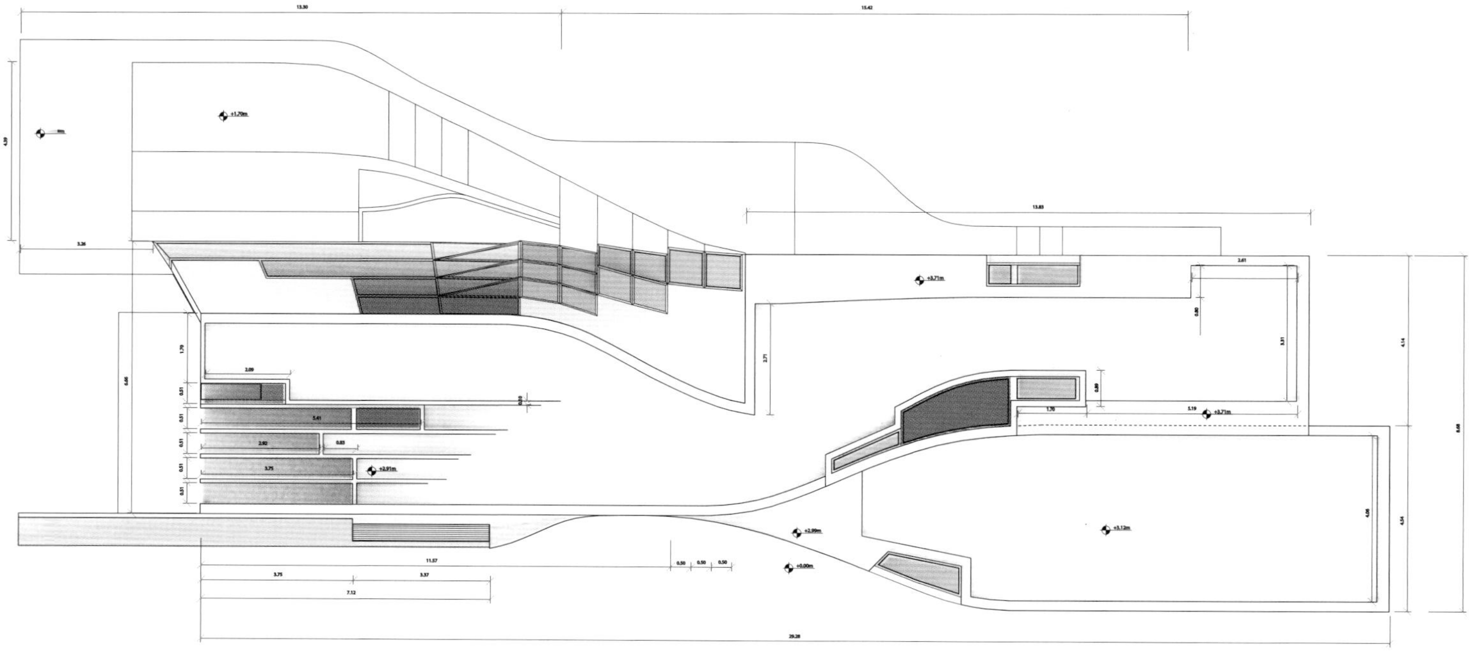

015

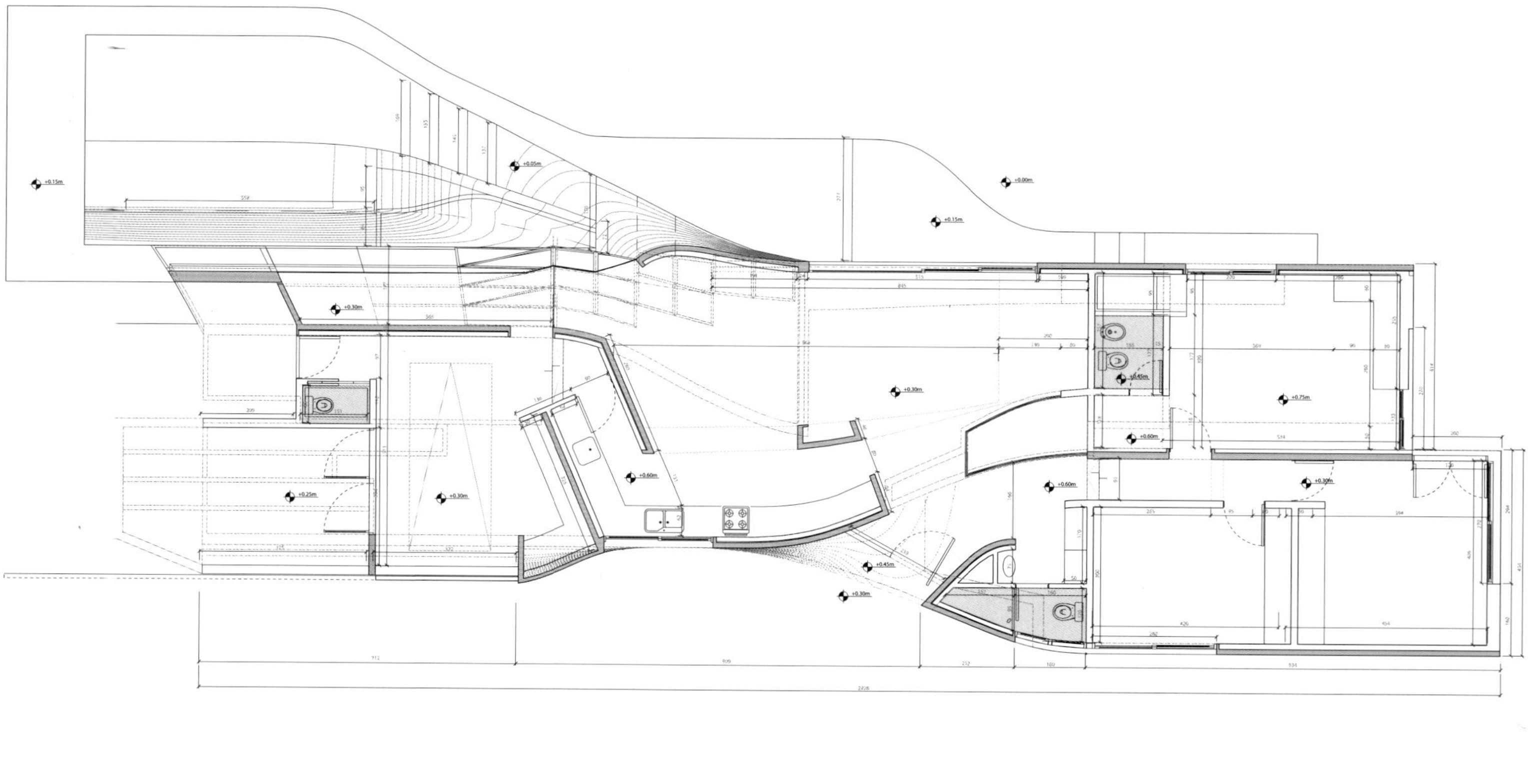

SG LIGHT

The idea was to blend a sculpture image with architectural needs, making them ambiguous, which was the proposal made to the owner, as a work premise.
We used a 10° flexion in two volumes, in order to maintain among themselves a common language. The application of bending, runs one of the volumes in its horizontal axis, and the other in its vertical axis. This gesture created a distant positioning to a formal level between the two blocks, allowing however have several reading volumes. These large volumes almost blind, provides you a very strong image.
Between the "bodies" happens the entry, where highlights, through a sectioning of the volume on the horizontal axis.
The organization of space, starts in the north wing of the house, a relationship between the house and an existing elementary school. Sought to break with some of the architectural forms of identification, especially outside windows that were used in the smallest possible number.
Lighting/ventilation of rooms happens from individual small patios, that controls the temperature in a natural way without mechanisms.

The owners of the house SG Light are a young couple with interest and knowledge in contemporary architecture. As such, we had total freedom and support of the decisions taken. The site shape is a trapezoidal rectangle. The site has an area of 785 m² and the house 240 m² of deployment. The house is located in front of an elementary school, and children aroused the curiosity for the house and the architecture in general. It was also well accepted by the neighborhood ... At first it was received with skepticism but was later welcomed.
This is a low budget home.

COMPANY	GRAU.ZERO
PHOTOGRAPHER	Manuel Correia
COUNTRY (DISTRICT)	Portugal

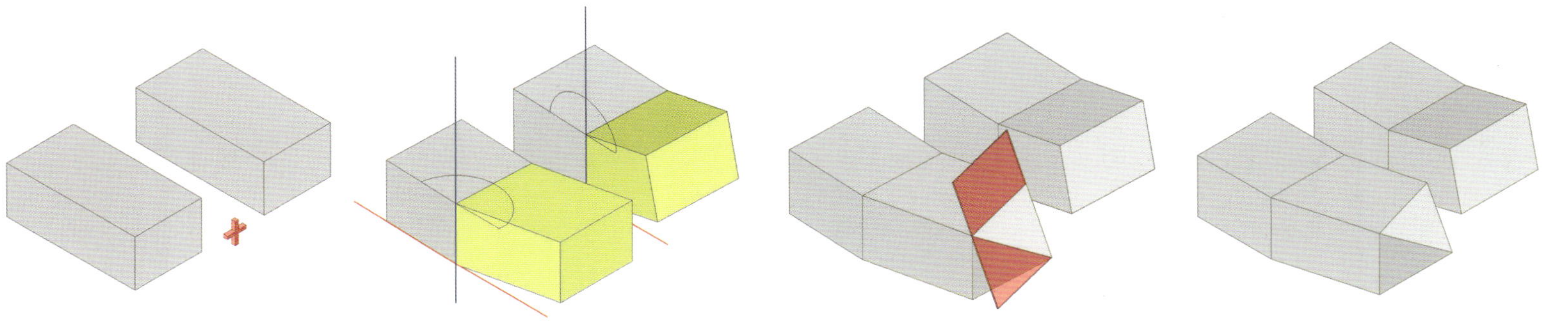

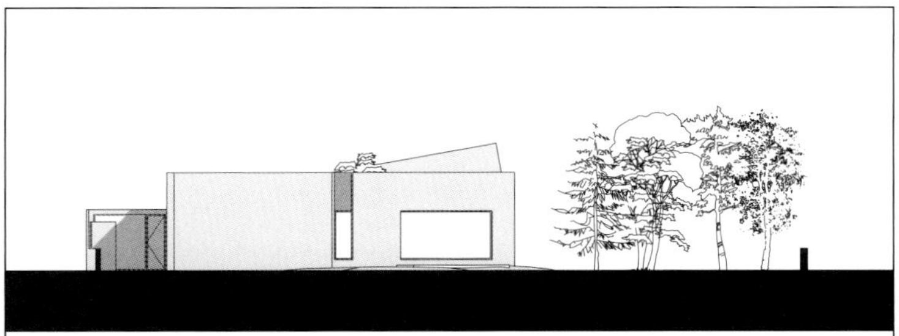

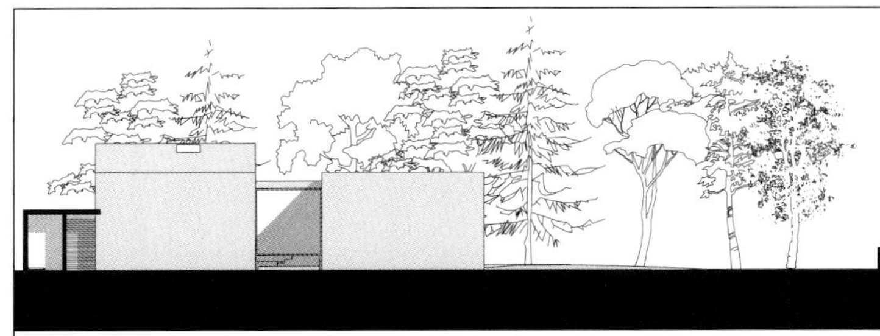

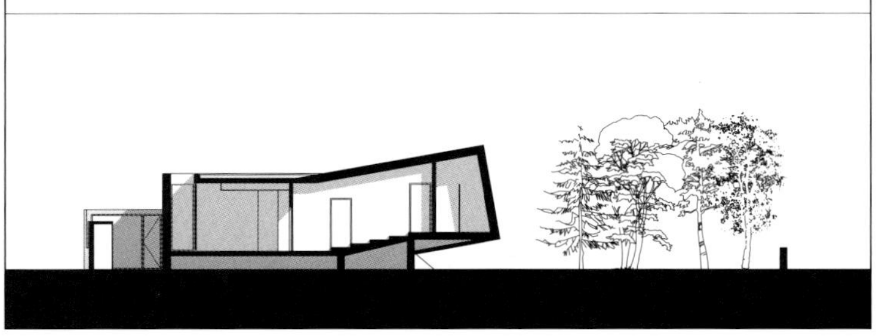

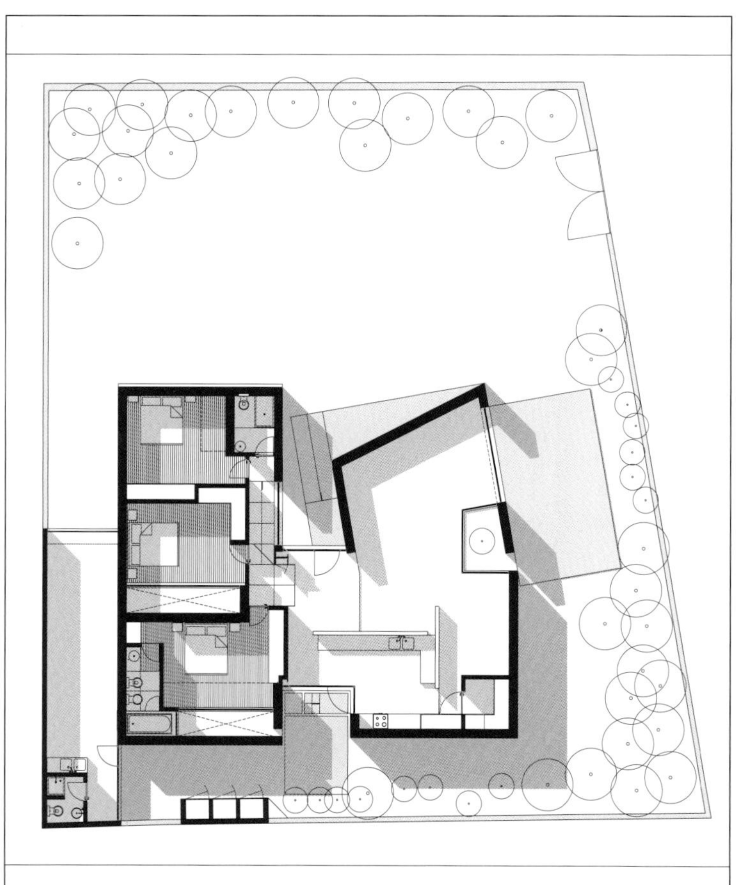

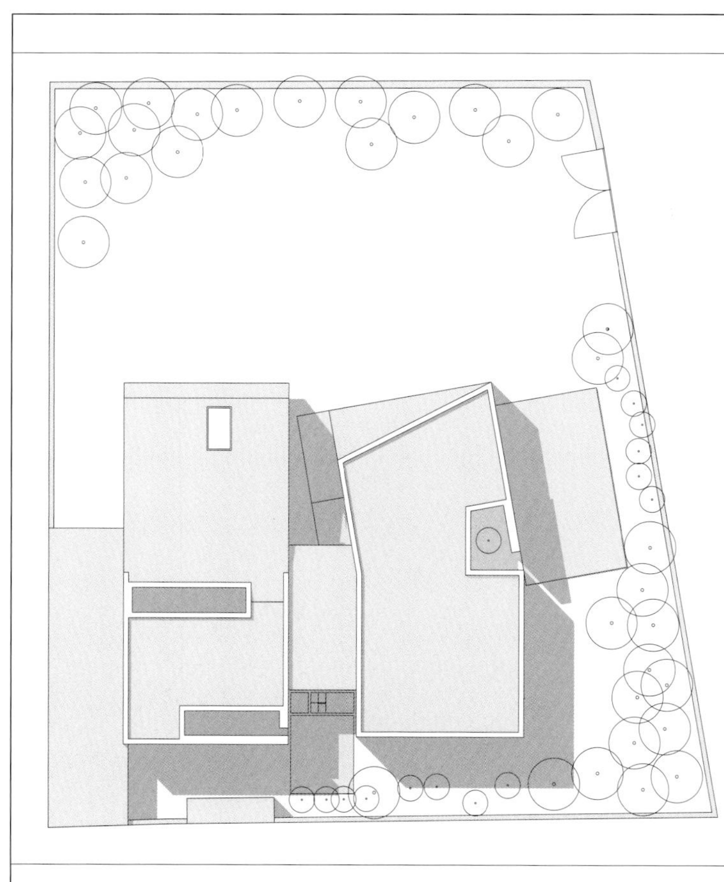

HOUSE OF MISTER R

The house has solid-cast reinforced concrete frame with piers and bridging and walls made of brick. One wall is sloped (hacking brickwork). There are two apartment floors and a basement storey deepened to 1.20 meters below ground level (the only thing deeper is a wine cellar). The services: water pumps, blowing wells, an emergency diesel-generator and a fuel storage tank are located in the basement storey. A sanitary piping, gas and electricity supply are also arranged in the basement.
The rooftop is made of one-piece and has the maximum slope of 12 angle degrees. It is provided with clerestories to lighten a stair shaft and a dormer. There is an accessible roof area for sunbathing or picnic located between the house wings.
There are two balconies and one recessed balcony on the second apartment floor. The recessed balcony adjoins a closet and is sheltered from rainfall by glass shed with a metal frame.
Outflows made of thin stainless pipes are being raised above the rooftop level and sloped against the house space to intensify an aesthetic impression.

COMPANY	za bor architects
DESIGNER	Peter Zaytsev,Arseniy Borisenko
PHOTOGRAPHER	Peter Zaytsev, Zinur Razutdinov
COUNTRY (DISTRICT)	Russia

VILLA G

Architect Todd Saunders landed a creative and dynamic client when he got the job to design a house on the south-west coast of Bergen, Norway. The result is rare and beautiful, and Saunders has said that the process has made him into a better architect.

Villa G lies like a white landmark in the soft landscape at Hjellestad, near Bergen. The house is large yet not dominating, modern but not pretentious. The house has a futuristic form but is built with traditional Nordic materials and architectural elements with a good basis in Norwegian building methods.

The wooden cladding on the house consists of 3 different size mounted in a random pattern. The house has an over built outside space and covered and the second floor covers the entrance below helping the house work together with the rough climate on the west coast of Norway. Villa G is now another plus in Todd Saunders consist portfolio of work.

The architect and the client started out on good terms and ended up having a very good working collaboration in all stages of the project. The architect liked the larger lines while the client was a perfectionist in regards to the details. The process was very symbiotic. All parts of the house were a fruitful discussion between the architect and the client.

The stair for example was developed together with the client and evolved after at least 10-12 suggestions that ended up as this final stair. The stair is one solid piece of 1cm thick steel, galvanised with white sand corn making it slipped resistant. The stair is produced locally, weighs almost a tonne, and had to be lifted into place by a crane through the window in the roof.

The architect and client have an enthusiastic description of the design and building process. Saunders say, "The client is very intelligent and has an acute interest in architecture. He challenged us the whole time, but never can get in the way of out design process. The family has documented their wants and needs. These clear and concise wishes help us come up with simple design principles for the project.

When commenting his own experience of the how the design of the house evolved, the owner said: "yes, we had an exact number of how many meters of closets we needed and so on. We have built a few houses before this and have learned from our experiences and mistakes. We knew that we wanted a house with clean lines without any visual noise and clutter." This is one of the reasons that most of the closets and storage spaces are integrated into, so – called, thick wall – walls that are at least 60-70cm deep. The kitchen bench is 8 meters long and has plenty of drawers for kitchen equipment and even other things that need to be stored away. None of the electrical outlets are visible and all technology controlled by a main control panel in the kitchen. The client admits that he is a "gadget freak" and the house reflects this part of his personality.

All the previous houses that the client has built were based on the fact that they will be sold again in the near future. Now, however, the owner says that "we have made a house where we will live for a very long time".

COMPANY	Saunders Architecture
DESIGNER	Todd Saunders
PHOTOGRAPHER	Bewt Rene' Synnevåg
COUNTRY (DISTRICT)	Norway

1. ETG _1:200

1.floor plan:

1. Entrance
2. Hall
3. Living Room
4. Bedroom 1
5. Walk-in Closet
6. Bedroom 2
7. Bedroom 3
8. Bathroom
9. Storage/ Utility Room
10. Washroom
11. Garage

TOTAL AREA: 208 m^2

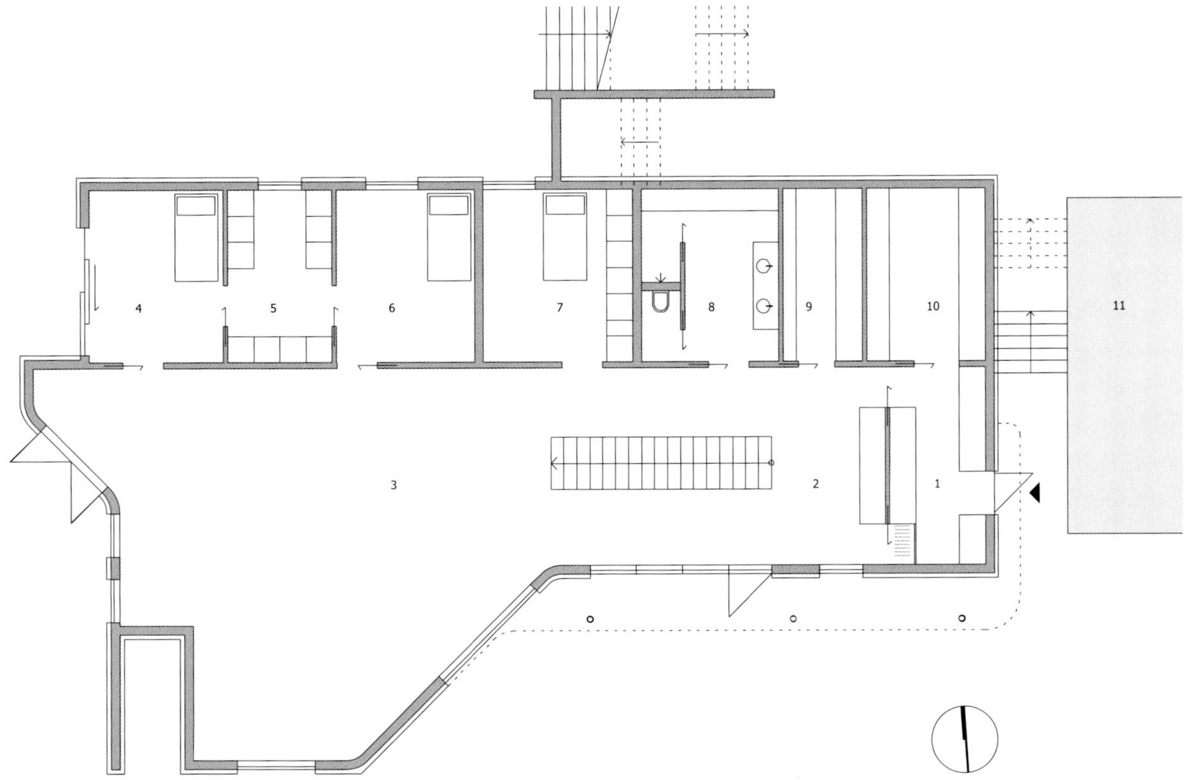

2. ETG _1:200

1.floor plan:

1. Terrasse
2. Living Room
3. Kitchen
4. Bathroom
5. Bedroom
6. Walk-in Closet
7. Bedroom
8. Storage
9. Opening under skylight

TOTAL AREA: 160 m^2

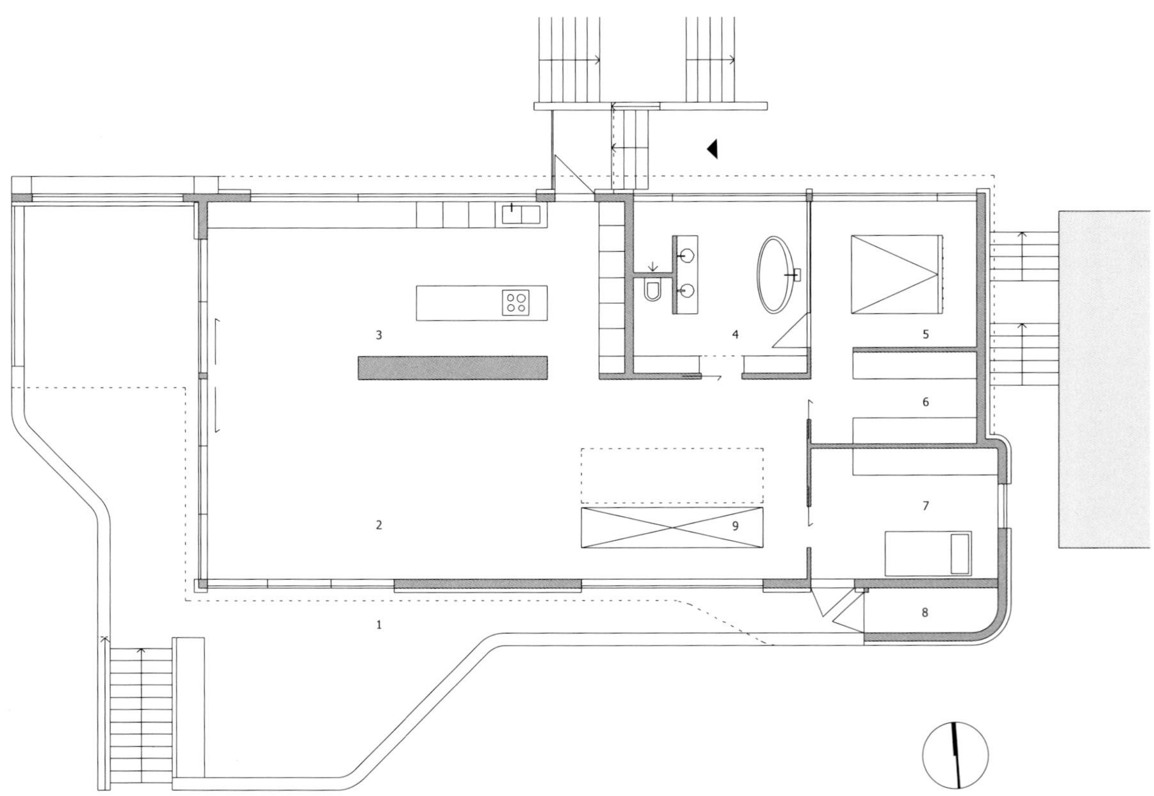

THE HOUSE ON NIKOLINA GORA

The name of the house is not incidental — "The House on Nikolina Gora" — which relates both to the geographical location of the house — near the elite village of Nikolina Gora (Rus: Hill of Nikolas), and the fact that the building is actually built-in to the hill.

The architectural design comes from the complexity of the landscape. The two level lot allocated for the construction of the house has the elevation difference of 3.5 meters. The main entrance is on the second floor and the first floor overlooks a beautiful meadow.

Mostly hidden inside the hill, the two sections of the house — a small and a large one — tower above the upper platform. In the small section — there are guest and staff apartments, technical facilities and the boiler. Public areas such as the living room, kitchen and the dining room are in the large section. Private zones are on the bottom floor, which is hidden from the road and other houses located higher on the hill.

The top public section is painted white. It is designed as a console over the private section and stretches wider on both sides by 3.5 meters. The private section is built into the slope of the hill.

Such an arrangement required some specific design solutions, for example the beam-counter in the basement, sunk by 1.5 meters into the ground to support the massive console above.

Since the private section is in the hillside and the solar exposure is not optimal — in the central part there has been a clerestory cut, which adds to the volume on the upper level. The clerestory has a clever design and is equipped with the chute to drain the rain water onto the slopes where the plants are.

A similar clerestory is also on the roof. The roof has a minimal slope going toward the center of the roof, allowing rain water to be collected in the central part and flow down the inclined plane of the clerestory into the gutter and water the plants on the other side of the house.

This elegantly solves the problem of water-saving and improves solar exposure areas.

COMPANY	za bor architects
DESIGNER	Arseniy Borisenko, Peter Zaytsev
PHOTOGRAPHER	Peter Zaytsev
COUNTRY (DISTRICT)	Russia

VILLA BH

Villa BH is a modern, (environment) friendly house with a remarkable experience of space, light and the natural context.
The villa is positioned on a rectangular plot of 34.75 x 50m, that is enclosed at 3 sides with similar plots and freestanding houses. On the back (north east) of the plot there's an old embankment with several tall trees, which existence is protected by local regulations. From the living program; the kitchen, dining area and living are all orientated on this embankment with the large trees. Here the villa has a facade width of 20 meters.
Villa BH is inhabited by a couple 60+ of age. To optimize the accessibility of the house all the program is situated on the ground floor level around a patio. This enclosed outdoor space provides the owners of the house the privacy they admired. As at the same time the patio makes the living area an enlightened space and gives it a facade to the south.
On the other side of the patio is the main bedroom situated. By making the facade of the patio totally from glass panels, the main bedroom has a great see through towards the existing embankment with the several tall trees as a central focus point on the plot.
The ceiling of the living area has an extra height in the shape of a sloped roof. The physical appearance of this area becomes hereby more specific and highly qualitative. Lifting the roof in this area also allows perspectives to the existing treetops, that give this plot its specific character, from all the different areas inside the building.
The villa is designed as environmental friendly with extra insulated facades, with 30cm of insulation. With this thick insulation there's a timber construction, that suits the thickness of the package. The roof is as well extra insulated and covered with sedum, which also regulates the distribution of the rainwater more gently. On the flat roof are 20 solar panels for electricity. A heat pump warms the interiors in the winter and cools them in the summer with natural temperature differences retrieved deep in the ground. As an extra heating there are 2 fireplaces for wood, one in the living and one in the TV room.

COMPANY	WHIM architecture
CREATIVE DIRECTOR	Ramon Knoester
DESIGNER	Ramon Knoester, WHIM architecture
PHOTOGRAPHER	Sylvia Alonso
COUNTRY (DISTRICT)	the Netherlands

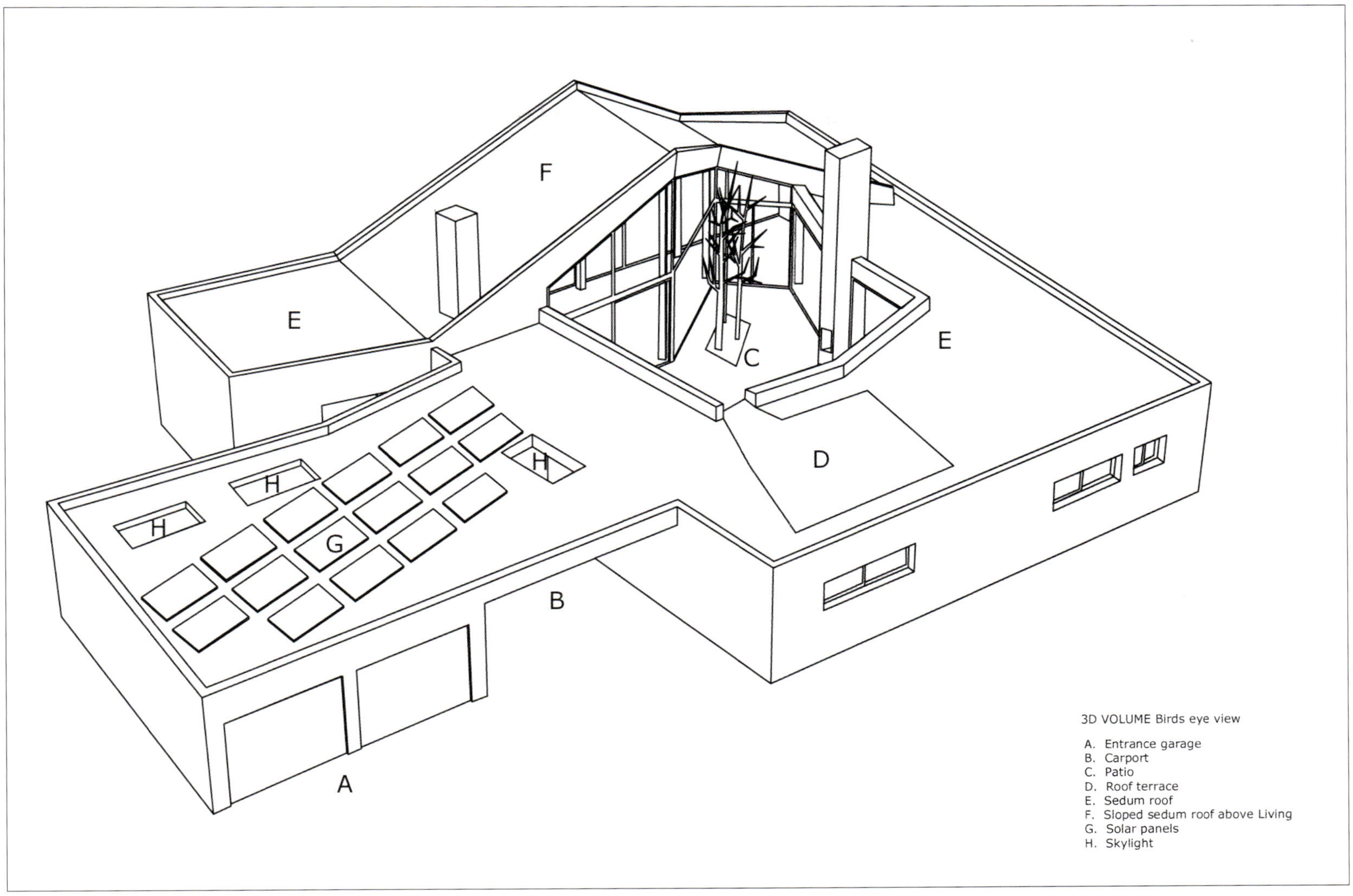
F
E
E
C
D
H
H
H
G
B
A
3D VOLUME Birds eye view
A. Entrance garage
B. Carport
C. Patio
D. Roof terrace
E. Sedum roof
F. Sloped sedum roof above Living
G. Solar panels
H. Skylight

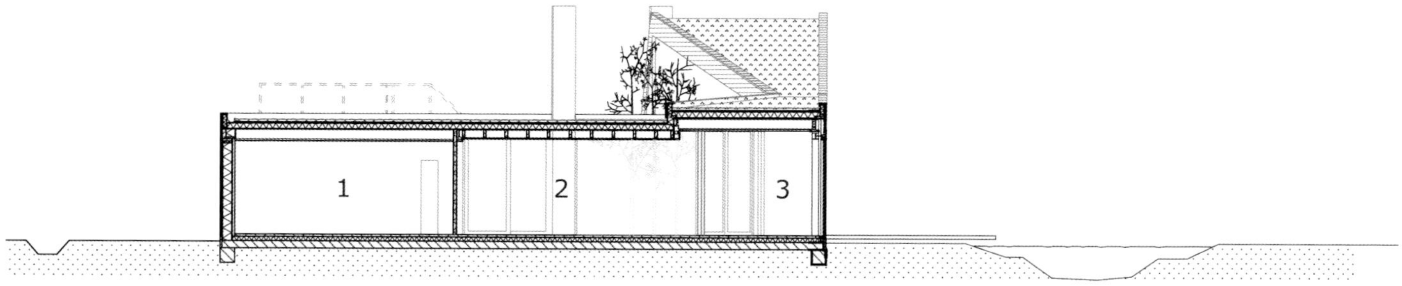

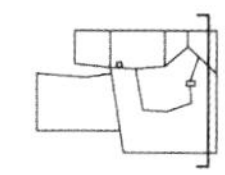

Section
1. Guestroom
2. TV-room
3. Living

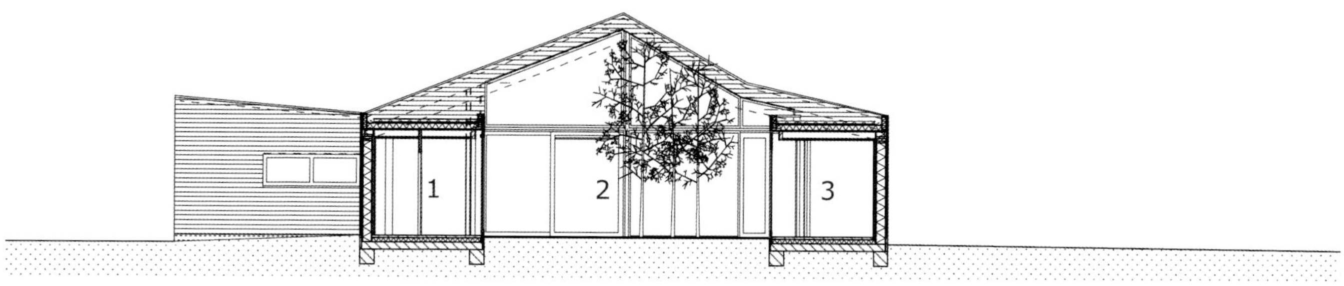

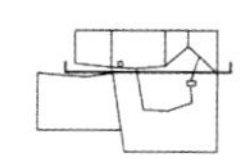

Section
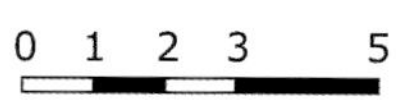

1. Corridor
2. Patio
3. TV-room

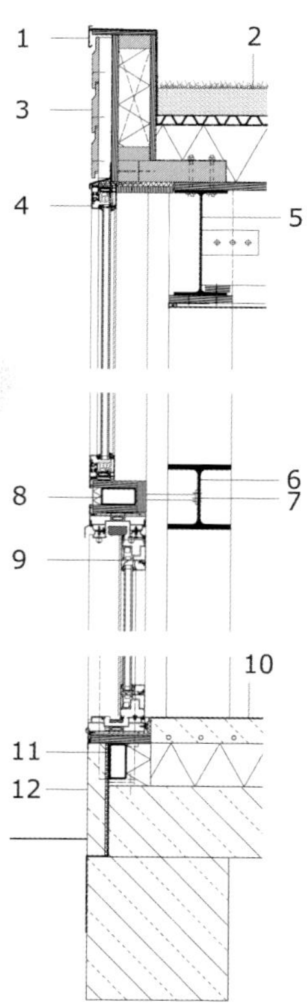

Vertical detail North-East facade

1. Sheet aluminium covering
2. Roof construction:
   .Substrate layer 80mm
   .Filter mat
   .Drainage 25mm
   .protective layer
   .Waterproof foil
   .Insulation 160mm
   .Vapour-retarding layer
   .Plywood 22mm
   .Structural beams 96x271
   .Acoustic ceiling
3. Siberian Larch tongued-and-grooved, Waxed
4. Aluminium window frame with double insulated glass
5. Steel beam IPE 300
6. Steel beam HEB 180
7. Steel connection 15x15
8. Steel tube 100x50
9. Aluminium sliding door with double insulated glass
10. Floor:
    .Synthetic seamless floor finishing 3mm
    .70mm screed around underfloor heating
    .Insulation 120mm
    .Reinforced concrete slab 200mm
11. Steel tube 50x100
12. Prefab concrete

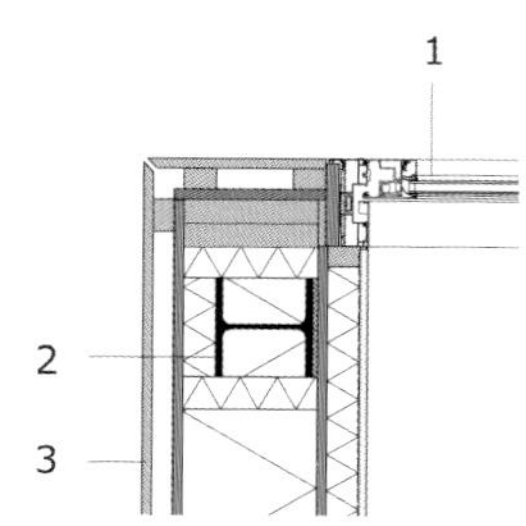

Horizontal detail corner North-East facade

1. Aluminium sliding door with double insulated glass
2. Structural steel column, HEB 180
3. Wall:
   .Siberian Larch tongued-and-grooved, Waxed
   .Cavity 38mm
   .Waterproof vapour transm. foil
   .Plywood 18mm
   .Insulation + wood construction 246mm
   .Plywood 18mm
   .Insulation 59mm
   .Vapour-retarding layer
   .Plasterboard 15mm

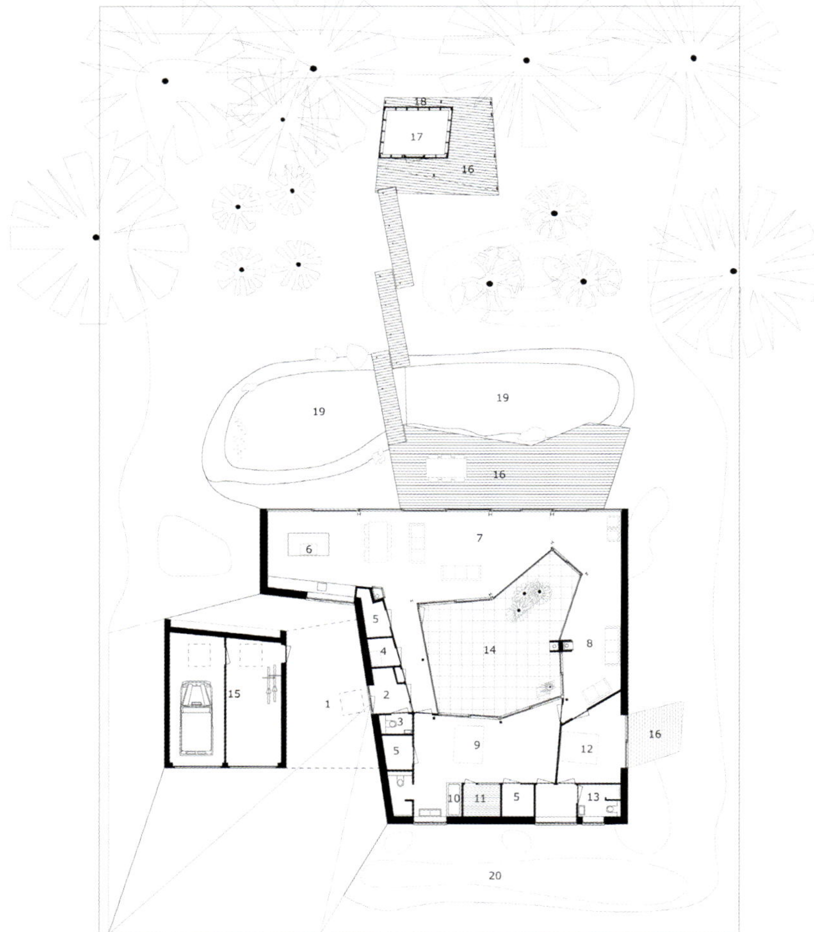

1:200 PLAN

1. Carport
2. Entrance
3. Toilet
4. Installation room heat pump
5. Closet
6. Kitchen
7. Living
8. TV-room
9. Main bedroom
10. Bath
11. Sauna
12. Guestroom
13. Guest bathroom
14. Patio
15. Garage
16. Terrace
17. Garden house
18. Wood storage for fireplaces
19. Pond
20. Wadi

RESIDENCE IN KURAKUEN

This building is fixed on the site so that most construction is so.
It has a site and interaction necessarily that it is fixed on the site. I formed the frame of the building by talking with a site and schemed that the interaction took you as construction, and it was generated good environment. I do not see the site where this building stands from front road at an extreme flag-shaped site. The level ground where open was stormy earlier of the alley which curved loosely along the waterway such as the brook is the site of this building.
The neighboring land of the level that 3M is high in the north side and the west from this site. The East is the neighboring land where 5M fell down to, but an existing building of 4 stories blocks up the view.
The south side sandwiches the waterway, and it is almost the neighboring land of the level, but high trees of 10m which mushroomed in a waterway verge, the neighboring land blocks up the view with this site. It is open view at the southeastern corner that it was slightly had.
Seemingly it is poorness place without the how to treat. The house where the program of the building added an office.
While each becomes independent, has seamless relations. Two entrances. A garage for 3 and the carriage porch which the visitor use included.
That I let these elements form while talking with a site was demanded.
The placement of the building was decided necessarily by letting a roadway and a carriage porch, the position of the garage talk with the shape of the site. I use a wall, and the building itself is intercepted with circumference by the north / the east / facing to the west.

I freed only a southern aspect and did it with depth and space constitution with the feeling of freedom by making use of the surrounding landscape in the design of a garden in the inside space. It is far from the second floor level and, from the southeastern corner that opened out of the view, can face the Osaka gulf alone. The rise of the room temperature by the case light of the sun is concerned about so that all living rooms do a southern aspect, but 2.5m evades it by the big eaves which stretched.
With the site as a result of having talked, it was be with a building felt green and water, the sky and wind close. By interaction through the talks with the site, the poorness ground know how to treat changed in quality to good environment.

COMPANY	Shunichiro Ninomiya+Tomoko Morodome/NRM Architects Office
CREATIVE DIRECTOR	Shunichiro Ninomiya+Tomoko Morodome/NRM Architects Office
PHOTOGRAPHER	Eiji Tomita
COUNTRY (DISTRICT)	Japan

1:200

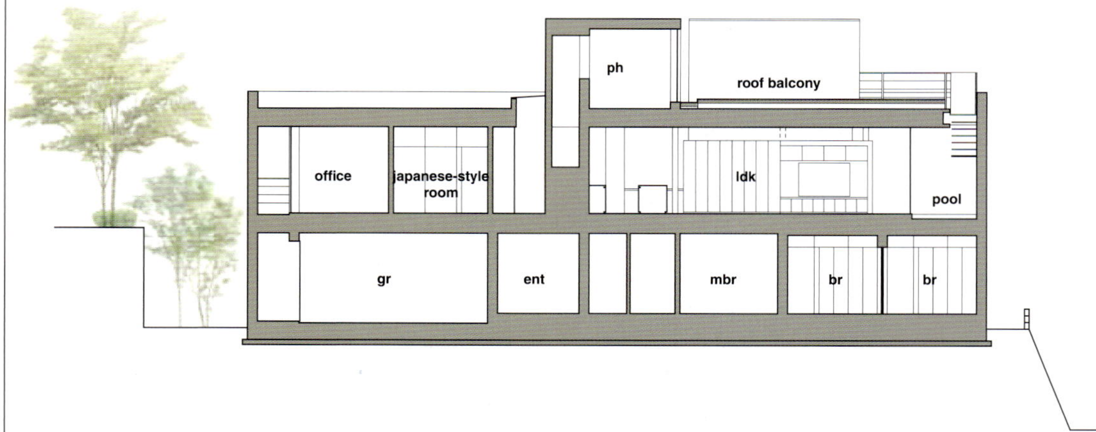

A-A SECTION

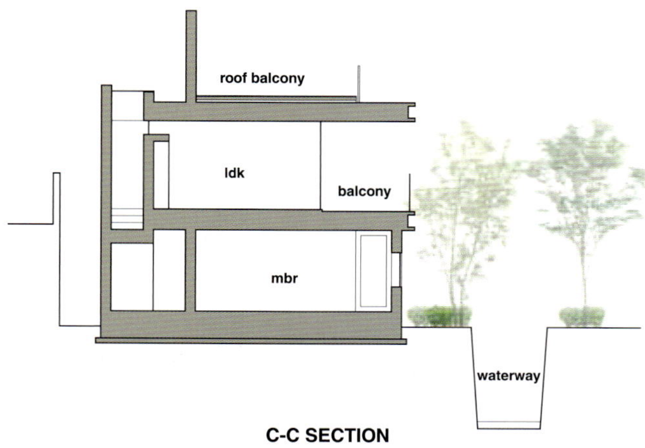

C-C SECTION

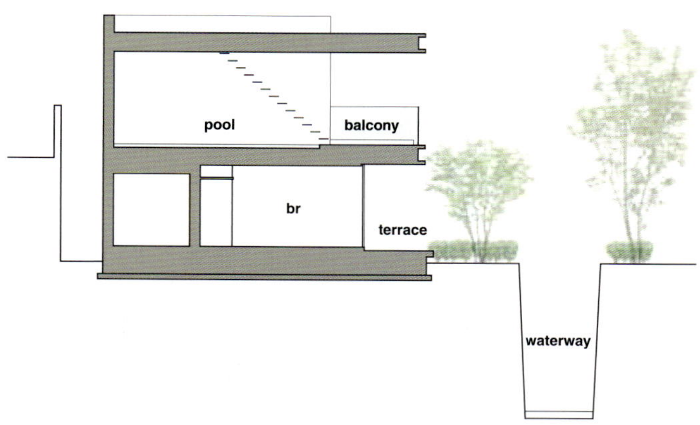

B-B SECTION

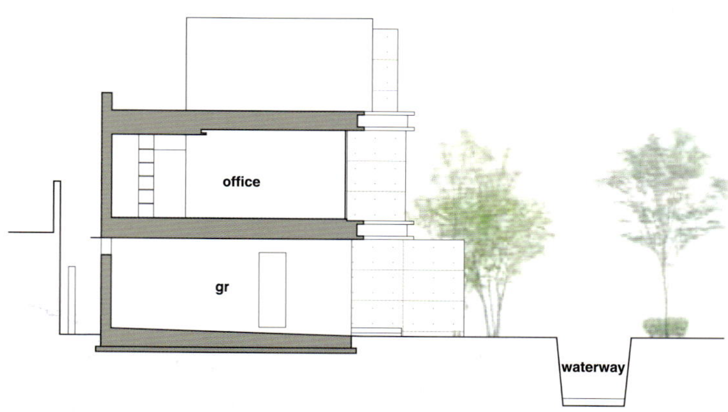

D-D SECTION

A
B
C
D
br
terrace
br
mbr
wcl
ent
gr
waterway
1F PLAN
1:200
pool
ldk
balcony
japanese-style room
office
2F PLAN
roof balcony
ph
PHF PLAN

MONTBLANC HOUSE

The plan of a house with a small beauty shop on the first floor. A house for a family of four: the young couple running the shop, their 3 year-old girl, and their newborn.
The site, surrounded by neighboring houses in 3 directions, is in a quiet residential area.
Most houses in the area have only 2 stories and one is able to see the mountains far away.
However, the neighboring houses and apartments stand close to the site with their windows opening on to it.
So I began to consider how to create an open space in such a tightly enclosed site.
The building has a gable-house-shape with a continuous exterior space from the 1st to the 3rd floor under a large inclined roof.
5 large openings in the inclined roof bring sufficient natural light and air, as well as scenery, into the building.
The windows, as "voids," lacking sashes, have a totally different scale from the windows of the neighboring houses.
That's why there is a wondrous scale around the area as if the model had been enlarged.
As for the inside of the building, when you're walking in a forest in the mountains, you feel as though you're being gently embraced though you're not actually inside anything.
Along the path, where the breezes encircle the leaves above, where one can hear the murmur of the wind in the trees, the sounds of the birds singing, and the footsteps of creatures in the hush, there is, I think, an interior-like sense of place, a state that is wholly distinct from urban spaces or open skies.
Or else, from amongst a thicket, finding a view of the city at the foot of the mountain, or the blue sky streaming through the leaves and so one encounters many such "exteriors" along the way.
Can we create a place for such experiences in a crowded residential area?
One encounters "outside" at various points as you walk upstairs since the semi exterior spaces are connected and gently covered with a large luminous roof.
I hope to create a diversity of "exteriors" with the various angles and heights of the site, appropriately hiding away the views from the neighboring sites, as well as a sense of the neighboring houses' existence.

COMPANY	studio velocity
DESIGNER	studio velocity
PHOTOGRAPHER	Kentaro Kurihara
CLIENT	passer piece
COUNTRY (DISTRICT)	Japan

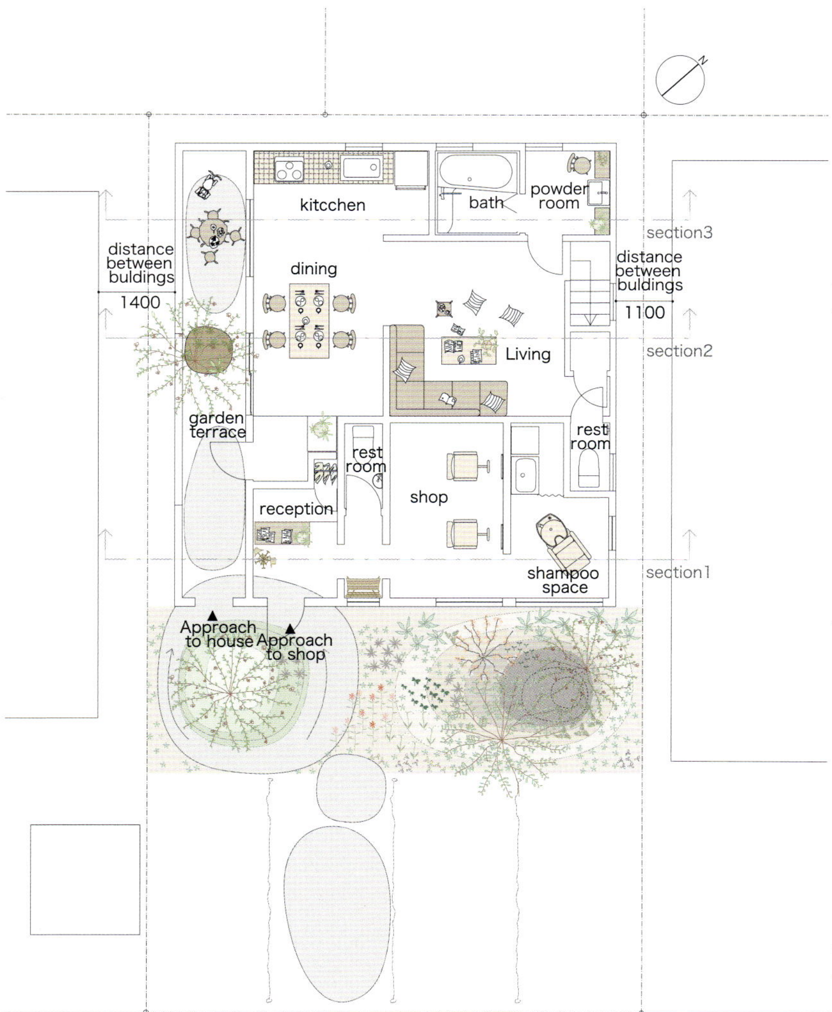

1th floor plan 1/100

2th floor plan 1/100

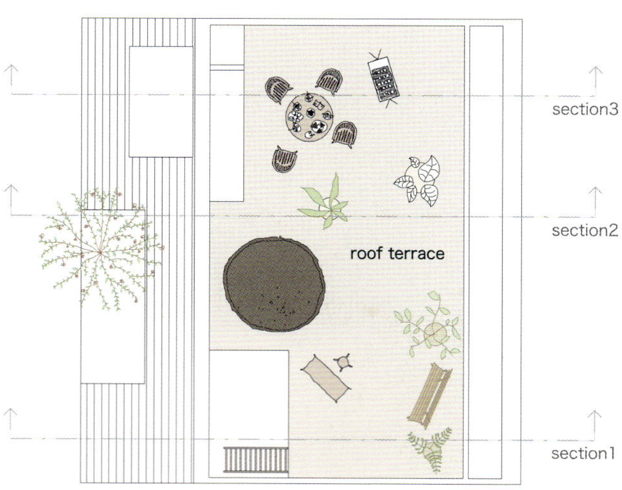

roof plan 1/100

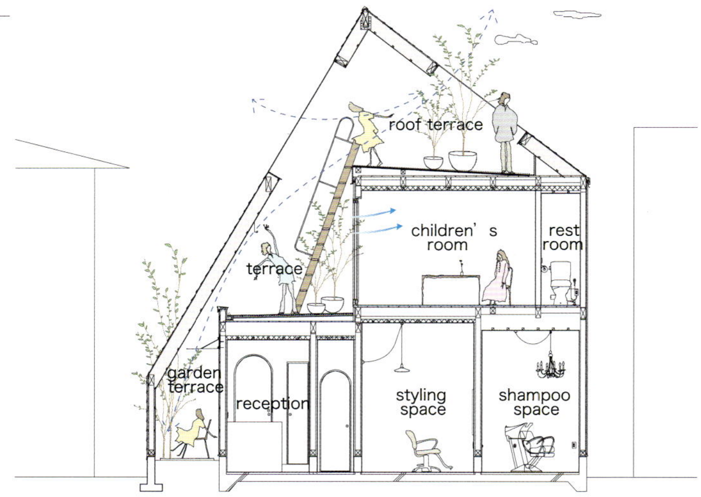

section1 1/100

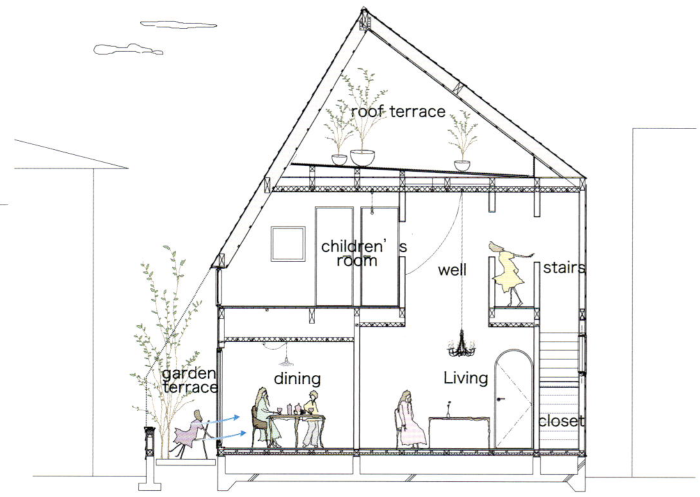

section2 1/100

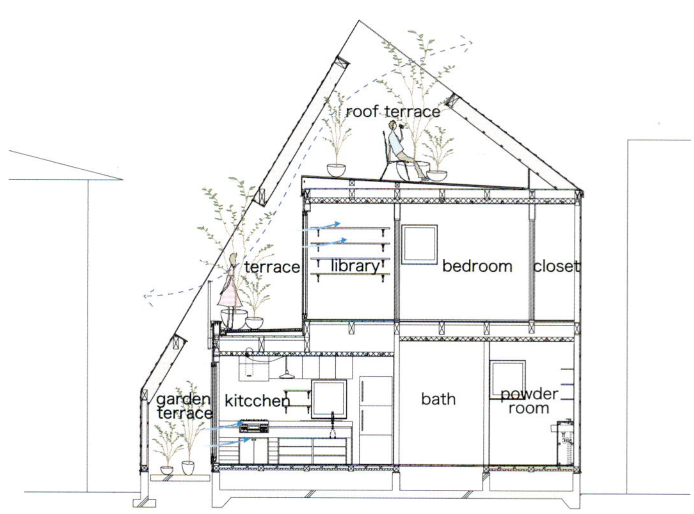

section3 1/100

INDEX

3DELUXE'S

Email: interior@3deluxe.de

The collective title 3deluxe connotes an interdisciplinary team of about 40 individuals from the fields of architecture, interior design, art, graphic design, media design and product design. On the basis of this broad spectrum of specialist knowledge, 3deluxe devises holistic design solutions that range from graphic identities via media installations to architecture and all boast a coherent aesthetics.
3deluxe's characteristic, organically inspired visual idiom has proven as much of a style icon in international context as the virtually expanded space concepts and the striking graphic design that redefines the interface between two- and three-dimensionality.
3deluxe was formed in 1992 in Wiesbaden by communication designers Andreas and Stephan Lauhoff as well as interior designer Nikolaus Schweiger and designer Dieter Brell. Since 1999 system modern gmbh - with industrial engineer Peter Seipp as MD - has been responsible for the development, production and management of 3deluxe's common projects.
Alongside joint interdisciplinary projects the following units work separately in specific fields of functions:
3deluxe graphics — realisation of graphic and multimedia designs under the direction of Andreas and Stephan Lauhoff.
3deluxe in/exterior — specialised in interior design and architecture, run by Dieter Brell (until 2005 along with Nik Schweiger) and Peter Seipp (Commercial Management).
3deluxe motion — conception of filmic and interactive brand and product presentations. Established in 2006 as collaboration between Andreas and Stephan Lauhoff and communications designer Sascha Koeth.
In 2005 Nik Schweiger left the 3deluxe constellation in Wiesbaden and started his own office 3deluxe Biorhythm, trading under the name Biorhythm — modern recreation GmbH, in Berlin. He initially contributed to the project "Leonardo Glass Cube" which was completed in 2007.

CEBRA

Email: jav@cebra.info

CEBRA is a Danish architectural office with its background in the architectural circles of Aarhus. The office was founded in 2001 by the architects Mikkel Frost, Carsten Primdahl and Kolja Nielsen - all are graduated from The Aarhus School of Architecture.
In 2008 CEBRA received the most prestigious award in Scandinavia the 'Nykredits Architecture Award' and in 2006 CEBRA received the Golden Lion at the Venice Biennale 2006 for the project Co-evolution, which has been exhibited at the Biennale, São Paolo, Beijing, Manchester, Copenhagen and Venice 2006/2007. In 2008 CEBRA participated in the Biennale once again - this time curating the Danish pavilion at the Venice Biennale ECOTOPEDIA - Walk the Talk. The Bakkegaard School was nominated for the Mies van der Rohe award in 2006.
The office has worked with numerous architectural functions and scales but dwellings, sports facilities and school buildings have been predominant.

AGC Design Limited

Email: agc@agcdesign.com.hk

Founded in 1999, AGC Design Limited is a professional services firm comprised of a strong, creative design and production team of about 70 professionals. The firm delivers comprehensive professional services in master planning, urban design, architecture and interior design. The primary goal and intent of AGC Design Limited is to provide client with the highest level of professional service while realizing design excellence. The firm believes in working closely with client which results in the best project functionally, technically and aesthetically, in addition to it being completed on time and within budget. "We consider each project in its own context. The design methodology is to be specifically tailored to the place, the people it serves and the business environment at the same time." It is probably this considerate and sensitive approach that allowes AGC Design Limited to be commissioned in the design and project management of end user-orientated and specialist building types.
Currently, AGC Design Limited is involved in projects in Hong Kong, Macau and China. The firm's body of work includes residential, serviced apartment, hotel, office, alteration and addition works, data center, retail and entertainment facilities. The firm also has long-standing and effective team relationship with overseas architectural practice in relation to local projects. "Our project partners include Altoon + Porter Architects (U.S.A.), Benoy (U.K.), Tod William Billie Tsien & Associates (U.S.A), Arquitectonica (U.S.A.), Zaha Hadid Architect (London) and WATG (Singapore). The joint expertise provides broad-based design experience and technical support to respond to client's need and project's multiple program elements." AGC Design Limited has established its Beijing office in 2005. Professional service can be extended more effectively and efficiently to the clients in China.

3LHD

Email: info@3lhd.com

3LHD is a collaborative architectural studio, particularly interested in the integration of architecture, art and (urban) landscape, an approach which has resulted in a series of projects and realizations in Croatia and abroad. 3LHD has an integrative approach to projects and believes that in addition to function, architecture must respond to many other issues. Basic principles of the practice are woven into the modernity of the early 21st century.
"Our design approach is each time with different realities, and with many different parameters that we give ourselves and which are given to us. It is integral, analytical and iterative. It is based on modification of opinions of different people, which we seek to bring into production. They are various specialists, experts in various areas and with them we try to achieve highest quality. This is where our approach is like that of a producer and we often bring ourselves in the role of a director or a DJ who performs the best editing. In such a way we investigate the most appropriate concept and try to create new value. We always make a kind of a prototype, which is sometimes, like in automobile industry, a redesign, and sometimes a research undertaking."

Andres Remy Architects

E-mail: info@andresremy.com

After emerging in the international market at Rafael Viñoly's studio in New York, the architect Andres Remy founded Andres Remy Architects, developing innovative projects, with a unique architecture language.
It is a principle in our design to mix functionality and design. We carefully study every project's detail in order to get the best quality we can produce.
Over its six years of existence, the studio's designs have been awarded nationally and internationally. Currently, the studio is considered one of the best studios that offer premium designs in Argentina.
Orchid House was awarded in the 2009 Buenos Aires Architectural Biennale.
Black House and Orchid House have won the House of the Year Award by Clarin in 2009 and 2010 respectively.
On March 2008, Waterfall House was awarded by the World Architecture Community.
Although most of the firm's projects are in Argentina, there are projects under development in Spain, the Netherlands and the UAE.
Andres Remy Architects organizes its work with multidisciplinary professional teams, which carefully study the local culture, available technology, as well as geographic and climatic context. The office counts on a solid group of professionals committed to design premium projects for high-end clients. It is a priority to collect process and produce information regarding the client needs, project's local culture, available technology, geographical and climatic conditions.

Christina Zerva Architects

Email: ARCH@CHRISTINAZERVA.COM

Christina Zerva Architects, founded in 1991, is a worldwide practice, working globally with project offices in Washington DC, Larissa and Belgrade. Christina Zerva leads the office with partners Paola Nena Nastasia Sakic and Milan Li. The practice works internationally on residential, cultural and commercial projects. "With each project we explore new ways to ensure that the best results are achieved through integration of concept and context with the programmatic and functional essence of a building. Through the continuity of the design process and extensive research involved in the analysis of site, program, social context, emerging construction and contemporary technologies, our approach and methodology introduce new perspectives and new dynamics, reinvigorating both landscape and cityscape."
"We provide full architecture, master planning, project management, interior design, product and furniture design services for both the private and public sectors."
"We use materials and sense of order that constitute the discipline and practice of modern architecture."
The practice has initiated systematic research into a responsible approach on systems that reduce energy consumption and regulate harmful emissions.
"Our architecture seeks to reduce waste of energy, water and materials. By taking advantage of a system of holistic design using technologies, methods and products that not only protect your health and the world around you, but actually enhance the spiritual, emotional, and mental quality of your daily experience."

Colboc Franzen & Associates

Email: architectes@cfa-arch.com

Colboc Franzen & Associates is a French, young and dynamic architecture firm based in Paris and founded in 2004. The team is composed of nine architects, one technician and administrative manager. So far the firm has mostly been working on public facilities, housing and offices in France and abroad. Benjamin Colboc and Manuela Franzen have been working together since 2000 and have won several awards including the competition CIBBAP-accommodation for homeless in 2001 and "The album of young architects" awarded by the French Ministry of Culture in 2004. In 2007, Arnaud Sachet became an associate. In 2009 the agency delivered their first project: housing in Laval, Extension of Chamber of Trades of Val d'Oise, offices for a French company named Actualis in Chateau-Gontier, a loft in Paris or even a private house in Sèvres (Parisian suburb) and offices for a French private accounting company - Fiteco - in Laval...More projects are under studies and several others, under construction.

Jarmund/Vigsnæs AS Architects MNAL

Email: jva@jva.no

Jarmund/ Vigsnæs AS Architects MNAL was established in 1996 by Einar Jarmund and Hakon Vigsnæs. In 2004 Alessandra Kosberg became a third partner. The firm is located in Oslo, Norway, and recent number of employees is 19.
"We are not only working in a wide architectural range with commissions mainly in Norway but also in other European countries. The majority of our finished works are public building and housing projects. We are also involved in urban planning and building interiors: aiming to cover all corners at the architectural field. We are focusing on the independent concept for every single project, avoiding general stylistic approaches. We give priority to early participation in creative programming and an attentive relation towards the surroundings."

GRAU.ZERO

Email: office@grauzero.com

Sérgio Manuel Pereira Nobre was born in Paris in 1974 and lives in Oporto, studied architecture at the Lusiada University in Oporto until 2001 and graduated in Management of Urban Centers in the Moderna University in 2003.
He created the Studio GRAU.ZERO in April 2004.
"Our approach is based on the start again, in every new project comes a new approach, a new concept, without references ... so the GRAU. ZERO named. We do not have a style, a label. We do architecture. Simply, our ambition is to continue to challenge convention and redefine limits. Highly creative and imaginative, we live a pro-active attitude and committed to the design of buildings, spaces and places that are innovative, socially, economically and environmentally responsible."
"We believe in the supreme art which is the architecture, in emotions... in the role of the architect to innovate and break down barriers between creative disciplines. We seek to meet the increasingly individualized needs of man. In the era of globalization we want to give more than identity projects."
"Our scope of work is essentially private demand, focusing mainly in the area of restoration and tourism."

MOON HOON: MOONBALSSO

Email: dollshoii@naver.com

Moon Hoon was born in 1968, in Sangdong Gangwon_do, and lived his teenage years in Tasmania, Australia. He was educated in architecture in Korea, and US, also had work experience in both countries. He has been running his studio Moon_Bal_Sso since 2001. He is interested in breaking the boundaries of architecture by experimenting crashing, fusing, mixing, and so forth with various other disciplines.
He is open-minded about boundaries of architecture. His major works include Rock It Suda, S_Mahal, Mookdong Multi House, Ongdalsam, and Sangsang Museum which was awarded KIA prize for year 2005. His drawings and installations have been exhibited in solo and group format at various museums. He also directs short films related to his architecture with the desire to expand the expressive potential of Architecture.

Giancarlo Mazzanti

Email: gmazzanti@gmail.com

Architect, Javeriana Pontific University of Bogotá - Colombia (1987)
Master in History and Theory of Architecture, and Industrial Design - University of Florence - Italia (1991)
After the completion of his studies in Architecture at the Javeriana Pontific University of Bogotá, Giancarlo worked at "Studio Cino Zucchi" and "Unimarck International Independente" in Milan, Italy. (1991-1992)
During this time he completed his Master in History and Theory of Architecture and Industrial Design at the University of Florence and later formed companies such as "Fischer & Mazzanti", "Santos & Mazzanti" and "EHM Arquitectos." He currently formed " Mazzanti Architectos", a firm that generates the main urban and architectural projects, representatives of the contemporary architecture in Colombia, covering social issues, violence, citizenship identity, technology and esthetics, such as The España library in Medellin Colombia, the Kindergarten El Porvenir and The Gerardo Molina School in Bogota Colombia and among others.

Pacific Environments NZ Ltd Architects

Email: info@pacificenvironments.co.nz

We are an enthusiastic & accomplished team of skilled design, professionals & 3d problem solvers that provide creative people-focused environmental solutions that literally 'bring out the best' in your project, your environment, your lifestyle.
We are based in Auckland, NZ and develop a strong communicative and open rapport with our clients and work alongside them to deliver exciting projects that often far exceed their initial dreams & expectations.
As recognised pioneers in environmentally friendly and energy conscious design with almost 50 years experience, our diverse portfolio includes residential, apartments, education, commercial, industrial, retirement villages, tourism, government and civic buildings, alpine, resorts and wineries and the innovative Yellow Treehouse Restaurant. ESD (Environmentally Sustainable Design) as it is now known, which is integrated to the appropriate levels into our projects our design package offers 'the full architectural service' personalised for each project and draws upon our close network of trusted design consultants.
Our enjoyment comes from working through unique and often complex design challenges and delivering innovative and exciting pragmatic outcomes. Our positive, energetic & 'hands-on' approach along with our focus on understanding our client's needs, means that we deliver real tailored solutions, (not generic answers) in a fun-filled process.
We draw upon our unique and beautiful local environment in the Pacific as our inspiration. With our technical & creative skills and 'can do' attitude, we continue playing significant roles and influence New Zealand architecture and its place in the world.

Studio Nicoletti Associati

Email: studio.nicoletti@inwind.it

Manfredi Nicoletti - Studio Nicoletti Associati, founded in 1957, delivers world-class professional design and management services. Studio Nicoletti Associati offers award winning architectural design, highly ranked project and construction management and is known for his quality and professionalism. As a pioneer in Sustainability and Advanced Technologies, the diversified practice offers comprehensive architectural services with a wide range of related disciplines, from development of master plans to furniture detail.
At over 30 professionals and being one of the oldest and largest firms in Italy, S.N.A practices expansion through all major aspects of urban and building design in Italy, Europe, Africa, Asia, USA, Middle East.
Leading architect
Manfredi Nicoletti, Master in Architecture M.I.T., USA; appointed "Commandeur de l'Ordre des Arts et des Lettres" by the French Government; Emeritus Professor at the Rome University "La Sapienza"; Honorary Fellow of the American Institute of Architects and of the Royal Architectural Institute of Canada; Vice President of the International Academy of Architecture; Member of the Academy of Russia, the International Academy of Moscow and the Architecture Academy of France.
Manfredi Nicoletti is a pioneer in Megastructures and in Bioclimatic Urban and Architectural Design; Expert in Architectural Ecology for the Italian Government and the European Community, member of the Italian Institute of Bioclimatic Architecture, of Eurosolar, and of PLEA. He received the International Award of WREN.
Partner
Luca Nicoletti graduated cum laude at Rome University "La Sapienza". After intense collaboration with Manfredi Nicoletti since 1996, Luca Nicoletti joined the office as partner of Studio Nicoletti Associati in 2004. Member of Architect's Chamber, Visiting Professor and Lecturer at Rome University "La Sapienza"; President of the Young Branch of International Academy of Architecture. Luca Nicoletti is an expert in direction management of high complexity urban and architectural projects and winner of several international design competitions.

Judd Lysenko Marshall Architects

Email: info@jlma.com.au

Judd Lysenko Marshall is a new and energetic design consultancy committed to innovative and imaginative solutions in the fields of architecture and urban design. Our diversely skilled team brings creative thought, scholarship and intelligence to each project. Judd Lysenko Marshall focuses on the delivery of inspired design responses grounded in an absolutely functional architectural approach. "We strive for maximum impact within tight budgets. We aim to reveal a complete understanding of the diverse and specific needs of each and every client. Through creative thought, use of new technology and just plain hard work, we produce projects of environmental sustainability, true excitement and life long durability."

NABITO

Email: info@nabit.it

NABITO was born in Barcelona from the will and courage of The Architects Alessandra Faticanti and Roberto Ferlito in 2006.NABITO won the important European award "Nouveaux albums des jeunes architectes Paris 2006", given by the ministry of culture. They won several competitions in Europe and opened new offices in Rome and Frosinone.
In 2009 NABITO won the Award "cavalierato giovanile della provincia di Roma" for Art and Architecture and it is featuered in the book "annual of best creativity talents, young Blood" award given by the Ministry of culture, Rome.
In 2010 NABITO is selected on the TNT festival young Talent award by ministry of youth, Rome.
Nabito's design strategy focuses on answering the questions of sustainability, architecture, urbanism and territorial strategies in its projects. It is an active studio in the research field.
Objective of our design approach is to conceive a product that is culturally valid and complete at every level: from design at the urban and territorial scale, through restaurations, installations, temporary architecture, various inhabitable typologies, parks and gardens, public buildings, residential complexes of different entity and urban and territorial masterplan. They investigate the relation between social and intimate space, private and public systems with an inclusive behavior.

Jorge Mealha

Email: geral@jorgemealha.com

Jorge Mealha graduated from the Faculty of Architecture, Lisbon in 1987. Since then he has developed projects for a variety of constructions including commercial, housing, industrial premises, schools and sports buildings.
He is a teacher of Architectural Project at the Faculdade de Arquitectura e Artes of Lisbon University Lusíada since 1991 till today.
His works have been published in magazines from Portugal, Spain and Italy. Some projects have been awarded and others been showed in several Exhibitions.
Jorge Mealha has also been invited to adress conferences at Universities and other public places.

PATTERNS

Email: info@p-a-t-t-e-r-n-s.net

PATTERNS is a design research architectural practice based in Los Angeles and operating globally. Founded in 1999 and headed by Co-principals Marcelo Spina and Georgina Huljich, PATTERNS's work has gained international recognition for its innovative approach to design and architecture that fuses advanced computation with an extensive understanding of form, tectonics and materials. PATTERNS's vision is to generate innovative spatial forms that actively engage, enhance and influence the body, constantly challenging its relationship to the built environment akin to the complexity of contemporary life.

PATTERNS has received numerous prizes and awards including first prizes in the competitions for the Vertical Garden at the Schindler House in West Hollywood and the New SCI_Arc Café, the third prize in the prestigious Young Architect of the year Award in 2003 and most recently, they were finalist for the Ordos Prize and the Iakov Chernikov Prize. PATTERNS' award winning project "Prism", a contemporary art gallery located at the heart of the Sunset Strip, opens to the public on November 20th. Current projects include a recently completed FyF Residence in Rosario, Argentina; A Hybrid Office Building in Chengdu, China and Jujuy Redux, a vertical apartment building also in Argentina, scheduled for completion in spring 2011.

PATTERNS's work has been shown and exhibited worldwide, most notably at the Art Institute of Chicago, San Francisco Museum of Modern Art, the Venice Biennale in Italy, The Architectural League of New York, and its first solo show "UniBodies" at Artists Space also in New York. PATTERNS's work is part of the Permanent Architecture Collection of the San Francisco Museum of Modern Art, the MAK Center in Vienna, the Chicago Art Institute and the Sculpture Collection at Gyeonggi Cultural Foundation in Korea.

In addition to their work, Spina and Huljich were the curators of "Matters of Sensation" at Artists Space. One of the most important collective exhibitions in architecture that Artists Space ever organized, the influential show opened to great acclaim and is being followed by a catalogue to appear in early 2010 by SCI_Arc Press.

Spina and Huljich have lectured extensively in the US, South America and Europe and his work has been published internationally in books, exhibition catalogues, magazines and newspapers such as Next Generation Architecture, New Architecture, Architectural Record, Praxis, A+U, Casabella, ICON, Index Architecture, L'Arca, Los Angeles Times, and the recently released SCI_Arc Book "Sessions". In 2004, Architectural Record selected the work of the firm among 11 emerging practices worldwide to integrate their prestigious "Design Vanguard". Most recently, Mr. Spina has been nominated for the Prestigious Ordos Prize, the most important architectural prize for an emergent architect to emerge from Asia.

PATTERNS first comprehensive book /monograph "Embedded" is forthcoming by the Beijing based AADCU and will appear in January 2011.

Marcelo Spina holds a Professional Degree from the National University of Rosario and a Master in Architecture from Columbia University in New York where he was the recipient of several honors including the William Kinne Fellowship and the Honor Award for Excellence in Design. He previously worked for Reiser+Umemoto and Keller Easterling in New York before setting his own Practice. Marcelo Spina is a Design Faculty at The Southern California Institute of Architecture since 2001. Formerly the Coordinator of the Applied Studies Program, Mr. Spina teaches design studios and seminars in technology in the Graduate Program. He has been a Visiting Professor at the Graduate School of Design of Harvard University, a Distinguished Visiting Professor at Tulane University, the Friedman Visiting Professor at the University of California Berkeley and a Visiting Professor at the Technical University of Innsbruck, Austria. He has previously held positions at the National University of Rosario and The Di Tella University in Buenos Aires in Argentina.

Georgina Huljich holds a Professional Degree from the National University of Rosario and a Master in Architecture from UCLA where she graduated with Distinction and was the recipient of several design awards. She has previously worked at the Guggenheim Museum and the architectural firm Dean/Wolf Architects in New York, as a project designer at Morphosis in Los Angeles, and as the co principal of fl-oz she was awarded one of the Six Winning Entries for the 21st. Century Park Competition organized by the Graham Foundation in Chicago and designed the exhibition 'Pass Through' at the School of Cinema and Television at USC. She has also participated at Beyond Media '05 Script Show in Florence, Italy with her video installation Fairy_Tails in collaboration with video artist Gaby Hamburg. She is currently a Design Faculty at the Department of Architecture at UCLA, having previously taught at UC Berkeley as a Maybeck Fellow and the University of Southern California.

WHIM architecture

Email: info@whim.nl

The architecture firm WHIM architecture allows possibilities to create innovative design solutions generating an outstanding approach that synthesizes the international experience of the Rotterdam based firm. The office was founded in 2005 by Ramon Knoester (NL).

The work is a combination of design and research. Committed to innovative and enjoyable architecture, WHIM seeks to respond to the unique circumstances and inherent potentialities of each project. Programmatic layout and sculptural form are the main assets of the office. Great care and attention is paid to the relations and dimensioning of program. Each building design results in a sculpture; a carefully studied form.

It is the opinion of the office that where society changes, architecture should adapt.

A lot of time is paid to research, on how society changes and on how to react to it by architecture. WHIM made an award winning proposal on how to react on the growing amount of single households and a study on the ageing population. End of 2009 the office started a research project to make a new floating island, from the existing plastic waste that is floating in our Oceans. Recycled island is a proposal to clean our oceans from all the plastic pollution, created new land and set an example how to create a new sustainable habitat. This project can be followed on www.recycledisland.com.

Gudmundur Jonsson Architecture office

Email: gjonsson@online.no

Gudmundur Jonsson Architecture office was founded in june 1987 after winning the Scandinavian Competition for the Icelandic Concerthouse. The office has 5 employees that serve a broad spectre in the field of Architecture, Interior Design, Exhibitions, City Planning, and Design.
Gudmundur Jonsson Architecture office has projects in a wide geographical range both nationally and internationally. Some of the National projects count f.ex. Hardangervidda National Park Centre, NORVEG Coast-Cultural Centre, and Norwegian FJORD Centre in Geiranger, together with the Weidemann-Gallery.
Some of the International Projects are f.ex. The Icelandic Embassy in Washington, Attached House in Malmö, Sweden, Library in Akureyri, Iceland among other projects in Iceland.
The main substances of the projects are Cultural buildings and Exhibitions together with Family-houses. Office building and projects for Hotels are to be mentioned as well.

ROEWU

Email: info@roewu.com

ROEWU is a young office with a global pedigree. Currently based in London the office was founded in New York City in 2003 as collaboration between Stephen Roe (Ireland) and Chiafang Wu (Taiwan). Since then the office has won many awards including the Young Architects Award from the Architectural League of New York in 2005, First Prize in the Competition for Ephemeral Structures for the Athens Olympics in 2004, the Kalil Fellowship for Smart Design in 2003 and the Kevin Kieran Award from the Arts Council of Ireland in 2007 among others. The office represented the UK at the 2006 Beijing Biennale, and is currently undertaking a major funded research project on the Weather and Architecture.
The partners have taught and carried out research at schools in the US and the UK focussing mainly on architectural materials, digital technologies and qualitative relations between buildings and their environments. Both partners were 2004-05 Emerging Practitioner Fellows at the Ohio State University and have also taught a graduate level Diploma Unit at the Architectural Association in London.

Avanto Architects Ltd

surname@avan.to

Avanto Architects Ltd was established in 2004 by Ville Hara and Anu Puustinen, after winning an open competition for a cemetery chapel. The office currently works for public communities, private companies and private customers. The scope of work varies from small scale art projects to urban planning. The office is a member of the Association of Finnish Architects' Offices (ATL). The office has special knowledge on the use of wood and designing sacral buildings.

Sporaarchitects

Email: spora@sporaarchitects.hu

Sporaarchitects is a Budapest based office - architects, designers, and thinkers operating within the fields of architecture, urbanism, research and development. The four partners, Tibor Dékány (1968), Sándor Finta (1973), Ádám Hatvani (1972) and Orsolya Vadász (1976) opened practice in 2002, after gaining experience working for different Hungarian and international studios. All of them were graduated from the Budapest University of Technology and Economics (BME). Among others, they currently work on one of Hungary's most significant projects, the construction of the underground line called Metro4. This challenging design process requires matching innovative architecture with complex technological points of view. Sporaarchitects was founded in order to develop an architectural practice that turns intense research and analysis of practical as well as theoretical issues into the driving forces of design. Often projects focus on ordinary aspects of everyday life, including the unappreciated or negative, that are enhanced or twisted in order to bring to the fore the unexpected potential of the things that surround us. At the core of our architecture is the ability to take a fresh look at things through experienced eyes. Rich of multiple expertises the office is fueled by designers and experienced architects that jointly develop projects from early sketches to on-site supervision. The mutual use of the complementing teams as consultants ensures that the projects will never suffer from being neither too conventional nor too naive. By continually developing rigorous methods of analysis, experimentation and execution, Sporaarchitects is able to combine experimental design research with efficient production.

Rai Studio

Email: info@raistudio.com

Rai Studio was founded in June 2007 by Iranian architect Pouya Khazaeli Parsa with the aim of reviving what he considers to be the lost spirit of architecture.
Khazaeli Parsa earned his Master's degree in architecture from Tehran Azad University in 2000.
He has since worked with several internationally renowned offices, including Shigero Ban Architects, Shirdel and Partners, NJP Architects.
Khazaeli Parsa is one of Iran's foremost architects and has been recognized as such in numerous architectural competitions and art biennials, most notably;
A world Pavilion Competition-2004, The 4th Tehran sculpture biennial-2005 (Kamalledin Behzad Prize), Memar Award-2006 ("Best Residential Building"), Memar Award-2009 ("First Prize").
As an international firm, Rai Studio has world wide partners in Tokyo, Rio de Janeiro,Sydney and Milan.

SUBARQUITECTURA

Email: para@subarquitectura.com

SUBARQUITECTURA [ABR 05] is formed by Andrés Silanes [NOV 77], Fernando Valderrama [AGO 79] Carlos Bañón [OCT 78]. All three are architects by the University of Alicante [OCT 04] and Master in COMPLEX ARCHITECTURES UA [05-07].
They've built transport projects like the TRAMSTOP in Alicante (awarded in the IX Bienal of Spanish Architecture and in the European Bienal Balthasar Neumann Prize and Nominated to the last edition of Mies Van der Rohe Awards 2009) and research buildings like RESEARCH LABORATORIES in Orihuela (First Prize in Ideas Competition and Awarded in Isover Sustainable and Ecological Buildings).
Now they're finishing the construction of public and private residential buildings: TOURIA tower in SOCIOPOLIS (Valencia), the 360 HOUSE in Madrid, a LIVING UNIT FOR STUDENTS in Alicante, and 1 VPO in San Anton, Alicante (First Prize in Ideas Competition). Also they're developing at this moment two First Prizes obtained in Competitions of Sports Buildings: the Sports Pavillion in Pedreguer and the New Hercules C.F. Football Stadium in Alicante. They have recently finished their Double Athletics Court in Elda, Alicante (2010). Different solutions, obtained by applying the same way of thinking to multiple uses, scales and places.

Saunders Architecture

Email: post@saunders.no

Saunders Architecture is a firm owned by Canadian Todd Saunders (born 1969 in Gander, Newfoundland) who has lived and worked in Bergen, Norway since 1997. Saunders has worked in countries such Austria, Germany, Russia, and Latvia. Currently, the office is working mostly in Norway, and has projects in England, Denmark, Sweden, and Canada. The work of Saunders Architecture has been published in newspapers, magazines, and books worldwide. Todd Saunders received a Bachelor of Environmental Planning & Design from the Nova Scotia College of Art and Design, Halifax, Canada. While doing his bachelors, Saunders spent a semester as an exchange student at the Rhode Island School of Design, Department of Architecture. He subsequently received a Masters of Architecture from McGill University, Montreal, Canada. Saunders has been a part-time teacher at the Bergen Architecture School, since 2001. He has lectured at various architecture and design schools in Scandinavia, Canada, and England. In 2005 Saunders taught a one-week design/build course in the International Architecture Program in Oulu, Finland. In the spring of 2006, Saunders was a visiting professor at The University of Québec in Montreal, Canada.

Massimiliano Fuksas

Email: office@fuksas.it

Native of Lituania, Massimiliano Fuksas was born in Rome in 1944, where he graduated in Architecture at "La Sapienza" University in 1969. In 1967 he created his own studio in Rome, followed by a second one in Paris in 1989. He opened an office in Vienna in 1993 and in Frankfurt in 2002, active until 2001 and 2009. From 2008 he has an office also in Shenzhen, China. From 1998 to 2000 he was the Director of the VII Biennial of Architecture in Venice "Less Aesthetics, More Ethics". Since 2000 he is the author of the architectural column founded by Bruno Zevi in the weekly magazine "L'Espresso". In 1999 he received the Grand Prix d'Architecture Française. In 2000 he was awarded "Commandeur de l'Ordre des Arts et des Lettres de la République Française". In 2002 he was awarded Honorary Fellowship AIA -American Institute of Architects-. Since 2006 he has been an honorary member of the Royal Institute of British Architects. At the same year he received the Award of Excellence for the New Trade Fair, Rho-Pero, Milan, Italy, from ULI-Urban Land Institute, Washington DC, USA. He was Visiting Professor at several universities, such as the École Speciale d'Architecture in Paris, the Akademie der Bildenden Kunste in Vienna, the Staadtliche Akademia des Bildenden Kunste in Stoccarda, and the Columbia University in New York. For many years he has been devoting special attentions into urban problems in large metropolitan areas.

Doriana O. Mandrelli

Email: office@fuksas.it

Doriana O. Mandrelli was born in Rome where she graduated in History of Modern and Contemporary Architecture in 1979 at "La Sapienza" University. She attended the faculty of Architecture at "La Sapienza" University. She graduated in architecture at ESA-L'Ecole Spéciale d'Architecture, Paris, France. She was the member of the executive board of INARCH (National Institute of Architecture). She did didactic activities at the Institute of History of Art in the Faculty of Letters and Arts in Rome at the University "La Sapienza". Since 1985 she has been cooperating with Massimiliano Fuksas. Since 1997 she has been responsible for Fuksas Design. She was the curator of the Architecture's Section at the VII Biennial of Architecture in Venice (2000) "Less Aesthetics, More Ethics", she was in charge of four special branches dedicated to: Jean Prouvé, Jean Maneval, the Peace Pavillon and Architecture of Spaces, and the Art Section. Her projects are characterized by a continuous research in new materials and innovative technology. They work and live between Rome and Paris.
Recent awards and recognitions: 2009 "Gold Medal" with the project Zenith Music Hall, Strasbourg, France, and "Honorable Mention for Public Spaces and Infrastructures" with the project S Paolo parish complex, Foligno, Italy 2009 finalist for the prize to contemporary architecture "Mies van der Rohe" with the project Zenith Music Hall, Strasbourg, France.

THAM & VIDEGÅRD ARKITEKTER

Email: info@tvark.se

Tham & Videgård Arkitekter is a progressive and contemporary practice that focuses on architecture and design - from large scale urban planning through to buildings, interiors and objects.
The practice objective is to create distinct and relevant architecture with the starting point resting within the unique context and specific conditions of the individual project. Taking an active approach, the office is involved throughout the whole process, from developing the early sketch to the on-site supervision. Commissions include public, commercial and private clients in Sweden and abroad.
The practice approach to architecture is inclusive; with practical, theoretical, social and environmental issues analysed and integrated within the process. When required and relevant the office involves a network of multidisciplinary external consultants. This use of complementing resources ensures that all projects address the right challenges, in order to make the most of the opportunities that each represent.
Within the office architects combine straight forward solutions with extensive research. The method of work encourages innovative thinking to drive the development of the project, which in turn facilitates the subsequent realization within the logics of efficient contemporary production.
From working with and completing several public, educational, exhibition and commercial buildings, the T&V team is experienced in managing projects that comply with the highest international standards regarding climate, security and long term sustainability. As a result the practice is well prepared to meet and organize the many different demands and factors that follow with buildings of complex programme and specialized functions.
T&V are based in Stockholm, Sweden, and directed by co-founders and chief architects Bolle Tham and Martin Videgård.
The T&V practice has been awarded prizes and nominations in several open international competitions and has also attracted attention for its experimental and innovative projects.
As an integrated part of the architectural practice, Bolle Tham and Martin Videgård also teach and lecture at schools of architecture in Sweden and abroad.

Cyrille Druart

Email: info@cyrilledruart.com

Designer, Interior Architect, also passionate about Photography, Cyrille Druart excels in many fields. He grew up in an artistic environment, immersed in surrealism on his mother's side, which has had a profound influence on his work and interest in the imagination. His father, an industrial designer, exposed him to the technical side of the profession. A creator at heart, he strives to design modern, non-decorative environments, but with an underlying language and sense of wonder. Architecture thus becomes a platform for introspection.

Art'Ur Architectes

Email: arturbordeaux@wanadoo.fr

Philippe PASCAL, architecte DPLG (French State diploma in architecture) Philippe is from Madagascar and strengthened his early interest for the wild fauna and flora while working for ORTSOM (Overseas Bureau for Scientific and Technical Research) and the Tsimbazaza zoo in Tananarive. He has developed a close collaboration with his brother, who heads a research team at the INRA (National Institute for Research in Agronomy) in Rennes, in order to understand the interaction between construction and the environment.
Eric de CHAMBURE, architecte DESA (Diploma of the Special School of Architecture, Paris) On top of his job as an architect, Eric also breeds horses and is sometimes called upon as an animal expert, particularly in the design of stud farms.
Philippe and Eric have been close to the Green movement since the 1980s, when they started developing projects about DIY-construction and the use of live materials: Wood, earth, stone are used for the structure, the coverings, the ceilings, the floors, both inside and outside. These materials breathe, move, and change through the seasons. The building evolves. It goes through time.
Their architectural vision was first fully embodied in the Bordeaux Technical Centre for Wood and Furniture, which was selected to represent France at the 2000 International Conference on Construction and the Environment in Maastricht.
A high environmental quality is an integral part of our architectural vision. We always aim at revealing the symbolic, social and cultural dimensions of our projects, in order to set humans at the heart of our processes, at the heart of our projects, and at the heart of life.
Art'Ur Architectes's young and dynamic team is divided between two agencies in France: one in the heart of Paris, not far from the Eiffel Tower, and the other by the Garonne river in Bordeaux.

SAKO Architects

Email: info@sako.co.jp

Keiichiro Sako

2004 to 2005	Visiting Scholar at Columbia University. Overseas artist dispatched by Agency for Cultural Affairs.
2004	Established SAKO Architects Jointly presided over Asian Architects Associates
1996 to 2004	Worked with Riken Yamamoto & Field Shop
1996	Obtained a Masters Degree from theTokyo Institute of Technology
1994	Graduated from Tokyo Institute of Technology
1970	Born in Fukuoka, Japan

ENOTA

Email: karmen.bovha@enota.si

Enota was founded in 1998 by Aljoša Dekleva, Dean Lah and Milan Tomac with the ambition to create contemporary and critical architectural practice of an open type based on collective approach to development of architectural and urban solutions. Over the years Enota has been constantly developing and from the beginnings it has served as creative platform for more than fifty architects. Since 2002 Enota's partner architects are Dean Lah and Milan Tomac. Enota's team of architects focuses on research driven design of the environment where contemporary social organisations, new technologies and arts are interwoven. Enota's solutions are always the result of research, reinterpretation and development of social, organizational and design algorithms that derive from nature and strong binding of the buildings with the environment that surrounds them.

OFIS architects

Email: ofis@ofis.si

OFIS arhitekti (OFIS architects)
Based in Ljubljana formed by Rok Oman and Spela Videcnik (1998).
rok oman
(born 1970) studied architecture at the Ljubljana School of Architecture
(grad.1998) and at the Architectural Association in London (grad.2000).
spela videcnik
(born 1971) studied architecture at the Ljubljana School of Architecture
(grad.1997) and at the Architectural Association in London (grad.2000).

Clavienrossier

Email: nicolas@clavienrossier.ch

Valéry Clavien graduated from the Fribourg School of Engineers and Architects in Switzerland. After his studies he worked in Zurich, then in Geneva at the office of Devanthéry and Lamunière. Nicolas Rossier, graduated from Fribourg also, worked in New York, then in Berlin at Daniel Liebeskind office. After several missions spent with ICRC he follows a Master's degree in Architecture in Geneva where he is teaching at the present as a scientific assistant.
With all their experiences, they join and start their own office in 2009 and are currently working on various projects in Switzerland and abroad.

Söhne & Partner

Email: office@soehnepartner.com

No task is too complicated for Söhne & Partner. Their works, their designs could be described as a quest for the optimum, as a highly diversified approach that is refined with every intricate and complex problem they find a solution for. Every project is different. And is treated as such. No off-the-shelf products but individual ideas. Precise analysis and research leads to solutions that are custom tailored to the needs of clients, projects and building sites. Let's be open-minded!
Söhne & Partner was founded in 2001 by Thomas Bärtl, Michael Prodinger and Guido Trampitsch.
The company is engaged in the sectors:
Architectural design
Architectural planning
Construction supervision
Project managment
Interior Design
Town Planning

za bor architects

E-mail: vadim@zabor.net

za bor is a Moscow based architectural office founded in 2003 by principals Arseniy Borisenko and Peter Zaytsev.
The bureau's objects are created mainly in contemporary aesthetic. What distinguishes them is an abundance of architectural methods used both in the architectural and interior design, as well as a complex dynamical shape which is a visiting card of za bor projects. The interiors demonstrate this feature especially brightly, since for all their objects Peter and Arseniy create built-in and free standing furniture themselves.
za bor architects have been involved in more than 30 projects including three residential houses, an office building, a cottage settlement, more than ten offices. Among the clients of za bor architects there are media, business and government companies such as Forward Media Group, Yandex, Inter RAO UES, Moscow Chamber of Commerce and Industry and others.

Takeshi Hosaka Architects

E-mail: info@hosakatakeshi.com

1975 Born in Japan
1999 Bachelor Degree of Architecture from Yokohama National University
1999 Established Architecture Speed Studio/ Principal
2001 Master Degree of Architecture from Yokohama National University
2004 Established Takeshi Hosaka Architects/ Principal
2004 Lecturer at Kokushikan University
2010 Lecturer at Hosei University

NRM-Architects Office

Email:ninomiya@nrm-a.com

Work contents Plans,design, supervision of buildings and plans, nvestigation,reserch relating to the regional and urban planning
Awards 2010: The 3th TASC Award for GAPs
2010: The 3rd TASC Award for House with Tiny Pool
2008: The 28th INAX Design Contest for HIDAMARINO-IE
2007: The 9th Warm Living Space Design Competetition for aH: 1
2007: The 27th INAX Design Contest for kH: 3
2005: Residential Lighting Awards 2005 for aH: 1
2003: Good Design prize, Good Design Award 2003(Japan ndustrial Design Promotion Organization) for sH: 1
2003: Interior Industry Association Award for sH: 1

Wingårdh Arkitektontor AB

E-mail: wingardhs@wingardhs.se

Wingårdhs is the generic name for Wingårdh Arkitektkontor AB and Wingårdh and Medarbetare AB.Gert Wingårdh, architect SAR/MSA, and CEO is owner and manager.

The office is today among the five largest architect groups in Sweden, and among the ten largest in the Nordic Region. This falls well in line with the target set in the office's general objective that we must be one of Scandinavia's leading architect offices.

"We work on projects in all phases, everything from pilot studies and surveys, to finish construction documents. The office has extensive experience of both reconstruction and new construction work."

"Our clients are from the business sector, government authorities, municipalities, real-estate companies, contractors and private ndividuals."

Donaire Arquitectos

E-mail: estudio@donairearquitectos.com

DONAIRE ARQUITECTOS was born in Seville in 2000.

Youth team with a large experience working in innovated architecture with traditional and new materials.

"We design public and private buildings, furniture and graphic design."

Exit

Email: exit@exitstudio.it

Exit is an architecture studio founded in 2004 by architects Francesco Loschi, Giuseppe Pageno and Panetto. Based in Treviso, Exit focuses on architectural and urban design, interior and landscape design and leverages the professional experience and insight of its founders in Italy, Spain and Portugal.

COOP HIMMELB(L)AU

Email: ecker@coop-himmelblau.at

COOP HIMMELB(L)AU was founded by Wolf D. Prix, Helmut Swiczinsky, and Michael Holzer in Vienna, Austria, in 1968, and is active in architecture, urban planning, design, and art. In 1988, a second studio was opened in Los Angeles, USA. Further project offices are located in Frankfurt, Germany; Paris, France; and Hongkong,China. COOP HIMMELB(L)AU employs currently 150 team members from nineteen nations.

The architectural studio COOP HIMMELB(L)AU is directed by Wolf D. Prix, Wolfdieter Dreibholz, Harald Krieger, Karolin Schmidbaur and Project Partners. Those are Andrea Graser, Hartmut Hank, Helmut Holleis, Paul Kath, Markus Pillhofer, Markus Prossnigg, Frank Stepper, and Michael Volk.

After Michael Holzer left the team in 1971, and with the retirement of Helmut Swiczinsky in 2001 from COOP HIMMELB(L)AU's daily operations and in 2006 from the office, Wolf D. Prix is leading the studio as Design Principal/ CEO. In 2000, Wolfdieter Dreibholz joined COOP HIMMELB(L)AU as CEO of COOP HIMMELB(L)AU Mex S. A. de C. V. and became a partner of COOP HIMMELB(L) AU Wolf D. Prix / W. Dreibholz & Partner ZT GmbH, and CEO of the main studio in 2004. In 2003 Harald Krieger has benn designated as Partner of COOP HIMMELB(L)AU Wolf D. Prix / W. Dreibholz & Partner ZT GmbH and is managing director of COOP HIMMELB(L) AU Europe GmbH, Frankfurt/ M., Germany, since 2006. Karolin Schmidbaur has been made Partner of the office in 1996 and is currently Design and Managing Partner of COOP HIMMELB(L) AU Vienna (since 2009) as well as the Director of the office in Los Angeles, California (since 2003).

Pascal Arquitectos

Email: carlos@pascalarquitectos.com

Pascal Arquitectos was founded in 1979 by Carlos and Gerard Pascal with the main purpose of achieving ultimate and integral development in architecture, interior, landscape, lighting and furniture design.

Atelier's production ranges from luxurious residential projects, residential complexes, institutional and religious buildings, restaurants, to corpatare and offices buildings and hotels.

Major restorations of two historic monuments, both recognized by the National Institute of Fine Art (INBA), had been completed: Edificio Bolivio, an original masterpiece of artitect Jose Villagron Gorcia nowadays corporate headquaters of Ford Motor Company de maeico, and the grand hetitage mansion located in Avenida Refomo and Rio Elba street, for "El Divino" restaurant.

In 2003 investment project Hotel Sheraton Centro Historico was conduded. This was the first project developed in the area since the 1985 earthquakes and also the first one done in 40 years in Mecixo's City historical downtown.

Dominique Coulon et associés

E-mail: agence@coulon-architecte.fr

Dominique COULON was born in 1961. In 1989 he was graduate with the professor and architect Henri Ciriani and he created his own studio.
Concepts for sustainable development, respect for historical context and responsibility towards the environment and its ecologies are amongst the main concerns for the agency.
As a way to find a new dynamic approach to each architectural project, the agency's methodology draws upon the rich exchange of information stemming interdisciplinary work. Complexity becomes the catalyst for the architectural project.
Since 2008, Sarah BREBBIA and Olivier NICOLLAS joined the office as associates, thereby becoming Dominique Coulon et Associés.
In 2010 the agency received The International Architecture Award from the Chicago Athenaeum Museum of architecture and Design, for its Conservatory of Music in Maizières-les-Metz.

SHED Architecture & Design

E-mail: info@shedbuilt.com

SHED believes in architecture that solves problems. In partnership with our clients, consultants and contractors, we strive to realize work that is resource efficient, pragmatic and original.
The following beliefs are the foundation of our design approach:
We believe that architecture is a practical art.
We believe that a pragmatic approach yields progressive design solutions.
We believe that buildings must use resources wisely.
We believe that architecture must sustain the way people live, work and play.
This approach strives to create work with the following qualities:
Design solutions consider site, climate, material, light, and space holistically.
Design solutions use resources efficiently over the long term.
Design solutions are purposeful in their use of material, light and space.
Design solutions are more than the sum of their parts.
Design solutions are direct and durable.
Design solutions support the life of the client.
We are committed to designing projects that meet the highest expectations of our clients and highest design standards of economy, efficiency and quality. We look forward to discussing your project with you.

Enproyecto Arquitectura

E-mail: info@enproyecto.es

Field Architecture

E-mail: jess@fieldarchitecture.com

Field Architecture (fA) is an internationally recognized father and son team, the recent winner of multiple Progressive Architecture (P/A) Awards. Founded by Stan Field and Jess Field, based on Stan's 40 years of practice, fA is a multi-generational firm dedicated to deepening the connection between people and the places they love. Stan and Jess draw inspiration from the unique qualities and character of each site, to create architecture that is congruous with the landscape, and buildings that are beautiful, practical, and provide lasting places of interchange between the built, and natural world.
"We approach each project with imagination and rigor, drawing on the marriage of the art and science of architecture - both creative and technical - to impart a sense of wonder and inspiration."

OPPENHEIM ARCHITECTURE+DESIGN

E-mail: beat@oppenoffice.com

Oppenheim Architecture + Design (OAD) is a full service architecture, interior design and planning firm with offices in Miami, Los Angeles, New York and Basel. Founded by Chad Oppenheim, OAD specializes in creating powerful and pragmatic solutions and has world-wide experience in hospitality, office, high-rise and single family residential, retail and mixed-use design as well as the complete masterplanning and design of new cities.

Takeshi Hamada

E-mail: info@hamada-design.com

TAKESHI HAMADA
1975 Born in Osaka,Japan
2003 Completed the Master Course, Kyoto Institute of Technology
2003-2005 Compas Architects
2005- Hamada Design Co.,Ltd.

WORKS
2007 Office K
2010 Apartment K
2010 House D
2010 Office A
2011 House A

AWARDS
2007 Good Design Award/JIDPO

BUSINESS
Architecture Design, Interior Design, Structural Design,
Civil Engineering Design, Seismic Diagnosis Survey work.